ENTREPRENEURSHIP
IDEAS IN ACTION | Cynthia L. Greene

6e

PRECISION EXAMS EDITION

SOUTH-WESTERN
CENGAGE Learning

Australia • Brazil • Mexico • Singapore • United Kingdom • United States

SOUTH-WESTERN
CENGAGE Learning·

**Entrepreneurship: Ideas in Action,
Sixth Edition; Precision Exams Edition**

Cynthia L. Greene

SVP, GM Skills & Global Product
Management: Jonathan Lau

Product Director: Matthew Seeley

Product Manager: Nicole Robinson

Sr. Content Developer: Karen Caldwell

Consulting Editor: Peggy Shelton, LEAP
Publishing Services, Inc.

Product Marketing Manager: Abigail Hess

Manufacturing Planner: Kevin Kluck

Art and Cover Direction, Production,
Management, and Composition:
Lumina Datamatics, Inc.

Cover Image: © Piccia Neri | Dreamstime.com

Intellectual Property
Analyst: Kyle Cooper
Project Manager: Lisa Brown

Two Students With Folder And Backpack
Isolated Over White Background
Credit: Andrey_Popov/Shutterstock.com

Casual group of college students smiling -
isolated over a white background
Credit: Andresr/Shutterstock.Com

Black abstract tablet computer (tablet pc)
on white background, 3D render.
Modern portable touch pad device
with white screen. Credit: mkabakov
/Shutterstock.com

Abstract background
Credit: StudioADFX/Shutterstock.com

For product information and technology assistance, contact us at
Cengage Learning Customer & Sales Support, 1-800-354-9706

For permission to use material from this text or product,
submit all requests online at **www.cengage.com/permissions**
Further permissions questions can be emailed to
permissionrequest@cengage.com

The Career Clusters icons are being used with permission of the States'
Career Cluster Initiative, 2011, **www.careerclusters.org**

Student Edition ISBN: 978-1-337-90469-8

Cengage Learning
20 Channel Center Street
Boston, MA 02210
USA

Cengage Learning is a leading provider of customized learning solutions with employees residing in nearly 40 different countries and sales in more than 125 countries around the world. Find your local representative at **www.cengage.com**.

Cengage Learning products are represented in Canada by Nelson Education, Ltd.

For your course and learning solutions, visit **ngl.cengage.com/school.**

Printed in the United States of America
Print Number: 05   Print Year: 2023

Contents

Chapter 3

Develop a Business Plan   64

IDEAS IN **ACTION**
An Online Community for College Women   65

Chapter 4

Identify and Meet a Market Need   94

IDEAS IN **ACTION**
The Art of Targeting Your Market   95

Chapter 7

Select a Type of Ownership   184

Chapter 8

Locate and Set Up Your Business   218

Chapter 11

Human Resource Management   **312**

IDEAS IN **ACTION**
Working for a Worthy Cause   313

Chapter 12

Risk Management   **346**

IDEAS IN **ACTION**
Making Friends Is Her Business   347

Chapter 13

Management for the Future 378

About the Author

Cynthia L. Greene is an educational consultant and teacher educator. She has developed entrepreneurship and small business development curriculum for the Small Business Incubator for the Newton College and Career Academy in Covington, Georgia, and the Nicholas County School System in Kentucky. Greene taught business education at the high school level for 25 years in the Fulton County School System in Atlanta. She was the program specialist for Business and Information Technology for the Georgia Department of Education for six years. An active member of the National Business Education Association, Greene served as president and has chaired the Entrepreneurship Standards Committee.

Photo courtesy of Cynthia L. Greene

PRECISION EXAMS This Edition of **Entrepreneurship** is aligned to Precision Exams' *Business Management & Administration* Career Cluster. The *Entrepreneurship & Management* pathway connects industry with skills taught in the classroom to help students successfully transition from high school to college and/or career. Working together, Precision Exams and National Geographic Learning, a part of Cengage, focus on preparing students for the workforce, with exams and content that is kept up to date and relevant to today's jobs. To access a corresponding correlation guide, visit the accompanying Instructor Companion Website for this title. For more information on how to administer the *Entrepreneurship* exam or any of the 170+ exams available to your students, contact your local NGL/Cengage Sales Consultant.

Comprehensive Teaching and Learning Tools

cognero® **Cengage Learning Testing by Cognero** is a flexible, online system that allows instructors to author, edit, and manage test bank content from multiple Cengage Learning solutions, create multiple test versions in an instant, and deliver tests from wherever they want. ISBN: 978-1-305-65411-2

MindTap **MindTap** is a personalized teaching experience with relevant assignments that guide you to analyze, apply, and improve thinking. The Build Your Business Plan feature is integrated into the Learning Path so that students have a complete business plan by the end of the course. ISBN: 978-1-337-90470-4

Student Workbook ISBN: 978-1-305-65310-8
Instructor's Resource CD ISBN: 978-1-305-65319-1

Transforming Innovations!

Have You Ever Wanted to Start Your Own Business? An entrepreneur is someone who organizes, manages, and assumes the risks of a business or enterprise. *Entrepreneurship: Ideas in Action, 6e* helps you prepare to become an entrepreneur, provides you with the skills needed to realistically evaluate your potential as a business owner, and guides you in building a business plan.

Each lesson begins with a list of terms and objectives to help you focus your reading.

Learning Objectives outline the main objectives of the lesson to help keep you on track.

Key Terms are the new terms defined in the lesson.

Focus on Small Business introduces concepts and provides a thought-provoking introduction to each lesson.

Locate and Set Up Your Business

8.1 CHOOSE A LOCATION

8.2 OBTAIN SPACE AND DESIGN THE PHYSICAL LAYOUT

8.3 PURCHASE EQUIPMENT, SUPPLIES, AND INVENTORY

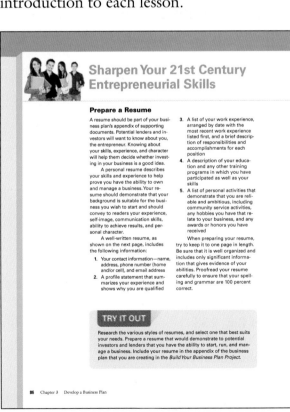

Sharpen Your 21st Century Entrepreneurial Skills

Prepare a Resume

A resume should be part of your business plan's appendix of supporting documents. Potential lenders and investors will want to know about you, the entrepreneur. Knowing about your skills, experience, and character will help them decide whether investing in your business is a good idea.

A personal resume describes your skills and experience to help prove you have the ability to own and manage a business. Your resume should demonstrate that your background is suitable for the business you wish to start and should convey to readers your experience, self-image, communication skills, ability to achieve results, and personal character.

A well-written resume, as shown on the next page, includes the following information:

1. Your contact information—name, address, phone number (home and/or cell), and email address
2. A profile statement that summarizes your experience and shows why you are qualified

3. A list of your work experience, arranged by date with the most recent work experience listed first, and a brief description of responsibilities and accomplishments for each position
4. A description of your education and any other training programs in which you have participated as well as your skills
5. A list of personal activities that demonstrate that you are reliable and ambitious, including community service activities, any hobbies you have that relate to your business, and any awards or honors you have received

When preparing your resume, try to keep it to one page in length. Be sure that it is well organized and includes only significant information that gives evidence of your abilities. Proofread your resume carefully to ensure that your spelling and grammar are 100 percent correct.

TRY IT OUT

Research the various styles of resumes, and select one that best suits your needs. Prepare a resume that would demonstrate to potential investors and lenders that you have the ability to start, run, and manage a business. Include your resume in the appendix of the business plan that you are creating in the *Build Your Business Plan Project*.

86 Chapter 3 Develop a Business Plan

One key competency employers value is the ability to think creatively in order to solve problems.

Sharpen Your 21st Century Entrepreneurial Skills offers 21st Century skill-building information and poses critical-thinking questions.

Abundant Real-Life Examples!

Ideas in Action presents stories of successful young entrepreneurs. "What Do You Know?" critical-thinking questions are followed up with "What Do You Know Now?" at the end of the chapter.

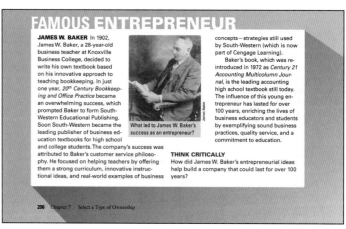

What Went Wrong? highlights the pitfalls of real entrepreneurs and includes critical-thinking questions to help students analyze the situations.

Famous Entrepreneurs profiles contributions of successful entrepreneurs throughout history.

Business Plan and Career Coverage!

Build Your Business Plan Project
concludes each chapter and is designed to help you prepare a complete business plan by the end of the course.

BUILD YOUR
BUSINESS PLAN PROJECT

This activity will help you plan the operations management of your business.

1. Describe the management style you will use for managing your business. Will you always use the same style? How will you determine when to use a different style?
2. Locate and contact two professionals in your area who specialize in strategic planning. What are their credentials? What are their fees? Do you think it would be helpful to utilize the services of a strategic planner? Why or why not?
3. Develop an operating procedures manual for your business. Include the rules, policies, and procedures that your business will follow to run effectively.
4. If your business has an inventory, list all of the items you will have in inventory and your cost for each. Create a purchasing plan for your inventory.
5. Set up inventory records for your business using either a paper system or an electronic system. Be sure to list all of the items discussed in Lesson 10.2. How did you determine your reorder point? What inventory carrying costs are relevant to your business? How can you reduce your carrying costs?
6. Analyze your sales by creating a table that lists each of your products and the total sales (or estimated sales) for each. What is the percentage of total sales for each product? Based on this information, will you make any changes to your inventory?
7. Develop internal accounting controls for your business. Explain why you chose the controls you did.

PLANNING A CAREER IN COMPUTER REPAIR

Information Technology

"My stepsister, who is a high school senior this year, has become our household computer expert. She recently attended a summer technology camp sponsored by a national computer retailer that provides a variety of computer support services. The camp was established as a way to help fulfill future labor needs. After completing camp, she's become the 'go to' person in our house for any high-tech gadget issues."

Computer service specialists help resolve a variety of complex technological issues that affect computer efficiency and reliability. This ranges from repairing computer parts, such as a hard drive or monitor, to removing spyware and viruses. They must be familiar with various operating systems and software packages. Some computer service specialists work from repair shops, while others travel to customers' locations.

Employment Outlook
* A faster-than-average rate of employment growth is anticipated.
* The use of the newest forms of technology, which are often complex, will help fuel demand.
* Growing demand will be somewhat offset by the trend to outsource tech support jobs to foreign countries with lower wage rates.

Job Titles
* Software Support Specialist
* Help Desk Analyst
* Application Specialist
* Technical Support Associate
* MIS Support Technician

Needed Education/Skills
* Education requirements vary. A bachelor's degree is required for some computer service specialist positions, while an associate's degree is adequate for some jobs.
* To keep up with changes in technology, many computer support specialists continue their education throughout their careers.
* Strong customer-service, problem-solving, and troubleshooting skills are needed.

What's it like to work in Computer Repair? Milo is a computer service specialist. He has his own business and provides on-site repair services.

Today, Milo is updating the rates on his company website. These rates include the trip charge to arrive at a client's home or place of business, the one-hour minimum labor charge, and the additional fees for a partial hour beyond the one-hour minimum.

After receiving a call from a frantic client, Milo dashes off to the client's home. The client, who has a home-based consulting business, has a hard drive that is failing. The client accidentally dropped his flash drive into a cup of coffee, and he has no backup for his files. Consequently, he needs help retrieving critical files from his hard drive.

After saving the files to a new flash drive, Milo suggests to his client that he consider investing in an automated data backup service. For a monthly fee, designated data can be automatically saved to a personalized website that would be password accessible for security purposes.

What about you? Would you like to help a variety of individuals and businesses solve their computer technology problems? What would you find appealing (or not appealing) about this job?

310

Planning a Career in... incorporates Career Clusters for a variety of careers as an entrepreneur.

Special Features Enhance Learning!

Winning Edge helps you prepare for competitive events.

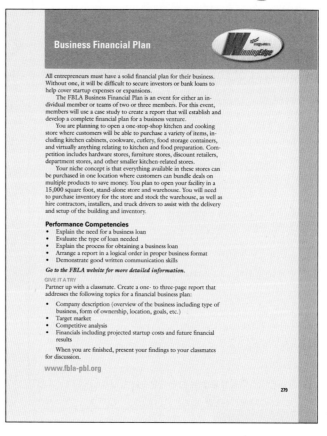

Did You Know? offers additional information that relates to chapter topics.

Develop Your Reading Skills provides exercises to reinforce reading skills.

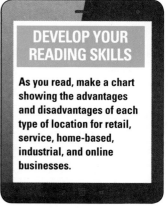

DEVELOP YOUR READING SKILLS

As you read, make a chart showing the advantages and disadvantages of each type of location for retail, service, home-based, industrial, and online businesses.

 BE YOUR OWN BOSS

You own a toy store. Some of the stuffed animals that you carry have become very popular with children, and you cannot keep them in stock. In the past, your reorder point was three and you never ran out of the animals, but now you are losing sales because of empty shelves. You know you could sell more stuffed animals if you had them. Outline a plan that will meet your business's inventory needs as well as your customers' needs.

Be Your Own Boss gives you the opportunity to complete the same types of activities that a real entrepreneur might do.

Abundant Review and Assessment!

An abundance of ongoing lesson and chapter assessments ensure you understand and can apply what you've learned.

Think About It contains activities to help you apply what you have learned in the lesson.

Make Academic Connections provides the integrated curriculum activities that show you how entrepreneurial concepts relate to other courses of study.

Teamwork provides you with opportunities to work with classmates on cooperative learning projects.

Chapter Assessment provides a summary of the main points and contains questions and activities to test your knowledge.

Summary presents key chapter concepts for quick review.

Key Terms Review matches terms with definitions to confirm understanding of key terms.

Review Your Knowledge provides questions with multiple choice answers that summarize key concepts to reinforce learning.

Apply What You Learned provides activities to reinforce, review, and apply concepts you've learned.

Make Academic Connections provides exercises that connect to other disciplines.

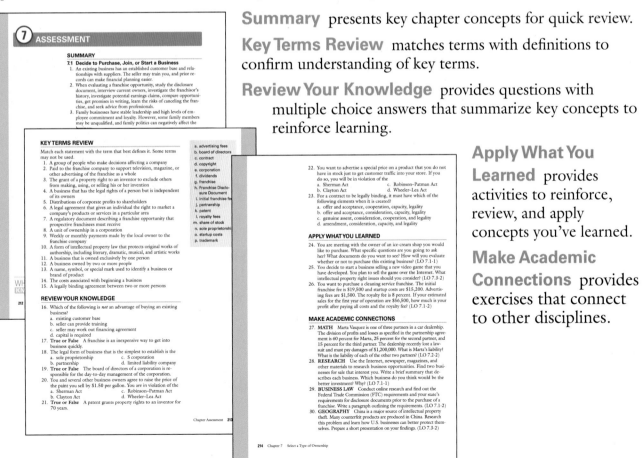

PhotoInc/iStockphoto.com

Should You Become an Entrepreneur?

1.1 ALL ABOUT ENTREPRENEURSHIP

1.2 ENTREPRENEURSHIP AND YOU

1.3 EXPLORE IDEAS AND OPPORTUNITIES

1.4 PROBLEM SOLVING FOR ENTREPRENEURS

Gaming and Financial Literacy Equal Success

Photo by Jason Young

Jason Young, CEO, MindBlown Labs

MindBlown Labs has a mission. It aims to create interactive, experience-based tools that help young people learn about finances. The company plans to reach 20 million teens and young adults by the year 2020. It is well on its way with Thrive 'n' Shine, a mobile app/game that explains personal finance. It all began with a young entrepreneur from Inglewood, California.

Jason Young was 9 years old when he started his first business, a one-man candy shop. By age 13, he was selling travel agency services. At age 17, he was running an e-commerce business selling vitamins. However, despite his success as a young entrepreneur, Jason was no stranger to hardship. His family was evicted from their home the day after Christmas during his sophomore year at Harvard. That experience set Jason on a course to meet his personal and professional mission—to help young people become financially literate. He and his college friend Tracy Moore co-founded MindBlown Labs to help young people develop money-management skills.

MindBlown Labs' game, Thrive 'n' Shine, provides an interactive experience for students. The game combines fun with financial concepts. Topics include auto loans, budgeting, credit cards, credit scores, savings, college loans, and taxes, among others.

MindBlown Labs has attracted attention along the way. It won a $610,000 research contract from the U.S. Department of the Treasury. President Barack Obama appointed Jason to the President's Advisory Council on Financial Capability for Young Americans. The Council advises the President and the Secretary of the Treasury on how to use technology to promote financial capability among young people in schools, families, communities, and the workplace. The magazine *Black Enterprise* wrote a story about Jason and his company. *Entrepreneur* magazine recognized MindBlown Labs as one of 100 Brilliant Companies. Co-founders Jason and Tracy and their team believe an award-winning gaming mobile app is the best way for America's youth to learn about financial responsibility.

WHAT DO YOU **KNOW?**

1. What event set Jason on course to his personal and professional mission?

2. Would you use a mobile app such as Thrive 'n' Shine to play a game that teaches you financial literacy? Why or why not?

3. Do you think an entrepreneur needs to keep up with changing technology? Explain your answer.

1.1 ALL ABOUT ENTREPRENEURSHIP

The Essential Question What role has entrepreneurship played in the U.S. economy?

LEARNING OBJECTIVES

LO 1.1-1 Define entrepreneurship.

LO 1.1-2 Recognize the role entrepreneurs play in the U.S. economy.

LO 1.1-3 Determine the reasons businesses succeed or fail.

KEY TERMS

- entrepreneurs
- entrepreneurship
- employees

FOCUS ON SMALL BUSINESS

Should you be your own boss?

"I'm so tired of someone telling me what to do all the time. It seems like there should be some way we could be in charge," Delia said to her friend Gloria.

"I know what you mean, because I feel the same way," Gloria answered. "But I've got an idea—let's be entrepreneurs. Mr. Rivera talked about them in my business class last week. They are people who start and run their own businesses. We could do that!"

"What would we have to do? Would we make a lot of money? Would it be fun?" Delia's mind was overflowing with questions.

Gloria was getting very excited as she replied, "We could be our own bosses! If we were the owners, we would be in charge!"

"This sounds pretty good," said Delia. "We could decide when we work, what we do, and how we do it. And we can make lots of money! I can't wait. When do we start?"

WORK AS A TEAM Many people go into business just so they can be in charge and make lots of money. Do you think this is the most important reason to start your own business?

Entrepreneurs can be of any age.

LO 1.1-1 Entrepreneurship

The U.S. economy includes thousands of small businesses. Many of these small businesses are owned and operated by men and women who created their own companies. Some of these individuals have become legends as you hear stories about their path to success. But what makes someone an entrepreneur? What impact have entrepreneurs had in history? What impact do they have today?

Would you like to own your own business? Why or why not?

What Is an Entrepreneur?

People who own, operate, and take the risk of a business venture are called entrepreneurs. They are engaged in entrepreneurship, the process of running a business of one's own. Entrepreneurs of all ages and from all types of backgrounds create all kinds of businesses. Entrepreneurs try to identify unmet needs in the marketplace. Then they provide a service or product to meet those needs. When they succeed, their business flourishes and profits are earned. But if their business idea is unsuccessful, they may lose the money they invested.

EMPLOYEES VS. ENTREPRENEURS Entrepreneurs assume risk. This makes them different from employees, who are people hired to work for someone else. Both may make decisions, but only the entrepreneur is directly affected by the consequences of those decisions.

Sara Jones manages a record store owned by Felipe Santiago. Sara decides to keep the store open later during the week. If the additional hours increase profits, Sara may be praised or even get a raise. However, Sara won't directly receive any of the profits because she is an employee. The additional earnings will flow to Felipe, the owner.

Some employees, usually found in large companies, may take on some of the characteristics of an entrepreneur. Called *intrapreneurs*, these employees are managers who take direct responsibility for turning an idea into a profitable finished product through risk-taking and innovation.

WHY DO PEOPLE BECOME ENTREPRENEURS? People go into business for themselves for many reasons. Some want to leave the fast-paced corporate environment and set their own schedules. Others want to be at home but still earn an income. Still others want to pursue a personal dream. You might choose to become an entrepreneur for completely different reasons.

INTEGRITY AND ETHICAL BEHAVIOR An important part of being an entrepreneur involves operating with integrity and exhibiting ethical behavior in all areas of business. Ethical business practices

DEVELOP YOUR READING SKILLS

As you read this chapter, write down questions related to headings and photos. Share your questions with the class.

by entrepreneurs ensure that the highest standards of conduct are observed in their relationships with everyone affected by the business's activities.

When operating with integrity, entrepreneurs behave consistently in actions, values, methods, measures, principles, expectations, and outcomes. When considering whether behavior is ethical, both the actions taken by the entrepreneur and the results of those actions should matter.

Types of Entrepreneurial Businesses

There are generally four types of businesses, as shown in the chart below, and there are many opportunities for entrepreneurs in each category. *Manufacturing businesses* actually produce the products they sell. Using resources and supplies, they create everything from automobiles to paper. *Wholesaling businesses* sell products to other businesses rather than the final consumer. For example, a wholesaler supplies your local greeting card store with items such as cards and wrapping paper. *Retailing businesses*, such as the greeting card store, sell products directly to the people who use or consume them. *Service businesses* sell services rather than products. They include hotels, hairdressers, and repair shops, to name a few.

OTHER BUSINESS AREAS Two other categories of businesses are (1) agricultural and (2) mining and extracting businesses. *Agricultural businesses* generate fresh produce and other farm products, such as wheat. *Mining and extracting businesses* take resources like coal out of the ground so that they can be consumed.

GREEN ENTREPRENEURSHIP Many types of businesses focus on being organic or "green." Because of the growing movement toward environmentally friendly products, entrepreneurs who have a passion about

TYPES OF BUSINESSES			
Manufacturing	Wholesaling	Retailing	Service
Apparel and other textile products	Apparel	Auto and home supply stores	Automotive repair
Chemicals and related products	Electrical goods	Building materials and supply stores	Babysitting
Electronics and other electrical equipment	Groceries and related products	Clothing stores	Bookkeeping
Food products	Hardware, plumbing, and heating equipment	Furniture stores	Dance instruction
Industrial machinery and equipment	Lumber and construction materials	Gift, novelty, and souvenir stores	Electrical services
Printing and publishing	Machinery, equipment, and supplies	Grocery stores	Florists
Stone, clay, and glass products	Paper and paper products	Hardware stores	House cleaning
		Jewelry stores	Lawn care
		Retail bakeries	Plumbing
		Shoe stores	Travel agency
		Sporting goods and bicycle stores	Tutoring
			Web design and maintenance

Source: Small Business Administration

being green have an advantage when introducing their product or service in the market. It is important for green entrepreneurs to educate their customers about how their products or services benefit the earth or conserve resources. In addition to offering green products, entrepreneurs who use green business practices, such as recycling and working with other green-minded companies, are often favored by customers.

SOCIAL ENTREPRENEURSHIP   Some entrepreneurs have a strong desire to help others who are in need. Social entrepreneurship uses business techniques to find innovative solutions to society's most pressing social problems. Social entrepreneurs find societal needs that are not being met by the government or other business sector. Then they work to change the system, implement practical solutions, and persuade others to support their efforts. Social entrepreneurs often commit their lives to making a positive impact on society.

CHECKPOINT

Describe different types of entrepreneurial businesses.

LO 1.1-2   Recognizing Opportunity

Many of America's most successful companies started with one person who recognized an opportunity and came up with an idea for a business in response to that opportunity. Entrepreneurs have played an important role in the history of America's economy and will continue to shape our economy in the future.

The Small Business Administration's Office of Advocacy defines a small business as an independent company having fewer than 500 employees. In 2012, the U.S. Census Bureau reported that there were over 22 million companies in the United States. Small businesses with fewer than 500 employees make up 99.9 percent of these companies. Just over 18,000 U.S. companies are considered large.

Small businesses contribute billions of dollars to the U.S. economy every year and generate jobs that drive economic growth. According to the National Small Business Association, small businesses created 14.3 million jobs over the past 20 years compared with 8.6 million jobs created by large businesses. Since the end of the recession in 2009, small businesses have generated the majority of new jobs. These small businesses are found in virtually every sector of the economy.

Entrepreneurs Who Changed America

Entrepreneurs change American business decade after decade. They establish new companies and fill unmet needs. They continuously change how things are done and contribute to the overall good of the nation. There are many businesses today that started small and have grown into large companies that are making a major impact in our economic system.

STARBUCKS COFFEE COMPANY   Founded in 1971, Starbucks Coffee Company opened its first location in Seattle's Pike Place Market. Starbucks is named after the first mate in Herman Melville's novel *Moby Dick*. It is the world's leading brand of specialty coffee. In 2014, Starbucks had more than 21,000 stores in over 65 countries. When Howard Schultz first joined the company in the early 1980s, Starbucks was already a highly respected local roaster and retailer of whole bean and ground coffees. A business trip to Italy, where he was impressed with the popularity of espresso bars in Milan, helped Schultz recognize an opportunity to develop a similar coffeehouse culture in Seattle. Espresso drinks became an essential element of Schultz's vision. He purchased Starbucks with the support of local investors in 1987. In addition to its well-situated coffeehouses, Starbucks markets its coffee and tea products through its website and through many national retail supermarkets. Today Starbucks strives to make a positive impact on the businesses it works with and the customers it serves.

MICROSOFT   Bill Gates and Paul Allen founded Microsoft, a multinational computer technology corporation, in 1975. Current best-selling products include the Microsoft Windows operating system, Microsoft Office software, Xbox, and the Internet search engine Bing. The name "Microsoft" was formed by combining the words

FAMOUS ENTREPRENEUR

MADAM C. J. WALKER You may have heard it said that "necessity is the mother of invention." Many entrepreneurs got their start by creating something that they themselves needed and then sharing their product with others. That's exactly what made Madam C. J. Walker a millionaire. Walker, originally known as Sarah Breedlove, suffered from a scalp ailment during the 1890s and began experimenting with homemade remedies. Her remedies worked well, so she began offering them to other African-American women. In 1905, she moved to Denver, married newspaperman Charles Joseph Walker, and started her own company. She sold her products door to door and bought ad space in newspapers. Walker later opened Lelia College, where she and her daughter trained other women to use and sell the product line, which had expanded to include items such as complexion soap and dental cream. At least 20 women completed the program every six weeks. Besides becoming a millionaire from the sales of her products, Walker made a huge contribution to the African-American community by empowering women to make their own mark in the business world.

Why do you think Madam C. J. Walker became such a successful entrepreneur?

© A'Lelia Bundles/Walker Family Collection/madamcjwalker.com

THINK CRITICALLY
Why is it important for entrepreneurs to make contributions to their community in addition to offering a product or service?

"microcomputer" and "software." Paul Allen retired in 1983, and Bill Gates went on to head the growing company.

Bill Gates became interested in computers at the age of 13, when he wrote a tic-tac-toe program that allowed users to play against the computer. While still in high school, Gates and his childhood friend Paul Allen wrote a computer program to monitor the traffic patterns in Seattle, Washington, giving them their first early experience with microprocessors. Gates pursued his interest when he attended Harvard University, but remained in contact with Paul Allen. In 1975, they collaborated on the development of a software program to run the Altair, an early personal computer, and soon after they started Microsoft.

In 1980, Microsoft formed a partnership with IBM and provided the operating system for IBM computers. In 1985, Microsoft launched its own operating system. By the 1990s, Microsoft Windows was the dominant operating system, and Microsoft had captured over 90 percent market share of the world's personal computers. As of 2014, Microsoft had a global annual revenue of more than $86 billion and employed over 128,000 people worldwide.

HARPO PRODUCTIONS, INC. While attending Tennessee State University, Oprah Winfrey worked at a local radio station. She got her start in TV as a news anchor on a Nashville TV station. In 1986, she began hosting *The Oprah Winfrey Show*, which went on to become the highest-ranked talk show in television history. It remained on the air until 2011. Winfrey's love of acting and her desire to bring quality entertainment projects into production prompted her to form her own production company, HARPO Productions, Inc., in 1986. Today, HARPO is a formidable force in film and television production. The company also is a partial owner of the Oprah Winfrey Network (OWN), a cable network joint venture with Discovery Communications. Harpo Print LLC publishes the popular *O, The Oprah Magazine*. In addition, Oprah has won praise for her humanitarian work, such as the formation of the Leadership Academy for Girls in South Africa. Oprah's immense influence has far-reaching effects in many aspects outside of media.

Entrepreneurial Opportunities in Our Economy

Small businesses drive innovation and job creation in industries across the country. Even during downturns in the economy, entrepreneurial opportunities still exist. While big businesses tend to be more conservative in their approach to economic slowdowns by scaling back production, conserving cash, and laying off workers, small businesses that have less to lose are more willing and able to make changes quickly. They can be more creative and take more risks than large companies. Their experimentation and innovation lead to technological change and increased productivity. This makes small businesses a significant part of the economic recovery process.

The American Recovery and Reinvestment Act of 2009 was passed to stimulate the American economy after the 2008 economic slowdown. It supported a number of provisions to help small businesses, including $30 billion in tax relief for small businesses and $13 billion in loans, lines of credit, and equity capital.

Since 2009 the U.S. economy has gained momentum. The Small Business Administration continues to provide support to ensure that entrepreneurs have the access and opportunity they need to grow their operations, reach new customers, and create jobs in our communities. The government offers various tax incentives and even grants in some areas to support small businesses. By taking advantage of the incentives offered, small businesses can benefit and help the economy thrive.

 CHECKPOINT

Describe how one of the entrepreneurs discussed above recognized an opportunity to develop a successful business.

LO 1.1-3 Business Success or Failure

Although there are many opportunities for entrepreneurial success, there is also a risk of failure. According to a recent study by the Small Business Administration's Office of Advocacy, about half of new businesses survive at least five years, and one-third survive at least ten years. This means that more than half of all new businesses do not survive beyond ten years. These results are similar for different industries. Major factors in a firm's success include having adequate capital and being large enough to have employees. The owner's education level and reason for starting the business in the first place, such as freedom for family life or wanting to be one's own boss, are also important factors.

The owner's business experience is a factor that contributes to the likelihood of success. Experienced businesspeople have an understanding of how to purchase products and services. They know how to plan, negotiate with suppliers, raise money, negotiate leases, sell and market their product or service, and manage finances. Many businesses fail because the owner lacks business knowledge. Someone may have an idea for a product or service but may lack the necessary business skills he or she needs to run a successful business. There is a major difference between having expertise regarding a product or service and running a business based on that product or service.

Entrepreneurs who lack the skills necessary to develop an idea into a viable product can find help. One way is to participate in a pitch contest or a business plan contest. A *pitch* outlines an idea for a product, service, or project. Often a pitch is made in a minute or less. A business plan describes how a business is going to achieve its goals. Both contests are ways entrepreneurs can get their ideas noticed. Help for an entrepreneur also may come from a *mentor*. However, even for those working in a company, the trend is away from traditional mentoring and toward making the entrepreneur's professional development his or her own responsibility. *Social networking* allows the entrepreneur to connect, build, and maintain a network of mentors. Entrepreneurs also may be helped by a *business incubator*. This is a company that provides services such as management training or office space to new and startup companies. Incubators often are associated with academic institutions, non profit development corporations, for-profit property development ventures, venture capital firms, or a combination of the above.

CHECKPOINT

What factors contribute to helping a business succeed?

1.1 ASSESSMENT

THINK ABOUT IT

1. What are your reasons for wanting to become an entrepreneur? Do you think your reasons are common to all entrepreneurs, or are some of them unique?

2. Explain how integrity and ethical behavior apply to a small business.

3. Why do you think entrepreneurship is important to the U.S. economy? Provide specific examples of how entrepreneurs affect the economy.

4. What do you think is the most important thing an entrepreneur should do before starting a business to ensure its success?

MAKE ACADEMIC CONNECTIONS

5. **MATH** Suppose there are 28,200,000 small businesses in the economy today. Twenty-five percent of those businesses have no employees. What is the number of businesses in the economy with no employees?

6. **SOCIAL STUDIES** Before Starbucks grew nationwide, there were few places that people could go to have coffee and meet with friends and business associates. Write at least one paragraph about how Starbucks and other coffee shops have changed the way people view coffee and its role in society.

7. **COMMUNICATION** Entrepreneurs can be any age. Research a teen entrepreneur. Write a one-page paper about his or her business. Discuss whether you think the business idea is a good one. Make recommendations for expanding the business.

Teamwork

Work in teams to choose a successful entrepreneur. List the traits and aptitudes this person has that have contributed to his or her success. Develop a presentation about the entrepreneur to share with the class.

The Essential Question Refer to The Essential Question on p. 4. Entrepreneurship has played an important role in the U.S. economy by providing job creation and product and service innovations.

1.2 ENTREPRENEURSHIP AND YOU

The Essential Question What does it take to be a successful entrepreneur?

LEARNING OBJECTIVES

LO 1.2-1 Identify the characteristics of successful entrepreneurs.

LO 1.2-2 Identify the characteristics of good team members.

LO 1.2-3 Assess whether you have what it takes to succeed in your own business.

KEY TERMS

• self-assessment
• aptitude

FOCUS ON SMALL
BUSINESS

Think it through!

Gloria and Delia were excited about starting their own business, but as they continued their discussions, Gloria realized they needed to slow down and think through the process carefully. "You know, Delia, it's not really easy to start our own business. When we talked about this in class, Mr. Rivera said that there are a lot of things to consider before starting a business. First, we need to decide what we like to do and what we are good at. Then we have to do a lot of research and planning if we want to be successful."

Thinking about what Mr. Rivera told her in class, Delia sighed. "This entrepreneur thing sounds like a lot of work. What do you think we should do?"

WORK AS A TEAM Many people go into business without first taking time to examine their strengths and weaknesses and what they really like to do. Why do you think it's a good idea for Gloria and Delia to slow down and examine their interests before starting the business?

Consider your strengths and weaknesses before starting a business.

LO 1.2-1 Characteristics of Successful Entrepreneurs

Many people dream of running their own businesses. They would like to become entrepreneurs. Entrepreneurship can be exciting, but many go into it not realizing how difficult it is to run their own business. In fact, statistics show that most new businesses will fail within a few years. These startup businesses can fail because of the owner's poor planning, lack of business knowledge, lack of entrepreneurial characteristics, inability to work with others, or failure to choose the right business. The success or failure of a business is generally the direct responsibility of the entrepreneur.

Researchers have identified several characteristics that distinguish successful entrepreneurs from those that fail.

1. **Successful entrepreneurs are independent.** They want to make their own decisions and do something they enjoy.

2. **Successful entrepreneurs are self-confident.** Entrepreneurs make all of the decisions. They must have the confidence to make choices alone and bounce back from a poorly made decision. They are not afraid to make quick decisions when necessary, which helps them beat their competitors.

3. **Successful entrepreneurs have determination and perseverance.** Entrepreneurs persist through hard times until goals are met. Many entrepreneurs experience failure long before they are successful. They must be willing to keep trying.

4. **Successful entrepreneurs are goal-oriented.** They know what they want, and they are able to focus on achieving it. They are motivated by setting and achieving challenging goals.

5. **Successful entrepreneurs are creative.** They think of new ways to market their businesses and are always looking for new solutions to problems.

6. **Successful entrepreneurs have a strong work ethic.** Being a business owner is hard work. Entrepreneurs must be willing to work beyond the traditional 40-hour work week. They may have to work flexible hours to accommodate customers or suppliers and to get the job done. Entrepreneurs must also continue to learn about their field and stay on top of trends to keep their business operating successfully. Learning does not end when school does.

7. **Successful entrepreneurs are master networkers.** By attending conferences, seminars, and workshops, entrepreneurs can *network*, or meet others who can be valuable resources. These contacts may offer their business expertise or turn into potential customers.

8. **Successful entrepreneurs keep up to date with technology.** New technologies emerge that can help with many business activities. To run their business efficiently, entrepreneurs should always be on the lookout for new technology they can apply to their business.

Ryan Nelson has many entrepreneurial characteristics. Since he was 14, he has played for his high school basketball team. Other boys of his height—just 5'8"—would not have enjoyed competing with much taller boys. Ryan accepted that he would have to work harder to win. He needed to be creative in handling the ball. Most of all, he had to believe in himself. He did and became one of the top players on his team. If Ryan opened his own business, the characteristics he displayed as a ball player could help him succeed.

DID YOU KNOW?

In a recent year, there were over 9 million businesses owned by women, according to Womenable, a website that focuses on women's entrepreneurship worldwide. Women-owned firms have an economic impact of $1.4 trillion annually and have over 7.8 million employees.

LO 1.2-2 Characteristics of Good Team Members

Entrepreneurs realize that there are other stakeholders in their businesses—partners, investors, employees, suppliers, customers, creditors, and so forth. They must work with others to get their business up and running. They must have good team-building skills as well as be effective team members. Good team members display the following traits:

1. **Commitment**   They are committed to team goals and are willing to work hard to achieve the goals.
2. **Competency**   They have the right set of skills needed to get the job done and to help accomplish the team's goals.
3. **Communication**   They have good communication skills and can share ideas with others both verbally and in written form.
4. **Cooperation**   They work well with others and know that they will not always get their way. They are willing to accept the decision of the group for the good of the group.
5. **Creativity**   They are able to look at things from different perspectives and suggest new ways of doing things.

Ryan Nelson displayed these traits as a member of his basketball team. He competed as a team player, recognizing that every member of the team contributed to its success. He freely handed off the ball to other teammates, knowing he could count on them to help win the game. He openly shared his thoughts about the game plan and listened to his teammates' thoughts. His experience will help him work effectively as part of a team in the business world. If Ryan becomes an entrepreneur, he could apply these skills when working with other people who will be important to his success.

How can participation on a sports team help prepare you to become an entrepreneur?

monkeybusinessimages/iStockphoto.com

✓ **CHECKPOINT**

Why is it important for entrepreneurs to be good team members?

LO 1.2-3 Are You Right for Entrepreneurship?

Entrepreneurship is not for everyone. Some people lack the qualities needed to become successful entrepreneurs. Others lack the aptitude needed to run a business. For others, the advantages of entrepreneurship do not outweigh the disadvantages.

To determine if entrepreneurship is right for you, you first need to perform a self-assessment. A **self-assessment** is an evaluation of your strengths and weaknesses. You can do this in a number of ways. You can list what you believe to be your strengths and weaknesses on a sheet of paper. You can ask others what they believe your strengths are and where your weaknesses lie. There are also professional tests you can take to assess your abilities.

Assess Your Interests

Success as an entrepreneur requires a strong commitment to a business and a lot of energy. To be able to commit yourself fully to a business, you should choose a field that interests you and that will provide you with an experience you will enjoy. Many entrepreneurs center a business on an interest or hobby. Analyzing past experiences and jobs can also help. Have you had any jobs or experiences that you found fulfilling? Perhaps building a business around that activity could lead to success.

Assess Your Aptitude

Different jobs require different job aptitudes. **Aptitude** is the ability to learn a particular kind of job. Auto mechanics must possess an aptitude for solving mechanical problems. They must also be good with their hands. People who sell insurance must have good interpersonal skills. Answering questions like those in the Job Attributes Checklist can help you identify the kinds of entrepreneurial opportunities that might match your aptitudes and interests.

JOB ATTRIBUTES CHECKLIST

- ❑ 1. I enjoy working with numbers.
- ❑ 2. I enjoy working outdoors.
- ❑ 3. I enjoy working with my hands.
- ❑ 4. I enjoy selling.
- ❑ 5. I like working with people.
- ❑ 6. I prefer to work alone.
- ❑ 7. I like supervising other people.
- ❑ 8. I like knowing exactly what I am supposed to do.

Cengage Learning

Assess the Advantages of Entrepreneurship

Many people see significant advantages in owning their own business. Some of the biggest advantages include the following:

1. **Entrepreneurs are their own bosses.** Nobody tells an entrepreneur what to do. Entrepreneurs control their own destinies.
2. **Entrepreneurs can choose a business that interests them.** Entrepreneurs work in fields that appeal to them. Many combine hobbies and interests with business.

3. **Entrepreneurs can be creative.** Entrepreneurs are always implementing creative ideas that they think of themselves.
4. **Entrepreneurs can make large sums of money.** Entrepreneurship involves risk, but if the business is successful, the business owner will reap the profits.

Assess the Disadvantages of Entrepreneurship

As the disadvantages show, entrepreneurship is not for the faint of heart. All prospective entrepreneurs must weigh the advantages and disadvantages before making the decision to start a business. Disadvantages include the following:

1. **Entrepreneurship is risky.** Just as there is the chance to earn large sums of money, there is the possibility of losing money and going out of business.

What Went *Wrong?*

Experience Needed

Louise was a theater performer who sang and danced in Broadway-style musicals. She earned additional money working part time at a print and copy shop for several years. The elderly couple who owned the shop allowed Louise to work flexible hours so that she could pursue a music career. When the couple decided to sell the business and move away, Louise was excited about the opportunity to purchase the business.

The former owner helped Louise gather financial information and put together a business plan. Louise's uncle cosigned a bank loan, and she was in business. She modernized the décor of the shop but made few other changes. Louise contacted all the existing customers to assure them of equal or better service. Sales increased in the first two months. But then...

The former owner left town earlier than planned. Then the employee in charge of printer operations quit. Using part-time employees, Louise frantically tried to get large orders out on time. With no formal business training and no management experience, Louise couldn't deal with all of the problems. After all of her struggles, Louise ended up selling the business at a $50,000 loss.

Get some business training before starting a business.

THINK CRITICALLY

1. What characteristics did Louise possess that led her to become an entrepreneur?
2. What circumstances do you think led to the failure of this business?
3. Are there steps Louise could have taken to try to save her business?

2. **Entrepreneurs face uncertain and irregular incomes.** Entrepreneurs may make money one month and lose money the next. Unlike employees who receive a steady paycheck, entrepreneurs may not.

3. **Entrepreneurs work long hours.** Entrepreneurs are never really finished with their jobs. They can work long, irregular hours. They receive no paid days off and often work evenings and weekends.

4. **Entrepreneurs must make all decisions by themselves.** Unless they have partners, entrepreneurs are responsible for all decisions made regarding the business, which can be difficult without the right expertise.

 CHECKPOINT

What kinds of assessments should you make to determine if entrepreneurship is right for you?

 1.2 ASSESSMENT

THINK ABOUT IT

1. Entrepreneurs can fail even if they are committed and have the characteristics needed to be successful. How can this happen?

2. What traits do good team members have? Select one trait and explain why it is important.

3. Do you think the advantages of entrepreneurship outweigh the disadvantages? Why or why not?

MAKE ACADEMIC CONNECTIONS

4. **TECHNOLOGY**   Research new technology products and services that would be useful to a business owner. Describe one product or service and explain how it can help business owners run their companies more efficiently.

5. **CAREER SUCCESS**   Choose a business idea that interests you. Make a list of your interests and abilities. Now list the attributes that you think are necessary to succeed in this business. Compare your two lists. Would this business be a good choice for you? Explain.

Teamwork

Work in teams to list advantages and disadvantages of being an employee. Then list advantages and disadvantages of being an entrepreneur. Analyze each list and summarize your findings.

The Essential Question   Refer to The Essential Question on p. 12. Entrepreneurs must be independent, self-confident, persistent, goal-oriented, and creative. They must also have a strong work ethic and be able to work well with others.

1.3 EXPLORE IDEAS AND OPPORTUNITIES

The Essential Question How do entrepreneurs choose what business to start?

LEARNING OBJECTIVES

LO 1.3-1 Identify sources for new business ideas.

LO 1.3-2 Recognize different business opportunities.

LO 1.3-3 Identify your own personal goals.

KEY TERMS

- opportunities
- ideas
- trade shows

FOCUS ON SMALL BUSINESS

It starts with an idea.

Gloria and Delia realized that although there are many advantages to owning their own business, there are also many responsibilities and challenges they would face as business owners. They knew they had their work cut out for them. They needed to have a really good idea and be certain that there were people who would be willing to pay them for the product or service they wanted to sell.

"How do we decide what kind of business we should have?" Delia asked Gloria.

"There are so many businesses in our community," Gloria responded. "We have to come up with just the right idea!"

WORK AS A TEAM How do people come up with ideas for new businesses? How can they determine if the idea is worth pursuing?

Spend time determining a good idea for your business.

LO 1.3-1 Look for Ideas

Millions of entrepreneurs in the United States start their own business. You may wonder how they decided what business to operate. They may have acted on a new idea or an opportunity. An idea is different from an opportunity. Opportunities are possibilities that arise from existing conditions. Ideas are thoughts or concepts that come from creative thinking. Ideas can come from many different sources.

Hobbies and Interests

Many people get business ideas from their hobbies or interests. Making a list of hobbies and interests can help you decide what business is right for you.

Bill Taylor had always enjoyed working with his grandfather on the farm and had helped to build and maintain many farm structures. He built a garage and added a sunroom to his own home. He also was able to make plumbing, electrical, and carpentry repairs around the house. He started doing this for others in his spare time. Soon he had so many people calling on him for these services that he decided to start a general contracting business.

Past Experiences

Analyzing past experiences and jobs can help you come up with ideas for a business you might enjoy owning. People who excel at their jobs have generally learned much about their profession and how to satisfy customer needs. They also see how successful marketing is conducted. Through their work, they can build a network of potential customers, suppliers, employees, and distributors. When they feel confident that they can offer a product or service to this market more effectively than their current employer, they can start a new business. The experience and training they received on the job will increase their chances of success in running a new business.

Samantha Rodriguez worked as a computer network administrator for a large company. Recognizing that she could use her experience to perform the same computer services for other companies, Samantha started her own computer consulting service. She currently earns less money than she did working for a large company, but she enjoys working flexible hours and meeting new people.

Discovery or Invention

Sometimes a business opportunity arises from a discovery or invention. Someone may invent a new tool that works better than tools that are currently available. The next step is to research and find out if the idea can be patented, who the competition is, what the manufacturing process would be, and who the target market is.

Chandra Coe enjoyed working in her garden, but she did not like any of the tools she had for removing weeds from around the plants. She made modifications to one of her garden tools and found that it worked perfectly. After several friends tried out the garden tool and liked it, Chandra decided to investigate how to market and sell her invention.

 **CHECKPOINT**

Where do new ideas for businesses come from?

LO 1.3-2 Investigate Opportunities

People often conduct research to determine what is missing in a particular market—what needs exist that are not being met. By doing this research, they hope to find the perfect business opportunity.

Sources of Information

The Internet and the library have resources that can help you conduct research for different opportunities. These include books on entrepreneurship, magazines for entrepreneurs, trade magazines for certain businesses, and government publications. *County Business Patterns* is an annual series of publications providing economic profiles of counties, states, and the country as a whole. Data include employment, payroll, and the number of establishments by industry.

The Internet and the library are not the only places to investigate opportunities. The Small Business Administration (SBA) is an organization that exists to help small businesses and their owners. It publishes helpful information. It can also be beneficial to talk to entrepreneurs and attend **trade shows**, which are special meetings where companies of the same industry or related industries display their products.

Luanda Williams wanted to use her love of sports and dancing to create her own company. She found many magazine articles on the Internet that gave her information on various kinds of businesses. She also talked to owners of gymnastic centers, health clubs, and dance studios. She discovered that there were not enough children's fitness programs to meet the demand in her area. Her research revealed the many opportunities available in the children's fitness industry.

Compare Different Opportunities

Once you find appealing business opportunities, you need to identify which ones have the best chance for success. Now is the time to assess each business opportunity by asking yourself the following questions:

1. Is there a market in my community for this kind of business? Will people buy my product or service?
2. How much money would it take to start this business? Will I be able to borrow that much money?
3. How many hours a week is it likely to take to run this business? Am I willing to commit that much time?
4. What are the risks associated with this business? What is the rate of business failure?
5. Does my background prepare me to run this kind of business? Do most people who own this kind of business have more experience?
6. How much money could I make running this business?

▶ BE YOUR OWN BOSS

You are interested in starting your own business, but you are not sure what kind of business it should be. To help you get started, think about something you do that you really enjoy. Now think about ways that you might be able to turn this activity into a business. Make a list of businesses in your area that offer a related product or service. Write a paragraph explaining your business idea. How will your business be different from the existing businesses you listed?

CHECKPOINT

How can you find out about various business opportunities?

LO 1.3-3　Set Goals

For everything you do in life, you set goals. Goals help you stay on track and follow through with your plans. The best goals are SMART. SMART goals provide more direction, as shown below.

SMART GOALS	
Specific	Goals should be specific and answer "What?" "Why?" and "How?"
Measurable	Goals should establish ways to measure your progress.
Attainable	Goals should not be too far out of reach.
Realistic	Goals should represent things to which you are willing to commit.
Timely	Goals should have a time frame for achievement.
Goal	I will learn more about starting my own business.
SMART Goal	I will learn more about starting my own catering business by obtaining information from the Small Business Administration and talking with the owners of three local catering businesses by the end of the month.

As an entrepreneur, you will need to set many goals. Goals can be categorized as financial and nonfinancial.

Financial Goals

Set specific financial goals before starting a business. Financial goals can include how much money you will earn and how quickly you will pay off debts. Make sure your goals are realistic. If one of your goals is to make large sums of money early on, you almost certainly will be disappointed. It usually takes time for businesses to become well established and profitable. Setting SMART financial goals will help you develop a realistic plan for earning a profit.

Goals should be measurable and easily attainable in the time allotted. Mo Yang wants to start a mail-order business for model trains, planes, and cars. His income goal is to earn $27,000 by the end of the first year. He estimates that after expenses he will earn $9 for each item he sells. At this rate of profit, he would have to sell 3,000 models to meet his income goal. Mo realizes that this is not realistic. He will have to lower his income goal or find another business idea.

Nonfinancial Goals

Most people who own their own business do so for more than just monetary gain. They are looking for personal satisfaction. They may want to serve a community need, do something they like, or enjoy the personal independence. You should specify what nonfinancial goals you want to achieve by being an entrepreneur. For example, as a business owner, you may want to offer support to a charity organization, either by making monetary donations or by offering your business's services. Setting and meeting nonfinancial goals can help an entrepreneur live a more satisfying and fulfilling life.

CHECKPOINT

Why are financial goals important? Name some nonfinancial goals an entrepreneur may have.

1.3 ASSESSMENT

THINK ABOUT IT

1. Think about a business opportunity that appeals to you. For this business, answer the six assessment questions listed on page 20 on a sheet of paper. Is this a realistic choice for you? Why or why not?

2. In terms of annual income, what financial goals have you set for yourself for five years after you graduate? What nonfinancial goals have you set that you could fulfill by becoming an entrepreneur? Which are more important to you— financial or nonfinancial goals? Why?

3. Your friend has set the following goal: I plan to eat healthier. Is this a SMART goal? Explain why or why not. What suggestions can you make for improving it?

MAKE ACADEMIC CONNECTIONS

4. **MATH**   You live near the beach and want to give snorkeling lessons. You estimate that after expenses, you can earn $10 per lesson. Each lesson will be one-hour long, and you will offer lessons five days a week. Your income goal is $15,000 per year. How many lessons do you need to give to achieve this goal? Is this goal realistic?

5. **COMMUNICATION**   Write a letter to the Small Business Administration. Indicate your interest in starting a small business of your choice. Ask what specific services the SBA provides to people who wish to start this type of business. Give your letter to your teacher.

6. **SOCIAL STUDIES**   Write a personal nonfinancial goal involving your local community that you would like to achieve through entrepreneurship. Be sure the goal is SMART. Write an outline for a detailed plan you can follow to achieve this goal and explain how it can benefit your community.

Teamwork

Working with classmates who have similar interests, come up with an idea for a business. Brainstorm a list of resources for finding information about similar businesses.

The Essential Question   Refer to The Essential Question on p. 18. Entrepreneurs research ideas that match their interests and goals and find an idea that might work.

PROBLEM SOLVING FOR ENTREPRENEURS

The Essential Question Why do entrepreneurs need to be good problem solvers?

LEARNING OBJECTIVES

LO 1.4-1 List the six steps of the problem-solving model.

LO 1.4-2 Describe ways to improve your problem-solving skills.

KEY TERMS

• problem-solving model
• brainstorming

Research your ideas.

Gloria and Delia spent time on the Internet and in the local library researching ideas for their new business. As a result, they came up with several ideas. Now they have to decide what to do with these ideas.

As they discussed their options, Gloria said, "You know, Delia, we can talk about these ideas, but we really need a system that we can use for solving problems. We want to be sure that we make the very best decisions for our business."

"Yes," Delia responded, "You're right. I remember reading about a problem-solving model in one of the books we found at the library. Let's go back and find it and see if we can adapt it for our use."

WORK AS A TEAM How important do you think it is to use a system for solving problems and making decisions?

Research will help you examine opportunities.

PIKSEL/iStockphoto.com

FOCUS ON SMALL
BUSINESS

LO 1.4-1 Use the Problem-Solving Model

As an entrepreneur, you will be faced with making decisions and solving problems every day. Whether to become an entrepreneur is a big decision itself. Many entrepreneurs make decisions casually or base them on intuition. As a result, their decisions may be based on faulty assumptions or illogical thinking. The best entrepreneurs use formal problem-solving models to gather information and evaluate different options.

A formal **problem-solving model** helps people solve problems in a logical manner. The model consists of six steps: (1) define the problem,

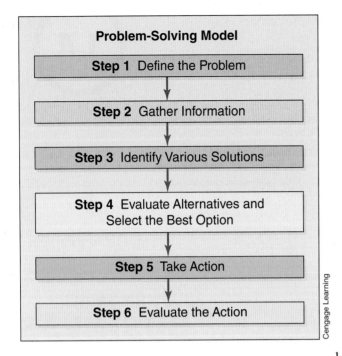

Problem-Solving Model

Step 1 Define the Problem

↓

Step 2 Gather Information

↓

Step 3 Identify Various Solutions

↓

Step 4 Evaluate Alternatives and Select the Best Option

↓

Step 5 Take Action

↓

Step 6 Evaluate the Action

Cengage Learning

(2) gather information, (3) identify various solutions, (4) evaluate alternatives and select the best option, (5) take action, and (6) evaluate the action.

Step 1 Define the Problem

Before you can solve a problem, you need to diagnose it. Write down what the problem is and why it is a problem. Try to quantify it too. For example, you may be trying to decide whether to start your own business or accept a job offer from another company. If you accept the job offer, your income would be $30,000 a year. If you reject the job offer, you would lose that income. Quantifying the problem helps you figure out how much it is worth to you to solve it.

Dan Parker knows what his problem is: Should he start a website design company? He took many computer courses throughout high school and is now attending college. He has worked in the food industry throughout high school and college to earn money to help pay for his college expenses. Dan enjoys working at restaurants and has gained valuable customer service and management experience. In addition, he also volunteers his web design skills on projects for his university and local community programs. He will be graduating in the next few months with a degree in Computer Science. Dan is considering starting his own website design business, but he is not sure whether that is the right choice for him.

Step 2 Gather Information

Once the problem has been defined, you need to gather information that could help solve it. Relevant information may be obtained from many sources, including company records, industry data, and trade magazines. It is also a good idea to interview other people in the industry to find out what their experiences have been and to learn how they have solved similar problems.

In Dan's case, it would be helpful for him to take a closer look at himself. He should do a self-assessment to determine his strengths and weaknesses. He also needs to consider his skills, experience, and interests. Does he have the characteristics of a successful entrepreneur? He also needs to examine the advantages and disadvantages of running a website design company. He should talk to other professionals in the business and read trade magazines to gather information. Dan needs to thoroughly explore every aspect of starting and running a website design company.

Step 3 Identify Various Solutions

Most problems can be solved in various ways. Identify all possibilities before you settle on a particular solution. Dan comes up with several possible solutions to his problem.

1. Work as an employee in a position that utilizes his customer service skills and management experience
2. Work as a website designer for another company to gain more experience and then start his own business in three to five years
3. Pursue his interests in the food industry and open his own restaurant
4. Start his own website design company upon graduation

Step 4 Evaluate Alternatives and Select the Best Option

The decision maker next needs to evaluate the alternatives to determine the best solution. In some cases, it may be possible to quantify the costs and benefits of each alternative. In other cases, quantifying each alternative may not be possible, and the decision maker may simply have to rank each alternative.

Dan ranks option 1 the lowest because of his desire to be his own boss. All of the information that Dan gathered indicates that he has a strong chance of succeeding as an entrepreneur. He ranks option 3 next to lowest. Dan has considerable experience in the food industry and enjoys that type of work, but he decides he would rather pursue his interests in website design. He ranks option 2 second because he is already confident in his level of computer knowledge and experience. After evaluating all of his alternatives, Dan decides option 4 is the best solution.

Why is it important to evaluate your options when making decisions?

Step 5 Take Action

Once you have selected the best solution to the problem, you need to take action to implement it. Dan begins putting together a business plan, which he will use to help obtain a loan from his family or a bank. He also starts spreading the word about his new venture.

Step 6 Evaluate the Action

The problem-solving process is not complete until you evaluate your action because even the best laid plans may not work. After being in business for six months, Dan evaluates whether he is achieving his financial and nonfinancial goals. It seems that Dan made the right decision because his business is profitable and he is enjoying his work. He has been able to fulfill his dream of working for himself while providing a valuable service to others. Dan will continue to use the problem-solving model to make the most effective decisions for him and his new business.

LO 1.4-2 Problem-Solving Skills

The more often you use the problem-solving model, the better skilled at decision making you will become. It will become a valuable tool to you throughout your career. There are also a few other things you can do to improve your problem-solving skills.

How can good communication skills help you succeed in business?

Communicate

Good communication is important in the problem-solving process. When trying to resolve problems and make decisions, you most likely will have to interact with others. You may have to ask questions, request information, and express your ideas and opinions. On such occasions, it is important that you communicate clearly and confidently. You must also be a good listener. You must carefully listen to information, opinions, and suggestions from others. Listening to others' input can help you make informed decisions.

Kris is the owner of a small boutique and is looking for ways to increase sales. She decides to conduct a meeting with her employees to communicate her sales objectives. During the meeting, she listens to her employees' thoughts and ideas for boosting sales. By communicating with others, Kris is able to gather lots of good information to help her solve her sales problem.

Brainstorm

Brainstorming is a creative problem-solving technique that involves generating a large number of fresh ideas. Brainstorming is often done in a group setting, but it is a very useful activity for an individual as well. Think about the problem you are trying to solve. Brainstorm by writing down as many possible solutions to the problem as you can think of. Do not be afraid to write down any idea you have. The point of brainstorming is not to judge your ideas as good or bad but to come up with as many ideas as possible. Once you have made a list of ideas, you can use the problem-solving model to determine the best alternatives.

Learn from Mistakes

If you want to become an entrepreneur, you cannot be afraid to make mistakes. Mistakes are likely to happen, but a negative situation can be turned into a positive one. You should view your mistakes as a learning experience. Mistakes can help you learn what to do or what not to do, which proves to be valuable in the problem-solving process.

When you read about some of the nation's most famous entrepreneurs, you will find that many of them failed before they came up with a winning idea. Colonel Sanders of KFC fame is a good example. He held many jobs and owned a motel chain, service stations, and other restaurants that were unsuccessful. While running his restaurant, he developed his secret recipe chicken. In 1952, at the age of 62, he began traveling across the country selling his chicken recipe. By 1964, there were 600 KFC restaurants in the United States and Canada, and Colonel Sanders sold KFC for $2 million.

 CHECKPOINT

How can you improve your problem-solving skills?

 ASSESSMENT

THINK ABOUT IT

1. Do the six steps in the problem-solving model have to be performed in the order described? Why or why not?

2. How do you think strong communication skills can improve the problem-solving process? Provide specific examples of how a business owner might use communication skills to resolve a problem.

MAKE ACADEMIC CONNECTIONS

3. **MATH**   In Step 3 of the problem-solving model (identify various solutions), you will list a variety of possible solutions to a problem. For the four options Dan Parker came up with on pages 24–25, assign a percentage weight to each based on Dan's reasoning. Give the decimal equivalent for each percentage. What must the decimal value of the four options total?

4. **PROBLEM SOLVING**   You own a successful shop that buys, sells, and services bicycles. The owner of the building you now lease tells you she plans to sell the property in six months, meaning you may have to move your business. Use the six-step problem-solving model to develop a plan for how to proceed.

Teamwork

Working as a team, identify some benefits to using a formal problem-solving model that are not discussed in the text. Provide some examples of how entrepreneurs might use the problem-solving model in their business.

The Essential Question   Refer to The Essential Question on p. 23. Entrepreneurs must be good problem solvers in order to make good decisions that will help the business succeed.

Sharpen Your 21st Century Entrepreneurial Skills

Effective Business Letters

As an entrepreneur, you might write letters to communicate your business ideas, solicit business, respond to customer questions, negotiate purchases, or deal with suppliers. To do so effectively, you need to develop your business writing skills. In today's world of social media, text messaging, and email, there has been a decline in communication skills. Texting and other social networking channels may lead to poor grammar, misspelled words, and an increased use of slang. Your business letter should demonstrate your strong communication skills.

When writing a business letter, a certain level of formality is necessary. That doesn't mean business writing should be difficult to understand. Good business writing communicates ideas clearly. It also gets results by being positive and persuasive and by convincing readers that they should accept what the writer is communicating.

Certain basic rules should be followed in writing business letters, as outlined below and as shown in the letter on the next page.

1. **Key all formal correspondence.** Send handwritten letters only when they are intended as personal letters.

2. **Spell all names correctly and have the correct address.** No matter how well written your letter is, its effect will be dramatically reduced if you misspell the recipient's name or the company's name. Addressing a letter incorrectly may cause it to arrive late or to be returned.

3. **Always date your business correspondence.** It may be necessary to refer to this date at a later time.

4. **Use names and titles appropriately.** Use the person's first name if you know him or her well. If you do not know the person or if the letter is very formal, use the person's last name, along with the appropriate title (Dr., Mr., Mrs., Ms., or Miss).

5. **Be direct and positive.** Always maintain a positive tone and portray your message in an optimistic light, even if your letter contains bad news.

6. **Be persuasive and specific.** Make sure the action or result you want from the reader is clear. Use nonthreatening language that will persuade the reader that this action or result is the most desirable.

7. **Avoid using fancy or complex language.** Use straightforward language that says exactly what you mean.

8. **Use an appropriate closing.** Make sure your closing corresponds with the content of the letter you have written. If you have written a letter to a supplier to complain about poor service, do not use "With warmest regards." Common closings are "Sincerely" and "Sincerely yours."

9. **Proofread for spelling and grammatical errors.** The most persuasive and positive letter can be ruined by a single mistake.

Creative Web Designs
10 E. 34th Street • Baltimore, MD 21218
(410) 555-4321 CWD@internet.com

April 11, 20—

Ms. Chelsey Wright
Advantage Marketers
692 Kemper Road
Baltimore, MD 21209

Dear Ms. Wright

Are you looking for new ways to energize your website? If so, I would like to introduce myself and talk with you about my company, Creative Web Designs.

As a recent graduate of Piedmont State University with an Associate degree in Computer Science, I am ready to put my skills to work for you. After providing web development services for the local university and for other local community programs for the past several years, I have decided to offer my services to other local businesses such as yours. Services provided include the following:

• Creation of visibly appealing and compelling web pages

• Revitalization of existing websites

• Hyperlink development

• Technical support

Please call for a free consultation to discuss how you can have a website that works effectively for your company. Samples of my website creations are available for you to review. References can be provided upon request. I look forward to hearing from you.

Sincerely

Dan Parker

Dan Parker
Owner

Cengage Learning

TRY IT OUT

You own a shop that sells comic books. Write a business letter to your main supplier, a comic book wholesaler. Tell the supplier that you have not received the shipment of the most recent edition of a popular comic that you ordered. Be sure to follow the basic rules for writing business letters. Create names for your business and your supplier's business.

SUMMARY

1.1 All about Entrepreneurship

1. Entrepreneurship is the process of running a business of one's own. The person who owns, operates, and takes the risks of a business venture is called an entrepreneur.
2. More than 99.9 percent of the 22 million businesses in the United States are considered small businesses. Small businesses contribute more to the U.S. economy than all large businesses combined and contribute to the economic recovery of the country during economic downturns.
3. Factors that contribute to a new business's success or failure include having adequate capital and being large enough to have employees. The owner's education level and business experience are also important factors.

1.2 Entrepreneurship and You

4. Successful entrepreneurs tend to be independent, self-confident, goal-oriented, and creative.
5. Entrepreneurs must have good team-building skills and be able to work well with others.
6. To determine whether entrepreneurship is right for you, you will need to assess your strengths, weaknesses, interests, and aptitudes.

1.3 Explore Ideas and Opportunities

7. Ideas for new businesses can come from many different sources, including your hobbies and interests, your past experiences, and a discovery or invention.
8. You may research business opportunities online and through the public library and the Small Business Administration. Other sources of information can be obtained by attending trade shows and talking to entrepreneurs.
9. Entrepreneurs should set SMART goals, which are specific, measurable, attainable, realistic, and timely. Goals can be categorized as financial and nonfinancial.

1.4 Problem Solving for Entrepreneurs

10. A problem-solving model consists of six steps: define the problem, gather information, identify various solutions, evaluate alternatives and select the best option, take action, and evaluate the action.
11. There are several ways to improve problem-solving skills, including communicating, brainstorming, and learning from mistakes.

WHAT DO YOU KNOW NOW?

Read *Ideas in Action* on page 3 again. Then answer the questions a second time. Have your responses changed? If so, how have they changed?

KEY TERMS REVIEW

Match each statement with the term that best defines it. Some terms may not be used.

1. People who are hired to work for someone else
2. An evaluation of your strengths and weaknesses
3. A creative problem-solving technique that involves generating a large number of fresh ideas
4. Special meetings at which companies of the same industry or related industries display their products
5. People who own, operate, and take the risk of a business venture
6. Thoughts or concepts that come from creative thinking
7. The ability to learn a particular kind of job
8. The process of running a business of one's own

a. aptitude
b. brainstorming
c. employees
d. entrepreneurs
e. entrepreneurship
f. ideas
g. opportunities
h. problem-solving model
i. self-assessment
j. trade shows

REVIEW YOUR KNOWLEDGE

9. Barbara Wall had a great recipe for sweet bell pepper sauce. Her friend Leonard Wilson convinced her that they should go into business together and sell the sauce. They now ship WW's Red Sauce to stores in 35 states. Wall and Wilson are examples of
   a. intrapreneurs
   b. entrepreneurs
   c. employees
   d. managers
10. Which of the following is *not* an example of an entrepreneur?
    a. Diane Molberg started By Request, a successful home bakery business.
    b. Donna Cook started a cleaning service ten years ago.
    c. Gene Morgan manages The Secret Garden, a business owned by her sister.
    d. Elmer Olsen created Bayfield Apple Jam and distributes the jam nationally.
11. Team members who have the right set of skills needed to get the job done are demonstrating __?__.
12. Jackson Hewitt, a tax preparation company, is an example of which type of business?
    a. manufacturing business
    b. wholesaling business
    c. retailing business
    d. service business
13. The plant where Goodyear tires are made is an example of which type of business?
    a. manufacturing business
    b. wholesaling business
    c. retailing business
    d. service business
14. According to the Small Business Administration's Office of Advocacy, how many new businesses survive for at least ten years?
    a. one-third
    b. one-half
    c. one-fourth
    d. three-fourths
15. Possibilities that arise from existing conditions are called __?__.
16. Which of the following is *not* an advantage of entrepreneurship?
    a. Entrepreneurs are their own bosses.
    b. Entrepreneurs can be creative.
    c. Entrepreneurs take all the risks involved with starting a business.
    d. Entrepreneurs can make large sums of money.

17. Which step of the problem-solving model involves performing research and interviewing customers, suppliers, and employees?
    a. define the problem
    c. identify various solutions
    b. gather information
    d. evaluate alternatives

APPLY WHAT YOU LEARNED

18. Types of businesses include manufacturing, wholesaling, retailing, service, agricultural, and mining and extracting. In small groups, compile a list of specific companies that belong to each category of business. Share your results with the class. (LO 1.1-1)

19. Is your personality suited for becoming an entrepreneur? Interview an entrepreneur about the personality traits that have been most beneficial for his or her success. As an alternative, read an article about a successful entrepreneur. Write a one-page paper comparing your personality traits to the entrepreneur's and describing whether you are suited for entrepreneurship. (LO 1.2-3)

MAKE ACADEMIC CONNECTIONS

20. **MATH** Edward Greenberg loves to make and fly kites. Edward is planning to open a shop that sells custom-made kites. He asks for your advice to help him set financial goals. Edward estimates that after expenses, he can make a $15 profit on each kite he sells. If his annual income goal is $15,450, how many kites will he have to sell? Assuming he can make only three kites per day and will work five days a week year round, is this goal realistic? (LO 1.3-3)

21. **HISTORY** Research online the life and career of a famous historical entrepreneur. Find out information such as birthplace, type of business started, and what effect the person had on the economy and history. Is the business still operating? Write a short report about your findings. (LO 1.1-2)

22. **COMMUNICATION** For the above History question, find a creative way to present your findings to the class. Use visual aids, skits, costumes, games, and so on. (LO 1.1-2)

 **What Would YOU DO?**

During their senior year of high school, Nancy told Gary about an idea she had for a business in the local community. She had done some research and thought that her idea could be turned into a profitable business.

After graduation, Nancy went off to college and Gary stayed home and attended the local community college. Since Nancy didn't act on her business idea, Gary decided that he would open a business using Nancy's idea. What do you think about Gary's actions? Is he doing the right thing?

BUILD YOUR
BUSINESS PLAN PROJECT

This activity will help you identify a business opportunity that may be right for you. You will use this business idea throughout the book.

1. Divide a sheet of paper into two columns. In the first column list all your interests. In the second column, list business opportunities that relate to each interest.

2. Do a self-assessment by listing your strengths and weaknesses. Compare this list with your list of business opportunities. For which business opportunities would your strengths most apply? For which business opportunities would your weaknesses hurt the most? Based on your strengths and weaknesses, cross out those business opportunities that no longer seem suitable for you.

3. Assess your aptitude, using the Job Attributes Checklist in Lesson 1.2. Put a checkmark next to the business opportunities that relate to your aptitudes.

4. For the business opportunities remaining on your list, assess the advantages and disadvantages of each. Cross out any where the disadvantages outweigh the advantages.

5. Conduct research to find and list sources of information that relate to the business opportunities that remain on your list. Locate at least one of these sources for each business opportunity and write a sentence stating the type of information it contains. On your list, cross out business opportunities for which you could not find any information.

6. Choose one of the business opportunities remaining on your list. Based on this business opportunity, answer the six questions listed in the "Compare Different Opportunities" section in Lesson 1.3.

7. Set personal financial goals for a five-year period based on the business opportunity you chose. Demonstrate that your goals are SMART (Specific, Measurable, Attainable, Realistic, and Timely). Assume you will need to borrow money to get started. How much profit do you hope to make in one year? Three years? Five years? Next, set nonfinancial goals you hope to achieve with this business. Be sure to include specific activities you can perform to help achieve each goal.

8. Write a letter to potential customers about the goods or services your business will provide. On paper, plan a telephone conversation you will use as a follow-up to the letter. Work with a classmate and do a mock phone conversation based on your plan.

9. Plan ahead to prevent any problems that may arise in your business. Describe a problem that could occur and use the six-step problem-solving model to deal with it now. Brainstorm solutions on your own or with family members or friends.

10. Save all of your materials from this project in a folder. You will continue to add to this folder as you build your business plan at the end of each chapter.

PLANNING A CAREER IN FITNESS TRAINING

"A new health club opened near my aunt's house, and she absolutely loves going there. The club is open 24/7. As my aunt was a bit intimidated by the high-tech exercise equipment at the club, she's hired a personal trainer to help her learn how to use the equipment and to hold her accountable for her efforts. She says she feels much more energetic and relaxed than she used to. She's even considering joining the volleyball team that's been established for health club members."

In a high-tech, convenience-oriented society that often results in inactive lifestyles, how do individuals maintain physical fitness? When the weather prohibits outdoor activities, where can people go to exercise?

Fitness facilities provide the location, equipment, and instruction necessary for club members to exercise. Personal trainers help individual clients customize a workout plan that will help them achieve their personal fitness goals.

Employment Outlook
- An average rate of employment growth is anticipated.
- Aging baby boomers, who hope to maintain fitness in later life, are fueling the demand for fitness workers.
- Parents' desire to keep children fit as well as employers who encourage employees to stay in shape will contribute to the ongoing need for fitness workers.

Job Titles
- Corporate Personal Trainer
- Fitness Advisor
- Certified Personal Trainer
- Fitness Consultant
- Personal Fitness Coach

Needed Education/Skills
- A high school diploma and CPR certification are usually needed.
- Fitness certification from a reputable certification organization is required.
- Continuing education is often mandatory.
- Being physically fit and extroverted and having strong interpersonal skills is necessary.

What's it like to work in Fitness Training? Nhu, a certified personal trainer, spent the weekend at a training seminar. The session was part of her ongoing training to stay current on developments in the personal training field.

This morning Nhu taught a group exercise class at a large fitness center. She enjoyed leading a large group of people and helping them improve their fitness level. The class also gave her the opportunity to meet many of the health club members. Some of the class attendees signed up for her personal training services at the club.

When signing up for personal training, club members can work with Nhu on their individual fitness goals for an hourly fee. If they elect to buy a ten-session pass, then the hourly fee is reduced.

Nhu has also established a private personal training service. When she attends a client's home for a training session, she charges a higher hourly rate. Many clients with busy schedules are more than happy to pay the higher rate for the convenience.

What about you? Would you find it gratifying to help individuals improve their physical fitness levels? What would you like or dislike about this type of career?

Impromptu Speaking

Impromptu speaking is an FBLA event that is perfect for the budding entrepreneur. Every entrepreneur must be able to effectively communicate with customers, employees, vendors, and potential investors. Imagine that you are on an elevator with a potential investor. You may have only 60 seconds to pitch your business to him. While speaking, you must show that you are confident, poised, and articulate. You want to be sure to make a great first impression.

Your speech should be four minutes in length and must relate to one or more of the FBLA-PBL goals. A topic will be given to you ten minutes before you are scheduled to perform. During those ten minutes, you may use two 4" × 6" notecards to prepare for your speech. You will not be allowed to use visual aids or a microphone during your speech.

You will present your speech to a panel of judges and spectators, who will judge you based on the content, organization, and delivery of your speech. When you finish your speech, your time will be recorded. You will be penalized five points if your speech is under 3:31 or over 4:29.

Performance Competencies
- Delivers a speech that is related to the topic
- States a central theme that is repeated throughout the speech
- Uses supporting evidence that is accurate and appropriate
- Provides strong support of the topic
- Gives effective and memorable introduction and conclusion
- Demonstrates self-confidence, poise, eye contact, and appropriate gestures
- Demonstrates use of professional tone and appropriate languages
- Delivers a sincere, interesting, creative, and convincing presentation

Go to the FBLA website for more detailed information.

GIVE IT A TRY

Your teacher will give you two 4" × 6" notecards. Set a timer for ten minutes. Prepare a speech using one of the topics below and make your speech to your class. Your teacher and your classmates will serve as judges.
1. Cell phones, texting, and cars are a dangerous mix. Explain why you agree or disagree with this statement.
2. Henry Ford said, "A business that makes nothing but money is a poor kind of business." Explain why you agree or disagree with this statement.
3. Nelson Mandela said, "Education is the most powerful weapon which you can use to change the world." How do you think education should be used to change the world?

www.fbla-pbl.org

Susan Chiang/iStockphoto.com

Entrepreneurs in a Market Economy

2.1 ENTREPRENEURS SATISFY NEEDS AND WANTS

2.2 HOW ECONOMIC DECISIONS ARE MADE

2.3 WHAT AFFECTS PRICE?

Providing Information Systems Solutions

©Photographer:David Fox/
www.ExclusiveConcepts

Scott Smigler, Exclusive Concepts founder and president

Entrepreneur Scott Smigler started on the road to success when he was a teenager. While working in his parents' retail store, he started a company that develops and markets a network of resource websites. These sites help companies stand out when someone uses a web search engine. As its founder and president, Scott built Exclusive Concepts into a multimillion-dollar-a-year company.

While building Exclusive Concepts, Scott balanced dual roles as a student and an entrepreneur through high school and college, maintaining a 3.7 GPA as a finance major at Bentley University in Burlington, Massachusetts. In the beginning, Scott ran the company alone from his parents' home and then his dorm room. Eventually he moved the company to offices in Burlington. Now his staff of 30 develops keyword strategies, writes attention-getting keyword ad copy, creates and optimizes bidding strategies, and analyzes results for continuous improvement for customers.

Scott's vision, along with his passion and dedication, has helped him become a leader in the field. He also founded the Bentley University Entrepreneurship Society and has participated in international forums for world energy planning.

Some important lessons Scott has learned include:

- **Perseverance** You must be organized and focused. Implementing dreams is not easy.
- **Mentorship** You need to have a network of mentors to help you with problems.
- **Communication** You need excellent communication skills. Written agreements between your company and clients are essential.
- **Capitalization** You should be prepared for everything to be more expensive than you think and plan for unanticipated expenses.
- **Marketing** You must work to acquire new relationships while continuing to build existing ones. Everyone is a potential customer or client.

Scott stresses the importance of finding a balance between work and play. Starting and running a business require focus, dedication, time, and energy, but it is also important to have a life outside the business.

WHAT DO YOU KNOW?

1. Which of the lessons that Scott has learned have you also learned through your experiences? Provide an example.
2. Why do you think it is important to be involved in societal concerns, such as world energy planning?
3. Why do entrepreneurs need to balance work and play?

2.1 ENTREPRENEURS SATISFY NEEDS AND WANTS

The Essential Question How do entrepreneurs satisfy needs and wants with the goods and services they sell?

LEARNING OBJECTIVES

LO 2.1-1 Distinguish between needs and wants.

LO 2.1-2 Describe the types of economic resources.

LO 2.1-3 Explain the role of entrepreneurs in the U.S. economy.

KEY TERMS

- needs
- wants
- economic resource

FOCUS ON
ECONOMICS

Do you *want* it or *need* it?

"Dad, I really need a new pair of shoes to wear to the Winter Dance," said Stephanie. "Do you *need* a new pair of shoes, or do you *want* a new pair of shoes?" her father responded. "Want or need—what's the difference?" Stephanie asked. "That's a good question, Stephanie. Let's look at it this way. Do you really need the shoes in order to survive, or will having the new shoes make you feel better?" asked her father.

Stephanie thought about it and then responded, "Well, Dad, it won't keep me from going to the dance if I don't have the new shoes, but I'd sure like to have them. So, I guess I'd have to answer you by saying they would make me feel better." "Then you *want* the shoes, but you don't *need* them!" her father responded. "That's what economics is all about!"

WORK AS A TEAM Do you sometimes have a difficult time telling the difference between a need and a want? Do you think peer pressure makes it more difficult to distinguish between a need and a want?

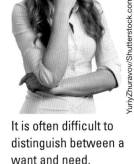

It is often difficult to distinguish between a want and need.

LO 2.1-1 Is It a Need or a Want?

Think about your favorite piece of clothing, such as a pair of jeans. First, you thought about what type of clothing you wanted, and then you went out and found it. Maybe you looked at several articles of clothing and compared prices before you decided to spend your money. If someone else gave you clothing as a gift, then that person had to think about what you might like and then make a choice. Economics is all about making choices and satisfying the wants and needs of consumers.

Do you know the difference between your needs and wants? Your **needs** are things that you must have in order to survive. Needs include food, basic clothing, and a place to live. Your **wants** are things that you think you must have in order to be satisfied. Wants add comfort and pleasure to your life. Wants would include things like smartphones, computers, and jewelry. The role of businesses is to produce and distribute goods and services that people need and want.

Needs

People have many needs. Some are basic needs, while others are higher-level needs. Abraham Maslow was a psychologist who developed a theory on the *hierarchy of needs*. It identifies five areas of needs—physiological, security, social, esteem, and self-actualization needs. The theory suggests that people's basic physiological needs, such as food, clothing, and shelter, must be satisfied first before they can focus on higher-level needs. Once basic needs are met, people will try to satisfy their security needs. When these needs are filled, individuals turn their attention to social needs, such as friendship. Esteem needs can be satisfied by gaining the respect and recognition of others. Self-actualization needs usually involve something that provides a sense of accomplishment, such as earning a college degree.

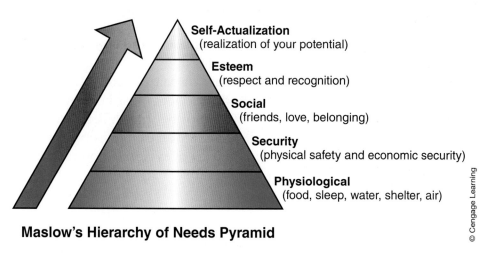

Self-Actualization (realization of your potential)
Esteem (respect and recognition)
Social (friends, love, belonging)
Security (physical safety and economic security)
Physiological (food, sleep, water, shelter, air)

© Cengage Learning

Maslow's Hierarchy of Needs Pyramid

Beyond basic needs, not all people have the same needs. Needs depend on a person's situation. You may live in a nice house in a gated community, so your security needs are met. Someone who lives in a high-crime area still may be trying to meet security needs.

Wants

Individuals have two different types of wants—economic wants and non-economic wants. *Economic wants* involve a desire for material goods and services. They are the basis of an economy. People want material goods, such as clothing, housing, and cars. They also want services, such as hair styling and medical care. No economy has the resources necessary to satisfy all of the wants of all people for all material goods and services. The goods and services that people want must be produced and supplied.

People also have *noneconomic wants*, or the desire for nonmaterial things. These wants would include such things as sunshine, fresh air, exercise, friendship, and happiness.

Needs and Wants Are Unlimited

Your needs and wants never end. You are limited only by what your mind can think of and what businesses make available for sale. One purchase often leads to another. For example, if you are going camping, you might need to buy a tent for shelter. After buying a tent, you might also want to buy other camping supplies. Then you might want a bigger backpack to carry your new supplies.

CHECKPOINT

What is the difference between a need and a want?

LO 2.1-2   Economic Resources

Economic resources are the means through which goods and services are produced. *Goods* are products you can see and touch. *Services* are activities that are consumed as they are produced. Entrepreneurs use economic resources to create the goods and services consumers use. Consumers satisfy needs and wants by purchasing and consuming goods and services.

Goods are products you can purchase. A pair of shoes, a jacket, food, and cars are all examples of goods. Services must be provided to you at the time you need them—they cannot be stored. A haircut, a manicure, lawn mowing, and car detailing are all examples of services. Thus, the difference between goods and services is based on tangibility. Where goods are tangible in nature, services are mostly intangible.

Factors of Production

In order to create useful goods and services, an entrepreneur may use three types of economic resources. These resources are called the *factors of production* and include natural resources, human resources, and capital resources.

NATURAL RESOURCES   Raw materials supplied by nature are *natural resources*. The earth contains oil, minerals, and the nutrients needed to grow crops and timber. Rivers, lakes, and oceans are the sources of both food and water. All products you use begin with one or more natural resources. The supply of many natural resources is limited. Increased use of natural resources and damage to the environment threatens the continued availability of natural resources in many regions of the world. Conservation practices and production of more efficient products help to preserve and renew resources. Compact fluorescent light bulbs (CFLs) are an example. CFLs cost more than old-style incandescent bulbs, but they last longer, use far less electricity, save consumers' money in the long run, and reduce greenhouse gases. Using CFLs helps preserve energy resources and the environment for future generations.

HUMAN RESOURCES The people who create goods and services are called *human resources*. They may work in agriculture, manufacturing, distribution, retail or some other type of business. As an entrepreneur, you would also be a human resource. Entrepreneurs have creative ideas and use these ideas to create new goods and services.

What are examples of natural resources, human resources, and capital resources used in the agriculture industry?

To increase the productivity of human resources, business owners may use specialization and division of labor. *Specialization* occurs when individual workers focus on single tasks, enabling each worker to become more efficient and productive. Even though a worker may be talented at many things, when he or she specializes in performing one task, generally, more can be produced. *Division of labor* divides the production process into separate tasks carried out by workers who specialize in those specific tasks. This division of labor allows the group as a whole to be more productive.

CAPITAL RESOURCES The assets used in the production of goods and services are called *capital resources*. Capital resources include buildings, equipment, and supplies. They also include the money needed to build a factory, buy a delivery truck, and pay the employees who manufacture and distribute goods and services.

Limited Resources

All economic resources have a limited supply. Most resources can be used to produce several different products and services. If resources are used to produce one type of product, they may not be available for the production of another product. Individuals, businesses, and countries compete for access to and ownership of economic resources. Those resources that are in very high demand or that have a limited supply will command high prices. Control of oil fields in the Middle East has been an ongoing issue for many years. The United States has a large demand for oil but a limited supply, so it is important to the United States to have access to oil from the Middle East. This high demand contributes to high gasoline prices.

Law of Diminishing Returns

To make the most efficient use of their resources, businesses should consider the law of diminishing returns. The *law of diminishing returns* states that if one factor of production is increased while others stay the same, the resulting increase in output (product produced) will level off after some time and then will decline. This means that extra workers, extra capital, extra machinery, or extra land may not necessarily raise output as much as expected. For example, increasing the number of workers (human resources) may allow additional output to be produced by using any spare capacity workers have, such as unused workspace or machinery (capital resources). Once this capacity is fully used, however, continually increasing the number of workers without increasing the workspace or number of machines will not result in an increase of output.

 CHECKPOINT

List the three types of economic resources, and give an example of each.

LO 2.1-3   Role of Entrepreneurs in the U.S. Economy

Entrepreneurs play an important role in the growth of the U.S. economy. Because all businesses that exist in the United States today began as an entrepreneurial idea, you could say that entrepreneurs are the backbone of the U.S. economy. The development and growth of small businesses help to ensure a strong economic future.

Supply and Demand

As business owners, entrepreneurs play an important role in supplying goods and services to meet the demands of consumers. They continually look for unmet needs or better ways to satisfy consumers' needs and wants. They use resources and their knowledge of markets and business to produce goods and services efficiently that meet consumers' needs and wants.

Capital Investment and Job Creation

Entrepreneurs need money to finance their businesses. Sometimes they use their own money; other times, they look to investors and lenders to supply the money they need. They may use the money to lease a building, buy equipment, or hire employees. By doing so, entrepreneurs are investing in their communities by contributing to the local economy and providing jobs.

How do entrepreneurs help meet the demands of consumers?

Change Agents

Many entrepreneurs create products that change the way people live and conduct business. For example, Steve Jobs, the founder of Apple Inc., invented the iPod MP3 player, the iPhone smartphone, and the iPad tablet computer. Bill Gates founded Microsoft. The works of these two individuals have revolutionized work and play. When you learn about American history, you see that many entrepreneurs have shaped the U.S. economy.

 CHECKPOINT

What are some things entrepreneurs contribute to the U.S. economy?

 ASSESSMENT

THINK ABOUT IT

1. What role do needs and wants play in determining what is produced in an economy?

2. How does the availability of economic resources in conjunction with the law of diminishing returns affect an entrepreneur's decisions?

3. Which of the contributions to the U.S. economy that entrepreneurs make do you think is most important? Why?

MAKE ACADEMIC CONNECTIONS

4. **SOCIAL STUDIES** Think of a business in your area. Make a list of the resources that the business uses for each factor of production.

5. **RESEARCH** Investigate and analyze the specialization and division of labor used by a business in your area. Write a paragraph explaining the impact of specialization and division of labor on the company's productivity.

6. **HISTORY** The needs of people in today's society vary greatly from the needs of people living a century ago. Conduct online research to learn about the life of the typical person living during that time period. Compare that person's needs with the needs of someone living today. Write a short report describing the differences and similarities.

Teamwork

Working in a team, make a list of the natural resources in your area. Using the Internet, almanacs, and other sources of information about your community, find out the impact these resources have on your local economy. Which businesses use these natural resources?

The Essential Question Refer to The Essential Question on p. 38. Entrepreneurs make decisions on how to best utilize their economic resources to produce the goods and services that satisfy the needs and wants of consumers.

2.2 HOW ECONOMIC DECISIONS ARE MADE

The Essential Question Why do entrepreneurs need to understand the various economic systems that exist throughout the world?

LEARNING OBJECTIVES

LO 2.2-1 Compare and contrast different types of economic systems.
LO 2.2-2 Describe the characteristics of the U.S. economy.
LO 2.2-3 Explain how scarcity affects economic decisions.
LO 2.2-4 Explain how business functions are used to satisfy consumers.

KEY TERMS

- capitalism
- profit
- economic decision making
- scarcity
- opportunity cost

FOCUS ON ECONOMICS

Choose between alternatives.

"Stephanie, weren't you thinking about buying a new iPod last week?" her dad asked. "Yes, Dad, I was," Stephanie replied, "but if I buy the new shoes I want for the Winter Dance, I won't have enough money to buy the iPod now." "You've just learned a lesson about opportunity cost. When you choose one item over another, the opportunity cost is the value of the item you give up—in this case, the iPod," her dad explained. "I understand, Dad. But if you took this opportunity to buy the shoes for me, then I wouldn't have any opportunity cost, would I?"

WORK AS A TEAM Discuss choices that you have made. Did you realize that in choosing one item over another there was an opportunity cost?

You often have to choose one option over another.

You can more/Shutterstock.com

LO 2.2-1 Economic Systems

Different economic systems exist throughout the world. However, all economies must answer three basic questions.

1. What goods and services will be produced?
2. How will the goods and services be produced?
3. For whom will the goods and services be produced (in other words, whose needs and wants will be satisfied)?

If all economies struggle with the same basic questions, what is it that makes economies different? The type of economic system will determine how these three economic questions are answered.

Economies must choose a way to allocate the goods and services that are available to the people who need or want them. These different allocation processes are what create different economies.

Command Economy

In a *command economy*, the government determines what, how, and for whom goods and services are produced. Because the government is making the decisions, there is very little choice for consumers in what is available. The government may see no reason to have more than one type of the same item. This means individuals may not always be able to obtain exactly what they want. There will be shirts and pants, but there will not be many styles and colors from which to choose.

Market Economy

In a *market economy*, individuals and businesses decide what, how, and for whom goods and services are produced. Entrepreneurship thrives in a market economy. Decisions about production and consumption are made by millions of people, each acting alone. Individual choice creates the market, so there are many items available that are very similar. If a product sells, it will remain on the market. If not, the manufacturer will not continue to produce it. Individual choice also exists in how items are produced. A furniture maker will make choices regarding the style, fabric, and durability of products made. In addition, products and services are always available to everyone who has the means to pay for them.

Traditional Economy

Before complex economic systems developed, simple economies operated according to tradition or custom. In a *traditional economy*, goods and services are produced the way they have always been produced. The traditional economy is used in countries that are less developed and are not yet participating in the global economy. Most of what is produced is consumed, and what is left over is sold or traded with people who live in nearby communities. Traditional economies lack the formal structure found in more advanced economic systems and usually have limited capital resources available to improve conditions.

Mixed Economy

When elements of the command and market economies are combined, it is called a *mixed economy*. In a mixed economy, individuals and businesses as well as the government are involved in making decisions in the marketplace.

A mixed economy often results when a country shifts away from a command economy toward a market economy. The former Soviet Union and China are examples of two countries making this shift. For over 70 years, the Soviet Union operated under a command economic system called *communism*.

bluecinema/iStockphoto.com

How does a country's economic system affect consumers' product choices?

Government control resulted in limited choices and a shortage in supply of many consumer goods. The Soviet Union disbanded and became 15 independent states in the early 1990s, resulting in a move toward market economies. China operates under a different type of communist government that controls most of the resources and decisions. The economy of China is adopting elements of a market system for a growing number of economic decisions. Entire regions of the country are enjoying a market economy based on greater individual freedom of choice. As a result, China is fast becoming a world leader in goods and services produced.

As countries with traditional economies develop, they often adopt mixed economies. The government makes many of the decisions about how the country's resources will be used to develop schools, hospitals, roads, and utilities. As people become educated, they are able to obtain jobs and earn money to purchase more goods and services. Often businesses from other countries will open a business in the developing country and offer jobs and locally produced products to the citizens.

 CHECKPOINT

How does the type of economy affect the way the basic economic questions are answered?

LO 2.2-2   The U.S. Economic System

What type of economic system do you think the United States has? To answer this question, you must look at who makes most of the decisions about what is produced and consumed. Since individual businesses and consumers make most of these decisions, the U.S. system is best described as a market economy. **Capitalism**, which is the private ownership of resources by individuals rather than by the government, is another name for the economic system in the United States. Another term often associated with the U.S. economy is *free enterprise*, due to the freedom of businesses and individuals to make production and consumption decisions. This individual freedom is vital to the success of the U.S. economy.

The U.S. economic system is based on four basic principles: private property, freedom of choice, profit, and competition.

Private Property

As a U.S. citizen, you can own, use, or dispose of things of value. You are free to own anything you want, and you can decide what to do with it as long as you operate within the law.

Freedom of Choice

You can make decisions independently and must accept the consequences of those decisions. Business owners are free to choose where to open a business, what to sell, and how to operate the company. Consumers are free to choose where to shop, what to buy, and how much they want to spend. Only when individual decisions will bring harm to others does the government regulate freedom of choice.

Profit

The difference between the revenues earned by a business and the costs of operating the business is called **profit**. The opportunity to earn a profit is at the heart of the free-enterprise system. One of the main reasons entrepreneurs invest resources and take risks is to make a profit. No business is guaranteed to make a profit, so entrepreneurs are challenged to work hard, invest wisely, and produce goods and services that consumers are willing to buy.

Why is profit one of the four basic principles of the U.S. economic system?

Competition

The rivalry among businesses to sell their goods and services is called *competition*. Consumers choose products and services based on the value they think they will receive. Competition forces a business to improve products, keep costs low, provide good customer service, and search for new ideas so that consumers will choose its products or services.

 CHECKPOINT

Describe the four basic principles of the U.S. economic system.

LO 2.2-3 Economic Choices

Individuals and businesses are faced with economic choices every day. Decisions about needs and wants must be made. **Economic decision making** is the process of choosing which needs and wants, among several, you will satisfy using the resources you have. Two factors commonly enter into economic decision making—scarcity and opportunity cost.

Scarcity

In every economy, there are limited resources to produce goods and services. However, individuals have unlimited needs and wants. This produces the basic economic problem of scarcity. **Scarcity** occurs when people's needs and wants are unlimited and the resources to produce the goods and services to meet those needs and wants are limited. For example, land is a scarce resource. Land is used for many purposes, such as for growing crops or as a site for a business or house. The same parcel of land cannot be used to meet all of these needs. A decision on how to use it must be made.

Decisions based on scarcity affect everyone. Individuals and families have many wants and needs. They must decide how to spread their income among all these wants and needs. National, state, and city governments collect taxes from their citizens. They must decide how to use the tax collections to provide all the services that citizens expect. In both cases, someone must make difficult choices.

Scarcity forces you to make choices or decisions. Suppose you earn $150 a week. If you decide to purchase a $75 concert ticket and you owe $75 for your monthly car insurance payment, you will not have any money left over to go out for pizza. Because you have only $150, you have limited resources. With limited resources, you cannot afford to buy everything you want. You may have to make a *trade-off* by giving up something so that you can have something else.

Opportunity Cost

When trying to satisfy your wants and needs, you most likely will have many alternatives from which to choose. Economic decision making will force you to explore all of your alternatives. When examining all of your alternatives, you should consider the opportunity cost of each one. **Opportunity cost** is the value of the next-best alternative—the one you pass up. For example, if your grandparents give you $300 for graduation, you have to decide what to do with it. If you decide to save the money for college, the opportunity cost would be the new smartphone that you really wanted and could have purchased with the money.

Diane Mayfield has $2,500 in extra cash that she wants to invest in her cake decorating business. Diane could use the money for advertising or she could purchase new equipment. If she decides to use the money for advertising, she will not be able to purchase new equipment. The opportunity cost of advertising will be the value of the new equipment—the next-best alternative. Like all entrepreneurs, Diane will have to choose between various investment options.

FAMOUS ENTREPRENEUR

PAUL REVERE Many remember Paul Revere as the American patriot who made a famous midnight ride, warning people that the British were coming. However, Paul Revere was also a successful entrepreneur. Trained as a silversmith, he used his engraving skills to create political cartoons to contribute to the movement for independence. He manufactured gunpowder, bullets, and cannons during the Revolutionary War. Afterwards, he developed new methods for

Why do you think Paul Revere was a successful entrepreneur?

his trade and founded the Revere Copper Company in 1801. The original company evolved into Revere Copper Products, Inc., which today manufactures a wide variety of industrial products that bear his name, a sure sign that his business lives on!

THINK CRITICALLY
Paul Revere was able to use his silversmith skills when starting his business. How important do you think it is to have a skill that you can use when starting a business?

LO 2.2-4 Functions of Business

In a market economy, an entrepreneur is free to produce and offer consumers any legal product or service. Knowledge of business activities will help entrepreneurs satisfy customers and make a profit. These activities, or *functions of business*, include the following:

- production
- marketing
- management
- finance

Each of these functions is dependent on the others for the business to be effective. Products can be produced, but if management is not functioning properly, if adequate financial records are not maintained, or if marketing is not getting the word out to consumers, the products probably will not be sold at a profit.

Production

The primary reason a business exists in a market economy is to provide products or services to consumers and to earn a profit. The production function creates or obtains products or services for sale.

Marketing

All businesses in a market economy need to complete marketing activities in order to make their products and services available to consumers. These activities make up the *marketing mix*, which includes the following:

- product
- distribution
- price
- promotion

The goal is to attract as many customers as possible so that the product succeeds in the marketplace.

Management

It is necessary for all businesses in a market economy to spend a great deal of time developing, implementing, and evaluating plans and activities. Setting goals, determining how goals can be met, and deciding how to respond to the actions of competitors is the role of management. Management also solves problems, oversees the work of employees, and evaluates the activities of the business.

Finance

One of the first responsibilities of finance is determining the amount of capital needed for the business and how the capital will be obtained.

 BE YOUR OWN BOSS

You are planning to open a sandwich shop. You begin to think about the four functions of business—production, marketing, management, and finance. Describe how each function will apply to your business. Explain how the functions will work together to ensure you run a successful sandwich shop. Be prepared to share your ideas with your classmates.

The finance function also involves planning and managing the financial records of the business.

CHECKPOINT

What are the functions of business?

2.2 ASSESSMENT

THINK ABOUT IT

1. Prepare a chart showing how the three basic economic questions are answered by a command, market, and traditional economy.

2. Explain how each of the four basic principles of the U.S. economy contributes to the success of our economy.

3. Opportunity cost can affect you personally. Name an item you wanted to purchase but did not because you wanted another item more.

4. Why is it important for all functions of business to work together?

MAKE ACADEMIC CONNECTIONS

5. **MATH** David Kalb started a pet-walking business. He charges $20 to walk one dog twice a day. He walks six dogs five days a week for four customers. He walks three dogs seven days a week for three other customers. How much money does David get from his customers each week? If his weekly expenses are $350, what is his profit?

6. **ECONOMICS** Research the economic system of another country. Explain the type of economic system the country has and the effect it has on the lives of the people in the country. Describe how the economic system would affect entrepreneurs in the country.

7. **PROBLEM SOLVING** You earned $75 for doing odd jobs around the house. You need $30 to fill your car with gasoline for the upcoming week, $10 for school lunch, $40 for prom tickets, and $30 for a deposit on your tuxedo/dress for the prom. How much money do you still need to cover all your expenses? Since your resources are limited, use the problem-solving model from Chapter 1 to decide how to spend the $75. Explain your choices.

Teamwork

Working in a team, choose a business with which you are familiar. For the business you choose, make a list of the activities that would take place involving each of the four functions of business.

The Essential Question Refer to The Essential Question on p. 44. Entrepreneurs must understand how each economic system will affect their functions of business so they can operate effectively within a global marketplace.

WHAT AFFECTS PRICE?

2.3

The Essential Question Why must entrepreneurs understand the impact of supply, demand, and competition on pricing?

LEARNING OBJECTIVES

LO 2.3-1 Recognize how supply and demand interact to determine price.

LO 2.3-2 Describe how costs of doing business affect the price of a good or service.

LO 2.3-3 Explain the effect of different market structures on price.

KEY TERMS

- supply
- demand
- equilibrium price and quantity
- fixed costs
- variable costs
- marginal benefit
- marginal cost
- economies of scale

Does supply match demand?

"Well, Dad, I went to the mall today to buy my new shoes and nobody had the ones I wanted," Stephanie told her father. "Every store I went to said it had sold out of the shoes because they were on sale. The manufacturer is supposed to send another shipment of the shoes next week."

"Oh," her father said, "so more people want the shoes because the price is lower. And the manufacturer is willing to make more shoes even at the lower price because it is still making a profit. This is the law of supply and demand at work."

Stephanie laughed. "There you go again, Dad. You're always trying to teach me a lesson about economics."

WORK AS A TEAM In the U.S. economy, you have many choices, but sometimes you might not be able to find exactly what you want. Think of products that you have wanted to buy but could not find. Why do you think you could not find them?

FOCUS ON
ECONOMICS

Nikitabuida/Shutterstock.com

Manufacturers must try to keep up with product demand.

LO 2.3-1 How Much Is Enough?

If a market economy is based on personal choice, why does there always seem to be just enough of everything? In a market economy, individual consumers make decisions about what to buy, and businesses make decisions about what to produce. Consumers are motivated to buy goods and services that they need or want. Business owners are driven by the desire to earn profits. These two groups, consumers and producers, together determine the quantities and prices of goods and services produced.

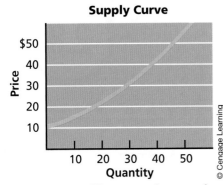

Supply Curve

Suppliers are willing to supply more of a product or service at a higher price.

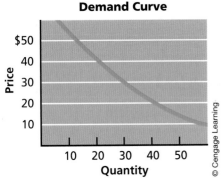

Demand Curve

Individuals are willing to consume more of a product or service at a lower price.

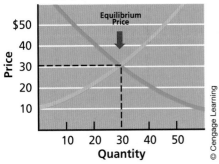

Supply and Demand Curves

The point at which the supply and demand curves intersect indicates the equilibrium price and quantity. The equilibrium price is $30 a unit, and 30 units will be produced.

Supply and Demand

To understand how this works, you need to understand two important forces: supply and demand. **Supply** is the quantity of a good or service a producer is willing to produce at different prices. Imagine that you supply car detailing services. Suppose that at a rate of $40, you are willing to spend eight hours a week providing car detailing services. If your customers are willing to pay just $20 for a car detail, you might decide not to bother detailing cars at all. If, however, the rate for car detailing rose to $60, you would probably increase the number of cars you would detail.

As the price of car detailing services rises, suppliers are willing to provide more services. The quantity of car detailing services supplied rises as the price for the car detailing services increases, as shown on the supply curve graph.

Now consider the demand side of the market economy. **Demand** is the quantity of a good or service that consumers are willing to buy at a given price. Suppose that you are interested in having your car detailed. At a rate of $40, you figure it is worth having your car detailed once a month. If, however, the rate fell to just $20, you might be willing to have your car detailed twice a month.

As the price of the service or product decreases, consumers are willing to purchase more of the product or service. Demand rises as the price falls, as shown on the demand curve graph.

When the demand for a product is affected by its price, this is referred to as *demand elasticity*. When a change in price creates a change in demand, you have *elastic demand*. When a change in price creates very little change in demand, you have *inelastic demand*. Demand is usually inelastic when

- There are no acceptable substitutes for a product that consumers need.
- The change in price is small in relation to the income of the consumer, so consumers will continue to buy the product if they want it.
- The product is a basic need for consumers, rather than just a want.

When Supply and Demand Meet

The point at which the supply and demand curves meet is known as the **equilibrium price and quantity**. This is the price at which supply equals demand. Above the equilibrium price, fewer people are interested in buying goods and services because they are priced too high. Below the equilibrium price, consumers are willing to purchase more of the goods or services at the lower prices, but suppliers are not willing to produce enough to meet their demand. Only at the equilibrium price does the amount that consumers want to buy exactly equal the amount producers want to supply.

LO 2.3-2   Costs of Doing Business

To determine how much profit they are earning, entrepreneurs need to know how much it costs to produce their goods or services. To do so, they must consider all the resources that go into producing the good or service to determine a price to charge. Resources may include office space, materials, labor, and equipment. A company that prices its product based only on the cost of materials involved in producing it will lose money and go out of business very quickly.

Fixed and Variable Costs

Every business has fixed costs and variable costs. **Fixed costs** are costs that must be paid regardless of how much of a good or service is produced. Fixed costs are also called sunk costs. **Variable costs** are costs that go up and down depending on the quantity of the good or service produced.

The Bread and Bagel Shop is a small business owned by Michael Miller. Whether or not Michael makes any sales, he must pay the same monthly rent, the same insurance fees, and the same interest on the loans taken out to finance his business. These are Michael's fixed costs. The store also has variable costs, including the expense of buying flour, sugar, and coffee. These expenses rise directly with the number of items sold. The more bagels, donuts, and cups of coffee the company sells the more resources it must buy to make more goods. In contrast, when customers purchase fewer loaves of bread, Michael uses less flour and other ingredients.

Understanding the difference between fixed and variable costs is important. A business with many fixed costs is a higher risk than a business with mostly variable costs because fixed costs will be incurred regardless of the level of sales. If sales are lower than expected, the business will have less revenue to pay the bills.

Marginal Benefit and Marginal Cost

Entrepreneurs make business decisions based on the concepts of marginal benefit and marginal cost. **Marginal benefit** measures the advantages of producing one additional unit of a good or service. **Marginal cost** measures the disadvantages of producing one additional unit of a good or service.

Michael Miller of The Bread and Bagel Shop wants to increase his sales. Michael is considering keeping the store open two extra hours every day. He estimates that during the last two hours of every day, he will sell an additional 50 baked goods and 20 cups of coffee, bringing in additional daily revenues of $100. This $100 represents the marginal benefit of keeping the store open an extra two hours a day.

Deklofenak/iStockphoto.com

How do fixed and variable costs affect a business?

To determine if staying open later makes economic sense, Michael needs to calculate the marginal cost of keeping the store open two extra hours every day. He will need to purchase additional ingredients to produce another 50 baked goods and 20 cups of coffee. He will have to pay overtime wages to at least two employees. He will also use more electricity. After adding up these costs, Michael estimates that staying open two extra hours will cost him $125 per day. Because the marginal cost of staying open ($125) exceeds the marginal benefit ($100), Michael decides not to change the store's hours.

Economies of Scale

When a business owner decides to grow the business, he or she needs to consider the economies of scale, which are the cost advantages obtained due to expansion. Businesses can expand their scale of operations in many ways, such as expanding the size of their facility, obtaining specialized machinery, and using a greater specialization of labor. Economies of scale represent an increase in efficiency of production as the number of units of goods produced increases. A business that achieves economies of scale lowers the average cost per unit through increased production because costs can be spread over an increased number of units. Lower costs per unit allow businesses to lower the prices of their product or service, which may attract more customers and lead to increased sales.

What Went *Wrong?*

Avoid Personal Debt

Dave Chen, an entrepreneur from Silicon Valley, took on a great amount of debt when he founded a Web and database services company, Aslan Computing. He used his own personal savings and took out a second mortgage on his home to get the money he needed to get his business off the ground. At first, it appeared that Dave's venture was successful. He made $1.8 million in sales within two years. Upon closer examination of his financial records, however, things did not look as good. Although Dave's business generated a large amount of revenue, it did not generate much profit. Aslan Computing's costs exceeded its revenues, and it incurred a net loss of $50,000 the second year. On the brink of collapse, no bank would lend Dave additional funds. Fortunately, he managed to sell the business for enough money to pay off his debts, which had reached a staggering $120,000.

THINK CRITICALLY

1. Do you think it is wise for a business owner to take on a large amount of personal debt when starting a business?

2. What other options does an entrepreneur have if no bank is willing to loan money to help finance the business?

When starting your business, be sure to avoid personal debt.

LO 2.3-3 Market Structure and Prices

Market structure is determined by the nature and degree of competition among businesses that operate in the same industry. The main criteria used to distinguish between different market structures are the number and size of sellers and buyers in the market, the type of goods and services being traded, and the barriers to entry into the market for sellers. There are four major market structures: perfect competition, monopolistic competition, oligopoly, and monopoly.

Perfect Competition

A market with *perfect competition* consists of a very large number of businesses producing nearly identical products and has many buyers. Buyers are well-informed about the price, quality, and availability of products. Because consumers have so many choices of similar products, price is often the deciding factor, making it difficult for a single business to raise prices. This gives consumers more control of the market. Businesses can easily enter or leave this type of market. Examples of industries in perfect competition include gasoline suppliers and producers of agricultural products such as wheat and corn.

Monopolistic Competition

A market with *monopolistic competition* has a large number of independent businesses that produce goods and services that are somewhat different. Each business has a very small portion of the market share. This is also called a competitive market. In a competitive market, many suppliers compete for business, and buyers shop around for the best deal they can find. In this kind of market, prices are said to be determined competitively. Products offered are not identical but very similar, so differentiating products is important. Consumers usually select the product that provides the most satisfaction at the best price. Businesses can easily enter or leave a market that has monopolistic competition. Businesses in this market include retail stores and restaurants.

How does perfect competition affect pricing?

Oligopoly

When a market is dominated by a small number of businesses that gain the majority of total sales revenue, it is called an *oligopoly*. Businesses in this market sell similar goods and services that are close substitutes, and they have influence over the price charged. With the dominance of a few businesses, it is not easy for new ones to enter the industry. Examples include the automobile and airline industries.

Monopoly

Where there is only one provider of a product or service, a monopoly exists. A company that has a *monopoly* is able to charge whatever price it wants because consumers have nowhere else to go to find a better price. This is the opposite of a competitive market where consumers can simply switch to a lower-priced good or service offered by a competitor. Monopolies usually exist because of barriers that make it difficult for new businesses to enter the market. Examples include local water and electric utility companies.

CHECKPOINT

How does the market structure affect the price of a good or service?

2.3 ASSESSMENT

THINK ABOUT IT

1. Have you ever wanted to buy something, but you couldn't find it? What role do you think supply and demand might have played?

2. Name three fixed costs and three variable costs that you have. How can variable costs be similar to opportunity costs?

3. Think of an item you purchase often. If the price is similar at several stores, do you always buy at the same store? Why or why not?

4. Describe the important features of each of the market structures.

MAKE ACADEMIC CONNECTIONS

5. **MARKETING**   Find advertisements for two competing products. Analyze the ads to see how the products are differentiated. Make a poster of the two ads and label the items that are different.

6. **ECONOMICS**   Create a table with two columns. In the first column, list the four market structures. In the second column, list five to ten goods or services that would be available in each of the different market structures.

Teamwork

Working in a team, brainstorm a list of businesses in your state and your city. Discuss with your teammates the type of market structure in which you think each business operates. Give reasons for your choices. Share your list with your classmates.

The Essential Question   Refer to The Essential Question on p. 51. By understanding the impact of supply, demand, and competition on pricing, entrepreneurs can price their products and services appropriately to achieve maximum profit margins.

Sharpen Your 21st Century Entrepreneurial Skills

Effective Presentation Skills

Much of your communication as a business owner will be conducted verbally. You may have to make a presentation to sell your business idea to potential investors, or you may have to make a presentation to convince potential customers to purchase your product or service. How you present yourself will have a big impact on the people with whom you deal.

When preparing a presentation, you should consider your audience. The content should not be too complicated for the recipient(s) to understand. To help you plan your presentation, ask the following questions:

1. To whom will I be speaking?
2. What do they know about the topic already?
3. What will they want to know?
4. What points do I want them to know?

The answers to these questions will help you identify the purpose (goal) of your presentation and guide you in developing it. You want to be sure to present information that will enable you to achieve your goal.

When delivering your presentation, you should be concise, but give adequate information to cover the topic. An effective presentation has three parts.

1. **Introduction** You should begin your presentation with an attention-getting opener that introduces your topic. Asking a question or using a famous quote is a good way to get your audience focused on the topic.

2. **Body of Presentation** Try to limit your presentation to three main points. It is often helpful to provide a visual aid that lists your key points. Do not overwhelm your audience with too much detail. Use facts and other supporting information to reinforce your main points. Keep the presentation simple and avoid using complicated language.

3. **Conclusion** After presenting your main points, summarize what you have told your audience in a brief conclusion.

TRY IT OUT

To practice your presentation skills, research an entrepreneur who you believe has been a change agent. Prepare an effective presentation for the class explaining the impact this entrepreneur has had on other people's lives.

SUMMARY

2.1 Entrepreneurs Satisfy Needs and Wants

1. Economics is about making choices and satisfying the wants and needs of consumers. Needs are things that you must have to survive. Wants are things that you think you must have to be satisfied.

2. Three kinds of economic resources (factors of production) are used by entrepreneurs to produce goods and services—natural resources, human resources, and capital resources.

3. Entrepreneurs play an important role in the U.S. economy. They supply goods and services, provide capital investment and job creation, and serve as agents for change.

2.2 How Economic Decisions Are Made

4. Different economic systems exist throughout the world. In a command economy, the government determines what, how, and for whom goods and services are produced. In a market economy, individuals and businesses decide what, how, and for whom goods and services are produced. A mixed economy combines elements of the command and market economies. Traditional economies are simple economies operated according to tradition or custom.

5. The U.S. economic system is based on the principles of private property, freedom of choice, profit, and competition.

6. Economic choices are necessary because of our unlimited desires and the scarcity of resources available to satisfy them. Every economic decision incurs an opportunity cost.

7. The functions of business are production, marketing, management, and finance. Each function is dependent on the others.

2.3 What Affects Price?

8. Supply is the quantity of a good or service a producer is willing to produce at different prices. Demand is the quantity of a good or service that consumers are willing to buy at a given price.

9. Fixed costs must be paid regardless of how much of a good or service is produced. Variable costs go up and down depending on the quantity of the good or service produced.

10. Market structure is determined by the nature and degree of competition among businesses that operate in the same industry. The four major market structures are perfect competition, monopolistic competition, oligopoly, and monopoly.

WHAT DO YOU KNOW NOW?

Read *Ideas in Action* on page 37 again. Then answer the questions a second time. Have your responses changed? If so, how have they changed?

KEY TERMS REVIEW

Match each statement with the term that best defines it. Some terms may not be used.

1. Things that you think you must have in order to be satisfied
2. The means through which goods and services are produced
3. Occurs when people's needs and wants are unlimited and the resources to produce the goods and services to meet those needs are limited
4. The process of choosing which needs and wants you will satisfy using the resources you have
5. The value of the next-best alternative—the one you pass up
6. The point at which supply and demand meet
7. Measures the advantages of producing one additional unit of a good or service
8. The private ownership of resources by individuals rather than the government
9. The quantity of a good or service that consumers will buy at a given price
10. Costs that go up and down depending on the quantity of the good or service produced

a. capitalism
b. demand
c. economic decision making
d. economic resource
e. economies of scale
f. equilibrium price and quantity
g. fixed costs
h. marginal benefit
i. marginal cost
j. needs
k. opportunity cost
l. profit
m. scarcity
n. supply
o. variable costs
p. wants

REVIEW YOUR KNOWLEDGE

11. An example of a noneconomic want is
    a. clothing
    b. housing
    c. friendship
    d. cars
12. Which of the following is *not* an example of a service?
    a. lawn care
    b. car wash
    c. bicycle
    d. cable TV installation
13. If a product has inelastic demand, a price increase will cause
    a. consumers to buy more
    b. competitors to enter the market
    c. consumers to buy less
    d. little or no change in the demand for the item
14. What are the three basic economic questions that countries must answer?
15. What determines the type of economic system a country has?
    a. the political beliefs of the country's ruler
    b. the way the basic economic questions are answered
    c. the resources of the country
    d. the demands of the people
16. Which of the following is *not* a role played by entrepreneurs in the U.S. economy?
    a. supply goods and services to meet consumer needs and wants
    b. provide capital investment and job creation
    c. determine how to allocate natural resources
    d. serve as agents for change

17. Another name for economic resources is
   a. factors of production
   b. goods and services
   c. supply and demand
   d. command economy
18. The four basic principles of the U.S. economic system are
   a. private property, freedom of choice, loss, competition
   b. taxed property, freedom of choice, profit, competition
   c. private property, freedom of choice, profit, competition
   d. private property, limited choice, profit, competition
19. Which of the following is *not* a function of business?
   a. production
   b. marketing
   c. job creation
   d. finance
20. If you were going to start a small cake decorating business, which type of market structure would you most likely be entering?
   a. perfect competition
   b. monopolistic competition
   c. oligopoly
   d. monopoly

APPLY WHAT YOU LEARNED

21. You plan to start a grocery delivery service. Analyze the possible demand for such a service by brainstorming answers to the following questions: Who is likely to use this service? Besides delivering groceries, what other services could such a business offer? What other questions should you consider? (LO 2.1-3)
22. Susan Tran of Nails by Susan wants to increase her sales. Susan considers keeping the nail salon open two extra hours each day. She estimates that during the last two hours of each day, she and her staff could provide nail services to five more customers, bringing in additional revenues averaging $125 a night. Susan estimates that providing the services to five more customers each night would cost approximately $25 in supplies. Her operating expenses for electricity and water will increase by approximately $20 per night. She would also have to pay two employees to work the extra two hours at a cost of $30 each. What is the marginal benefit of staying open an extra two hours a day? What is the marginal cost? Do you think Nails by Susan should stay open two extra hours each day? (LO 2.3-2)

MAKE ACADEMIC CONNECTIONS

23. **MATH**   Find a cookie recipe that you would like to make and sell. Using this recipe, determine the quantity of ingredients you will need to purchase. For example, does one package of butter contain two cups? If not, you may need to buy more than one package of butter. Now determine how much it will cost to make the cookies. What are your costs of doing business? Are these fixed costs or variable costs? (LO 2.3-2)
24. **COMMUNICATION**   Marketing plays an important role as one of the functions of business. Research and write a report explaining how each of the other functions—production, management, and finance—depends on the marketing function. Present your report to the class. (LO 2.2-4)

25. **ECONOMICS** Identify and research economies in the process of converting from a command to a market economy. What events led to this change? What involvement, if any, do U.S. companies have in these countries' economies? Discuss your findings with the class. (LO 2.2-1)

What Would YOU DO?

You and a partner own a home security business, which sells a variety of home security devices, such as surveillance systems, alarms, and motion detector lighting systems. A senior citizen comes to your store to get some information about the types of security systems your company offers. Your partner asks the elderly customer for some basic information, such as where she lives. Using this information, your partner tries to falsely convince the customer that she lives in a crime-ridden neighborhood and, thus, needs several different security devices to ensure her safety. The customer is ready to sign a contract for the purchase of a very expensive home security package. Suddenly, your partner is called away to take a phone call and asks you to finish helping the customer. You overheard the entire discussion between your partner and the customer, and you don't believe she needs such an extensive home security system. Business is slow due to a downturn in the economy, and you need all the sales you can get. What will you do?

BUILD YOUR BUSINESS PLAN PROJECT

Based on the business idea you identified in Chapter 1, complete the following activities:

1. Decide on one item (product or service) that you would like to sell in your business. Determine the price you would charge for the item. Calculate the following amounts: price plus 50%, price plus 25%, price minus 25%, and price minus 50%. Poll 25 people to learn the highest price they would pay for the item. Use this information to determine how much you will charge for the good or service.

2. Determine the fixed and variable costs for your business. Estimate how much money you will need to cover these costs. Make a chart showing these expenses. Do you need to adjust your pricing for your business to make a profit?

3. Consider adding another product or service to your business. What are the marginal benefits and costs of adding this new product or service? Is it a good or bad idea to add the item?

Business Management & Administration

"Our softball coach threw a party for team members and their families at the pool in his neighborhood. A pool, playground, tennis courts, and clubhouse are shared and maintained by the community. He said that the day-to-day maintenance of the community was handled by a property management company."

Property management companies assist businesses by managing their daily operations. Retail locations, office parks, and residential communities often use their services. Property managers have a wide variety of tasks, including inspecting building facilities; arranging for repairs as needed; maintaining the grounds and equipment; contracting for trash removal, swimming pool maintenance, landscaping, and security; and preparing budgets and various financial reports.

Employment Outlook
- An average rate of employment growth is expected.
- Almost half of property managers are self-employed.
- As new home developments form neighborhood associations to manage common areas, the need for property managers should increase.

Job Titles
- Assistant Facility Manager
- Commercial Property Assistant
- Occupancy Specialist
- Homeowners Association Field Manager
- Community Association Manager
- Portfolio Manager—Property Management

Needed Education/Skills
- A bachelor's degree is recommended.
- Strong customer service, financial, organizational, and problem-solving skills are required.
- A background in real estate or facilities management is helpful.

What's It like to work in Property Management? Ari, the owner of a property management company, is posting the minutes of a neighborhood's annual meeting on the neighborhood's website. Website maintenance is just one of the many services provided by Ari's company.

Ari's next task is to analyze landscaping bids for a condominium community he is managing. He will prepare a report on the three most competitive bids and present them to the condominium's board at the monthly meeting. In addition to providing a financial summary of the bids, Ari will also provide information regarding the reliability of the various landscaping companies. Because he manages several communities, Ari is able to obtain feedback on the effectiveness of a variety of landscaping companies.

After lunch, Ari reviews the time cards for the lifeguards at a neighborhood community pool. Because the neighborhood lacks the resources to manage employees, it pays Ari's company to handle the contract for the community's lifeguards.

What about you? Would you like to manage the daily operations of communities to help them run smoothly? What would appeal to you most about this job?

Economic Research

It is essential for entrepreneurs to know the basics of the U.S. economy. Understanding the economic principles of private property, freedom of choice, profit, and competition can help an entrepreneur succeed. In addition, it is important for entrepreneurs to recognize how supply and demand interact to determine the price of a good or service.

The Economic Research Event will help you sharpen your knowledge of the economy. This event can be completed individually or as part of a team (two to four members). You will be given a preselected topic to research using a variety of resources. You must then write a research paper (up to five pages) and make an oral presentation to a panel of judges. Refer to BPA's *Workplace Skills Assessment Program Guidelines* for specific requirements for the report.

Performance Indicators

- Demonstrate knowledge and understanding of basic economic concepts
- Explore and analyze global and domestic economic issues
- Evaluate research and communicate findings both orally and in writing
- Explore basic economic concepts that affect the workplace
- Identify economic systems
- Explain how economic growth can be promoted and measured
- Conduct research using various resources and methods

Go to the BPA website for more detailed information.

GIVE IT A TRY

Select one of the following topics and then use a variety of sources to research it. Based on your research, write a two- to three-page report (typed, double-spaced, using 1" margins). Present your findings to the class.

1. Michelle Obama's school lunch nutrition program and its impact on local school budgets
2. Social Security and the economic impact of the depletion of Social Security funds
3. Career or college choices and their impact on an individual's future endeavors
4. Minimum wage increases and their impact on the economy

www.bpa.org

diego_cervo/iStockphoto.com

Develop a Business Plan

3.1 WHY A BUSINESS PLAN IS IMPORTANT

3.2 WHAT GOES INTO A BUSINESS PLAN

3.3 HOW TO CREATE AN EFFECTIVE BUSINESS PLAN

An Online Community for College Women

Her Campus Media

Stephanie Kaplan Lewis, Annie Wang, and Windsor Hanger Western, of Her Campus.

Ambitious entrepreneurs seize an opportunity when they see one. Stephanie Kaplan Lewis, Windsor Hanger Western, and Annie Wang, three students at Harvard University, did just that. The three met while working on a student magazine that focused on campus lifestyle and fashion. They worked together to convert an annual print publication to an online weekly magazine. Their efforts boosted readership significantly, and as a result, the women saw the potential for a new business.

While still students, the trio developed a business plan for their online enterprise, HerCampus.com, and then spent the summer putting it into action. The site launched in September of that year and soon became the number one online community for college women. Written by college journalists for college readers, the website now has more than 6,000 contributors and features content on style, beauty, health, love, life, career, and more. Her Campus also offers conferences, events, a blogger network, job listings, e-commerce, giveaways, and scholarships.

After Harvard launched Her Campus's first campus chapter, other colleges soon became interested in launching their own school-specific chapters. By the time Stephanie and Windsor (who were a year ahead of Annie) graduated, Her Campus had established campus chapters at nearly 30 schools, including Penn State, Syracuse University, and the University of Texas at Austin.

Journalists at each school create and maintain the local content on the website. Schools receive editorial and publicity templates for publishing content directly to Her Campus. The site earns revenue through digital, on-campus, and event-based marketing programs for companies that want to target the college market.

The three women, who won a Harvard business plan competition, have been hailed as successful innovators and businesspeople. They have been recognized in *BusinessWeek's* "25 Under 25 Best Young Entrepreneurs" and *Inc.* magazine's "30 Under 30 Coolest Young Entrepreneurs."

WHAT DO YOU **KNOW?**

1. What started the students on their course to professional success?

2. What strategic planning did the trio do that helped them launch Her Campus? Why is this important?

3. Besides planning, why do you think Her Campus has been so successful?

3.1 WHY A BUSINESS PLAN IS IMPORTANT

The Essential Question Why should an entrepreneur prepare a business plan?

LEARNING OBJECTIVES	KEY TERMS
LO 3.1-1 Explain the purpose of writing a good business plan. LO 3.1-2 Describe the importance of a business plan.	• business plan

---

Look before you leap.

Tony worked for a local automobile dealership as a technician for over 20 years. He was able to diagnose all types of mechanical problems and make the needed repairs. He always received very high customer service ratings. One day, Tony decided that because he was such a good technician, he could make more money working on his own than he was making at the auto dealer. At a local print and signage shop, he had business cards printed and a sign made that read "Tony the Technician." He quit his job at the dealership on Friday, put his sign up on Sunday, and was open for business on Monday.

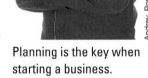

Planning is the key when starting a business.

WORK AS A TEAM What do you think are Tony's chances for success? Discuss what advice you would have given Tony if he had talked to you about his idea first.

LO 3.1-1 The Business Plan

Once you have settled on a business idea, it is time to start making a plan for the business. Often the plan will depend on your *business model*, which describes the way the company generates revenue and makes a profit. Business models can be classified into four types. The model for a manufacturer is a company that takes raw materials and creates a product. It also can apply to companies that assemble products from pre-made parts. Another model is the distributor, which is a business that purchases products directly from a manufacturer for resale either to retail outlets or directly to the public. A retail outlet is another type of business model. It purchases products from a distributor or wholesaler and then sells those products to consumers. The fourth is the franchise business model. A franchise adopts the business model of that franchisor, which can be a manufacturer, distributor, or retailer, depending on the type of franchise. Whatever type of business model you follow will become part of your business plan.

A **business plan** is a written document that describes all the steps necessary for opening and operating a successful business. A business plan does the following:

- Describes the nature of your business—what your business will produce, how you will produce it, which marketplace needs you are trying to satisfy, how your product or service meets these needs, and who will buy your product or service
- Explains who will run your business and who will supply it with goods
- States how your business will win over customers from competitors and what your business will do to keep customers
- Provides detailed financial information that shows how your business will succeed in earning a profit
- Describes plans for the future growth of your business

Writing a business plan is one of the most difficult and important things you will do as an entrepreneur. Writing a solid business plan is critical because the plan can make or break your business. Also, potential investors or lenders will want to see evidence of a well-thought-out plan. The business plan will also serve as a guide for you as you get your business started. It usually opens with a *mission statement*. This is a short sentence or paragraph that explains the company's purpose and eventually will help employees focus on the company's goals.

Purposes of a Business Plan

If you think preparing a business plan is unnecessary, you should think about the three important purposes it serves.

1. **A business plan explains the idea behind your business and spells out how your product or service will be produced and sold**. To convince banks or investors that your business idea is solid, you will need a completely new product or service or one that is better or less expensive than products or services that already exist. You will need to identify the marketplace needs you will satisfy and explain how your product or service meets these needs. You should define your target customer and show how your company will be able to obtain and keep customers.

2. **A business plan sets specific objectives and describes how your business expects to achieve them**. A good business plan includes sales projections for the short term (the first year), the medium term (two to five years after startup), and the long term (five years in the future). It describes products or services to be introduced over the next five years and other future plans.

DEVELOP YOUR READING SKILLS

As you read this chapter, make a list of the items that you will need to develop and research for your business plan.

3. **A business plan describes the backgrounds and experience of the leadership team of the business**. Banks and investors make financing decisions based on how well they think a company can meet its objectives. If you provide good information on the background and experience of the leadership team of your company, the bank or investor will be more likely to provide funding for your business.

CHECKPOINT

What are the three main purposes of a business plan?

LO 3.1-2   Importance of a Business Plan

Every new business must have a business plan. When comparing businesses that succeed to those that fail, there is often one important difference: Business owners that develop and follow a well-orchestrated business plan are more likely to succeed. The business plan is important for several reasons.

1. **A business plan makes you think about all aspects of your business**. It will help you during the development and startup phases of the business. Stan Meyer began a graphic design business from his home. He spent many hours thinking about the business and thought he was ready to start it until he sat down to write his business plan. He had not made sales and profit projections. He had also not thought about the possibility that he might need to hire staff if the business grew too large for him to handle alone. Drafting a business plan helped Stan gain even more confidence in his business idea. It showed him that building a successful business based on his concept would be possible. Working on his business plan also helped Stan think through business strategies, recognize limits, and identify any problems he might encounter.

How does creating a business plan help you see the "big picture"?

2. **A business plan may help you secure financing for your business**. You may have a great idea, but very little capital to invest in your business. You may need to go to a bank to obtain a loan or find other investors to get startup money. Lenders and investors require a business plan before they will consider financing a business. A well-written business plan shows lenders and investors that you are serious about your business idea and have spent sufficient time in the planning process. The loan officer at Stan Meyer's bank was very impressed

Denys Prykhodov/Shutterstock.com

with the work that Stan had put into his business plan. The plan showed the loan officer that Stan thoroughly understood all that was involved in starting his own graphic design business. The loan officer recommended that he be approved for a loan.

3. **A business plan helps you communicate your ideas to others.** By the time you write your business plan, you will have given much thought to the business you want to establish. You will proceed believing that your business can succeed. If you communicate your ideas well on paper, you will also convince the readers that your business can succeed. It will give suppliers confidence in extending credit to your company. Stan presented his business plan to the owner of the local office supply company to help convince her to sell him a computer and software on credit.

FAMOUS ENTREPRENEUR

WALTER ELIAS DISNEY

No one has entertained families more than The Walt Disney Company. Who has not experienced the Disney brand by seeing a movie, visiting a theme park, staying at a resort, buying merchandise, or watching TV?

As a young child, Walt Disney had an interest in art. To improve his drawing skills, he took art courses in high school, and at night, he attended the Chicago Academy of Fine Arts. In 1923, Walt arrived in California to peddle one of the cartoons he had made. Although the cartoon was not an initial success, Walt did not give up. He started working with his brother, Roy, in his uncle's garage. Success did not come quickly to the Disney brothers, but Walt's faith helped him persevere.

Walt's big breakthrough occurred with the creation of Mickey Mouse in 1928. Mickey made his screen debut in the world's first fully synchronized sound cartoon, *Steamboat Willie*. In the midst of the Great Depression of the 1930s, Disney took great risk and invested a then-unheard-of amount of $1.5 million to produce the first full-length animated musical feature, *Snow White and the Seven Dwarfs*. The film became the most successful motion picture of 1938. Following this success, Disney built a new campus for the Walt Disney Studios, and the staff grew to more than 1,000 artists, animators, story men, and technicians. Disney also expanded into other entertainment operations. He began television production in 1954, opened the Disneyland theme park in 1955, and created a company-owned record production and distribution entity in 1956.

The Walt Disney Company continues with innovation and success today. Through perseverance and an entrepreneurial spirit, Walt's dreams and the dreams of millions of others have come true!

Why do you think Walt Disney was a successful entrepreneur?

THINK CRITICALLY

Do you think success comes quickly for most entrepreneurs? What do you think Walt Disney's first business plan included as his vision for the company?

4. **A business plan can serve as a tool for managing your business**. Once your business is up and running, you can use the business plan in your decision making. Stan Meyer regularly uses his business plan to help him manage his company. Stan's plan laid out his vision of how the company would grow over time. By following the strategies in his plan, he has increased sales by offering innovative designs and reaching new clients.

CHECKPOINT

What are the benefits of a well-orchestrated business plan?

3.1 ASSESSMENT

THINK ABOUT IT

1. Why do you think the quality of the business plan is so critical to an entrepreneur's success?

2. Melinda Rosati wants to purchase her uncle's barber shop. Because it is an ongoing business, Melinda doesn't think she needs to write a business plan. Do you agree or disagree with Melinda? Explain your answer.

3. Putting your business plan in writing helps you communicate your ideas to others. Do you think discussing your business plan aloud with others can also help get your ideas across to them? Why or why not?

MAKE ACADEMIC CONNECTIONS

4. **PROBLEM SOLVING** André Kitaevich uses the business plan he wrote to help him run the day-to-day operations of his jewelry store. On what specific issues might André consult his plan?

5. **COMMUNICATION** You want to start a business in the home health care industry. Conduct research to learn more about this field. Based on your research, write a paragraph explaining your business idea. Be sure to spell out how you plan to market your services.

Teamwork

Working in a team, choose a well-known business in operation today. Research the history of the business. Find out who started the business, why the person had the idea to start the business, and when the business was started. Prepare a presentation for the class about the history of the business.

The Essential Question Refer to The Essential Question on p. 66. An entrepreneur should prepare a business plan as a way to think through all aspects of the business, to help secure financing for the business, to communicate ideas to others, and to serve as a tool for managing the business.

WHAT GOES INTO A BUSINESS PLAN

The Essential Question What elements must an entrepreneur include in a business plan?

LEARNING OBJECTIVES

LO 3.2-1   List and describe the basic elements of a business plan.

LO 3.2-2   List and describe the other elements of a business plan that capture readers' attention and provide supporting information.

KEY TERMS

- pro forma financial statement
- exit strategy
- cover letter
- statement of purpose
- executive summary

Create interest in your business plan.

Having always had a strong interest in electronics and computers, Andy wanted to start a business building customized computers for business and personal use. He knew that he would need about $5,000 to get his business started. He had $2,000 in savings that he could use, but he was going to have to get a loan from family, friends, or the bank for the remaining $3,000. He sat down one night to throw together a few facts about his business and handwrote a list of items that he needed to purchase. The cost of the items on the list totaled $1,950. He showed the information he had compiled to his parents, grandparents, aunt and uncle, and friend. No one was interested in making an investment in his business.

WORK AS A TEAM   Discuss why you think Andy could not interest anyone in making an investment in his business. How do you think a formal business plan would improve his chances of finding lenders?

FOCUS ON SMALL BUSINESS

Sergiy Zavgorodny/Shutterstock.com

A formal business plan is the best way to share your business idea.

LO 3.2-1   Basic Elements of a Business Plan

Every new business should have a business plan, but not all business plans are alike. The content of a business plan for a small, home-based, single-owner business will differ from a business plan for a large corporation with offices in many cities. But regardless of the business, all business plans serve the same basic purposes. They should also contain the same three basic components—introductory materials, the main body, and the appendix.

The main body of the business plan will contain the bulk of the information about the business idea. It provides details on how the business will succeed. A lot of time and effort will go into writing the main body of the plan, and it should be compiled before the other components in the business plan. The following parts, or elements, should be included in the main body:

1. Introduction
2. Marketing
3. Financial Management
4. Operations
5. Concluding Statement

Nora Ellis and Samantha Richards are qualified child-care providers who have worked together at a day care center for many years. The center frequently has to turn away children because it does not have the room or the staff to care for more toddlers. Because of the high demand for quality day care services, Nora and Samantha know they are well positioned to meet this need. They decide to work together to create a business plan.

Introduction

The introduction section of a business plan contains many important details about the proposed business idea. The following information should be included in the introduction section:

- A detailed description of the nature of the business and its goals
- The ownership of the business and the legal structure
- The skills and experience you bring to the business
- The advantages you and your business have over your competitors

What kinds of information do you think investors would want to know about a new day care center?

DETAILED DESCRIPTION Something inspired the idea for your business. Describing how you came up with your idea can help lenders, investors, and others understand what your business is about. Your business plan should also outline your short-term (three months to one year), medium-term (two to five years), and long-term (more than five years) goals. Stating goals will help provide you with direction and focus for your business activities.

Nora and Samantha know their short- and medium-term goals. In the first year of business, they want to get financing that will allow them to lease or buy a facility, equip it, and staff it with eight employees. In their second and third years of business, they want to invest in more equipment and possibly expand their facility to accommodate more children. They have not yet thought through what their objectives are for the long term. Writing a business plan will force them to think about these goals, such as whether they want to remain a single day care center or expand into a regional chain of centers.

OWNERSHIP AND LEGAL STRUCTURE In your business, you should have a section detailing your form of ownership. Will it be a sole proprietorship (one owner), a partnership (two or more owners), or a corporation (many owners that hold shares of stock

Christopher Futcher/iStockphoto.com

in the business)? Provide information relevant to your form of business, such as who will make up your leadership team and how many shareholders you have. This section of the business plan is important because each legal form of business has an effect on how the business works and makes profits. If you use your business plan to obtain financing, the lender will be interested in this information.

SKILLS AND EXPERIENCE   As the owner of the business, a written summary of your experience is an essential part of your business plan. This summary should emphasize all experience you have that relates to the business, including paid work experience, volunteer experience, and any hobbies associated with your proposed business. Along with you, any other individuals that you hire to serve as managers will make up the leadership team of your business. The skills and experience of the members of your leadership team will also be relevant.

Nora and Samantha have master's degrees in early childhood education. Together, they have more than 35 years of experience in day care, including 15 years in management. To show that they are well qualified to run a center, they include copies of their resumes and letters of reference from satisfied parents.

ADVANTAGES   List your company's advantages over the competition. These advantages may include the following:

- Performance
- Quality
- Price
- Reliability
- Promotion
- Distribution
- Location
- Public image or reputation

Marketing

The marketing section of your business plan should describe the products or services you will offer, the market, the industry, and your location. Developing a marketing plan will be examined in more detail in Chapter 5.

PRODUCTS/SERVICES   Describe your products or services, and explain how they differ from those already on the market. Highlight any unique features, and explain the benefits that customers will receive by purchasing from your business.

Nora and Samantha describe their vast experience in the day care industry. They also promote their plan for four large outdoor play structures and a state-of-the-art day care facility.

MARKET   Explain who your prospective customers are, how large the market is for your product or service, how you plan to enter that market, and how you plan to deal with competition.

Nora and Samantha's prospective customers are the parents of the 1,000 to 1,500 children between the ages of 2 and 5 who live in their area. Nora and Samantha determine that 90 percent of the families will be able to afford their center. They will advertise in local newspapers and send out fliers to their target market. They will also offer two months of care at a discounted rate for new customers.

INDUSTRY   Describe the industry in which you will operate. To find this information, you will need to perform research. Things you should include in this section are as follows:

- External factors affecting your business, such as high competition or a lack of certain suppliers
- Growth potential of the industry, including growth forecasts
- Economic trends of the industry
- Technology trends that may affect the industry

When providing information on the industry in which they will operate, Nora and Samantha include population data for their area. This information shows that demand for their service could grow over time. They also cite government sources reporting that the demand for day care services is expected to grow steadily.

LOCATION   Describe the location of your business. Lenders and investors want to know exactly where your business will be because the location of a business is often a critical factor to its success.

Nora and Samantha describe their plan to start the business in a prime location—in the heart of a suburb where most families have young children and both parents work outside the home.

Financial Management

The financial management section of your business plan will help determine your financial needs. It consists of the following three elements:

1. **Identification of Risks** Prospective lenders and investors will want to know what risks your business faces and how you plan to deal with them. Do not be afraid to list potential problems. Lenders know that every business faces risks. They will be reassured to see that you have clearly thought through the potential problems and have a plan for dealing with them. Risks typically faced by new businesses include competitors cutting prices, costs exceeding projections, and demand for your product or service declining over time.
2. **Financial Statements** A new business must include projected financial statements in its business plan. An existing business must include current as well as projected statements. A financial statement based on projected revenues and expenses is called a **pro forma financial statement**. Each of the statements that you will need to prepare is described in Chapter 9.
3. **Funding Request and Return on Investment** You must indicate how much you need to borrow and how you plan to use the money. You should give investors an idea of how much money they can expect to earn on their investment in your business.

You should state how much money you are personally investing and provide a personal financial statement. Investors will want to know who will maintain your accounting records and how they will be kept.

Nora and Samantha believe the biggest risk they face is safety. They must show concerned parents that they have addressed all safety issues that could arise on a daily basis as well as during emergencies. Nora and Samantha have prepared a pamphlet entitled "Safety and Your Child" to use as part of their marketing package. They include a copy of this pamphlet with the business plan.

Nora and Samantha have also included pro forma financial statements for their business, which show how much money and profit they expect to earn. They require $140,000 to start their business. Together they are contributing $85,000 of their own money. This means they need a bank to loan them $55,000. They include all of this information in their business plan.

Operations

The operation of your company is critical to its success. In this section of your business plan, you should explain how the business will be managed on a day-to-day basis and discuss hiring and personnel procedures. You should also include information on insurance and lease or rental agreements. Describe the equipment that will be necessary for production of your product or service and how the product or service will be produced and delivered.

While planning the operations of your business, you must also think ahead and plan for ending the operations of your business. It is important to plan for this in the early stages of your business. You may plan to operate the business for many years until you retire. Or you may have a short-term plan in which you operate and grow a successful business and then sell it. In any case, you need to have an exit strategy.

An **exit strategy** (or *harvest strategy*) is the way an entrepreneur intends to extract, or harvest, his or her money from a business after it is operating successfully. It details what strategy the entrepreneur has chosen and how much money he or she expects to gain. Plans for exiting could include selling the business to someone else or to another company, passing the business onto other family members, merging with another company, going public by selling shares of stock in the company to new investors, or closing the business and selling the assets such as the building or equipment. Having an exit strategy in place gives you control over how you will end the operation of your business.

As part of the operations section of their business plan, Nora and Samantha describe hiring plans to ensure their day care center is well staffed. They also devote a section to health and safety issues. They

Why should a business owner have an exit strategy for ending the business?

describe procedures for dealing with allergies, illnesses, and injuries because these are common occurrences among preschool children. Currently, Nora and Samantha plan to run their business for the long term and then sell it upon retirement.

Concluding Statement

In this section, you should summarize the goals and objectives you have for your business. You should also emphasize your commitment to the success of the business.

CHECKPOINT

List the elements of the main body of a business plan, and explain why each one is important.

LO 3.2-2 Complete the Business Plan

After you have completed the main body of your business plan, you will need to focus your efforts on the other components—the introductory elements and the appendix. Then you must pull all the components together into a well-organized, attractive document.

Introductory Elements

Every business plan should begin with a cover letter, a title page, a table of contents, a statement of purpose, and an executive summary. These elements grab the readers' attention and help set the tone for the body of your business plan.

COVER LETTER   A letter that introduces and explains an accompanying document or set of documents is called a **cover letter**. The cover letter for your business plan should include your name, the name of your business, and your address, phone number, and email address. It should briefly describe your business, its potential for success, and the amount of capital you need. Nora and Samantha's cover letter is shown on the next page.

TITLE PAGE   Your business plan should have a title page that indicates the name of your company, the date, the owner of the company, the title of the owner, and the address and phone number of the company.

TABLE OF CONTENTS   A table of contents is a listing of the material included in a publication. It shows the reader what each page covers. It is similar to a table of contents in a textbook. It is important that your table of contents is accurate, so make sure the sections are listed in the proper order and the given page numbers are correct.

STATEMENT OF PURPOSE   A brief explanation of why you are asking for a loan and what you plan to do with the money is called a **statement of purpose**. It should be no more than one or two paragraphs. Nora and Samantha's statement of purpose is shown on the next page.

THE MT. WASHINGTON

Children's

CENTER

5813 NORTH AVENUE, BALTIMORE, MARYLAND 20215

(410) 555-4445

MWCC@Internet.com

April 11, 20—

Ms. Jane Stewart
Vice President
First National Bank
E. 35th Street
Baltimore, Maryland 20215

Dear Ms. Stewart

Enclosed please find a copy of the business plan for The Mt. Washington Children's Center, a proposed new day care center in northwest Baltimore that will serve approximately 50 young children. We believe that the acute shortage of high-quality day care in this part of the city will allow us to generate significant revenues for the center and that we will be earning a profit within a year of opening.

To establish the kind of center we envision, we plan to put up $85,000 of our own capital. We will need additional financing of $55,000. As you will note from our pro forma financial statements, we plan to repay the loan within five years.

Please let us know if there is any additional information you would like to receive. We look forward to hearing from you.

Sincerely yours

Nora Ellis
Nora Ellis

Samantha Richards
Samantha Richards

STATEMENT OF PURPOSE

The Mt. Washington Children's Center will operate as a private day care center serving approximately 50 children in northwest Baltimore. The Center will offer excellent supervision in a clean, safe, and intellectually stimulating environment.

The project is requesting $55,000 in financing. This money will be used to:

- rent and remodel 4,000 square feet of indoor space
- prepare 18,000 square feet of outdoor space for use as a playground
- purchase equipment such as swings, jungle gyms, sandboxes, and supplies
- pay salaries of eight employees until sufficient cash flow is generated to allow operating expenses to be covered

EXECUTIVE SUMMARY   Before getting into the detail of the main body of the business plan, readers will want to read an **executive summary**, which is a short restatement of the report. It should capture the interest of its readers. If the executive summary is unconvincing, a lender may decide not to read your entire business plan. This makes a strong, convincing executive summary critical to the success of your business.

The executive summary should be no longer than one or two pages, and it should be written in a clear, simple style. Your executive summary should do all of the following:

- Describe your business concept and communicate what is unique about your idea
- Include your projections for sales, costs, and profits
- Identify your needs (inventory, land, building, equipment, etc.)
- State how much you want to borrow

Although the executive summary appears before the body of the business plan, it should be written *after* the main body of the business plan has been completed. Go through the business plan and find the most important and persuasive points you have made. Then draft an outline of an executive summary based on these points. Nora and Samantha's executive summary is shown below.

EXECUTIVE SUMMARY

The Mt. Washington Children's Center (MWCC) will be established as a partnership in Baltimore, Maryland. It will be owned and operated by Nora Ellis and Samantha Richards, highly respected child-care professionals with more than 35 years of experience in the field. Three experienced teachers and three teacher aides will supervise approximately 50 boys and girls between the ages of 2 and 5. In addition, a receptionist/bookkeeper and a cleaning/maintenance person will be hired.

MWCC is being established in response to the shortage of high-quality child care in northwest Baltimore. Only two small day care centers now serve a population of 45,000 upper-middle-class professionals. In 75 percent of these households, both parents work outside the home. The accessible location of the Center will make it an extremely attractive day care option for parents in the area. When completed, its facilities, which will include four large outdoor play structures and eight personal computers, will represent state-of-the-art day care. Its staff will comprise the finest day care professionals in Baltimore, led by a management team that is recognized throughout the region.

Market research indicates that MWCC could expect to fill 90 to 100 percent of its student positions immediately upon opening and that the center would be profitable as early as the third year of operation. Expansion could begin in the third year. To finance the startup of the company, its owners are seeking $55,000 in financing, which they would expect to repay within five years.

Why should you ask someone else to review your business summary before finalizing it?

Once you have created a draft of your executive summary, ask people who do and do not understand your business to read the summary. If readers do not come away with a clear sense of what you plan to do and why you will succeed in doing it, your executive summary needs more work.

Appendix

The appendix to the business plan includes supporting documents that provide additional information and back up statements made in the body of the report. To help you determine what supporting documents to include, you should ask yourself what you would want to know about a business before you would lend it money. Documents that might be contained in the appendix include the following:

- Tax returns of the business owner for the past three years
- Personal financial statement of the owner
- Copy of proposed lease or purchase agreement for the building space
- Copy of licenses and other legal documents
- Copy of resume of the owner
- Letters of recommendation
- Copies of letters of intent from suppliers
- Copies of any large sales contracts the owner has already negotiated

Put It All Together

Your business plan should follow a standard format and be organized as shown here. Because your business plan is your best opportunity to let other people know what you want to do with your company, its appearance should make a good first impression. Your business plan gives you

OUTLINE OF BUSINESS PLAN
Introductory Elements

- Cover Letter
- Title Page
- Table of Contents
- Statement of Purpose
- Executive Summary

Main Body

- Introduction
- Marketing
- Financial Management
- Operations
- Concluding Statement

Appendix of Supporting Documents

the chance to convince others that your idea is sound and that you have the talent and resources to make your idea a successful business venture. To make the best of this opportunity, you will want to create an attractive document that is neat, well organized, and inviting to read. Handwritten business plans are not acceptable. All business plans must be created, edited, and printed using a computer.

 CHECKPOINT

Why should you include supporting documents in your business plan?

3.2 ASSESSMENT

THINK ABOUT IT

1. Why is it possible to write an executive summary only after you have written the main body of your business plan? Why might the executive summary be more important than the body of the plan?

2. Why do you think it is important to include management and staffing in the operations section of your business plan?

3. A group of investors is planning to open a new theme park. What supporting documents should be included in their business plan?

MAKE ACADEMIC CONNECTIONS

4. **MATH**   You plan to start a company. You have $67,500 in savings, but need $165,000 total to begin your business. How much money will you need from investors? What will be your percentage of ownership? If you have four outside investors, how much will each investor provide if the investment is split equally? What percentage will each investor own?

5. **COMMUNICATION**   Write short-, medium-, and long-term goals for an entrepreneur starting a new ice-cream parlor.

Teamwork

Working with team members, choose a business in your community. Make a list of the items you think this business would include in each component of its business plan—introductory elements, main body, and appendix.

The Essential Question   Refer to The Essential Question on p. 71. A business plan should include introductory materials (a cover letter, a title page, a table of contents, a statement of purpose, and an executive summary), the main body (an introduction, a marketing section, a financial management section, an operations section, and a concluding statement), and an appendix.

HOW TO CREATE AN EFFECTIVE BUSINESS PLAN

3.3

The Essential Question How can an entrepreneur ensure that the business plan is effective?

LEARNING OBJECTIVES

LO 3.3-1 Describe resources available for researching your business plan.

LO 3.3-2 Name common mistakes to avoid in business planning.

KEY TERMS

- Small Business Administration (SBA)
- Small Business Development Centers (SBDCs)
- SCORE
- trade associations

Where do I start?

Marta loved working with children. All of the parents in her neighborhood wanted her to babysit for them. She was always thinking up fun games to play and creative activities for the children to do. She wondered if she could do even more with these activities to earn money for college. She talked with her mother and some of the parents and came up with an idea. She would run an activity center where she could host parties and let the children read, play games, and watch movies. Once Marta came up with a business idea, she knew it was time to make a detailed plan. However, she did not really know how to get started on a plan.

WORK AS A TEAM What kind of information do you think Marta needs to gather? Prepare an outline of the topics that Marta needs to research. Where might Marta find this information, and whom might she talk with to learn more about starting a business?

Your interests and hobbies can lead to a new business.

LO 3.3-1 Research the Business Plan

Your business plan needs to convince readers that you have come up with a practical business idea. To do this, you must include information and data from objective sources to show that your idea is founded on solid evidence. Researching and writing a business plan takes many hours. The process requires patience, research, thought, and a great deal of writing and editing.

Pulling together the information you will need to write your business plan involves researching all aspects of your business, from leasing space or equipment, to determining what you will charge for your product or service, to dealing with competitors. Researching all the parts of your business will teach you a great deal about running a business and may provide you with specific ideas for starting a company.

Community, Government, and Professional Resources

When writing a business plan, you will likely need to seek out advice from others. People from many organizations can help you with your business plan. Available resources include the SBA, your local SBDC, SCORE, your local chamber of commerce, trade associations, professional business consultants, and financial institutions.

THE SBA   The U.S. **Small Business Administration (SBA)** is an independent agency of the federal government that was created to provide support to entrepreneurs and small businesses. Since its founding in 1953, the SBA has delivered millions of loans, loan guarantees, contracts, counseling sessions, and other forms of assistance to entrepreneurs and small businesses. The SBA has at least one office in each U.S. state.

SBDCs   **Small Business Development Centers (SBDCs)**, which are cosponsored by the SBA, provide technical assistance to small businesses and prospective entrepreneurs. SBDC advisors provide a variety of low-cost training and free business consultations in the areas of business plan development, financial projections, market research, manufacturing assistance, and many others. Assistance from an SBDC is available to all populations. Many SBDCs are located at community colleges and state universities.

SCORE   Another source of valuable assistance is SCORE (formerly the Service Corps of Retired Executives). **SCORE** is a nonprofit association made up of working and retired business professionals who volunteer their time to provide small businesses and entrepreneurs with free real-world advice and know-how. SCORE volunteers represent every business area. Some have worked as executives at Fortune 500 companies, whereas others were small business owners themselves.

You can set up a meeting with a SCORE volunteer, or you can work with one of the SCORE online mentors by email. SCORE can provide assistance to you in just a few sessions or for a number of years, based on your needs. In addition to mentoring, SCORE also offers inexpensive local business seminars and workshops and free online webinars on a variety of important small business issues, from business planning and marketing to web-based retailing.

CHAMBER OF COMMERCE   In many communities, the local chamber of commerce offers assistance and information to entrepreneurs. It can provide information on trends affecting local businesses, local resources, and zoning and licensing information.

 BE YOUR OWN BOSS

You have taken horticulture classes in school and want to find a way to turn your acquired knowledge and love of plants into a profitable nursery business. You start working on your business plan and realize that you need help. You decide to contact SCORE for assistance.

Prepare for your first meeting with the SCORE volunteer. Write a brief summary explaining your business idea, why you want to start the business, and what you hope to accomplish by starting the business. Compile a list of questions you want to ask the SCORE volunteer.

TRADE ASSOCIATIONS Organizations made up of professionals in a specific industry are called **trade associations**. They exist to provide information, education, support, and networking opportunities to individuals in their industry. These associations can be valuable sources of information to entrepreneurs.

PROFESSIONAL CONSULTANTS Some entrepreneurs hire experts to help them. Professional business consultants can be found in directories available in your library or online.

FINANCIAL INSTITUTIONS Many entrepreneurs are not familiar with the financial aspect of starting and running a business. When writing the financial section of your business plan, it may be beneficial to talk with a banker and an accountant. They can help answer any questions you may have about loans and financial statements.

Print Resources

Information for your business plan can come from many print resources. Your public library will have a number of books on entrepreneurship. In addition, books on marketing, financing, staffing, purchasing a business, and operating a franchise can be helpful. The library will also have books about writing a business plan, including sample business plans.

Magazines may also prove to be helpful. Many are devoted to small business ownership and to the industry in which you will be competing.

Government documents, including publications issued by the SBA and other federal agencies, may provide you with useful information. The SBA district office nearest to you will have many publications that can help you complete your business plan.

Online Resources

The Internet is a good resource for finding information that can help you prepare a business plan. The websites of the SBA, SCORE, and your local SBDC contain much of the same information that is provided in their print publications. In addition, there are many websites specifically for entrepreneurs and small businesses.

The Internet is also useful for finding programs that can help you prepare a business plan. These programs provide an easy-to-use template that allows you to plug in your specific information and get a professional-looking finished report. Many websites provide these templates for free. The SBA's website contains a Business Plan Tool, which provides a step-by-step guide on creating a business plan. SCORE's website contains a generic business plan template that you can modify.

 CHECKPOINT

What are some resources that are available to help you develop your business plan?

LO 3.3-2 Mistakes in Business Planning

Many entrepreneurs will not take the necessary time to carefully plan their business and prepare their business plan. This can contribute to difficulties in getting their business started and may lead to business failure. To create an effective business plan, avoid making the following common mistakes:

1. **Unrealistic Financial Projections**   When making financial projections, they should be based on solid evidence that supports the potential growth of the company.
2. **An Undefined Target Market**   You must clearly define your market and give an accurate picture of your potential customers. Explain why these customers will buy your product.
3. **Poor Research**   Many potential business owners do not spend adequate time conducting research. Use up-to-date research information, and verify the facts and figures that will go in your business plan.

What Went *Wrong?*

Conduct Market Research

While working as a salesperson for a custom exhibit display company, Leo Hunt found a unique product that was not currently being marketed in the United States. It was a lightweight, portable, full-color display that could be set up and dismantled quickly. A company in Sweden was the manufacturer of this display. Leo thought it was ideal for trade shows and conventions and decided to become a distributor.

Market research can help business owners avoid many frustrations.

He quickly prepared a business plan focusing on the unique features of the product and the lack of competition in the United States. He estimated that he could generate more than 5,000 sales in the first quarter of the year. He did very little research and assumed that everyone who exhibited at a trade show would be part of his target market. He hired a staff of ten salespeople, placed a large order with the manufacturer, and was ready to go! Within six months, Leo had taken only 250 orders for the product, spent 95 percent of his startup capital, and found that many exhibitors had no need for his product. With bills piling up and unhappy employees, Leo decided to close his business.

THINK CRITICALLY

1. What mistakes did Leo make when preparing his business plan?
2. What could Leo have done (or not have done) to improve his chances of success?

4. **Ignored Competition**   Do not overlook the competition, and do not focus only on what the competition has done wrong. Investors want to know who your competition is and how you plan to compete in the market. Outline how you will differentiate yourself from the competition.

5. **Inconsistencies and Omissions in the Business Plan**   You should review your final business plan to ensure no pertinent information is missing. Be sure that the information provided is consistent from section to section. It is a good idea to have an objective person review your final plan before you show it to investors.

 CHECKPOINT

List some common mistakes that are made in business planning.

 ASSESSMENT

THINK ABOUT IT

1. Some elements of the business plan require outside source information. If your business manufactures clothing, what specific sources might you need to consult?

2. Why is it important for financial projections to be as realistic and as accurate as possible when writing your business plan?

MAKE ACADEMIC CONNECTIONS

3. **TECHNOLOGY**   Using web search engines or advertisements from magazines and newspapers, research business plan software programs. Choose three of these and make a list of their features and costs. Evaluate your selections and decide which one you would choose to prepare your business plan. Justify your decision.

4. **MATH**   If you intend to borrow 20 percent of the $174,500 you need to start a business, how much of your own funds are you investing?

Teamwork

Working in a team, review a business plan that you obtained from the Internet or from a local company. List the features of the business plan that you think are the most effective and the features that you think need improvement, explaining why. Provide suggestions for improving the ineffective features.

The Essential Question   Refer to The Essential Question on p. 81. To ensure the business plan will be effective, entrepreneurs must conduct extensive research and make sure that the plan is realistic, complete, and consistent.

Sharpen Your 21st Century Entrepreneurial Skills

Prepare a Resume

A resume should be part of your business plan's appendix of supporting documents. Potential lenders and investors will want to know about you, the entrepreneur. Knowing about your skills, experience, and character will help them decide whether investing in your business is a good idea.

A personal resume describes your skills and experience to help prove you have the ability to own and manage a business. Your resume should demonstrate that your background is suitable for the business you wish to start and should convey to readers your experience, self-image, communication skills, ability to achieve results, and personal character.

A well-written resume, as shown on the next page, includes the following information:

1. Your contact information—name, address, phone number (home and/or cell), and email address
2. A profile statement that summarizes your experience and shows why you are qualified

3. A list of your work experience, arranged by date with the most recent work experience listed first, and a brief description of responsibilities and accomplishments for each position
4. A description of your education and any other training programs in which you have participated as well as your skills
5. A list of personal activities that demonstrate that you are reliable and ambitious, including community service activities, any hobbies you have that relate to your business, and any awards or honors you have received

When preparing your resume, try to keep it to one page in length. Be sure that it is well organized and includes only significant information that gives evidence of your abilities. Proofread your resume carefully to ensure that your spelling and grammar are 100 percent correct.

TRY IT OUT

Research the various styles of resumes, and select one that best suits your needs. Prepare a resume that would demonstrate to potential investors and lenders that you have the ability to start, run, and manage a business. Include your resume in the appendix of the business plan that you are creating in the *Build Your Business Plan Project*.

Brian Johnson

1650 Sweetwater Boulevard
Sugar Land, TX 77479
(555) 980-7117
bjohnson@Internet.com

PROFILE

Lifelong sports enthusiast and collector wants to share knowledge and experience with others by starting a business selling sports-related memorabilia and other sporting goods products

WORK EXPERIENCE

Sales Clerk, Sports and More, Sugar Land, TX, 20— to present

Accomplishments:
- Outstanding customer service skills
- Mastery of inventory management system
- Cash management skills

EDUCATION

Sugar Land High School, will graduate May 20—

Business Preparation:
Introduction to Business
Entrepreneurship
Accounting
Business Law
Sports and Entertainment Marketing

PROFESSIONAL SKILLS

Public Speaking (FBLA)

Microsoft Office certification

Accounting/Bookkeeping

Filing

Proper telephone etiquette

ACTIVITIES/ SERVICE

FBLA President

Habitat for Humanity Volunteer

Foreign Missions Project, Local Church

Regular Community Service at Assisted Care Center

HONORS AND AWARDS

First place in Texas FBLA Financial Services Team
Decision-Making Event

Honor Roll every year at Sugar Land High School

Character Award, Sugar Land High School

SUMMARY

3.1 Why a Business Plan Is Important

1. A business plan is a written document that describes all the steps necessary for opening and operating a successful business. It explains the idea behind your business and spells out how your product or service will be produced and sold. It sets specific objectives and describes how your business expects to achieve them. It describes the backgrounds and experience of the leadership team of the business.

2. Writing a business plan is important because it makes you think about all aspects of your business, helps you secure financing for your business, enables you to communicate your ideas to others, and serves as a tool for managing your business.

3.2 What Goes into a Business Plan

3. The main body of the business plan will contain the bulk of the information about your business idea and should include the following sections: Introduction, Marketing, Financial Management, Operations, and Concluding Statement.

4. To complete the business plan, you need to prepare introductory elements consisting of the cover letter, title page, table of contents, statement of purpose, and executive summary. The executive summary is the most important element. It should not be written until the main body of the plan is complete. You also need to compile an appendix, which includes supporting documents that provide additional information to the readers of the plan.

3.3 How to Create an Effective Business Plan

5. To show you have a practical business idea, you must include information and data from objective sources. People from many organizations—including the SBA, the SBDC, SCORE, your local chamber of commerce, trade associations, business consultant agencies, and financial institutions—can help you with your business plan. Print resources can be obtained at the public library and through government agencies. An extensive amount of information is also available on the Internet.

6. Common mistakes made in business planning include unrealistic financial projections, an undefined target market, poor research, ignored competition, and inconsistencies and omissions in the business plan.

WHAT DO YOU KNOW NOW?

Read *Ideas in Action* on page 65 again. Then answer the questions a second time. Have your responses changed? If so, how have they changed?

KEY TERMS REVIEW

Match each statement with the term that best defines it. Some terms may not be used.

1. A written document that describes all the steps necessary for opening and operating a successful business
2. A financial statement based on projected revenues and expenses
3. A letter that introduces and explains an accompanying document or set of documents
4. A short restatement of a report
5. A brief explanation of why you are asking for a loan and what you plan to do with the money
6. An independent agency of the federal government that was created to provide support to entrepreneurs and small businesses
7. An entrepreneur's plan for extracting his or her money from a business after it is operating successfully
8. A nonprofit association made up of working and retired business professionals who volunteer their time to provide small businesses and entrepreneurs with free real-world advice and know-how

a. business plan
b. cover letter
c. executive summary
d. exit strategy
e. pro forma financial statement
f. SCORE
g. Small Business Administration (SBA)
h. Small Business Development Centers (SBDC)
i. statement of purpose
j. trade associations

REVIEW YOUR KNOWLEDGE

9. A business plan is *not* intended for
   a. your competition
   b. potential investors
   c. your bank
   d. any of the above
10. Purposes of a business plan include which of the following?
    a. it explains your idea for a product or service
    b. it sets specific objectives and describes how they will be achieved
    c. it describes the backgrounds and experience of the people who will run the business
    d. all of the above
11. A business plan is important for all of the following reasons *except*
    a. it makes you think about all aspects of your business
    b. it helps you communicate your ideas to others
    c. it guarantees you will get financing for your business
    d. it can serve as a tool for managing your business
12. Which of the following is *not* a true statement regarding risks?
    a. Identifying the possible risks your business faces will alarm lenders and investors and cause them to withhold funds.
    b. Potential investors and lenders want to know the risks your business faces and how you plan to deal with them.
    c. Lenders will appreciate the fact that you know the risks you face and have a plan for dealing with them.
    d. Lenders know that every business faces risks.
13. The purpose of including supporting documents in a business plan is to
    a. make the plan lengthy
    b. provide additional information
    c. give the readers more information than they might need
    d. explain your business idea

14. Writing a business plan
    a. is a quick and easy process
    b. is quick but difficult
    c. requires patience, research, thought, and time
    d. none of the above
15. Which of the following organizations can provide assistance when writing your business plan?
    a. bank
    b. chamber of commerce
    c. SBA
    d. all of the above
16. Organizations made up of professionals in a specific industry are called
    a. entrepreneurs
    b. trade associations
    c. trade shows
    d. SBDCs
17. The main body of a business plan includes which of the following?
    a. executive summary
    b. statement of purpose
    c. financial management
    d. supporting documents
18. Mistakes to avoid when preparing a business plan include all of the following *except*
    a. providing unrealistic financial projections
    b. wasting time on research
    c. ignoring the competition
    d. failing to define the target market

APPLY WHAT YOU LEARNED

19. Obtain a sample business plan. Review the business plan and discuss whether the five common mistakes in writing a business plan were avoided. Provide reasons to support your decisions. (LO 3.3-2)
20. You plan to open a skateboarding park. What kind of research should you do? What sources will you consult for your research? (LO 3.3-1)

MAKE ACADEMIC CONNECTIONS

21. **COMMUNICATION** You are preparing a business plan for a self-storage facility (U-Store-It). You are requesting a $75,000 loan to buy the property and storage lockers. Write the cover letter to the bank loan officer and a statement of purpose. (LO 3.2-2)
22. **RESEARCH** Choose a business with which you are familiar. Research trade associations that could provide useful information to the business. Make a list of the trade associations and the type of information that each one provides, and explain why it would be useful to the business. (LO 3-3.1)
23. **COMMUNICATION** Think about a business you would like to start. Assume you will need a startup loan. With a partner, role-play a meeting between you and the loan officer. Based on your role-play experience, write a short report describing the do's and don'ts of requesting a loan. (LO 3-1.2)

What Would YOU DO?

You have a great idea for a business you want to start. Because you are going to school full time and working nights and weekends, you really don't have much time to prepare a business plan. But you know you need one to help secure a loan for the business. While searching the Internet, you find a business plan for a company that is very similar to the one you want to start. It would save you time if you copied this plan, changed the business name, and added your personal information. What would you do? What problems might this cause?

BUILD YOUR BUSINESS PLAN PROJECT

This activity will help you get started on the development of a business plan for your business idea.

1. Create a well-defined company description. Write a paragraph explaining the nature of your business.

2. Describe how you came up with the idea for your business project. List the marketplace needs you are trying to satisfy, and explain how your product and/or service meets these needs. Interview five or more people about your product or service. How many of them would buy it? Did any of them make suggestions? Prepare a one-page report that fully describes your product or service and how it differs from what is currently available.

3. List your short-, medium-, and long-term goals. What steps do you need to take to achieve each of these goals? Do you foresee any obstacles in attaining them? If so, describe them and explain how you will overcome them.

4. Use appropriate technology to obtain information about the industry in which you will be competing. Also, contact the SBA, your local SBDC, or SCORE and ask for information about your type of business. Use this information to write a summary about the industry in which you will be competing. What are the economic, technological, or growth trends in this industry? Is the location of your business a critical factor in its success? Why or why not?

5. Begin the financial section of your business plan by writing a report that identifies the risks that your business faces. Explain how you will overcome each risk. Provide examples from magazine articles about businesspeople in your field who have succeeded when faced with similar problems.

6. Present the information you have compiled to your teacher or representatives from your local business community. Explain your choices and be prepared to defend them.

"We got a great deal on our house. Not only was the lawn in chaos, but there was also a problem with storm water runoff. My stepdad hired a landscape architect to re-route the storm water to comply with local regulations. Now our yard looks healthy and inviting. The city and our downhill neighbors are all quite pleased with the improved storm water routing."

Landscape architects plan and design land areas for recreational facilities, private homes, public parks, college campuses, and other open spaces. Through their work, they not only seek to enhance the natural beauty of a space but also provide environmental benefits.

Employment Outlook
- An average rate of employment growth is expected.
- About one-quarter of landscape architects are self-employed.
- New construction and an increasing need to meet environmental regulations will drive employment growth.

Job Titles
- Landscape Consultant
- Open Space Planner
- Residential Landscape Architect
- Historical Landscape Architect

Needed Education/Skills
- A bachelor's degree in landscape architecture may be necessary; some positions require a master's degree.
- Most states require licensing based on the Landscape Architect Registration Examination.
- An appreciation of nature, a creative vision, and strong analytical and communication skills are needed.

What's it like to work in Landscape Architecture? Givon, a self-employed landscape architecture consultant, is developing a bid for a new 300-home community that has many landscaping needs. To complete the bid for this project, Givon needs to meet with the developer's architects, visit the site, and meet with city officials regarding zoning requirements. The final bid will include a completion timeline and landscaping sketches.

After lunch, Givon meets with his city's urban renewal team. The city is renovating a blighted residential area. Givon's input is needed to develop a landscaping plan that will optimize the use of a small amount of land set aside for landscaping.

After dinner, Givon prepares for his meeting tomorrow morning with a retail developer. Givon's recommendations for the retail parking lot design include planting many trees and shrubs throughout the parking lot. This greenery not only improves the aesthetics of the parking lot, but it also helps lessen "heat buildup," which is a common problem during hot summer weather.

What about you? Would you like to help develop landscaping plans that have a long-term beautifying effect on communities and businesses? Why or why not?

Business Presentation

Thoroughly communicating your thoughts and ideas is an important skill for every entrepreneur. Add in the use of visual aids, as well as questions from your audience, and you could be in for a challenge if you are not prepared!

The FBLA Business Presentation Event is for either an individual or a team of two or three members. Your task is to use presentation software as a visual aid in delivering a business presentation. The current year's topic can be found on the FBLA website. You may also use handouts during your presentation, but nothing can be left with the judges or audience after you present. You will have five minutes to set up your equipment and seven minutes to give your presentation, followed by a three-minute question-and-answer session.

Performance Competencies
- Develop a business presentation based on a given topic
- Comply with all federal and state copyright and fair use of information laws
- Effectively use presentation software
- Demonstrate ability to make a businesslike presentation
- Demonstrate effective verbal communication skills
- Demonstrate project development and implementation
- Explain content logically and systematically
- Answer questions effectively

Go to the FBLA website for more detailed information.

GIVE IT A TRY
1. You have been asked by your local chamber of commerce to speak at its upcoming meeting on one of the following two topics:
   a. How to prevent identity theft
   b. How the Affordable Care Act's rules, regulations, and tax implications will impact businesses
2. After choosing your topic, research it to become more knowledgeable on it. Be sure to take good notes and cite all of the sources that you use.
3. Using multimedia presentation software, create a presentation that is 10 to 12 slides in length. Your presentation should be professional, entertaining, and creative.
4. Create a one-page flyer that you can give to the members of the chamber of commerce as part of your presentation.
5. Present your work to your teacher and classmates. Answer any questions that they may have when you are finished.

www.fbla-pbl.org

4

Dusit/Shutterstock.com

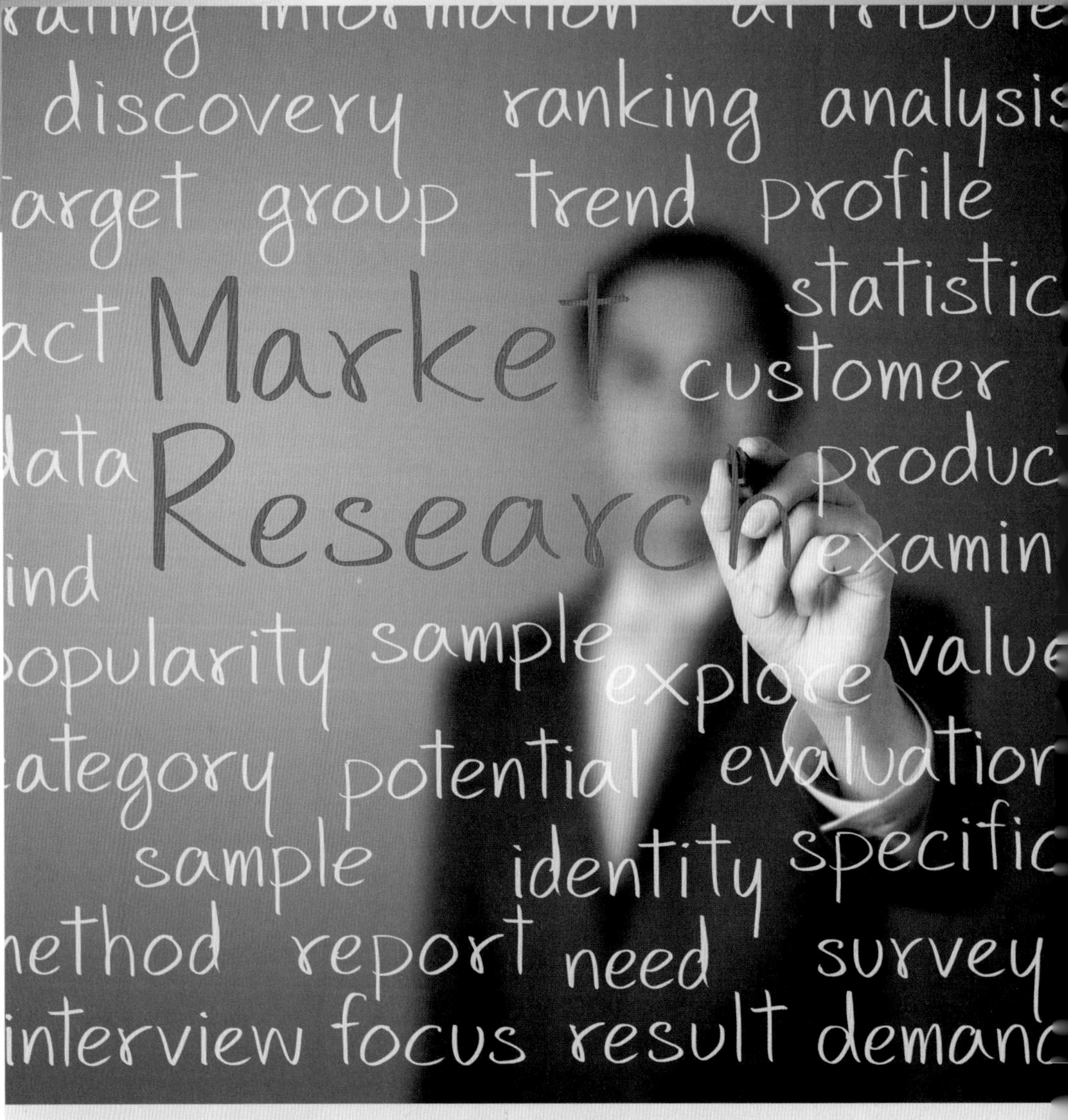

Identify and Meet a Market Need

4.1 IDENTIFY YOUR MARKET

4.2 RESEARCH THE MARKET

4.3 KNOW YOUR COMPETITION

The Art of Targeting Your Market

Photo courtesy of Ben Cathers

Ben Cathers, author of *Conversations with Teen Entrepreneurs.*

When Ben Cathers was 12 years old, he started his first business. That business, an online advertising and marketing firm geared toward teenagers, grew to ten employees. As a teenager, he launched a national syndicated radio talk show for teens. He also became a successful author with his book *Conversations with Teen Entrepreneurs.* Now in his mid-20s, Ben attributes his success to researching and understanding his target market—high school students.

Before starting his Internet company, Ben spoke to business owners and researched how to make money through web advertising. He shares what he learned in his book. The book covers many topics but focuses on teenage entrepreneurs. It also explores the hardships and successes that go along with entrepreneurship. Ben urges teen entrepreneurs to get out and talk to as many people as possible. He also recommends that new entrepreneurs target their own age group. According to Ben, "It is easier to recognize needs when you are living in that market. If you don't have an understanding of the market, how can you convince a client you know what you are doing?"

After graduating from Boston University School of Management, Ben moved to New York City to be a social media consultant and to create his next startup business. He also writes a blog that covers topics such as entrepreneurship and social media, among others. Ben believes that blogging is an inexpensive way to reach potential clients or future employers. Teens can reference their blog posts in conversations, giving them a leg up.

Ben encourages young people to find what they like and start their business early. He advises that even small failures can be beneficial if they are used as learning experiences. Ben is quick to warn, however, that young entrepreneurs will have to work long hours to succeed, so passion and drive are necessary.

WHAT DO YOU KNOW?

1. To what does Ben Cathers attribute his success?
2. How can teen entrepreneurs use social media and blogging to their advantage?
3. Why is passion such an important trait for successful entrepreneurs to have?

4.1 IDENTIFY YOUR MARKET

The Essential Question Why do entrepreneurs need to define their target market and how can they do so?

LEARNING OBJECTIVES

LO 4.1-1 Identify a target market by analyzing the needs of customers.

LO 4.1-2 Explain how market segmentation can help an entrepreneur analyze a target market.

KEY TERMS

- target market
- market segments
- customer profile
- demographics
- psychographics
- use-based data
- geographic data

FOCUS ON SMALL
BUSINESS

Who is your customer?

Roseanna and John had their own restaurant in Los Angeles, California, when their daughter was born. Deciding that they wanted a different lifestyle for their family, they began to think about relocating and starting a new restaurant in a small-town setting. They talked about the kind of restaurant they wanted to open. They decided that they would target middle- to upper-middle-class families who had a love for good food, were willing to drive up to 30 miles to get it, and were willing to pay $10 to $15 per meal.

WORK AS A TEAM Roseanna and John put a great amount of thought into the type of customer they wanted to attract before they began to look for a location. Why is this important?

Think about the type of customer you want to attract.

fatihhoca/iStockphoto.com

LO 4.1-1 Target Market

Entrepreneurs with exciting new ideas are sometimes so focused on their products or services that they forget about the customer. Coming up with a good idea for a business is not enough to guarantee success. Customers are the people or organizations who buy the products and services that businesses offer. Before establishing your new enterprise, you need to determine who your primary customers are and whether these customers will be willing to buy your product or service. Market research is the key to finding out this information. Understanding people's wants and needs will allow you to identify business opportunities. The more you know about your customers, the better you will be at giving them what they need and want.

As an entrepreneur, you will need to estimate demand for your products or services by identifying your target customers. The **target market** includes the individuals or companies that are interested in a particular product or service and are willing and able to pay for it. Identifying your target market helps you reach the people who desire your products and services. Target customers are the customers you would most like to attract. For example, a car dealer selling moderately priced minivans would target middle-class families with children, whereas a car dealer offering expensive sports cars might target single people with higher incomes.

DEVELOP YOUR READING SKILLS

As you read this chapter, develop questions for each section that you can use as a study guide for the chapter.

Identify Your Target Market

To identify the target market for your product or service, you will need to answer the following questions:

1. Who is my potential market? Are my customers individuals or companies?
2. If my customers are individuals, how old are they? How much money do they earn? Where do they live? How do they spend their time and money?
3. If my customers are companies, what industries are they in? Where are those industries located?
4. What needs or wants will my product or service satisfy?
5. How many potential customers live in the area in which I want to operate?
6. What is the demand for my products or services?
7. Where do these potential customers currently buy the products or services I want to sell them?
8. What price are they willing to pay for my products or services?
9. What can I do for my customers that other companies are not already doing for them?

Why should a clothing store identify its target customers?

As an entrepreneur, you should put yourself in your customers' shoes before you start your business. Then you should continually evaluate your market to be ready to respond to changes in communities, consumer tastes and buying habits, and competitors' offerings.

CHECKPOINT

What questions should you ask when identifying your target market?

LO 4.1-2 Market Segments

Groups of customers within a large market who share common characteristics are known as **market segments**. Market research can be used by a business to identify market segments. Segmenting, or dividing your target market into several small groups, can help you develop a product or service that will meet specific customer needs and wants.

The process of market segmentation is important because most products and services appeal to only a small portion of the population. The leisure services market is a large market that includes many segments, such as outdoor adventurers, people who vacation frequently, couples who eat at restaurants, and more. Targeting the entire leisure market would not make sense. You would never be able to meet the needs of the entire market. Even the restaurant segment of the leisure services market has subsegments. Some people eat fast food on a regular basis, whereas others like a sit-down meal at a nice restaurant. Some people like Italian food, whereas others prefer seafood.

Businesses can make decisions based on the information gathered about market segments. However, if the data are not analyzed correctly, the product or service may not meet the needs of the customers, or the business might ignore a segment of the market that would be very interested in the product or service.

SAMPLE CUSTOMER PROFILE FOR A SPORTING GOODS STORE

- Individual 23 to 52 years of age
- Participates in sports
- Wants good-quality sports equipment
- Looks for good prices
- Lives in city of Blanchester
- Average household income: $42,000 per year

Customer Profile

A market segment is made up of people with common characteristics. The more you learn about them, the better strategy you can develop for reaching them. A very useful part of analyzing your data is the creation of a customer profile. A **customer profile** is a description of the characteristics of the person or company that is likely to purchase a product or service. A customer profile can help you understand what you need to do to meet customer demand. Customers may be profiled based on many types of data, including demographics, psychographics, use-based data, and geographic data.

By analyzing these types of data, you will be able to develop a marketing strategy that identifies those customers you can serve more effectively than your competitors can. The data can

What are some of your demographic and psychographic characteristics?

help you determine the size of your market and how many people would be willing and able to purchase your product or service. You can design your product or service, set prices, and direct promotional efforts toward those customers.

DEMOGRAPHICS Data that describe a group of people in terms of age, marital status, family size, ethnicity, gender, profession, education, and income are called demographics. Women business owners between the ages of 25 and 40 who earn at least $50,000 per year would be an example of a market segment based on demographic data.

PSYCHOGRAPHICS Data that describe a group of people in terms of their tastes, opinions, personality traits, and lifestyle habits are called psychographics. People who prefer to live in a downtown setting and whose musical preference is jazz would be an example of a market segment based on psychographic data.

USE-BASED DATA Data that help you determine how often potential customers use a particular service are called use-based data. If you were starting a travel agency, you would want to know how often your potential customers travel.

GEOGRAPHIC DATA Data that help you determine where your potential customers live and how far they will travel to do business with you are called geographic data. If you were thinking of opening a coffee shop, it would be important for you to know that people are not willing to drive more than one mile for coffee.

 CHECKPOINT

Name four types of customer data that may be analyzed in developing a customer profile.

THINK ABOUT IT

1. Why is it so important to identify your target market?

2. How are market segments useful to an entrepreneur?

3. You are thinking about offering golf lessons in your town. What types of data (demographics, psychographics, use-based, or geographic) would you collect to create a customer profile?

MAKE ACADEMIC CONNECTIONS

4. **MATH**   Marcel wants to open a car wash after graduating from high school. For several days, he observed the cars being washed at a local car wash and recorded the following information:

Day 1	**Day 2**	**Day 3**	**Day 4**	**Day 5**	**Day 6**
50 cars	45 cars	48 cars	26 cars	47 cars	55 cars

   What is the average number of cars washed each day? If the car wash were open only five days a week, how many cars might be washed per year? (Hint: There are 52 weeks in a year.)

5. **GEOGRAPHY**   Think of a business you would like to open. Obtain a map of the area where you would like to locate the business. Mark the areas on the map that represent the farthest distance you believe customers would be willing to travel to do business with you. Draw a circle that encompasses the points where your customers live.

6. **COMMUNICATION**   Interview a business owner. Ask the owner the nine questions listed in the lesson about identifying a business's target market. Write a one-page report based on what you find out about the owner's target market.

7. **MARKETING**   Think about a television station or network that has a particular focus (such as the Food Network or the Travel Channel). Identify several characteristics of a market segment that enjoys the shows that are broadcast on the station or network. Use the characteristics to create a customer profile for the television network.

Teamwork

Working with team members, look through magazines and newspapers for an advertisement of a new product. Based on the type of publication and the material contained in the advertisement, answer the nine questions listed in the lesson about identifying a target market. Can you determine who the target market is for the product?

The Essential Question   Refer to The Essential Question on p. 98. Entrepreneurs must define their target market to estimate demand for their products or services. Entrepreneurs should segment their target market by defining their customer profile using demographics, psychographics, use-based data, and geographic data.

RESEARCH THE MARKET

The Essential Question Why is market research important to an entrepreneur?

LEARNING OBJECTIVES

LO 4.2-1 Explain the role of market research.

LO 4.2-2 Identify the six steps involved in market research.

LO 4.2-3 Explain the role that technology plays in market research.

KEY TERMS

- market research
- primary data
- survey
- focus group
- secondary data
- customer relationship management (CRM)
- social media marketing

Get to know your market.

Roseanna and John decided that they would like to locate their business in South Carolina close to the areas where they grew up. They knew that it would be important to do research in that area to be sure that there was a market for the type of restaurant they wanted to open. They decided to interview groups of potential customers to gather their thoughts and opinions. They also developed a survey and hired some local high school students to call residents in the community to collect more data. Finally, they explored how they could utilize technology and social media to conduct market research.

WORK AS A TEAM Do you think that Roseanna and John are using good methods to gather data? Can you suggest any other ways they can find out what their potential customers think about the business idea?

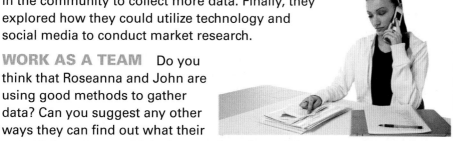

Mehmet Dilsiz/Shutterstock.com

Interviews are just one way to gather market research.

LO 4.2-1   Role of Market Research

For your business to succeed, you need to identify potential markets, analyze demand, and determine how much customers are willing to pay for your products or services. To collect this information, you will perform market research. **Market research** is a system for collecting, recording, and analyzing information about customers, competitors, products, and services. Based on the findings of market research, a business will be able to determine which marketing strategies will be most effective and most profitable. Spreadsheets and databases are used for collecting and analyzing market research data. Market research has its limits because it can be very expensive and time-consuming, but it is worthwhile when major decisions must be made.

You will draw on primary data and secondary data to help you identify ways in which you can meet customer needs. As an entrepreneur, you will need to determine how much primary and secondary market research data you need to collect.

Primary Data

Many market researchers collect primary data. Information collected for the very first time to fit a specific purpose is **primary data**. A researcher collects primary data to help identify and understand the target market. Primary data can provide up-to-date and useful information. There are a few ways to collect primary data.

SURVEY The most common type of primary market research is a questionnaire, or survey. A **survey** is a list of questions you would like to ask your customers to find out demographic and psychographic information. A survey can be conducted by mail, over the phone, on the Internet, or in person.

Creating a good survey is important. Surveys should be kept to a page in length when read over the phone or mailed to respondents. Longer surveys can be used if an interview is face to face. Questions should be clear and easy to answer, and only the most important questions should be asked.

OBSERVATION Market research can also involve observation. For example, someone who is considering opening a juice bar in a shopping mall could go to the mall and count the number of people purchasing drinks at various food outlets to get an indication of how many customers he or she could attract. Likewise, an entrepreneur interested in starting a motorcycle repair shop might count the number of motorcycles at a busy intersection.

FOCUS GROUPS Another way to find out about the market is by conducting interviews with small groups of people. A **focus group** is an in-depth interview with a group of target customers who provide valuable ideas on products or services. You can ask the same kinds of questions in a focus group that you would ask in a survey, but the group setting allows for more discussion and interaction. Focus groups usually are led by a moderator, who asks questions about buying habits, likes and dislikes, and interests in particular products and services. The focus group session is recorded so that the comments can be reviewed carefully after the session.

Secondary Data

Entrepreneurs also use secondary data to research their target market. **Secondary data** are found in already-published sources. Data on population, family size, household income, economic trends, industry forecasts, and other information can be found in secondary data resources. Places to find secondary data include the following:

1. Publications issued by government and community organizations, such as the U.S. Census Bureau, the Small Business Administration, and your local chamber of commerce
2. Books about specific industries
3. Information on websites for government and businesses
4. Books about other entrepreneurs who set up similar businesses
5. Trade magazines and journals
6. Newspaper articles and statistics

Kisha Nichols wanted to expand her family-owned chain of retail shoe stores. She decided to perform some secondary data research. She visited her local chamber of commerce website, which provided her with population demographics for her city and county and industry forecasts for local communities. This information allowed Kisha to identify the largest markets as well as any growing markets. Magazines provided information on the average income of retail shoe store owners in her state. Newspaper articles gave Kisha psychographic data on the lifestyles of people in her area. Most of them worked in professional office settings, which meant they had a need for comfortable dress shoes. The secondary data gave Kisha a good idea of which community might provide the best prospects.

 CHECKPOINT

What types of data can be collected through market research?

LO 4.2-2   Six Steps of Market Research

Collecting primary data can be time-consuming and expensive, but it is extremely valuable. It will tell you exactly what you want to know and uncover information you may not find through secondary sources. Conducting primary market research involves six steps.

Step 1   Define the Question

In the first step in the market research process, you need to define exactly what you need to know. Entrepreneurs have many concerns and questions about the businesses they are planning. By determining what they need to know, they are defining the question that will be the focus of their research.

Maggie Blandin is thinking about starting a dog-walking service. Before she invests in her business, Maggie needs to determine who would be most likely to use her service (her target customers).

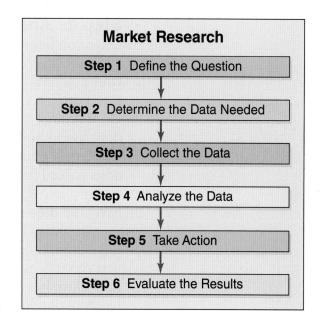

Market Research

Step 1 Define the Question

↓

Step 2 Determine the Data Needed

↓

Step 3 Collect the Data

↓

Step 4 Analyze the Data

↓

Step 5 Take Action

↓

Step 6 Evaluate the Results

Step 2 Determine the Data Needed

Once you have defined the market research question, you should determine what data you need to collect to answer the question. Entrepreneurs need to be sure that the data they collect will be helpful.

Maggie needs to know how many people living in the area are dog owners who don't have time to walk their dogs.

Step 3 Collect the Data

Before you begin collecting data, you need to decide how you will go about gathering the data. Should you use a survey? Should you use an observation method? Is a focus group appropriate? The method you use will depend on what type of information you want to gather. For example, you can find out people's opinions in a survey or focus group but not by observation. You should find some secondary market research first to familiarize yourself with your market. Demographic and psychographic data, as well as information on economic trends and industry forecasts, will help you determine what kind of primary data research to perform. You can then choose the best research method for the information you want to gather.

If you use observation to do your research, you need to determine where and when to get the best information. If a focus group is needed, you should think about what kinds of individuals to include and what questions to ask them. If you choose a survey, think carefully about how long it should be, what questions it should include, how it should be administered, and how many people you should survey.

Maggie decides that a survey is the best way for her to find answers about customer preferences for a dog-walking service. Through her secondary data research, Maggie learned that 60 percent of the households in her area own one or more dogs and that the average annual household income is $75,000. Most households have one or more adults working in a professional field. Using this information, Maggie put together the survey shown on the next page.

Step 4 Analyze the Data

Once you have collected all your data, you will need to analyze and interpret the information. The data may be used to find out about your potential customers and to forecast sales. The analysis should be in a written format so you can refer to it later.

Through her secondary data research, Maggie found that 2,500 dogs live in her area. From her primary data research, she found that 30 percent of dog owners in her area would pay $20 to have their dogs walked for 30 minutes. Many would pay to have them walked two or three times a week. Maggie determines that she could easily have 750 dogs to walk each week.

Data may be analyzed through use of a canvas. A *canvas* is a graphic tool that maps the key elements about the company's products or services. A specific type of canvas, the *value proposition,* graphically illustrates a company's product or service as well as the wants and needs of potential customers.

MARKET RESEARCH SURVEY

Thank you for participating in this market research survey. We appreciate your assistance in helping us identify the needs of pet owners in our community.

PLEASE CHECK THE BOX THAT BEST DESCRIBES YOUR SITUATION.

Age: UNDER 18 ❑   19–30 ❑   31–40 ❑   41–50 ❑   51–65 ❑   OVER 65 ❑

Gender: MALE ❑   FEMALE ❑

Number of pets: 0 ❑   1 ❑   2 ❑   3 ❑   4 OR MORE ❑

Kinds of pets: DOG ❑   CAT ❑   FISH ❑   BIRD ❑   OTHER ❑ (PLEASE SPECIFY)

IF YOU OWN A DOG, PLEASE ANSWER ALL OF THE FOLLOWING QUESTIONS.

How often do you walk your dog?

EVERY DAY ❑   A FEW TIMES A WEEK ❑   ONLY ON THE WEEKENDS ❑   NEVER ❑

Would you be willing to pay someone you trusted to take your dog for walks?

YES ❑   POSSIBLY ❑   NO ❑

If you would be willing to pay someone to walk your dog, how many times a week would you use this service?

EVERY DAY ❑   2–3 TIMES A WEEK ❑   ONLY ON THE WEEKENDS ❑

How much would you be willing to pay to have your dog(s) walked for 30 minutes?

$10 ❑ $15 ❑ $20 ❑ $25 ❑   I WOULD NOT PAY TO HAVE MY DOG WALKED ❑

How often do you travel out of town?

ONCE A YEAR ❑   2–3 TIMES A YEAR ❑   SEVERAL TIMES A YEAR ❑   NEVER ❑

Who takes care of your dog when you are out of town?

KENNEL ❑   FRIEND ❑   NEIGHBOR ❑   OTHER ❑

Would you be interested in having someone you trust take care of your pets while you are away?

YES ❑   POSSIBLY ❑   NO ❑

Step 5   Take Action

Once you have analyzed and interpreted your data, you will need to determine how to use the data to make a decision. You will develop a plan of action based on the information you found in your market research.

Maggie Blandin's market research has helped her conclude that her idea for a dog-walking service is profitable. From her market research, she has created a target customer profile of 31- to 50-year-olds who travel often, work long hours, and earn $50,000 to $100,000 a year. She also knows the amount of money her target customers are willing to pay for her service and how much income she can expect to make.

In her first effort to get customers, Maggie plans to create a flyer aimed at her target market, which she will distribute in neighborhoods and veterinarian offices. She also plans to distribute the flyer downtown and in other business areas where many of her target customers work.

Step 6   Evaluate the Results

Evaluation is the last step in the market research process. It is not enough just to develop a plan of action. Entrepreneurs must regularly evaluate the actions they take as a result of the plan.

Once Maggie has developed and distributed the flyer, she will need to evaluate the results. If she feels that she is getting a good response from her target market, she can assume that her plan of action is effective. However, if she is not getting a good response, then she will need to revise her plan of action.

CHECKPOINT

What are the six steps of market research and how are they used to make decisions?

LO 4.2-3   Technology-Driven Marketing

Technology has brought many changes to the marketing field. As an entrepreneur, it is important that you keep up to date with new trends in marketing and that you are aware of the types of technology that are influencing your customers.

Customer Relationship Management

Customer relationship management (CRM) refers to a company's efforts to understand customers as individuals instead of as part of a group. It is a business strategy designed to increase profitability and customer satisfaction. CRM uses technology to track customer interactions and to organize business processes in a way that will produce customer-satisfying behaviors.

INTERACTIONS WITH CUSTOMERS   In a CRM system, companies identify customer relationships, including information on who customers are, where they are located, and what products and services they buy. This is done by collecting data on all types of interactions a customer has with the company. These can include phone, web-based, or salesperson contacts. Other *touch points* where a customer might have contact with the company include a product or service registration, a request for product information, the return of a completed warranty card, or a customer talking with delivery personnel and product installers.

Many companies are now using websites as a touch point for customers to communicate with them. On the Web, companies provide forms that customers can complete to purchase products, make reservations, enter product and service preferences, and give customer feedback. This information is transmitted through *electronic data interchange (EDI)*, which is the movement of data between locations in a structured, computer-retrievable format. The information is then used to define market segments, adjust marketing strategies, develop new products, and improve customer relationships.

CUSTOMER DATABASE   Large amounts of data can be obtained from the interactions between a company and its customers. A business must decide what types of data it wants to acquire and how it can use the data to enhance customer relationships. Data collected can include customer contact information and data pertaining to the customer's current relationship with the company—past purchase history, quantity and frequency of purchases, average amount spent on purchases, and reactions to promotional activities.

The data are stored in a *data warehouse*, which is a large computerized database containing all of the information collected in the CRM process. Data stored in the data warehouse by one department within the company are available to other departments or to anyone else who has access to the database.

Data mining is used to find hidden patterns and relationships in the customer data stored in the data warehouse. The value of data mining is the ability of a company to transform individual bits of data into usable information that marketers need to develop successful marketing strategies. By using data mining, marketers can search the data warehouse to find relevant data, categorize significant characteristics, and develop customer profiles. Once the most profitable customers and prospects are identified, marketing strategies that will appeal to them are created.

Social Media Marketing

Social media isn't just about being social. In today's world, both wired and wireless, it's also about marketing. Potential customers are closer than ever—literally at your fingertips—but you still have to build relationships and establish trust. That's where social media marketing comes in. **Social media marketing** is a form of Internet marketing that utilizes social networking sites as a marketing tool. The goal of social media marketing is to produce content that users will share with their social network to help a company increase exposure and reach more customers.

Social networking sites act as word of mouth. They allow users to "retweet" or "repost" comments made by others about a product, service, brand, or company. As a result of the message being repeated, more people are reached and, thus, more traffic is brought to the product and/or company. Also, because the message comes from a friend or trusted source, as opposed to the brand or business itself, it is viewed more positively and results in "free" media rather than paid media.

One of the key components of social media marketing is *social media optimization (SMO)*, which works hand in hand with search engine optimization (SEO). Many users perform searches on social networking sites to find certain topics. These searches then impact the results displayed by search engines such as Google and Bing.

THE SOCIAL MEDIA MARKETING CONVERSATION Conversations are usually the best way for businesses to build relationships. Customers love to share their opinions about products or services they buy.

FAMOUS ENTREPRENEUR

MARK ZUCKERBERG The social networking site Facebook has recreated how humans communicate and has transformed lives globally. Cofounder Mark Zuckerberg developed an interest in computers and began writing software in middle school. One of Zuckerberg's earliest ventures was a software program called "ZuckNet" that allowed all of the computers in the house and his father's home-based dental office to communicate with each other. It is considered a "primitive" version of AOL's Instant Messenger. During high school, Zuckerberg created the Synapse Music Player, an early version of the music software Pandora. Microsoft and AOL both expressed an interest in buying the software and hiring Zuckerberg before he graduated. He declined the offers to attend college at Harvard University.

While at Harvard, Zuckerberg was recruited by other Harvard students to work on a social networking site they called Harvard Connection. This site was designed to create a dating site for Harvard students. Zuckerberg soon dropped out of this project and, with some other friends,

How do entrepreneurs change the way we live?

catwalker/Shutterstock.com

created a site that allowed users to create their own profiles, upload photos, and communicate with other users. Initially called "Thefacebook," Zuckerberg and his friends launched the site in February 2004. Membership was initially restricted to Harvard students. The group quickly expanded the site to more universities and colleges, and Zuckerberg and his team moved their operations to Palo Alto, California.

By August 2005, Zuckerberg had officially changed the company's name to Facebook and, after raising $12.7 million in venture capital, was ready to move the company to the next level. The site gradually expanded from college networks and now is accessible to anyone age 13 or older. The site has over one billion users and has made Zuckerberg the world's second-youngest billionaire!

THINK CRITICALLY
Why do you think Facebook has become so popular all over the world? What are some of the marketing applications for businesses using Facebook?

Though buyers have access to more product information online than ever before, they are still motivated most by the opinions of other consumers. Many shoppers say that consumer opinions, ratings, and reviews they read on websites affect their purchasing decisions. When readers share real-life experiences about the benefits of a product or service, potential buyers can see themselves in their place and make an emotional connection to the business.

Social media also allows customers to interact directly with the company. Consumers have the opportunity to ask questions or voice complaints and feel they are being heard. In turn, social media marketing helps a company get direct feedback from customers.

 CHECKPOINT

What are the goals of CRM and social media marketing?

 ASSESSMENT

THINK ABOUT IT

1. What are the limitations of market research?

2. Why is it important to define the question you want your market research to answer?

3. How is data mining used?

MAKE ACADEMIC CONNECTIONS

4. **PROBLEM SOLVING**   Your family-owned business processes and sells orange juice to food distributors. In order to grow, the business needs to expand its product line. Describe how you would apply the six market research steps to help determine an additional product that your business could offer.

5. **RESEARCH**   Identify the sources of primary and secondary data that you would use to make decisions about expanding the product line for your orange juice business in the previous question.

6. **TECHNOLOGY**   Choose a company with which you are familiar. Research the company's website and make a list of the different ways the company uses CRM and social media marketing.

Teamwork

Working in a team, come up with an idea for a new product that you think will be useful for students in your school. Develop a survey for potential consumers of this product to gauge their interest. Have students from your school complete the survey. Tabulate the results and determine if the product is a good idea. Report your findings.

The Essential Question   Refer to The Essential Question on p. 101. Market research can help entrepreneurs understand their target markets and, in turn, help satisfy the wants and needs of their customers.

4.3 KNOW YOUR COMPETITION

The Essential Question How can entrepreneurs better understand their competition?

LEARNING OBJECTIVES

LO 4.3-1 Explain the importance of knowing and understanding your competition.

LO 4.3-2 Prepare a competitive analysis.

LO 4.3-3 Describe strategies for maintaining customer loyalty.

KEY TERMS

- direct competition
- indirect competition
- competitive analysis

FOCUS ON SMALL BUSINESS

Who is your competition?

Roseanna and John needed to find out who their competition would be for their new restaurant. They drove 30 minutes in all directions from the location they chose for their restaurant and made a list of all the restaurants they saw on their trips. They also obtained menus of the restaurants to see what type of food they offered. They even ate at several of the restaurants and observed the restaurants' strengths and weaknesses. Roseanna and John determined that their restaurant would offer a different type of food from any of their competition and that the customers in their target market would be willing to try a new restaurant.

WORK AS A TEAM Roseanna and John have determined that there is a market for their restaurant. How can they differentiate their restaurant from competing restaurants? How can they keep customers coming back?

It is beneficial to check out the competition in person.

LO 4.3-1 Impact of Competition

The U.S. economic system is based on private property, freedom of choice, profit, and competition. Because consumers are free to buy whatever they want from whomever they want, companies compete for their business. Most new businesses face *competitors*—companies offering similar or identical products and services to the same group of target customers. As the owner of a new business, you will have to persuade customers to buy from you instead of from your competitors. You must always watch the competition and be sure that you are offering products that are of equal or better quality at the same or lower prices.

Understand the Competition

Knowing about your competition will also help you define your target market. Businesses have to identify some special customer need or want that is not being met. Customers may be happy with the products or services, but they may be unhappy with the prices. Customers might be dissatisfied with the quality of a product or service and would be willing to pay more for better quality. In either case, a customer need is going unmet by a competitor, indicating a possible opportunity for an entrepreneur.

Know the Types of Competition

Competitors may be categorized as either direct or indirect competition. You will need to find ways to identify and differentiate yourself from both types of competition.

DIRECT COMPETITION A business that makes most of its money selling the same or similar products or services to the same market as other businesses is **direct competition**. For example, Macy's and Nordstrom's are direct competitors. A direct competitor of The Coca-Cola Company is PepsiCo.

How can businesses that are similar compete with one another?

Secondary data resources can give you information on your direct competition. Your direct competitors may be in the same geographic area as your business. The telephone directory or an Internet search will help you find the number and locations of competing businesses. Your local chamber of commerce will also have information on competitors in your business field. Observation methods can help you learn more about your direct competitors. If you start a retail business, you can visit all of the malls, shopping centers, and retail outlets in your area.

For some businesses, direct competitors may be located far away. For example, Carmen Quinterro publishes a travel newsletter about Ireland. Carmen's target customers live all over the United States. Her competitors include five other newsletters about Ireland as well as several travel websites.

INDIRECT COMPETITION A business that makes only a small amount of money selling the same or similar products and services to the same market as other businesses is **indirect competition**. For example, a large department store in your area may stock some of the most popular products carried by a privately owned specialty shop. However, the department store offers many other lines of merchandise as well and, thus, makes only a small amount of money on the same items that the specialty shop offers. This makes the department store an indirect competitor to the specialty shop.

Locating your indirect competition can be difficult. You must think of all of the possible businesses that can compete with you indirectly. The number of indirect competitors can be significant, making it easy to overlook some of these competitors.

LARGE RETAILERS   When a large retailer enters a community, it can be a source of direct and indirect competition for many other businesses. Large retailers such as Walmart bring lower prices and jobs to a community, but many small businesses find it difficult to compete with them for the following reasons:

1. **Large retailers usually are able to keep larger quantities of products in stock.** They can purchase inventory in bigger quantities because they have more revenue and larger storage areas. Bigger orders result in volume discounts, and the savings can be passed to consumers in the form of lower prices.

2. **Large retail chains do not rely on a single product line.** Because it has other successful product lines, a large retail store does not go out of business if one product line sells poorly. Small businesses face risks associated with having only one product line. If its product falls out of favor with consumers, it has no other product lines to make up the difference.

What Went *Wrong?*

Price War

U-Corp was the first company in the computer industry to offer removable hard disk drives for personal computers. For years, U-Corp had a unique position in the industry and had little direct competition. Eventually, the company was making $300 million in annual revenue.

U-Corp's first competition came from A-Corp, which offered a product similar in price and performance. A-Corp spent heavily on advertising and ran frequent reduced-price promotions. As a result, A-Corp took a large amount of business from U-Corp. U-Corp decided to try to take back the market it had lost to A-Corp and launched a multimillion-dollar marketing campaign aimed at its target market.

The two companies went head to head, selling hard drives at lower and lower prices. However, consumers do not generally need to buy multiple hard drives because of their large storage capacity. Only one company could win, and it was A-Corp. In less than two years, U-Corp suffered losses, and A-Corp bought it out.

THINK CRITICALLY

1. What was U-Corp's major disadvantage in competing with A-Corp?
2. What did each company fail to realize about its customers?
3. How might the price war for removable hard drives have been avoided?

Don Farrall/Getty Images

Consider other strategies before engaging in a price war.

3. **Large companies usually have more resources to devote to advertising.** A larger company makes more revenue and can hire marketing professionals to create effective advertising to attract more customers.

CHECKPOINT

Why is it important to understand the competition your business faces?

LO 4.3-2 Competitive Analysis

Identifying and examining the characteristics of a competing firm is called a **competitive analysis**. Analyzing the strengths and weaknesses of your competition will help you identify opportunities and threats against your business. Follow these steps to begin your competitive analysis:

1. **Identify your competitors.** Explore the area in which you plan to locate your business, and perform online research to identify your competition. Talk to potential customers to find out with whom they are currently doing business. Review trade magazines and newspapers to see who is advertising the product or service you plan to offer.

2. **Summarize the products and prices offered by your competitors.** Investigate the products or services that your competition offers for sale. How are they different from yours? Examine the price ranges of your competitors and determine how they compare to what you plan to charge. Are your prices higher or lower?

3. **List each competitor's strengths and weaknesses.** What does the competitor do that no one else does, or what does it do better than everyone else? Is the competitor lacking in any areas? How does the quality of the competitor's product compare to yours? Are the competitor's location and facilities better, worse, or about the same as the planned location and facilities for your business? What attracts customers to your competitor?

4. **Find out the strategies and objectives of your competitors.** A copy of each competitor's annual report would have this information. In addition, looking at competitors' websites or advertising can give you clues about their strategies and objectives.

5. **Determine the opportunities in the market.** After identifying your competitors' weaknesses, determine if you can use them to your advantage. Is there an increase in demand for the product or service you plan to offer? What are the industry forecasts? If demand is predicted to increase, more opportunities exist for those wanting to enter the market.

6. **Identify threats to your business from the competition.** What would make a customer choose the competition over you? Examine your competitors' strengths. These strengths can be viewed as threats to your business. How will you compete with these strengths?

Competitive analysis may lead to pivoting. *Pivoting* has occurred within some of the world's most innovative companies when, after developing an idea or product that was not successful, it reexamined its ideas until it came up with something successful. Pivoting also can be a tool to discover additional growth. Some analysts believe there is a virtue in "failing fast," because it allows entrepreneurs to reduce their losses and in some cases to pivot to a more successful strategy.

Interjit Singh wants to start a premier car wash in an expensive suburb of Washington, D.C. He does a competitive analysis as shown below. He researches his direct and indirect competition. He finds that Royal Hand Wash is able to charge twice the price of the other competitors even though its location is not the best. Royal Hand Wash guarantees nonscratch car washes and waxes done by hand, not machines. Because Interjit's business will also offer car washes, waxes, and detailing done by hand, Royal Hand Wash is the direct competition. All other car wash businesses, including gas stations with automatic car wash machines, are his indirect competition. Interjit considers Royal Hand Wash's location and prices to be two of its biggest weaknesses, which open up opportunities for Interjit. He plans to capitalize on these opportunities by choosing a prime location for his car wash and charging lower prices. The biggest threat posed by Royal Hand Wash is its excellent facility. Interjit believes that having a convenient location and offering better service will stamp out this threat.

ANALYSIS OF COMPETITORS						
Competitor	Price	Location	Facility	Strength	Weakness	Strategy
Standard Gas	$6.00	Excellent	Good	Excellent location	Car wash not easily accessible	Target a different market
Lakeland Car Wash	$5.50	Fair	Good	Low price	Location	Target a different market
Ray's Car Wash	$5.00	Good	Fair	Low price	Facility	Target a different market
Royal Hand Wash	$11.50	Fair	Excellent	Excellent facility	Location, high price	Offer lower prices, better service, more convenient location

 CHECKPOINT

What is the purpose of a competitive analysis?

LO 4.3-3 Maintain Customer Loyalty

Getting customers to buy your products and services instead of your competitors' is only one step in running a successful business. Once you get the customers, you must make sure they remain loyal to you and keep coming back.

Listen and Respond to Feedback

To retain customers, you will need to continually ask customers for their opinions about your business and respond to their feedback. Businesses that ignore customer concerns will not stay in business long. Businesses stay in touch with their customers' needs in different ways. Some businesses may call customers after sales are made to ensure they are satisfied with their purchase. Many companies have a customer feedback box where customers can put complaints or positive comments about the business. You can also design a survey for your customers to complete.

Jason Rose's business, the Metropolitan Athletic Club, closed because of his failure to respond to customer feedback. Club members had repeatedly complained about the lack of cleanliness in the locker rooms and the lack of available weight machines during peak hours. Jason ignored his customers' complaints, believing that the excellent location and low monthly membership fee would ensure his success. Jason learned from his mistake. When he opened his next athletic club, he immediately tried to find out what customers wanted by conducting a market research study. His study revealed, among other things, that he should offer more strength training classes and put high-speed hair dryers in the locker rooms. Due to his focus on customer satisfaction, Jason's club is doing very well and attracting new members all the time.

Satyrenko/Shutterstock.com

How can customer feedback be used to maintain customer loyalty?

Other Strategies for Maintaining Loyalty

To maintain customer loyalty, businesses use many strategies. The main purpose of these strategies is to keep customers happy so that they return to the business. The strategies also give the business a means for gathering data about their customers and their shopping and spending habits that can help in future decision making. Some of the most basic customer loyalty strategies businesses use include superior service and more convenient hours than other businesses, easy return policies, store-specific credit cards, personal notes or cards for birthdays or to say thanks for the business, and frequent-buyer programs.

Frequent-buyer programs have become popular among businesses. To join, customers must fill out a registration form that asks for personal information, such as your name, address, phone number, and email address. Customers are then given a card, which they can use each time they make a purchase. The cashier scans the magnetic strip or bar code on the card to keep a running total of the purchases made by the customer. Rewards are given to the customer based on the frequency of

 BE YOUR OWN BOSS

You opened The Sweet Shop, a candy and ice-cream store, on the grounds of a beach resort hotel. You get a steady stream of new customers because guests from the hotel visit your shop. However, you want to attract local residents from the community to your business to help grow a customer base year round. You decide that a frequent-buyer program is one way to get customers to visit and return to your business. What type of frequent-buyer program would be good for The Sweet Shop? Design a flyer that would introduce the program to customers. Also, design a card that you would give customers to identify them as frequent buyers.

purchases. The rewards help attract customers to the business. In addition, the business can collect information electronically about the buying habits of its customers, helping it know what items to stock.

Kathleen McGuire, the owner of Flower Markets, offers a frequent-buyer program at her store. Every time customers make a purchase, Kathleen scans the bar code on their frequent-buyer card to record the purchase. When customers have made purchases totaling $200, she offers them a 25 percent discount on their next order. Kathleen also uses the purchasing data she collects from the cards to notify customers about sales on items they frequently purchase.

 CHECKPOINT

What are some strategies for maintaining customer loyalty?

 4.3 ASSESSMENT

THINK ABOUT IT

1. Why should entrepreneurs analyze both direct and indirect competitors?

2. Why is a competitive analysis important to an entrepreneur?

3. Why is customer feedback considered valuable market research?

MAKE ACADEMIC CONNECTIONS

4. **MARKETING** Devise a plan to maintain customer loyalty for a hair salon. Create an advertisement to let your customers know about this plan.

5. **COMMUNICATION** Shontel Washington just started a website design company. She would like feedback from the people who have used her services. Develop a short survey that would help Shontel learn more about her customers' feelings toward her business. How can she use the data collected to beat her competition?

6. **TECHNOLOGY** Using the car wash data shown on page 114, enter the prices into a spreadsheet. Use the spreadsheet to create a bar graph that will help Interjit Singh analyze the data.

Teamwork

Working with team members, choose a successful business in your area. Then choose three competing businesses. Prepare a competitive analysis for the business using the six steps listed in this lesson.

The Essential Question Refer to The Essential Question on p. 110. Entrepreneurs can perform a competitive analysis to fully understand the strengths and weaknesses of their direct and indirect competition.

Sharpen Your 21st Century Entrepreneurial Skills

Use Spreadsheets to Analyze Data

Spreadsheets are a powerful tool for analyzing, sharing, and managing numerical data. Entrepreneurs can use spreadsheets to analyze market research, prepare budgets, measure performance, and create financial statements. One of the most valuable uses of spreadsheets is creating charts and graphs. Charts and graphs can improve decision making by presenting data in an easy-to-read, understandable format. Line graphs, bar charts, and pie charts are among the most commonly used visual aids.

Gena has decided that she wants to open a coffee shop in her community. She wants to determine the age of her target market. She surveys 25 people in each of the following age groups: 18–25, 26–30, 31–35, and 36–40. She enters her survey results into a spreadsheet and creates the pie chart shown below. The pie chart clearly shows that consumers in the 18–25 age group are more likely to buy coffee on their way to work.

Consumers Who Buy Coffee on the Way to Work

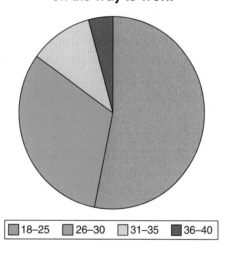

- 18–25
- 26–30
- 31–35
- 36–40

TRY IT OUT

Maggie Blandin conducted research for her dog-walking business by surveying 2,500 dog owners. She asked them what price they would be willing to pay for a dog-walking service. She collected the following data:

Number of People	Price
500	$10
250	15
750	20
500	25
500	0 (not interested)

Enter the data into a spreadsheet and create a pie chart to help Maggie determine the price she should charge for her dog-walking service. Experiment with the different kinds of charts and graphs you can create.

SUMMARY

4.1 Identify Your Market

1. Before starting a new business, you should conduct market research to determine who your target market is and whether your target customers will be willing to buy your product or service.

2. You should develop a customer profile and decide which segment(s) of the market to target. Markets may be segmented based on many factors, including demographics, psychographics, use-based data, and geographic data.

4.2 Research the Market

3. Market research is important because it helps you learn about your customers and your competition. Primary data are collected for the very first time to fit a specific purpose. Secondary data are found in already-published sources.

4. The six steps of market research are: (1) define the question, (2) determine the data needed, (3) collect the data, (4) analyze the data, (5) take action, and (6) evaluate the results.

5. Technology now plays an important role in the field of marketing. Customer relationship management (CRM) uses technology to track customer interactions on an individual level. Social media marketing utilizes social networking sites to help a company increase exposure and reach more customers.

4.3 Know Your Competition

6. Direct competition comes from a business that makes most of its money selling the same or similar products and services to the same market. Indirect competition comes from a business that makes only a small amount of money selling the same or similar products to the same market.

7. Creating a competitive analysis involves the following steps: (1) identify your competitors, (2) summarize the products and prices offered by your competitors, (3) list each competitor's strengths and weaknesses, (4) find out the strategies and objectives of your competitors, (5) determine the opportunities in the market, and (6) identify threats to your business from the competition.

8. There are many ways to maintain customer loyalty, such as by asking for customer feedback, providing superior service, and offering frequent-buyer programs.

 WHAT DO YOU KNOW NOW?

Read *Ideas in Action* on page 95 again. Then answer the questions a second time. Have your responses changed? If so, how have they changed?

KEY TERMS REVIEW

Match each statement with the term that best defines it. Some terms may not be used.

1. A description of the characteristics of the person or company that is likely to purchase a product or service
2. Data that describe a group of people in terms of age, marital status, family size, ethnicity, gender, profession, education, and income
3. An in-depth interview with a group of target customers who provide valuable ideas on products or services
4. Information collected for the very first time to fit a specific purpose
5. A company's efforts to understand customers as individuals instead of as part of a group
6. Data that describe a group of people in terms of their tastes, opinions, personality traits, and lifestyle habits
7. Data found in already-published sources
8. A business that makes most of its money selling the same or similar products or services to the same market as other businesses

a. competitive analysis
b. customer profile
c. customer relation-ship management (CRM)
d. demographics
e. direct competition
f. focus group
g. geographic data
h. indirect competition
i. market research
j. market segments
k. primary data
l. psychographics
m. secondary data
n. social media marketing
o. survey
p. target market
q. use-based data

REVIEW YOUR KNOWLEDGE

9. Which of the following is *not* a reason that entrepreneurs need to know who their customers are?
   a. customers won't buy products that don't meet their needs
   b. companies cannot remain in business without customers
   c. customers have no influence on products or services offered
   d. customers can help businesses estimate demand for products and services
10. To identify your target market, you need to know
    a. who your customers are
    b. how old your customers are
    c. where your potential customers currently shop
    d. all of the above
11. Data that help you determine where your potential customers live and how far they will travel to do business with you are
    a. demographics
    b. psychographics
    c. use-based data
    d. geographic data
12. Which of the following is *not* an example of primary data?
    a. a survey
    b. statistics from a government website
    c. observation of customer behavior
    d. all of the above are examples of primary data
13. Sources of secondary data include all of the following *except*
    a. customer feedback from a survey
    b. publications issued by government and community organizations
    c. trade magazines and websites
    d. newspaper articles
14. **True or False** Collecting primary data can be time-consuming and expensive.

15. It is difficult for small businesses to compete with large retailers because
    a. large retailers usually are able to keep larger quantities of products in stock
    b. large retail chains do not rely on a single product line
    c. large companies usually have more resources to devote to advertising
    d. all of the above
16. Which of the following is *not* a step involved when preparing a competitive analysis?
    a. identify your competitors
    b. create a customer profile
    c. list each competitor's strengths and weaknesses
    d. summarize the products and prices offered by your competitors
17. **True or False** Businesses do not need to identify their target market in order to succeed.
18. Which of the following is *not* a good way to get customer feedback?
    a. check with your competition
    b. call customers the day after they make a purchase
    c. use a customer feedback box
    d. have customers complete a survey after shopping with you
19. Which of the following is a strategy for maintaining customer loyalty?
    a. keeping standard business hours
    b. adhering to strict return policies
    c. offering superior service
    d. none of the above
20. **True or False** Longer surveys are always better because you can collect more information.

APPLY WHAT YOU LEARNED

21. Set up an interview with a local entrepreneur to find out how he or she identified the target market, what kind of market research was conducted and whether any of it was technology-driven, what kind of competition the business faces, and how customer loyalty is maintained. Before conducting the interview, compile a list of questions to ask. Present your findings to the class. (LO 4.3-2)
22. You want to start a company that prepares professionally formatted term papers and resumes for students in your school. Design a survey to help you determine if there is a market for your company. Determine the best way to administer the survey. (LO 4.2-1)

MAKE ACADEMIC CONNECTIONS

23. **MATH** You have collected primary data that indicates three-quarters of the people in your town would switch dry cleaners if they could save 50 percent on their dry cleaning. If the average resident in your town spends $7 a week on dry cleaning and the town has 5,000 residents, how much revenue could you expect to earn per year by opening a discount dry cleaner? (LO 4.2-1)

24. **MANAGEMENT**   Maggie Blandin, who wants to open a dog-walking business in your town or city, has asked for your help in collecting data. Call your local chamber of commerce to gather demographics and psychographics for your community. Also ask for statistics on dog ownership in your area. (LO 4.1-2)

25. **RESEARCH**   Use the Internet to find three market research companies. Create a table to compare the companies. Record information including the company's name, location, number of years in business, types of market research the business does, and any other information that would be pertinent to a business owner. (LO 4.2-2)

What Would YOU DO?

You are having a lunch meeting with one of your suppliers at a local restaurant. Across the restaurant, you see the owner of a business that is your main competitor having lunch with someone else. They leave while you are still at your table.

Afterwards you notice that a portfolio was left at their table. You go to the table, pick up the portfolio, and see that it is your competitor's marketing strategy for the upcoming year. What would you do? Would you read the business's strategy, or would you turn it in to someone at the restaurant? Why did you choose the action you did?

BUILD YOUR BUSINESS PLAN PROJECT

This activity will help you conduct a market analysis for your business idea. Use online sources to conduct research and obtain information.

1. Identify the target market for your business. Use secondary data to help you assess demand for your product or service.

2. Using the secondary data, develop a customer profile for your business. Which market segment of your industry are you targeting? Be specific.

3. Conduct primary data research for your business using the six steps outlined in Lesson 4.2. Develop a survey that will give you the information you need. Ask at least 30 people in your target market to complete the survey. Analyze your results and determine what course of action you will take.

4. Describe how you would use social media marketing to help you gain attention for your business.

5. Prepare a competitive analysis for your business. Be sure to identify strengths, weaknesses, opportunities, and threats related to the industry, competition, and customers.

6. Describe your strategies for maintaining customer loyalty and explain why you think they will work.

PLANNING A CAREER IN MARKET RESEARCH

"My sister decided to start a babysitting service. To tailor her business to meet client needs, she asked neighbors with children to complete a free online survey regarding their child-care needs. The results she compiled from the survey helped her put together a service and fee schedule."

Market research helps companies decide how to best meet the needs of their customers. Market research analysts help a company market its products or services by conducting research and gathering data about consumers. They collect data using a variety of methods, such as surveys, questionnaires, focus groups, and opinion polls. They also help determine a company's position in the marketplace by researching its competitors and analyzing their prices, sales, and marketing techniques.

Employment Outlook
- A much faster-than-average job growth is anticipated.
- Globalization, an increasingly competitive marketplace, and better educated consumers all contribute to the increased need for market research.
- Outsourcing will create opportunities at consulting and market research firms.

Job Titles
- Market Research Analyst
- Market Research Coordinator
- Marketing Communications Specialist

Needed Education/Skills
- A bachelor's degree in market research is required. Some jobs require a master's degree.
- Work experience in business, marketing, or sales is beneficial.
- Strong math and analytical skills are essential.

What's it like to work in Market Research? Sales at a local gift shop have been lagging, and the owner has contracted with Tess, a self-employed market research analyst, to create a market research study. The store is an independent store with a limited budget, so Tess decides to use one of the free online survey services to gather data from existing customers. The store's mailing list will be used to send customers an electronic invitation to participate in the survey. As an incentive for participating in the survey, customers will be offered a 5 percent discount on their next purchase.

During the afternoon, Tess works on preparing a summary report for a restaurant chain. The restaurant wanted to obtain feedback on its service, the environment, and quality of food while all were still fresh on customers' minds. So Tess used a survey service that collects data via smartphones. Upon receiving their restaurant bills, customers were instructed how to access a website where they could answer a brief online survey about their dining experience. Customers received a coupon via email for a free dessert upon their next visit as a reward for survey participation.

What about you? Would you like to help businesses improve their understanding of customer preferences by conducting market research? Why or why not?

All entrepreneurs must be able to sell. Not only do entrepreneurs need to sell their product or service to customers, but they also need to be able to sell their business ideas to potential investors. Successful selling skills can help an entrepreneur get the business off to a great start right from the beginning.

The DECA Professional Selling Event will give you an opportunity to demonstrate selling and consulting skills. In this role-play event, you will organize and deliver a sales presentation or consultation for one or more products, services, or customers. You must research an actual company and represent an actual product that the company sells. The topic of your sales presentation can be found in the current year's DECA Guide.

Performance Indicators

- Explain the selling process
- Acquire product information for use in selling
- Explain the role of customer service as a component of selling relationships
- Explain business ethics in selling
- Describe the use of technology in the selling function

Go to the DECA website for more detailed information.

GIVE IT A TRY

1. Select one of the following topics:
   a. You are a sales representative for a major electronics company. A large hospital is searching for wearable technology to help its workforce be and stay healthy.
   b. You are a sales representative for a major tablet maker. A large school system is looking to purchase tablets to aid in instruction and reduce textbook expenses.
   c. You are a sales representative for a bicycle tire manufacturer. A major bicycle manufacturer is looking for a tire supplier for the company's new entry-level mountain bike.
2. Research both the company for which you work and the company to which you will be presenting.
3. Create a sales presentation that includes the following elements:
   - An engaging opening and effective closing
   - An understanding of your client's needs
   - A recommended product along with an explanation of that product, including features and benefits
4. Create at least one visual aid to go along with your presentation.

www.deca.org

baona/iStockphoto.com

NEW ARRIVAL

Market Your Business

5.1 DEVELOP THE MARKETING PLAN

5.2 THE MARKETING MIX—PRODUCT

5.3 THE MARKETING MIX—PRICE

Marketing to an Engaged Audience

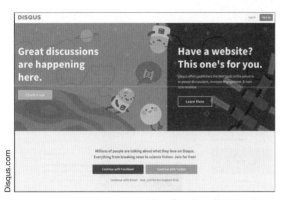

Disqus.com was founded by Daniel Ha and Jason Yan

You become part of a community when you visit one of the millions of sites using Disqus.com, and for advertisers, it's a windfall. A new form of social media, Disqus, differs from traditional sites in that users can "explore a personal passion in an optimal place to discover new ideas, new people, and new stories that they couldn't find anywhere else," according to Daniel Ha, co-founder and CEO.

Disqus serves three groups: readers, publishers, and advertisers. Readers log on to Disqus to join a conversation about a subject of interest, such as TV shows, movies, music, or sports. Advertisers insert sponsored comments about their brand into the discussion, allowing them to reach an active, already engaged audience. Website owners (Disqus publishers) add Disqus to their site to drive traffic along with discussion to their site. Advertisers get the opportunity to engage with the audience (readers) through promoted content. Disqus shares the revenue earned from advertisers with the publishers.

It all began when 9-year-old Daniel put his love of video games to good use, using them to teach himself to write computer programs. In middle school he became friends with Jason Yan. Daniel and Jason became involved in online communities by running discussion forums and writing software for them. They understood the power of these communities in connecting people. Folks from all around the world could connect with others who were passionate about the same topic.

In 2007, while students at the University of California, Davis, Daniel and Jason launched Disqus.com. It has reached over one billion monthly visitors, and the company is still growing. Disqus's philosophy is that the freedom to express yourself in the way you want allows you to be truly authentic. The site provides the opportunity for readers and advertisers to do just that.

WHAT DO YOU **KNOW?**

1. Why do you think Disqus is so popular with readers? With advertisers?

2. How did Daniel's and Jason's early experiences help them in their careers?

3. How does Disqus help readers and advertisers be authentic? What does being authentic mean to you?

5.1 DEVELOP THE MARKETING PLAN

The Essential Question Why do entrepreneurs need to develop a marketing strategy?

LEARNING OBJECTIVES	KEY TERMS
LO 5.1-1 Explain the importance of marketing a business.	• marketing
LO 5.1-2 Discuss how to develop a marketing strategy for a business.	• marketing concept
	• marketing mix
LO 5.1-3 Describe what information is included in a marketing plan.	• marketing strategy
	• marketing plan

FOCUS ON SMALL BUSINESS

Is a marketing plan always necessary?

Wanda loves jewelry and has spent much time studying the work of famous jewelry designers. She also has taken some beading classes. She decides that she wants to open her own jewelry design business. She conducts market research and finds that there is an interest in custom-designed jewelry in the target market she defines. Now she's ready to think about how to market her business. She contacts the SBA, and it advises her to develop a marketing plan. She is not sure that this is a wise use of her time, but she sets out to learn more about a marketing plan.

WORK AS A TEAM Because Wanda has already found that there is a market for her jewelry designs, discuss whether she would be wise to spend time developing a marketing plan. Should she just start making jewelry and see what happens? Make a recommendation to Wanda and explain your reasoning.

A marketing plan lays the foundation for success.

LO 5.1-1 What Is Marketing?

As defined by the American Marketing Association, "marketing is the activity, set of institutions, and processes for creating, communicating, delivering, and exchanging offerings that have value for customers, clients, partners, and society at large." To simplify this definition, **marketing** is all of the processes— planning, pricing, promoting, distributing, and selling—utilized by a company to place its products in the hands of potential customers. This definition demonstrates the importance of the customer.

It is very important to conduct market research to discover what products or services customers want to buy. Using the primary and secondary data that is gathered through market research helps entrepreneurs develop a marketing concept for the business. The **marketing concept** uses the needs of customers as the primary focus during the planning, production, distribution, and promotion of a product or service. To use the marketing concept successfully, businesses must be able to:

- Identify what will satisfy the customers' needs and wants
- Develop and market products or services that customers consider better than other choices
- Operate profitably

How can the marketing mix help meet consumer needs?

DEVELOP YOUR READING SKILLS

As you read this chapter, make a list of the marketing strategy components and the information you will include about each one in your marketing plan.

An important part of implementing the marketing concept is developing a marketing mix that helps meet customer needs and enables the business to earn a profit. The **marketing mix** is a blending of the product, price, distribution, and promotion used to reach a target market. For example, once you have determined what product or service meets customers' needs, you must determine the right price for it, make it available to customers in the right places, and then let your target market know about it.

 CHECKPOINT

Why is marketing important to a business?

LO 5.1-2 The Marketing Strategy

As a business owner, you will need to outline the goals you want to accomplish through your marketing efforts. Once you have identified your goals, you will need to develop a **marketing strategy**, which is a plan that identifies how these goals will be achieved. In your startup marketing plan, your strategy should address:

- Product introduction or innovation
- Pricing
- Distribution
- Promotion
- Sales or market share
- Projected profitability

It is important that your marketing strategy be consistent with the overall goals you have set for your business. Be sure that the strategy will actually work for you and is within the resources you have available. Your marketing goals should be written following the SMART guidelines you learned in Chapter 1. SMART goals are specific, measurable, attainable, realistic, and timely. Your goals should reflect your short-, medium-, and long-term plans for your business. What do you want your marketing efforts to achieve for your business? Do you want to offer additional products or services after one year? Perhaps in three years, you want to find a larger building or add on to your current one. After five years, maybe you want to sell your product internationally. Establishing short-, medium-, and long-term marketing goals ensures that the marketing you do today fits in with the vision you have for your business tomorrow.

Short-Term Goals

Short-term goals are what you want your business to achieve in the next year. They can be stated in terms of number of customers, level of sales, level of profits, or other measures of success.

FAMOUS ENTREPRENEUR

SERGEY BRIN AND LARRY PAGE What would the Internet be like if there was no Google? Just what is a Google? Thanks to Sergey Brin and Larry Page, we have Google and an explanation of the name. "Googol" is the mathematical term for a 1 followed by 100 zeros. The term was coined by the nephew of Edward Kasner, an American mathematician. Brin and Page chose a variation of this term for their company. When they started their business, Brin and Page's mission was "to organize the world's information and make it universally accessible and useful!"

Brin and Page developed a new approach to online searching while they were students at Stanford University. Using that approach, they launched Google in September 1998 as a privately held company. Google began generating revenue by selling advertising space. Ads are

How has the Internet provided new opportunities for entrepreneurs?

Gautam Singh/AP Photo

displayed on search results pages that are relevant to the content on the page. Google tracks customer traffic to measure the cost-effectiveness of the online advertising.

Google is one of the world's best-known brands. It now offers email (Gmail), an office suite (Google Docs), a cloud storage service (Google Drive), and a social networking service (Google+). In addition, it developed the Chrome OS operating system to run its Chromebook computers. Google also purchased the popular video-sharing site YouTube. Today, Brin and Page share a net worth of about $59 billion. That's not bad for a research project that began in a dorm room by two college students!

THINK CRITICALLY

Have you ever used Google or a Google product? Why do you think Google is so popular?

Identifying your short-term goals will help you determine how to target your marketing. If your goal is to build a customer base, you may decide to keep prices low and spend more money on promotion. If your goal is to have a positive cash flow, you may decide to price your products or services higher.

Luisa Ramirez, a 32-year-old entrepreneur, wants to open a gourmet food shop in her community. In the short term, Luisa wants to bring traffic into her store. Because of that goal, her marketing strategy focuses on establishing a customer base. She creates a list of short-term goals based on product, price, distribution, and promotion.

How can goals help entrepreneurs succeed?

Medium-Term Goals

Medium-term goals describe what you want your business to achieve in the next two to five years. Although your marketing strategy will be determined largely by your short-term goals, you will need to make sure that the strategy you are planning will make it possible for you to achieve your medium-term goals.

Luisa wants her business to become the most successful gourmet food shop in her community by increasing her customer base and her total sales. She hopes to expand the offerings in her store to include more international foods and specialty items from local suppliers. In addition to running her store, in five years Luisa hopes to expand her business to include catering.

Long-Term Goals

Long-term goals show where your business will be 5, 10, and even 20 years from now. Thinking about what you want the business to do in the long term can help you think about how to market your business today.

Luisa eventually would like to establish an Internet branch of her business to allow customers to place orders online. She does not let her long-term plans for an online store change her thinking about how to market her store today. Knowing what she wants in the long run, however, motivates her to work very hard to make her store a success so that she can use it as a foundation to develop a second business.

 CHECKPOINT

Why is goal setting important when developing a marketing strategy?

LO 5.1-3 Write Your Marketing Plan

When your goals and marketing strategy have been determined, you will be ready to write your final marketing plan. The purpose of the **marketing plan** is to define your market, identify your customers and competitors, outline a strategy for attracting and keeping customers, and recognize and anticipate change. A written marketing plan will help you determine whether it is solid and all parts are consistent. Your written plan becomes a guiding document as you operate your business. You can always review it later to determine if you need to change the way you are marketing your business.

The marketing plan becomes a part of your business plan. Having a marketing plan as part of your business plan is essential when you seek financing for your business. Investors will expect your marketing plan to answer the following questions:

- What product or service will I offer?
- Who are my prospective customers?
- Is there a constant demand for this product or service?
- How many competitors are providing the same product or service?
- Can I create a demand for the product or service I want to offer?
- Can I compete effectively in price, quality, and delivery of my product or service?

To effectively answer these questions, the marketing plan for your business must include information on the following topics:

1. Product or Service
2. Target Market
3. Competition
4. Marketing Budget
5. Business Location
6. Pricing Strategy
7. Promotional Strategy
8. Distribution Strategy

As part of your marketing plan, you should include performance standards that will help you measure your effectiveness. Researching industry norms and past performances will help you develop

jamievanbuskirk/iStockphoto.com

What kinds of information do you think should be included in a marketing plan for a small, locally owned lawn care business?

appropriate standards. After your marketing plan has been implemented, you should compare your actual results to your performance standards to see how well you are progressing. It is helpful to examine your performance quarterly. Questions to ask yourself include:

- Am I meeting sales forecasts?
- Is my promotional campaign reaching the target market?
- Is my company doing everything it can to meet customers' needs?
- Is it easy for my customers to find what they want at a competitive price?

 CHECKPOINT

Why is it important to put your marketing plan in writing?

 5.1 ASSESSMENT

THINK ABOUT IT

1. What is the marketing mix?

2. What is the relationship between short- and medium-term goals?

3. What topics should be included in the marketing plan?

MAKE ACADEMIC CONNECTIONS

4. **MATH** Akeo Goto has opened a pet grooming business. He estimates the annual sales of the pet grooming market in his community to be about $325,000. There are two other pet grooming businesses in town. If Akeo achieves his five-year goal of capturing 45 percent of the market, how much will he earn in his fifth year?

5. **COMMUNICATION** Think of a local business with which you are familiar. Make a list of questions you would like to ask the owner about the marketing plan for the business. Contact the business owner and make an appointment to discuss the questions. Report your findings to your classmates.

Teamwork

Working in a team, choose one of the following businesses: Mexican restaurant, wholesaler, health-food store, or advertising agency. Brainstorm a list of short-, medium-, and long-term goals for the business. Make a list of these goals and post them on the wall in your classroom. Discuss the goals that your team sets with your classmates.

The Essential Question Refer to The Essential Question on p. 126. A marketing strategy helps entrepreneurs focus on how they will accomplish the marketing goals related to the product, price, distribution, and promotion.

5.2 THE MARKETING MIX—PRODUCT

The Essential Question What types of decisions will entrepreneurs have to make about their products?

LEARNING OBJECTIVES

LO 5.2-1 Explain how the marketing concept affects decisions regarding the product mix.

LO 5.2-2 Define and describe the importance of product management.

KEY TERMS

- product mix
- features
- brand
- positioning

FOCUS ON SMALL
BUSINESS

Does location affect image?

Chase has a strong interest in men's clothing. During high school and college, Chase worked at several upscale men's stores in the Seattle area. When he graduated from college with a degree in retail marketing, he decided that he wanted to open his own upscale clothing store for men. In determining the startup costs for his business, he realized that the rent for the space in an upscale mall with specialty boutiques was too expensive. In looking for space he could afford, he found a site in a medium-sized strip mall. The other stores in the mall are discount stores, but he wants to promote his business as an "upscale, specialty store."

WORK AS A TEAM Do you think the location of Chase's store will affect its image and ability to attract the target customer? What do you think Chase should do? Should he change the focus of his business for this location?

Location can help you reach your target customers.

Elnur/Shutterstock.com

LO 5.2-1 The Marketing Concept and the Product

Once you have determined what kind of business you will run, you will need to decide what to sell by thinking carefully about which products or services most appeal to your target market. If you can convince your customers that your products satisfy their wants and needs better than any competitor's products, then your products become a marketing tool for your business. The marketing concept is the belief that the wants and needs of customers are the most important consideration when developing any product or marketing effort.

Consumer-Driven Market

Over the past 50 years, consumers have become more educated, and competition has increased to include the global market. This has led the U.S. market to change from a product-driven market to one that is consumer-driven. The marketing concept can give small businesses an advantage over larger businesses. Small businesses can get to know their customers better than larger businesses can. They can be more responsive and have more flexibility when trying to satisfy customer needs.

In the newspaper in Luisa's community, there was a recipe for a pasta dish using a special type of cheese that Luisa did not carry in her gourmet food shop, and she knew none of the local grocery or food specialty stores stocked it. Knowing that many of her customers like to try the recipes from the paper, she immediately placed an order with a supplier to get the cheese in stock the next day.

Product Mix

The different products and services that a business sells are its **product mix**. In a consumer-driven economy, entrepreneurs realize that sometimes they must include products in their mix as a convenience for customers even though those products may not be profitable. This will give the appearance to customers that the store has everything they need. It has been found that often a small percentage of the product mix makes up the majority of the sales revenue.

Luisa's Gourmet Luxuries will offer hundreds of different packaged goods, such as imported Italian olive oil and pastas. Luisa will also offer a wide selection of fresh foods, including cheeses, fruits, vegetables, and baked goods. To determine her product mix, Luisa lists the various departments she plans to establish in her shop and the products that each department will carry. Luisa knows that most

How does a business's product mix help to satisfy customers?

of her customers are looking for gourmet foods, but she decides to carry a small selection of pasta-making machines and coffee makers. Although these items will not be a large source of revenue, they will show customers that she can meet all their needs.

CHECKPOINT

How does the marketing concept affect decisions made about the product mix?

LO 5.2-2   Product Management

Consumers buy a product because it meets their wants or needs. However, there is much more to a product than consumers may realize. The many aspects of a product that a business must spend time developing and managing include its features, branding, packaging, labeling, and positioning.

Select Product Features

Every product has **features**, which are product characteristics that will satisfy customer needs. Features include such things as color, size, quality, warranties, delivery, and installation. You will need to consider your target market when selecting product features.

Luisa has many choices when she is deciding what types of olives to stock in her store. There are green and black olives and olives stuffed with pimentos, blue cheese, and almonds. There are olives that come in jars and in cans and fresh olives that are available loose. There are olives that are produced in the United States, Italy, Greece, and France. There are so many different types of olives that there is no way Luisa can offer every single type to her customers. She needs to decide how many types of olives she can carry and what kinds her target market prefers.

How does a product's packaging affect consumers' buying decisions?

Consider Branding, Packaging, and Labeling

Making your product stand out from all the others in the market is a challenging task. The **brand** is the name, symbol, or design used to identify your product. The Nike "swoosh" is a very recognizable brand. When you see the Nike symbol, you know what quality you can expect from this product.

The package is the box, container, or wrapper in which the product is placed. The label is where information about the product is given on the package. The brand, package, and label that you choose for your product will help differentiate it from others on the market.

Niloo/Shutterstock.com

Position Your Products or Services

Different products and services within the same category serve different customer needs. For example, both Jaguar and Honda sell automobiles, but these two product lines are positioned very differently in the marketplace. **Positioning** is creating an image for a product in the customer's mind. Businesses position a product in a certain market to get a desired customer response. Product features, price, and quality may be used for positioning. Jaguar's luxury cars are positioned in the market to meet the needs of those consumers who desire high quality and status, whereas Honda positions its products to satisfy a need for a reliable family automobile at a good value. Examining the competition's positioning strategy can help you determine the best positioning strategy for your target market.

What Went *Wrong?*

Product Identity Problems

What if you were "nouncering" instead of "tweeting" your messages of 140 characters or less? If Eran Hammer-Lahav had been a bit quicker to get his product to market, that might be what you would be doing! Having a vision of a microblogging web service, Eran began working on Nouncer in 2006. However, because microblogging was not being used at that time, Eran found it difficult to explain his business concept. He did not communicate a clear vision for it. One day, Eran might describe Nouncer as a tool to help small businesses target local customers, while on another day, he might describe it as a tool to enhance existing social networks. By not sticking with a single vision, Eran created a lot of confusion about the product, making it difficult to create a brand.

After Twitter came on the market and became the leading microblogging service, Eran decided to shift the focus of Nouncer. He moved from building an interactive consumer website to being a corporate infrastructure provider and software developer. In doing so he found that his overhead costs rose, the amount of time to get his product to market increased, and the resources he needed were difficult to find. Finally, after two years of development, Eran decided to pull the plug on Nouncer.

THINK CRITICALLY

1. What impact do you think Twitter had on Eran's business idea?

2. What could Eran have done to avoid the problems with his product message?

3. What advice would you give to someone who is trying to develop a new product?

Because of its unique offering, Twitter quickly positioned itself as the leading microblogging service.

ymgerman/Shutterstock.com

Luisa knows that the other gourmet food shop in town is perceived as more upscale because it caters to professional cooks. Because of this, Luisa decides to position her store as the friendly gourmet store for anyone who loves to cook. To do so, she plans to offer in-store cooking classes and free samples of food items. She knows that having a cheerful and caring attitude will help convey her desired image to customers.

CHECKPOINT

Why is product management important?

5.2 ASSESSMENT

THINK ABOUT IT

1. How can a small business use the marketing concept to its advantage over a larger business?

2. Choose one of your favorite products. Make a list of the features of the product.

3. In the blue jeans market, which brands are positioned to satisfy customers' need for high quality and status? Which brands are positioned to satisfy a need for inexpensive clothing? Describe the consumers who are more likely to buy each of the brands you name.

MAKE ACADEMIC CONNECTIONS

4. **RESEARCH**   Choose a business in your community. Make a list of all the products or services it offers. Talk to the business owner about which of the products or services represent the largest revenue for the business. Find out which of the products or services are less profitable but are offered to customers as a convenience. Find out if the owner is thinking about adding any new products to the product mix or dropping any of the current products from the product mix and why. Share your findings in a one-page report.

5. **COMMUNICATION**   You have created a new energy snack bar for students at your school. Design a label for the snack bar package that will brand the product. You should incorporate your school's mascot in the design of the label.

Teamwork

Working with team members, make a list of products and services you would offer if you were opening a desktop publishing business. Make a list of the features of your products and services. Write a positioning statement that differentiates your business from your competitors.

The Essential Question   Refer to The Essential Question on p. 132. Entrepreneurs will have to make decisions about a product's features, branding, packaging, labeling, and positioning strategy in order to appeal to the target market.

THE MARKETING MIX—PRICE

5.3

The Essential Question What should entrepreneurs consider when pricing their products?

LEARNING OBJECTIVES

LO 5.3-1 Identify pricing objectives for a business.

LO 5.3-2 Calculate the price for products using various methods.

LO 5.3-3 Discuss factors to consider when pricing services.

LO 5.3-4 List and describe various pricing strategies.

KEY TERMS

- return on investment (ROI)
- market share
- demand-based pricing
- cost-based pricing
- competition-based pricing
- psychological pricing
- discount pricing

What price should I charge?

FOCUS ON SMALL BUSINESS

Marie was excited about her new business, "Straighten It Out," that offered laundry services, such as washing and ironing clothes, for busy people. She would go to the homes of her clients once or twice a week and do all of their laundry for them. She looked forward to the opportunity to make money while home from college, but she was not sure how much she should charge for her services. She thought about charging a flat hourly rate. But then she realized that some of the tasks would take longer than others and some would require extra care, such as having to treat stains, iron pleats, or handle delicates. After careful consideration, she concluded that an hourly rate might not be the fairest way to charge customers or the best way to earn money.

WORK AS A TEAM How should Marie decide how much to charge? What will happen if she charges too much or too little?

VGstockstudio/Shutterstock.com

Determine the best price for your product or service.

LO 5.3-1 Set Pricing Objectives

The price is the actual amount that a customer pays for a product or service. Prices you charge must be low enough so that customers will buy from you, not from your competitors. To earn a profit, though, your prices will need to be high enough so that revenues exceed expenses. Before you can select a pricing strategy, you will need to establish objectives for your pricing program. What is the most important thing you want the price to do? Examples of pricing objectives include:

- Maximize sales
- Increase profits
- Discourage competition
- Attract customers
- Establish an image

Return on Investment

When setting pricing objectives, you may want to consider your return on investment. Investment refers to the costs of making and marketing a product. The **return on investment (ROI)** is the amount earned as a result of the investment and is usually expressed as a percentage. Entrepreneurs must identify the percentage return they want from their investment. The target percentage in the beginning may be lower than it will be as the business grows. For example, if you invest $5,000 in your smoothie stand at a local park and you want a 15 percent return, you need to price your product so that you will earn $750 ($5,000 × 0.15).

Market Share

Market share is another consideration when setting pricing objectives. **Market share** is a business's percentage of the total sales generated by all companies in the same market. The total market for a product must be known in order for a market share to be determined. For example, if people in Luisa's community normally spend $1,750,000 a year on gourmet food products and Luisa's store sells products amounting to sales of $192,500, her market share will be 11 percent, calculated as follows:

Amount of sales	÷	Total market size	=	Market share
$192,500	÷	$1,750,000	=	11%

The chart below graphically illustrates Luisa's market share along with the expected market shares of her competitors.

Gourmet Market Share

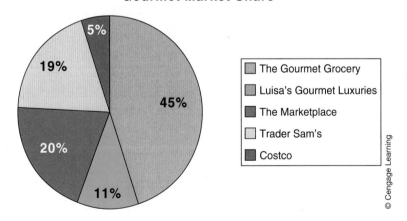

Your market share will depend on the level of competition in your market. If you create a market for an entirely new product, your market share will be 100 percent because you will be the only supplier, at least for a period of time. If you enter a market with many competitors or one in which a few large companies dominate the market, your market share will be small at first.

Companies in highly competitive environments must develop a plan to gain a higher market share. Companies can increase market share in many ways. One way is to lower prices. Advertising and promotional campaigns can help too. You can also network with potential customers. *Networking* involves establishing informal ties with people who can help your business grow. Attending trade association meetings and other gatherings can provide good opportunities to network and gain new customers.

How can networking contribute to a business's success?

One of Luisa's goals is to become the most successful gourmet shop in her community by having a market share of at least 40 percent and a 10 percent ROI. If Luisa wants a market share of 40 percent, she will need to generate annual sales of at least $700,000 ($1,750,000 × 0.40). Based on this, Luisa sets her pricing objectives carefully. She decides to set her prices low to build customer traffic. Once Luisa has increased her market share, she may raise prices slightly to increase her ROI.

To help increase her market share, Luisa will seek out networking opportunities. She plans to play softball in a local women's league in the summer. She also plans to attend chamber of commerce meetings monthly. She hopes that through both settings she will meet people who will become customers. She also hopes to meet other business professionals, such as lawyers, financial advisers, and other business owners, who might offer advice on ways to run her business more efficiently and, in turn, increase her ROI.

 CHECKPOINT

Why is it important to determine pricing objectives before pricing goods and services?

LO 5.3-2 Determine a Price for a Product

Once pricing objectives have been determined, the next step is to determine the possible prices for products. There will usually be more than one price that can be charged for a product. Pricing may be based on demand, cost, or the amount of competition.

Demand-Based Pricing

Pricing that is determined by how much customers are willing to pay for a product or service is called **demand-based pricing**. Potential customers are surveyed to find out what they would be willing to pay for the product. The highest price identified is the maximum price that can be charged.

If the bakery at Luisa's Gourmet Luxuries becomes widely recognized as the best in town, Luisa could begin charging higher prices for her baked goods. People will be willing to pay a higher price for a loaf of bread that they believe is the best available.

Cost-Based Pricing

Cost-based pricing is determined by using the wholesale cost of an item as the basis for the price charged. A *markup price* is calculated by adding a percentage amount to the wholesale cost of an item.

Luisa buys artichoke hearts for $1.77 a can. To cover her operating expenses and allow for a profit, she adds 40 percent to her wholesale cost, or $0.71. The new price of $2.48 is her markup price, or retail price.

Wholesale cost	×	Percentage markup	=	Markup amount
$1.77	×	0.40	=	$0.71
Wholesale cost	+	Markup amount	=	Retail price
$1.77	+	$0.71	=	$2.48

Sometimes business owners purchase too much of a particular item and want to sell more of it quickly. To do so, they mark down the retail price of the product. A *markdown price* is calculated by subtracting a percentage amount from the retail price of an item. You should be careful not to mark down an item below its cost. You do not want to lose money.

Luisa usually charges $10.50 for a large bottle of olive oil. To sell more, she decides to mark down its retail price by 20 percent.

Retail price	×	Percentage markdown	=	Markdown amount
$10.50	×	0.20	=	$2.10
Retail price	−	Markdown amount	=	Markdown price
$10.50	−	$2.10	=	$8.40

Competition-Based Pricing

Pricing that is determined by considering what competitors charge for the same product or service is called **competition-based pricing**. Once you find out what your competition charges for an item, you must decide whether to charge the same price, slightly more, or slightly less.

Luisa's business will compete with The Gourmet Grocery, which has been in her community for five years. She cannot charge more than her competitor for items that customers could purchase there. She decides initially to charge a few cents less than The Gourmet Grocery on all packaged goods. She will keep an eye on competitors to make sure she stays up to date on what they are charging for their products.

CHECKPOINT

List three methods for determining the price to charge for a product.

LO 5.3-3 Price a Service or an Idea

When setting the price for a service, it is important to consider not only the cost of any items used in providing the service but also the amount of time and anything that is included with the service. You may also have business ideas that you can sell to others. You should consider the different ways to structure payments for your ideas.

Time-Based Pricing

The price to charge for services can be determined by the amount of time it takes to complete the service. A plumber may charge $100 per hour. If a job takes 1½ hours to complete, the labor charge would be $150 ($100 × 1.5). A service provider must decide whether there will be a separate charge for materials or whether the materials will be included. For example, a plumber often charges an additional fee for the parts needed to make repairs because the cost of those parts can be quite expensive. If there isn't a separate charge for parts, then the hourly rate likely will be higher to recover those additional costs. Some service providers will negotiate the price. This is often done with legal services and construction projects.

One area in which Luisa would like to expand her business is catering. She will have to calculate prices based not only on the cost of the food but also on the time that it takes her to prepare and deliver the food. If she is responsible for serving at a catered event, she will have to charge for her time and the time of any helpers she may hire to serve guests at the event.

Bundling

Services can be *bundled*, or combined under one charge, rather than making the customer pay for each individual part of the service. When you go to a beauty salon and have your hair cut and styled, the price is bundled. The price you pay includes the services of the hair stylist as well as the cost of the hair products, water, and towels that were used on your hair.

Pricing an Idea

Ideas can be priced in different ways. You might be acting as a consultant to another business. When consulting, you could charge

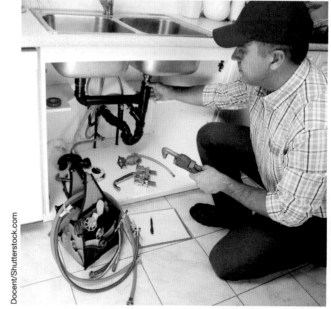

What are some advantages to a business owner of using time-based pricing?

an hourly rate for your time and the ideas you present during that time. You might have an idea that you want to license to another company for development. *Licensing* is the process of selling your idea to a company for the development and launch of a new product. When licensing your idea, there are different ways you can be paid, including:

1. *Up-front payment.* The licensee pays you a fee before development or sales begin. This may be the only amount you receive, or it could be an amount that is applied to future royalties.
2. *Royalties.* The licensee makes payments to you based on a percentage of the product sales. For example, you may be paid royalties of 2 percent of the total sales of a product developed from your idea.
3. *Annual minimum.* The licensee pays you a minimum amount each year regardless of the amount of sales.

 CHECKPOINT

Which method would be the best for a housepainter to use to price services? Why?

LO 5.3-4 Pricing Strategies

Pricing can make or break a business; therefore, it is important to set the right price for your products and services. When first introducing a product or service into the market, price skimming and penetration pricing strategies may be used. Afterwards, psychological pricing and discount pricing are two other pricing strategies that you should consider and incorporate when establishing permanent pricing for your products and services.

What pricing strategy might a company use for a new technology product?

Introductory Pricing

As a product is introduced into the market, sales will be low, marketing costs will be high, and little, if any, profit will be made. Two pricing strategies that are often used in the introductory stage of a product are price skimming and penetration pricing.

Price skimming, which is used when a product is new and unique, starts with a high price to recover the costs involved in developing the product. Then as more competitors enter the market with similar products, the price is dropped.

Penetration pricing uses a low introductory price with the goal of building a strong customer base. The low price also discourages competition.

©Canadapanda/Shutterstock.com

Psychological Pricing

Psychological pricing is based on the belief that certain prices have an impact on how customers perceive a product. This type of pricing is most often used by retail businesses. Strategies used in psychological pricing include the following:

- *Prestige pricing* is selling at a high price in order to create a feeling of superior quality and social status.
- *Odd/even pricing* suggests that buyers are more sensitive to certain ending numbers. Studies have shown that consumers tend to round prices ending in odd numbers to the next lowest monetary unit, thus perceiving the prices as lower than they actually are. For example, $4.99 is perceived as spending $4 rather than $5.
- *Price lining* involves offering different levels of prices for a specific category of product based on features and quality. A jeweler might offer three price lines of diamond necklaces and display them in different cases so that shoppers can go straight to the price level they can afford.
- *Promotional pricing* is offering lower prices for a limited time to increase sales. This type of pricing is temporary, and prices return to normal when the promotion ends.
- *Multiple-unit pricing* involves pricing items in multiples, such as 10 for $10. This type of pricing suggests a bargain. People will buy more items than they would if the items were priced individually.

Discount Pricing

Discount pricing offers customers a reduced price to encourage them to buy. Markdowns are a type of discount pricing. Other discount pricing strategies include the following:

- *Cash discounts* are offered to customers to encourage early payment of invoices. When this is done, the terms of an invoice will include the amount of the discount, the number of days in the discount period, and the invoice due date if the discount is not taken. For example, terms of "2/10, net 30" mean that a 2 percent discount may be taken if the invoice is paid within 10 days. If no discount is taken, the net or total amount of the invoice is due within 30 days of the date of the invoice. To find the last date available for the discount, add the number of days in the discount period to the date of the invoice. For example, if the invoice is dated April 1 with terms of "2/10, net 30," the last day of the discount period would be April 11.
- *Quantity discounts* are reductions in price based on the purchase of a large quantity. This is also called a volume discount. Selling a large quantity at once reduces a business's selling expenses.

 BE YOUR OWN BOSS

You plan to open a pizza delivery service near the University of Texas at Austin. Your target market includes students who live in dorms and houses on and near the main campus. You know that the price you charge is going to be critical to the success of your business as there are several restaurants in the area with which you will be competing. Develop a psychological pricing strategy for the pizza delivery service.

- *Trade discounts* are reductions on the list price granted by a manufacturer or wholesaler to buyers in the same trade.
- *Seasonal discounts* are used for selling seasonal merchandise out of season. Barbecue grills are in high demand in the spring and summer months but not in the fall and winter. Manufacturers offer discounts to customers who purchase grills out of season.

 CHECKPOINT

Name two strategies used in introductory pricing and provide an example of each.

 5.3 ASSESSMENT

THINK ABOUT IT

1. What pricing objectives are most important to a new business?

2. How can a new business compete against similar well-established businesses in a community?

3. What do you need to consider when pricing services?

4. Why is discount pricing used?

MAKE ACADEMIC CONNECTIONS

5. **VISUAL ARTS**   Look through advertisements in newspapers and magazines and find examples of introductory, psychological, and discount pricing. Prepare a poster of the advertisements and label each pricing strategy.

6. **MATH**   You have started manufacturing tote bags from vintage fabrics. It costs you $12 to have each tote bag manufactured. You decide that you are going to sell them with a 50 percent markup. What will your retail price be? If you have the bags in your inventory for more than three months, you plan to mark down the selling price by 25 percent. What will the markdown price be?

Teamwork

You and your teammates plan to open a home entertainment store. Locate distributors, wholesalers, and manufacturers of three products you would like to sell. Choose at least two brands for each item. Contact the distributor to obtain information about pricing and delivery. What is the wholesale price of each product? Find the same product in a local store. What is the retail price? What is the markup percentage?

The Essential Question   Refer to The Essential Question on p. 137. When pricing their products, entrepreneurs should consider their market, pricing objectives, and pricing strategies (introductory, psychological, and discount, for example).

Sharpen Your 21st Century Entrepreneurial Skills

Breakeven Point

As an entrepreneur, you will have to make decisions about pricing your products or services. Knowing how to calculate the breakeven price will help ensure you do not price products or services below your cost.

The lowest price identified in a price range is based on the costs of the product or service to the seller. All production, marketing, and administrative costs should be considered when determining the minimum price. The minimum price can be calculated through breakeven analysis. The breakeven point is the point at which sales revenue equals the total cost of acquiring or producing a product or service and selling it. At the breakeven point, a business has no profit and no loss—it simply breaks even. A business can use the breakeven point in units to analyze whether it is charging an appropriate price.

To calculate the breakeven point in units, a business must determine the selling price, fixed costs, and variable costs for one unit. Then total fixed costs are divided by the selling price minus the variable costs.

Luisa's Gourmet Luxuries sells stainless steel pasta pots. Luisa determines that her fixed costs are $35,000 a year and her variable costs per unit are $9. Luisa wants to determine how many pasta pots she would have to sell to break even if the price is set at $150. Her breakeven point for the pasta pots would be calculated as follows:

Total fixed costs ÷
(Selling price– Variable costs) =
Breakeven point
$35,000 ÷ ($150 – $9) = 248.23

The breakeven point in units would be approximately 249 units. Luisa must determine if she can sell 249 pasta pots. If she can, she can set the price at $150. If she wants to make a profit on the pasta pots, she will have to sell more than 249 units. Luisa can make additional calculations to determine the relationship between price and breakeven point.

TRY IT OUT

You own AAA Audio/Video Repair. You make service calls to customers' homes to repair their audio/video equipment such as television sets and home theater systems. Your fixed costs are $10,000 per year, and your variable costs for each service call are $20. If you charge $75 for each service call, how many service calls will you have to make in order to break even?

SUMMARY

5.1 Develop the Marketing Plan

1. Marketing is all of the processes—planning, pricing, promoting, distributing, and selling—utilized by a company to place its products in the hands of potential customers. Businesses that follow the marketing concept use the needs of customers as the primary focus. Implementing the marketing concept requires developing a marketing mix, or a blend of the product, price, distribution, and promotion.

2. A marketing strategy identifies how you will achieve your marketing goals. For a new business, a marketing strategy should address product introduction or innovation, pricing, distribution, promotion, sales or market share, and projected profitability.

3. A marketing plan should include information on the product or service, target market, competition, marketing budget, business location, pricing strategy, promotional strategy, and distribution strategy. Putting it in writing helps you determine whether your marketing plan is solid and acts as a guiding document as you operate your business.

5.2 The Marketing Mix—Product

4. The different products and services that a business offers are its product mix. The marketing concept keeps you focused on meeting the wants and needs of customers as you develop a product mix.

5. Product features are the characteristics of the product that will satisfy customer needs. Branding is the name, symbol, or design that identifies your product. The brand, package, and label will help differentiate your product from others on the market. Positioning is creating an image for a product in the customer's mind.

5.3 The Marketing Mix—Price

6. A business may set pricing objectives aimed at maximizing sales, increasing profits, discouraging competition, attracting customers, or establishing an image.

7. Pricing may be based on demand, cost, or competition.

8. Services may be priced based on time, materials used, and bundling. Ideas can be licensed and priced in different ways.

9. Introductory pricing strategies include price skimming and penetration pricing. Psychological pricing techniques include prestige pricing, odd/even pricing, price lining, promotional pricing, and multiple-unit pricing. Discount pricing includes cash discounts for early payment, quantity discounts, trade discounts, and seasonal discounts.

WHAT DO YOU KNOW NOW?

Read *Ideas in Action* on page 125 again. Then answer the questions a second time. Have your responses changed? If so, how have they changed?

KEY TERMS REVIEW

Match each statement with the term that best defines it. Some terms may not be used.

1. All of the processes—planning, pricing, promoting, distributing, and selling—utilized by a company to place its products in the hands of potential customers
2. Pricing that is determined by using the wholesale cost of an item as the basis for the price charged
3. Uses the needs of customers as the primary focus during the planning, production, distribution, and promotion of a product or service
4. A blending of the product, price, distribution, and promotion used to reach a target market
5. Identifies how marketing goals will be achieved
6. The amount earned as a result of an investment
7. Pricing that offers a reduced price to encourage customers to buy
8. Product characteristics that satisfy customer needs
9. The name, symbol, or design used to identify your product
10. Pricing that is based on the belief that certain prices have an impact on how customers perceive a product
11. A business's percentage of the total sales generated by all companies in the same market
12. Creating an image for a product in the customer's mind
13. The different products and services that a business sells
14. Pricing that is determined by how much customers are willing to pay for a product or service

a. brand
b. competition-based pricing
c. cost-based pricing
d. demand-based pricing
e. discount pricing
f. features
g. market share
h. marketing
i. marketing concept
j. marketing mix
k. marketing plan
l. marketing strategy
m. positioning
n. product mix
o. psychological pricing
p. return on investment (ROI)

REVIEW YOUR KNOWLEDGE

15. To successfully use the marketing concept, a business must do which of the following?
    a. identify what will satisfy the customers' needs and wants
    b. develop and market products or services that customers consider better than other choices
    c. operate profitably
    d. all of the above
16. List six elements that should be addressed in a company's marketing strategy.
17. A marketing strategy should be consistent with the overall __?__ that a business sets.
18. **True or False**   Opening two more restaurants in other locations around the city would be an example of a short-term goal for the owner of a new restaurant.
19. The branding, packaging, and labeling of your product should accomplish all of the following *except*
    a. identify your product
    b. describe the company's product mix
    c. differentiate your product from others in the market
    d. provide information about the product

20. Which of the following would be a good addition to the product mix for a health club?
    a. diamond rings
    b. chocolate chip cookies
    c. fitness apparel
    d. photo print service
21. Which of the following is *not* a pricing objective?
    a. to maximize sales
    b. to increase profits
    c. to attract customers
    d. to decrease expenses
22. A new computer device that acts as a watch but also lets you surf the Internet, text, use voice commands, track your fitness levels, access GPS navigation, and much more has just been released. There are people who want this device so badly they are willing to pay any price for it. This device should be priced using
    a. demand-based pricing
    b. cost-based pricing
    c. competition-based pricing
    d. time-based pricing
23. During late summer, Nordstrom department stores offer fall and winter clothes at a discounted price for a short period of time. After that time, the price of this clothing goes up and is not reduced again until the end-of-season clearance. This is an example of
    a. prestige pricing
    b. price lining
    c. promotional pricing
    d. multiple-unit pricing
24. You own an office supply store. You purchase desk lamps at a wholesale cost of $14 each. You use a markup of 45 percent to determine the selling (retail) price. At the end of the season, you offer a discount price using a markdown of 20 percent of the selling price. The discount price for desk lamps is
    a. $20.30
    b. $17.50
    c. $16.24
    d. $11.20
25. Which of the following pricing strategies is often used when introducing a new product into the market with the goal of developing a strong customer base while discouraging competition?
    a. price skimming
    b. penetration pricing
    c. prestige pricing
    d. price lining

APPLY WHAT YOU LEARNED

26. You want to open a gardening business that offers planting, weed pulling, and watering services to busy homeowners in your neighborhood. Write a positioning statement for your business. (LO 5.2-2)
27. You think that networking would be a good way to increase your market share for your gardening business described above. Outline a networking strategy to implement. (LO 5.3-1)

MAKE ACADEMIC CONNECTIONS

28. **MATH** The annual sales of home entertainment equipment in your area is $23 million. You want to capture 15 percent of the market. How much will you have to sell to achieve your goal? (LO 5.3-1)
29. **COMMUNICATION** Write a paragraph describing how psychological pricing has affected one of your purchasing decisions. (LO 5.3-4)

30. **PROBLEM SOLVING** Your sporting goods store sells fitness equipment. Included in your product mix is a treadmill that is not selling well, and you do not understand why. List some possible causes. How can you determine the reason behind low sales? (LO 5.2-2)

31. **MATH** You want to download some special relaxation music that you will play in the nail salon you are going to open. The site from which you download music is offering a multiple-unit price on music downloads this month. For every three songs you download, you pay only $2.50. If you download only one or two songs, the price is $0.99 per song. You download 38 songs. How much will you have to pay for the downloads? (LO 5.3-2)

What Would YOU DO?

You offer a math tutoring service for children at the elementary and middle schools in your neighborhood. You normally charge $15 per hour. You recently received a message from the mother of a fifth grader inquiring about your services and pricing. She got your name from the mother of another student that you tutor. You recognize her name as being from a family that owns a very large business in your town. You would like to charge her more than $15 per hour because you know the family is wealthy. What would you do? Is it fair for you to raise your price just because you know the family has more money? What problems do you think you might experience if you charge customers different prices? Under what circumstances would you be justified in charging customers different prices?

BUILD YOUR BUSINESS PLAN PROJECT

This activity will help you get started on the development of a marketing plan for your business idea.

1. Define short-, medium-, and long-term marketing goals for your business.
2. Determine the product mix for your business and the features of each product. How do you plan on positioning your products?
3. Decide how you will develop brand recognition for your business. Design any logos, symbols, and/or product labeling and packaging you will use.
4. Determine your pricing objectives and how you plan to achieve them.
5. Develop a pricing strategy for your products and/or services. What price will you charge? How did you decide on this price?
6. Calculate the breakeven point based on your selling price. Is your breakeven point realistic? Do you need to adjust the selling price?

PLANNING A CAREER IN E-MARKETING

"My boss gave me one hour to use the Internet to research local competing businesses and their products. Some websites were informational with pages of text, while other sites were more visually appealing by using color and graphics. Some sites had movie-quality commercials, while other sites offered free products. Some sites had multiple links to other sites. My summary report gave my boss a lot to consider."

E-marketing refers to the application of marketing principles and techniques via the Internet and other digital media. It includes email marketing, website marketing, social media marketing, display advertising (such as web banner advertising), and mobile advertising. When you use the Internet to learn about a company, product, event, or other item, you likely will visit a site that was developed by an e-marketer.

Employment Outlook
- A faster-than-average growth is anticipated.
- As businesses increase their dependence on the Internet for the efficient distribution of product and marketing information, demand for these jobs will continue to grow.

Job Titles
- Online Marketing and Outreach Coordinator
- Website Designer
- Web Page Developer
- E-commerce Communication Manager
- Website Marketer

Needed Education/Skills
- A bachelor's degree in marketing is recommended.
- Knowledge of programming, especially HTML, and graphic design is needed.
- Computer science and business courses are helpful.
- Strong creativity, attention to detail, and problem-solving and analytical skills are required.

What's it like to work in E-Marketing? This morning Lev, a freelance website marketer, is meeting with a small group of investors who want to build a dozen windmills on property bordering a huge lake. As part of a public relations campaign to encourage community support for the project, the investors want to develop a website about the project. Lev has been contracted to develop a website that will promote all of the benefits of the windmill farm. The website needs to include photos of the windmill farm's proposed design, statistics on the number of homes that can be powered from wind energy, and data reflecting flight patterns of local birds. The site also needs to provide links to similar small-scale projects that have been successful.

In the afternoon, Lev will meet with a farmer's association that wants to provide support via a website for independent farmers who want to convert corn to ethanol. This meeting will focus on the site's content and design. To help make the project more appealing to farmers, Lev must ensure that the website is easy to navigate.

What about you? Would you like to design websites that are informative, easy to navigate, and profitable for their sponsors? What would you like or dislike about this career?

Website Design

We live in a highly technical society. Information is available with just the click of a mouse or the swipe of a finger. For this reason, businesses must have a strong web presence in order to be competitive. The FBLA Website Design Event allows students to demonstrate their ability to create and design a quality website.

This event consists of two components: a project and a performance. An individual or a team of two to three students will design and create a website based on the current year's topic, which can be found on the FBLA website. The topic changes with each school year.

Performance Competencies
- Show creativity and cohesiveness of design through the use of graphics, text, and special effects
- Demonstrate effective decision making and problem-solving skills
- Present a final product that indicates a clear thought process and an intended, planned direction with formulation and execution of a firm idea
- Explain content logically and systematically
- Effectively communicate required information
- Demonstrate ability to make a businesslike presentation

Go to the FBLA website for more detailed information.

GIVE IT A TRY
Ask your teacher for the current year's Website Design topic. Then use any form of software available to design and create a website based on the topic. As you develop your website, use the following guidelines:

- Be sure the overall design is aesthetically pleasing and consistent across all pages
- Ensure the design has a high level of usability
- Show creativity and originality and support the theme
- Use proper grammar, spelling, and punctuation
- Follow copyright laws

After you create and develop your website, create a five-minute oral presentation to give in class. During your presentation, address the following topics: development of the topic, the design process, and the use of media elements (sound, graphics, and video) and social media elements. When you are finished with your presentation, be prepared to answer questions from the audience.

www.fbla-pbl.org

IPGGutenbergUKLtd/iStockphoto.com

Distribution, Promotion, and Selling

6.1 THE MARKETING MIX—DISTRIBUTION

6.2 THE MARKETING MIX—PROMOTION

6.3 SELLING AND PROMOTING

Giving Young Entrepreneurs a Leg Up

Photo by Kyle Kesterson

Marc Nager, President of UP Global and CEO of Startup Weekend

Marc Nager believes entrepreneurship can be both taught and learned, and he's out to ensure that young people around the world know that. Both a U.S. and Swiss citizen, Marc is the president of UP Global and CEO of Startup Weekend.

UP Global supports entrepreneurs worldwide with action-based learning programs, resources, and networks. It powers such programs as Startup Weekend and the Young Entrepreneur Council (YEC) Startup Lab, among others. Startup Weekend offers 54-hour events where developers, designers, marketers, product managers, and startup enthusiasts come together to share ideas, form teams, and build and launch products. YEC Startup Lab is an international mentorship program to support young entrepreneurs and foster a global entrepreneurial ecosystem.

Marc, now in his late twenties, has a degree in International Business from Chapman University in Southern California. He turned his passion and curiosity about startup businesses into a way to help others pursue their dreams. Marc and his partner, Clint Nelsen, obtained Startup Weekend from founder Andrew Hyde in 2009 and converted it into a nonprofit organization.

Since then, they have held over 3,000 Startup Weekend events in more than 650 cities and 130 countries, including places like Syria, Iran, Nigeria, India, and Iceland.

"Our mission is education, inspiration, and empowerment," Marc said. "It's really amazing to be in a position to really change people's lives. People come in [to Startup Weekend] with ideas but don't have the skills and meet people who do. Or they bond and get inspiration."

His work has received media attention in national publications such as *Entrepreneur* magazine, *Forbes*, *Wall Street Journal*, *Harvard Business Review*, *TechCrunch*, and more. Marc considers himself an orchestrator of passion and talent. He believes entrepreneurship is a real option for anyone. His efforts are helping to pave the way for future entrepreneurs.

WHAT DO YOU KNOW?

1. Do you think having dual citizenship has influenced Marc's business? How?
2. Marc believes that entrepreneurship is a real option for anyone. How does he back up his belief?
3. How might you benefit from participating in a Startup Weekend event?

6.1 THE MARKETING MIX—DISTRIBUTION

The Essential Question How do products get from the manufacturer to the consumer?

LEARNING OBJECTIVES

LO 6.1-1 Describe the four basic options of channels of distribution.

LO 6.1-2 Apply channels of distribution to the specific needs of various types of businesses.

LO 6.1-3 Discuss factors to consider in the physical distribution of products.

KEY TERMS

- supply chain management
- distribution
- channels of distribution
- direct channel
- indirect channel
- intellectual property
- physical distribution

FOCUS ON SMALL BUSINESS

Avoid distribution mix-ups.

Dustin owns a small hardware store in southern Florida. During the winter, he placed an order for swimming pool supplies to be delivered in early spring. He knew that his customers' pool usage and maintenance needs would increase in the spring. He wanted to be sure he had everything in stock in time. His supplier processed the order and assured Dustin it would be delivered in late February. Imagine Dustin's surprise when he opened the box from the supplier and found a product used to melt snow on walkways and driveways!

WORK AS A TEAM What do you think happened to Dustin's order? How do you think Dustin should handle this situation?

Distribution problems can negatively impact a business.

Produktownia/Shutterstock.com

LO 6.1-1 Supply Chain Management

Supply chain management is the coordination of manufacturers, suppliers, and retailers working together to meet a customer need for a product or service. **Distribution** is an important component of supply chain management that involves the locations and methods used to make products and services available to customers. As you develop a distribution strategy for your business, you will determine how you will get your products and services to your customers.

Channels of distribution are the routes that products and services take from the time they are produced to the time they are consumed. Choosing the right channel of distribution for a product includes finding the most efficient way to ship it to desired locations. Using the right distribution channels saves time and lowers costs for both buyers and sellers.

Direct and Indirect Channels

Channels are either direct or indirect. A **direct channel** moves the product directly from the manufacturer to the consumer. An **indirect channel** uses *intermediaries*—people or businesses that move products between the manufacturer and the consumer. Agents, wholesalers, and retailers serve as intermediaries.

Getting a product to the market in a timely manner is an important component of the distribution phase. If a farmer in Georgia grows strawberries, the value of the strawberries will be maximized if they can be moved to northern markets quickly while they are fresh. Because there is a lack of fresh strawberries in northern markets, the demand will be higher, and they will command a better price. The strawberry farmer must determine whether to use a direct or indirect channel of distribution to get the product to customers.

Channel Options

There are four basic options of channels of distribution. They are illustrated and described below.

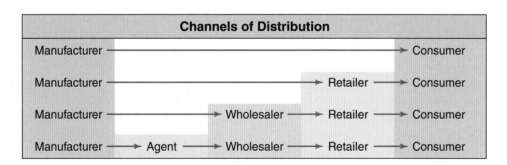

1. **Manufacturer to Consumer** The product can be sold by the manufacturer directly to the consumer using various methods, such as the Internet, direct mail, or television shopping channels. There are no intermediaries involved in this option, and it is the most cost-effective. Internet sales and direct downloads of books, software, and music have made it easier to reach consumers directly.
2. **Manufacturer to Retailer to Consumer** A sales force can sell manufactured goods to retail stores, and the retail stores can sell to the consumers. This is a more expensive option than selling directly from the manufacturer to the consumer.

3. **Manufacturer to Wholesaler to Retailer to Consumer** To reach a large market, the manufacturer can sell large quantities to a wholesaler, also called a distributor, who will then store and sell smaller quantities to many retailers. Even though more intermediaries are involved in this method, prices can be lower because the manufacturer is producing mass quantities of the product, resulting in lower production costs.

4. **Manufacturer to Agent to Wholesaler to Retailer to Consumer** With this option, the manufacturer does not get involved in selling. Selling is handled by an agent. This option is often used in international marketing.

 CHECKPOINT

What are the four basic options of channels of distribution?

LO 6.1-2 Distribute Goods and Services

Distribution increases the value of goods and services by getting them to customers when and where they are needed. Retail businesses, service businesses, and manufacturing businesses will choose different channels of distribution based on the needs of their businesses. Those needs can vary based on the size of the market, the type of product or service, and customer needs and wants.

Retail Businesses

Retail businesses have many ways of selling products. As the owner of a retail business, you can distribute products in various ways.

- Offer your product to consumers in a convenient location and during convenient hours.
- Use catalogs, fliers, and other advertisements to reach customers who live outside the area. Take orders by phone or fax and ship them directly to customers.
- Create a website. People with access to the Internet can visit your website to learn about your products and make online purchases.

Service Businesses

Most entrepreneurs who own service businesses sell their services directly to customers. These businesses have a single, direct channel of distribution because the production and consumption of a service happen at the same time. For example, electricians, restaurant owners, and lawyers deal directly with the people who purchase their services. It is important for a service provider to offer the service when it is needed

 BE YOUR OWN BOSS

You plan to open a kite shop in a beach resort town. You will sell custom-made kites as well as kites you plan to import. You know that you will have customers during the spring and summer when families are visiting the beach, but you are looking for ways to increase sales during the off-season when there are very few visitors to the area. Describe ways that you can distribute your products that will increase sales during the off-season.

by the customer to maximize the value of the service. If the service cannot be provided when needed, the customer will look for another provider. Some service businesses, such as film developers, use retail stores to distribute their services.

Manufacturing Businesses

Manufacturers usually don't sell directly to customers. Instead, they make their products and then sell the products to other businesses, such as retailers. The retail store then sells to the final consumer.

Some manufacturers distribute their products very broadly and use all possible channels of distribution. Other manufacturers distribute their products through selected outlets only. For example, high-priced cosmetics usually are sold in exclusive department stores, whereas inexpensive cosmetics are sold in discount stores and drugstores.

Intellectual Property

Intellectual property is the original, creative work of an artist or inventor and may include such things as songs, novels, artistic designs, and inventions. Intellectual property can be distributed in a number of ways. Songs and artistic designs may be distributed through outlets such as the radio or art museums. Consumers can also purchase intellectual property through retailers. But you no longer have to make a trip to the store to do so. You can get intellectual property delivered online instantly. Songs can be purchased and downloaded to MP3 players and other mobile devices from music sites such as Rhapsody. You can purchase and download digital e-books directly to your reader, tablet, or laptop or have books shipped to you from Amazon's website. The Internet has revolutionized the way creative and artistic works are distributed.

 CHECKPOINT

Why are channels of distribution different for different types of businesses?

LO 6.1-3 Physical Distribution

Physical distribution includes not only transportation but also storage and handling of products and packaging within a channel of distribution. A product may move through several channel members by various forms of transportation to get to the point where it will ultimately be sold to consumers. As the product is transported, it will be stored at various points along the channel before being moved to the next channel member. It is important that storage facilities along the channel provide safe and adequate space to protect the product.

Transportation

There are many choices when transporting goods. Products can be moved by airplane, pipeline, railroad, ship, truck, or a combination of methods. You must determine which method is best and most cost-efficient for your products. Factors to consider in making a transportation decision include what you are shipping (type of product) and where it is being shipped (geographic distance). If you are shipping a small product to someone in your city, you would probably choose a parcel delivery service. If you are shipping a large item to another state or country, you would probably send the item by air or ship and use a truck to get the product to and from the airport or shipyard. If the product is perishable, you may need to choose a carrier that provides refrigeration or that can move the product very quickly to its destination.

Product Storage and Handling

Efficient storage allows channel members to balance supply and demand of products. However, this adds to the cost of the products and also adds the risk that products may be damaged or stolen while stored. Most products are stored in warehouses at various points through the channels of distribution. An automobile manufacturer in Japan selling autos in the United States stores them in Japan at the factory and at the shipyard until they are shipped. Once they arrive in the United States, they will be stored at the port until they can be loaded onto automobile carriers to be distributed to the dealers. Dealers have to provide storage for the automobiles until they are sold to the consumer.

Packaging

Packaging is designed to protect the product from the time it is produced until it is consumed. If the product is not protected during the distribution phase, it could be damaged or destroyed, resulting in a loss of money to channel members. Packaging requirements will vary depending on the product, the way it is shipped, and where it is being shipped. The automobile manufacturer in Japan would package a small accessory item being shipped to the United States differently than the autos it ships.

Why is product storage and handling an important part of the distribution process?

Receiving Goods to Sell

All types of businesses must receive goods from suppliers. Whether or not they sell goods to customers, all businesses need paper, computers, raw materials, and more to be able to function. Retail businesses need to obtain goods to sell. A service business that grooms pets needs to buy cat and dog shampoos and flea combs. A blanket manufacturer must buy cotton.

You can use various sources to locate distributors, wholesalers, and manufacturers. Your public library and the Internet will have research materials that you can use. Some helpful sources include the following:

- The *American Wholesalers and Distributors Directory*, which lists suppliers in a wide range of industries
- The ThomasNet website, which lists all manufacturing companies
- Trade magazines that may include articles or advertisements pertaining to the suppliers for your industry

 CHECKPOINT

What factors are important to consider in the physical distribution of products?

 ASSESSMENT

THINK ABOUT IT

1. Which channel of distribution would be the best for a fruit and vegetable farm with limited production of a few products to be sold to a small group of local customers?

2. How is it possible to add intermediaries to the distribution channel and at the same time increase profits?

3. How does distribution add value to goods and services being sold, including intellectual property?

MAKE ACADEMIC CONNECTIONS

4. **GEOGRAPHY**   Think of a product that would have to be shipped from another country to the United States. Research the route that the product would follow while being shipped. Write a paragraph describing the places that the product would pass through, and describe the transportation method that would be used for shipping. Research and estimate the total costs associated with shipping the product.

5. **COMMUNICATION**   Make a list of products that are sold directly to consumers by the manufacturer. Share the list with your classmates.

Teamwork

Working in a team, choose one of the following products: fruit, smartphones, magazines, milk, motor oil, t-shirts, or software. Draw flowcharts tracing all of the possible channels of distribution for the product.

The Essential Question   Refer to The Essential Question on p. 154. Products get from the manufacturer to the consumer using one of the four channels of distribution. The needs of the business will determine the channel that is used, and the product will be shipped and packaged appropriately.

6.2 THE MARKETING MIX—PROMOTION

The Essential Question What role does promotion play in the success of a business?

LEARNING OBJECTIVES

LO 6.2-1 List the many forms of advertising and discuss advantages and disadvantages of each.

LO 6.2-2 Define publicity and describe ways to use publicity as a promotional tool.

KEY TERMS

- advertising
- mass media
- publicity
- press release
- public relations

FOCUS ON SMALL BUSINESS

Know the costs of promotion.

From the moment she got the idea to open her own spa, Chachi grew excited about Grand Opening Day! She prepared her business plan and secured financing for the business. Now Chachi is ready to get the word out to her target market. She wants to be sure that the information she shares motivates customers to visit the spa. She considers offering a free spa service with the purchase of a spa service on opening day. This promotion could cost her up to $120 per free service. Chachi has a staff of four, but only two of them are certified to perform certain spa services. So she knows she must consider any staffing problems that could occur on opening day as a result of the promotion.

WORK AS A TEAM

Do you think Chachi's idea for an opening day promotion is a good one? Why or why not? Can you suggest some alternative promotions that Chachi might use?

There are many factors to consider when developing promotions.

Africa Studio/Shutterstock.com

LO 6.2-1 Advertising

No matter how wonderful your products, pricing, and distribution methods are, you will not succeed as an entrepreneur if customers do not know about your business. You will have to promote your business to make customers aware of the benefits of buying from you. Promotion takes many forms, including advertising, publicity, personal selling, and sales promotion. The strategy created by adopting a blend of some, if not all, of these techniques is your *promotional mix*. Advertising is generally the most commonly used form of promotion.

Service industries, manufacturers, and retailers all advertise. **Advertising** is a paid form of communication sent out by a business about a product or service. It keeps your product or service in the public's eye by creating a sense of awareness. Advertising should help a business convey a positive image.

Advertising can be very important for small businesses, particularly new ones. Advertising helps you communicate with potential customers. Large companies generally use advertising agencies to create their advertisements. Using an advertising agency usually results in highly creative and effective ads, but it can be costly. As a small business owner, you probably will handle your own advertising.

Your advertising should clearly communicate your message and image. If, for example, your marketing strategy is to have low prices, advertisements should highlight your prices. If your aim is to target customers who are willing to pay higher prices for excellent service, advertising that describes your well-trained staff would fit your image.

Once you choose a message, you will need to decide which advertising media you want to use. **Mass media** is any means of communication that reaches very large numbers of people, such as the Internet, television, radio, and print publications. When choosing media, you have to consider their effectiveness in reaching your target audience.

You will also have to decide what percentage of your promotion budget will go toward advertising. As a guide, compare your percentage to the industry average, which can be obtained from trade associations, business publications, or business owners. Your promotional budget should be in line with similar businesses.

Online Advertising

Online advertising is a form of marketing and advertising that uses the Internet to deliver promotional marketing messages to consumers. It conveys messages visually using text, animations, videos, photographs, or other graphics. As Internet use has increased, online advertising has become widely used by businesses to promote their products or services. Online advertising can take many forms.

- **Display advertising**   Some common types of display advertising include *banner ads* (graphic images or animation displayed within a rectangular box across the top or down the side of a web page), *pop-up ads* (ads displayed in a new window that opens in front of the current window), *floating ads* (ads that move across the screen or float above the page content), and *interstitial ads* (ads displayed before a user can access content requested through a link).
- **Rich media ads**   These type of online ads use images or streaming video to interact with the user. Often, some kind of motion occurs in response to an interaction with the user. For example, by moving the mouse cursor over an image, scenes from a movie may be displayed.

DID YOU KNOW?

Forrester Research's Interactive Marketing Forecast estimates that marketing leaders will spend more than $103 billion on display advertising, email marketing, social media marketing, and search engine marketing over the next five years—more than they will on television advertising.

- **Email marketing** Some online advertisements are sent in the form of an email message. Email marketing may be unsolicited, in which case the sender may allow the recipient to opt out of future emails, or it may be sent with the recipient's prior consent (opt-in).
- **Search engine marketing** A business can increase its visibility as a result of search engine marketing. Customers are made aware of a business's website through keyword searches using Internet search engines.
- **Social media marketing** Many companies are now using social media marketing, which is promotion through social media websites, such as Twitter, Facebook, LinkedIn, YouTube, Instagram, and Pinterest, as well as through blogging. Companies can post information about product updates and provide special offers through social media.

PAYING FOR ONLINE ADVERTISING Because online ads can be tracked and analyzed in ways that don't apply to traditional advertising media, there are various methods of charging for online advertising, based on the effectiveness of the ads. Some of the most common ways to purchase online advertising include the following:

- **Cost per Mille (CPM)** The charge to the advertiser is based on the exposure of the message to a specific audience. CPM costs are priced per thousand viewers reached with the message. (Mille is the Latin word for "thousand.")
- **Cost per Click (CPC)** The charge to the advertiser is based on the number of user clicks on the advertisement. This method offers an incentive to the publisher of the ad to target it correctly. The ad will appear when certain keywords are used in visitors' searches that correspond with the content of the ad. Payment to the publisher is dependent upon viewers actually responding to the ad by clicking on the link within the ad.
- **Cost per Action (CPA)** The charge to the advertiser is based on the user taking some form of action that will lead to a sale, such as completing a form or registering for a newsletter. The publisher assumes all of the risks in running this type of advertisement. Advertisers prefer this type of charge for banner advertisements. *Cost per Engagement (CPE)* is a similar method that tracks Facebook likes, Twitter retweets, and other types of the viewer's engagement with the ad.

ADVANTAGES AND DISADVANTAGES OF ONLINE ADVERTISING The Internet allows advertisers to reach significantly more people than traditional advertising media at a fraction of the cost. Ongoing advancements in technology make it easier for customers to get the information they need. Online advertising can be targeted to ensure that your messages are seen by the most relevant audiences. Advertisers can customize ads based on preferences identified by individual users.

Although online advertising has many advantages, it also has disadvantages. Marketers have lessened the effect of online advertising with excessive *spamming*, which involves sending mass emails to Internet users. Excessive use of pop-ups, flashy banners, and spam has caused people to use pop-up blockers, spam control, and spyware to block promotions.

Luisa Ramirez, who is opening a gourmet food shop in her community, knows that the Internet is a cost-effective way to reach customers. She creates a website that provides information about her specialty food products. She also sets up Facebook and Twitter pages to interact with customers and to post updates and special promotions for her business.

Why might some people overlook Internet ads?

Television Advertising

Television has been used as an advertising medium for almost 75 years. With the general population spending an average of five hours per day watching television, TV advertising remains a powerful form of promotion.

TV ads usually come in the form of commercials or infomercials. Commercials are usually less than a minute in length and are run during breaks in television programming. They are very short promotions about a product or business. Infomercials can last a half hour or more and go into depth about the product being offered.

ADVANTAGES AND DISADVANTAGES OF TELEVISION ADVERTISING

Television advertisements on network and cable television reach millions of people every day. Television advertising allows businesses to appeal to multiple senses through its combination of text, images, sound, and motion. This allows television ads to make a lasting impression on viewers. Ads can be creative, entertaining, and informative.

Advertising on television is very expensive. Producing even a low-budget commercial can cost thousands of dollars. You will need to seek the help of video and production professionals when developing a television ad. In addition, you will have to pay a network or cable station to broadcast the commercial. For example, if a one-minute commercial costs $25,000 to produce, you pay the television station $2,000 for each minute it airs, and you plan to have it aired 30 times, the cost per minute would be $2,833.33 {[$25,000 + ($2,000 × 30)] ÷ 30]}.

Given its high cost, the effectiveness of television advertising is limited. Television reaches a broad audience, but if only 1 percent of the viewing audience is interested in a particular product, TV advertising may not be cost-effective. In addition, viewers often pay little attention to commercials because they are doing other things. Also, various technological innovations, such as TiVo, have enabled consumers to skip television commercials altogether.

Because of the excessive costs and its limited effectiveness, Luisa decides that television advertising is not right for her business.

Radio Advertising

Radio advertising can be effective for small businesses. One advantage is that you can be more certain that you are reaching your target market. Radio stations have different formats, from news/talk to classical to rock. News/talk and classical stations tend to attract an older audience, whereas rock stations are more likely to attract teenagers and young adults. Selecting a station whose listeners share the same demographics as your target market can increase the effectiveness of your advertising. You can contact stations and ask for a demographic profile of their listeners to make sure it fits your target market profile. In addition, the popularity of *podcasts*, which are digital audio files about various topics that can be downloaded from the Internet, makes targeting specific markets even easier.

Another advantage of radio advertising is that it is relatively inexpensive compared with television or print advertising. Production costs and air time for radio ads are lower.

Radio advertising does have some disadvantages. Radio is a purely audio message and cannot visually show your product. Radio listeners may not remember what they hear. They may tune out or even "surf the airwaves" during the commercial spots. Also, although the cost of radio advertising is less than TV advertising, you most likely will need to hire professional help when developing a radio ad.

Luisa decides to use the radio to target middle-aged, upscale customers. To reach this target audience, she advertises on the classical music station in her community.

Newspaper Advertising

Newspaper advertisements are print ads that run in local or national news publications. Newspaper advertising has been around longer than any other form of advertising, and it is relatively inexpensive. One of the benefits of newspaper advertising is its *reach*, or the number of people who read the newspaper within a given geographic area. Businesses can target specific geographic areas by advertising in local newspapers or gain greater exposure in national newspapers or newspapers with a larger reach.

Newspaper advertising also allows marketers greater flexibility. They can change their ads with ease compared to TV ads, which take a long time to produce. This is beneficial when dealing with time-sensitive ads.

Newspaper advertising does have some drawbacks. Newspaper readership has been dropping steadily, especially among younger consumers, as more people turn to the Internet for news and other information. Also, newspapers are not the best type of media when targeting a specific market—they are more effective for mass marketing. Finally, ads can easily be overlooked on busy pages containing news articles and competing ads.

Luisa decides to advertise in her community's local newspapers. She places a quarter-page ad in the morning paper serving the city-wide area. She also puts a half-page ad in all of the free newspapers that serve her community. The community papers reach a much smaller audience than the large city newspaper, but they target the geographic area Luisa is trying to reach.

Direct Mail Advertising

Direct mail advertising includes fliers, catalogs, letters, and other correspondence sent to target customers through the mail. Direct mail advertising is highly targeted. Companies can send direct mail pieces to specific groups based on key demographics, such as gender, age, household income, and household size. Mailing lists for target markets are available for purchase. For example, if your business sells hospital beds, you can purchase targeted mailing lists of people who would purchase your product. You can also get lists of people based on the geographic area. Companies that specialize in maintaining targeted mailing lists can provide almost any kind of list for any kind of business.

Although direct mail advertising can be effective if read, many people throw out direct mail advertising, calling it "junk mail." Furthermore, it has been shown that only a small percentage of recipients respond to direct mail offers. That is why if you use this method of advertising, you will want to come up with an attention-grabbing design, write a highly convincing sales pitch, and send it to the right target audience.

Luisa decides to use direct mail to target residents living in four zip code areas near her store. She creates an attractive brochure that showcases some of her unique food offerings.

Magazine Advertising

Magazine advertisements are print ads that run in national or local magazines. Magazine advertising is one of the most powerful promotion tools available for targeting specific markets. If you advertise a product or service closely tied to the magazine's theme, you will likely reach readers who have an interest in your products or services. For instance, if you sell athletic apparel and equipment, you can advertise in fitness magazines.

Why are magazines an effective advertising medium when you are trying to reach a specific target market?

Most magazines are nationally distributed. By advertising in them, you can reach people outside your geographic area. Many cities have local magazines, some of which are free to the public. Advertising in these magazines is an effective way to target a limited area.

Today, magazine advertising can be used in conjunction with online advertising. *QR (quick response) Codes*, which are bar codes that are readable by smartphones, can be placed in magazine ads. When the code is scanned by the smartphone, the user is directed to a website that provides product information.

Magazine publishers typically require an ad to be submitted weeks or even months in advance, which may not be possible for time-sensitive material. Also, magazine advertising is more expensive than newspaper advertising. The cost for prime space in a popular magazine can be too high for businesses with small promotion budgets.

The city in which Luisa is opening her gourmet shop has two local magazines. One focuses heavily on restaurants and entertaining. Luisa checks the demographics of the magazine's readership and finds that it targets the same market she is trying to reach. She decides to advertise in the magazine every other month.

Outdoor Advertising

Outdoor advertising is any advertising done outdoors that publicizes your business's products or services. Types of outdoor advertising include billboards and signs. Such advertising can be effective in keeping the name of your business in a place where many people can see it. But because people have only a few seconds to view your ad as they drive by, it cannot include much information. You'll need to keep your message short and to the point with large print that is easy to read. You'll also need to consider whether outdoor advertising will project the image you are trying to convey for your business.

Transit Advertising

Transit advertising is placed on modes of public transportation or in public transportation areas. Transit advertising includes ads placed on the inside or outside of buses, trains, and taxis, and in train, bus, and subway platforms. You typically can provide more information on a transit ad than you can on a billboard. In large cities that rely heavily on public transportation, transit ads receive high exposure. You will gain less exposure in smaller cities and towns that don't have subways or bus service.

Luisa's target market lives in the suburbs and rarely uses public transportation. For this reason, she rules out transit advertising, which would not help her reach her target market.

CHECKPOINT

What are the various advertising methods that a business can use for promotion?

LO 6.2-2 Publicity

Publicity is a nonpaid form of communication that calls attention to your business through media coverage. Publicity may be good or bad. Good publicity can be as helpful as advertising. Publicity is free, but staging an event or bringing in a celebrity to generate publicity usually is not.

While there are things that you can do to attract positive media attention, publicity is largely out of a business's control. Publicity can be negative if the media coverage is unfavorable. For example, some community newspapers publish listings of restaurants that have

What Went *Wrong?*

Too Much, Too Soon!

Nikki Pope started Toygaroo, an online toy rental service that operated similar to Netflix. Basically, parents who signed up for the service could choose a wish list of kids' toys to be sent to their home. Once the child was done with a particular toy, the parents could send it back to Toygaroo, where it was cleaned and sanitized before being shipped to other children.

Pope appeared on *Shark Tank*, a TV reality show in which aspiring entrepreneurs pitch their business concepts to a panel of potential investors (sharks). Sharks Mark Cuban and Kevin O'Leary liked the concept and invested in the business. Afterwards, Pope generated publicity for the company by appearing on countless local TV stations and network shows. The company also promoted its services through social networking sites.

For a short time, things seemed to be going well. Then problems surfaced: Toygaroo received negative publicity through comments posted on business review sites; the company's Facebook, Twitter, and LinkedIn pages disappeared; and Toygaroo stopped accepting new customers due to "tremendous growth." Barely a year after being funded by Cuban and O'Leary, Toygaroo filed for bankruptcy.

Until that point, the business had been growing. But exploding growth is a difficult thing for small businesses to handle. Toygaroo's former chief technology officer still believes in the business idea, but realizes that the business model needs to change.

Poznyakov/Shutterstock.com

Plan your promotions carefully.

THINK CRITICALLY

1. Do you think it was a good idea for Toygaroo to seek investors on *Shark Tank*?

2. What role do you think promotions played in the success of Toygaroo?

3. Do you think that the negative publicity online played a factor in the demise of the business?

violated health code laws. Customers may see this publicity and stop eating at those restaurants.

A **press release**, which is a written statement meant to inform the media of an event or product, is a good publicity tool. A press release should include seven components:

1. **"For Immediate Release"**   If you want your news to go public as soon as possible, you should include "For Immediate Release" in uppercase letters at the top of your document. If you submit your press release before you want it published, put "Hold Release Until" in uppercase letters followed by the date you want the story released.
2. **Headline**   The headline summarizes what your news is about. It should be set in bold type and placed on the line below "For Immediate Release."
3. **Dateline**   The dateline includes the date as well as the city and state where the press release is being issued. It precedes the first paragraph of the press release.
4. **Body**   The body should start on the same line as the dateline. The first paragraph includes all of the important details, such as who, what, when, where, and why. The subsequent paragraphs provide supporting details and often include a quote.
5. **Company/Organization Information**   Include a few sentences at the end of your press release that describes your organization.
6. **Contact Information**   Include the name, mailing address, phone number, email address, and other contact information for the person who is distributing the press release to the media.
7. **Close**   To indicate the end of the press release, type the word "Ends" in uppercase letters or insert three hash tags (###) at the bottom.

Luisa plans to have an open house to mark her first day in business. She hopes that the media will do a story on her grand opening. To increase this chance, Luisa hires a popular local jazz band to perform. She also invites her community's leaders and personalities. She writes and sends a press release to all of the local newspapers, magazines, and radio and television stations as well. Luisa's press release is shown on the next page.

To keep her name in the news, Luisa volunteers to write a weekly cooking column for one of the free newspapers in her community. She likes the opportunity to educate the public about gourmet cooking. And by doing so, she can also increase her store's visibility as a seller of gourmet foods.

Why is positive publicity important to the success of a business?

Wdstock/iStockphoto.com

FOR IMMEDIATE RELEASE

Gala Opening of Luisa's Gourmet Luxuries

Glendale, CT, September 12, 20— Come celebrate the opening of Luisa's Gourmet Luxuries on Friday, September 20, at 6:00 P.M. Hors d'oeuvres, imported champagne, gourmet cheeses, and French pastries will be served at the event. Music will be provided by Glendale's leading jazz ensemble, Jazz Expressions.

The opening of Luisa's Gourmet Luxuries marks the realization of a dream by owner Luisa Ramirez. "As a specialty cook," she says, "I could not always find the products I needed. And I was never happy with the selection of produce and baked goods in town." Luisa decided to open a store that would offer the kinds of products she could not find elsewhere in town.

Luisa's Gourmet Luxuries offers an astounding selection of products, including 14 different kinds of olive oil, 12 different kinds of rice, 6 different ancient grains, and pasta products from several different countries. "Everyone's taste is different," says Luisa, "so I offer a large selection."

You can find out more about Luisa's Gourmet Luxuries at www.luisasgourmetluxuries.com.

Contact:
Luisa Ramirez, Proprietor
Luisa's Gourmet Luxuries
1610 Marbury Road
Glendale, CT 06840
Phone: (275) 555-3983
Email: lramirez@luisas.com

###

Public Relations

Public relations is the act of establishing a favorable relationship with customers and the general public. Public awareness and positive public relations can be generated for your business when you show your community that you are involved and committed to it. There are many ways to support your community, including the following:

- Sponsor a community sports team.
- Become a member of the local chamber of commerce.
- Make a donation to a local charity or relief effort program.
- Get involved with the work-based program at your local high school or community college.
- Organize community programs such as cleaning up neighborhood parks.

Self-Promotion

A business should try to keep its name visible and in the forefront of people's minds. Self-promotion is a good way to do this. It's a simple way to generate "free" publicity. Self-promotion may include activities such as the following:

- Giving away t-shirts, hats, pens, notepads, coffee mugs, and other useful items displaying your company name and logo.
- Distributing business cards with the name, address, telephone number, website address, and logo of your business.

CHECKPOINT

What are the advantages and disadvantages of publicity?

6.2 ASSESSMENT

THINK ABOUT IT

1. Why is it important for a business to consider its target market when selecting advertising media?

2. How would you decide which methods of advertising are the best and most cost-effective for your business?

3. Describe some public relations activities that businesses in your area have performed.

MAKE ACADEMIC CONNECTIONS

4. **PROBLEM SOLVING**   You are offering a new gardening service in your community. You will help your customers plan their flower gardens and shop for the plants. You will also provide planting services if needed. Use the six-step problem-solving method in Chapter 1 to determine how to advertise the grand opening of your business.

5. **MATH**   You have produced a one-minute television commercial for $20,000. You plan to air it on a local television station for a cost of $1,000 per minute. You plan to air the commercial 20 times. What is the advertising cost per minute?

Teamwork

Working with team members, plan the grand opening activities for Fit For U, a fitness center that offers clients fitness equipment, exercise classes, personal trainers, and personalized fitness plans. Describe the promotional activities for the business. Write a press release about the grand opening.

The Essential Question   Refer to The Essential Question on p. 160. Promotion, including advertising and publicity, is the way that you get the word out about your business and make customers aware of the benefits of buying from you.

SELLING AND PROMOTING

The Essential Question What do salespeople need to know about their customers and products to close a sale?

LEARNING OBJECTIVES

LO 6.3-1 Explain the role of selling in a business.

LO 6.3-2 Determine how to meet customer needs and wants.

LO 6.3-3 Discuss other types of promotional activities.

LO 6.3-4 Evaluate the effectiveness of promotional campaigns.

KEY TERMS

- personal selling
- rational buying decisions
- emotional buying decisions
- sales promotion
- rebate
- telemarketing
- visual marketing

Expand the business.

FOCUS ON SMALL BUSINESS

JoJo started her dance studio five years ago. Over the years, many of her clients have expressed a desire for JoJo to sell dance attire and shoes at her studio. She looks into the idea of adding a clothing line and thinks that it would be a good addition to her business. She decides to hire Claire to run the clothing side of the business. Claire has worked in retail sales for over ten years and is very customer-oriented. By adding Claire to her staff, JoJo will be able to offer her clients other products and services to meet their needs. In addition to her dance clients, JoJo wants to make the clothing line available to the general public.

WORK AS A TEAM Do you think that JoJo is making a good decision by adding a retail clothing line to her dance studio? Why or why not? What kinds of promotions do you think JoJo should use to try to attract new customers?

Pavel Ganchev - Paf/Shutterstock.com

The right promotional mix will attract customers.

LO 6.3-1 Selling

Good selling skills are important to an entrepreneur. You will be selling your business ideas to potential investors in the beginning stages of developing your business, and you will be selling products or services to customers once you open your business. You may need to hire others with good selling skills to assist you with your business.

To many customers, the salesperson is the business. This may be the only representative of the company that customers ever come in contact with, so it is important for the salesperson to create a positive image for the company. Selling is the way a business makes money, so a salesperson plays a very important role.

Why is personal selling an important component to the success of a business?

Personal Selling

Personal selling is direct communication between a prospective buyer and a sales representative in which the sales representative attempts to influence the prospective buyer in a purchase situation. The salesperson should uncover and identify the customer's needs, issues, and concerns so that they can be addressed throughout the sales process.

Product Knowledge

To be successful at selling a product or service, a salesperson must have thorough knowledge of the features and benefits of the product or service. *Features* are the physical characteristics or capabilities of the product or service. *Benefits* are the advantages that could result from those features. Customers are mainly interested in the benefits they will receive from purchasing a product or service. Many times a salesperson builds a sales presentation around the features alone. However, customers who see the benefits of purchasing the product or service will be less likely to object to the price of the item as the sales transaction progresses. In addition, salespeople may promote *product extensions*, which are items offered in addition to the product to make it more attractive to the target market. Examples of product extensions include guarantees, warranties, and free technical support.

It is important for a business to spend time training salespeople about the product or service being sold. In addition, they need to be knowledgeable about the industry in which they are working and the market in which they are selling. They should also be familiar with their own company as well as their company's competition. The more salespeople know about the internal and external environment in which they are working, the more effective they will be.

 CHECKPOINT

Why is selling important to a business?

LO 6.3-2 Determine Customer Needs and Wants

Customers purchase goods and services in order to satisfy needs and wants. The need may be as basic as food, water, or shelter. Or, it may be a more complex need, such as the need for esteem. A salesperson must determine what need the customer is seeking to satisfy in order to sell a product or service to meet the need. To satisfy lower-level needs, customers do not usually need the assistance of a salesperson. Selling skills become more important as customers try to meet higher-level needs.

Needs Assessment

When a customer goes shopping, it is up to the salesperson to find out as much as possible about the customer's situation by conducting a needs assessment. This involves interviewing the customer to determine his or her specific needs and wants. The salesperson can then help identify the range of product or service options to satisfy those needs and wants.

Some customers will know exactly what they want. In this case, the fulfillment of their needs is referred to as *need satisfying*. Even though the customer knows what he or she wants, the salesperson must be flexible and willing to commit company resources and selling time in order to better satisfy needs. When the need is not identified, the process of satisfying the need is called *problem resolution*. Problem resolution requires the salesperson to adopt the customer's point of view, ask questions to assess the nature of needs, and act as a consultant to assist the customer in solving the problem.

Buying Decisions

Customers are influenced by rational and emotional buying motives. **Rational buying decisions** are based on the logical reasoning of customers. Customers evaluate their options and make a purchase only after careful thought. Rational buying motives include safety, simplicity, quality, reliability, value, savings, convenience, service, durability, knowledge, and ease of operation. **Emotional buying decisions** are based on the desire to have a specific product or service. Feelings, beliefs, and attitudes can influence buying decisions. Often, little thought or time is spent making an emotional decision. Some emotional buying motives include fear, protection, appearance, recreation, improved health, comfort, recognition, pride of ownership, imitation, prestige, and popularity.

Customer Decision-Making Process

Following a problem-solving process is the best way to make a decision. This is also true with customers when they are making a decision to purchase a product or service. The steps are to (1) define the problem, (2) gather information, (3) identify various solutions, (4) evaluate alternatives and select the best option, (5) take action, and (6) evaluate the action. A salesperson can assist customers through this process by helping them define their need, showing them the products or services that could meet the need, explaining the features and benefits of the various options, making the sale, and following up.

 CHECKPOINT

Why is it important to meet customer needs and wants in the selling process?

LO 6.3-3 Other Types of Promotion

Advertising, publicity, and personal selling are not the only ways to draw attention to your business. You can also offer sales promotions, use telemarketing, and develop a visual marketing strategy to promote your business.

Sales Promotions

A **sales promotion** is the act of offering an incentive to customers in order to increase sales. Examples of sales promotions include contests, free samples, rebates, coupons, special events, gift certificates, and frequent-buyer rewards. A **rebate** is a refund offered to people who purchase a product. Rebates are offered by either the retailer or the manufacturer of the product.

FAMOUS ENTREPRENEUR

JEFF BEZOS As a child, entrepreneur and e-commerce pioneer Jeff Bezos showed an early interest in how things work, turning his parents' garage into a laboratory and rigging electrical contraptions around his house. He pursued his love of computers at Princeton University, earning a degree in computer science. After graduation, Bezos worked on Wall Street at the investment firm D.E. Shaw, where by age 30, he had established a lucrative career.

In 1994, Bezos became aware of the fast-growing usage of the World Wide Web. He recognized the expansive opportunities of selling online and began exploring the entrepreneurial possibilities of starting his own Internet business. He decided to focus on books. Bezos realized that while the largest superstores could stock only a few hundred thousand books, a "virtual" bookstore could offer millions of titles. So Bezos quit his job at D.E. Shaw and made the risky move into the world of e-commerce by opening an online bookstore.

Named after the South American river, Amazon.com opened in 1995 and experienced rapid growth. Even with no press promotion, sales reached $500,000 by the end of the first year

JASON REDMOND/Reuters/Landov

Why do you think Amazon was initially so successful, even with no press promotion?

of operation. Over the years, Bezos diversified Amazon's offerings, starting with CDs and videos and later adding clothes, electronics, toys, and more. The company started selling its own line of consumer electronics with the introduction of the Amazon Kindle (a handheld digital book reader that allows users to buy, download, read, and store their book selections), the Amazon Fire (a tablet computer version of the Amazon Kindle), the Fire TV (a digital media player), and the Fire Phone (a smartphone). The company also has its own video-on-demand service (Amazon Instant Video) and online music store (Amazon Music). What does Jeff Bezos envision for Amazon in the future? How would you like to have your Amazon orders delivered to your home by drone!

THINK CRITICALLY

What entrepreneurial characteristics does Jeff Bezos have? Why do you think Amazon is so popular with consumers? How has the addition of new products contributed to its success?

As part of her sales promotions, Luisa plans to give away a $25 gift certificate each month. She also offers free samples and distributes discount coupons for selected merchandise. Luisa makes customers aware of all product rebates by posting a list in her store.

Telemarketing

Telemarketing is using the phone to market your product or service. It can be an inexpensive, effective way to let people know about your business or about special offers. Keep in mind, though, that some consumers consider telemarketing to be annoying.

Visual Marketing

Visual marketing involves the use of visual media to promote, sell, and distribute a product or service to a targeted audience. Visual images help a company build a brand or an identity in the mind of consumers. It begins with the company's identity materials—its logo, signage, promotional tools, and uniforms. Every point at which the company's identity is viewed by the public should create an image that is unique. Visual marketing spans across all company communications, including advertisements, promotions, and websites. Having a well-planned visual marketing strategy can help establish brand awareness, which can lead to customer loyalty and repeat sales.

 CHECKPOINT

What is the purpose of sales promotions?

LO 6.3-4   Evaluation Strategies

An important part of your promotional plan is to evaluate the effectiveness of the promotional strategies you use. Some factors to consider include:

1. **Is the volume of sales increasing?**   In addition to an increase in sales volume, you might also check the number of new leads or appointments being generated or determine if there is an increase in customer traffic in a retail establishment.
2. **How are you getting new customers?**   Ask your clients/customers where they learned about your business.
3. **Does your advertising and/or promotional activity produce direct responses?**   Be sure you are advertising in the right media. Choose media that your target market uses.
4. **Do your networking activities create new opportunities for you?**   To measure the effectiveness of your networking activities, track the source of new business and inquiries.
5. **Do your marketing tactics make it easier to sell your products?** Your marketing activities and materials should:
   - Focus on your customer/client needs.
   - Attract customers who have shown a specific interest in your products and who have the resources to pay for them.
   - Anticipate and answer questions from prospective customers.

6. **What is your sales conversion rate?** Review your records and determine whether the number of sales has increased. Evaluate your success rate at closing the sale.

7. **Does your plan have a positive return on investment (ROI)?** Does your promotional plan bring in enough new/repeat business to justify the expense? Evaluate the cost-effectiveness of each specific marketing activity. Even if you have a great ROI overall, you might improve your rate by changing or eliminating unproductive promotion tactics.

 CHECKPOINT

How can you determine the effectiveness of promotional activities?

 6.3 ASSESSMENT

THINK ABOUT IT

1. Why is personal selling used in a business?

2. What is the purpose of a needs assessment?

3. Name some sales promotions that an entrepreneur might use. Can you think of examples in addition to the ones listed in the lesson?

4. Describe how a business owner can evaluate the effectiveness of his or her networking activities.

MAKE ACADEMIC CONNECTIONS

5. **MARKETING** Prepare a display of the logos of five companies that you think have good visual marketing. See if your classmates can identify the companies that you selected.

6. **COMMUNICATION** You plan to use telemarketing to market your pressure washing business to people in your local community. You can wash driveways, walkways, patios, decks, vinyl siding, and lawn furniture. Write a script you will use when making the sales calls.

Teamwork

Working in a team, choose a business in your community. Make a list of all the marketing efforts that this business uses. Outline what you think the marketing plan for this business would look like.

The Essential Question Refer to The Essential Question on p. 171. By having a good knowledge of products (features and benefits), knowing the competition, and learning about the customers' needs, salespeople can match customer needs to the most appropriate products, making a sale more likely.

Sharpen Your 21st Century Entrepreneurial Skills

Marketing and Technology

Technology has greatly affected the way that businesses conduct marketing. There are many technology tools available. As an entrepreneur, you will need to analyze these tools to determine the best way to use them to market your business.

Some of the advantages of using technology tools include:

- **Cost savings**   It is much cheaper to use social media or send an email or a tweet to promote your products or services than it is to use traditional advertising media.
- **New customers**   Websites, social networking sites, and blogs can attract new customers from around the world to your business.
- **Networking opportunities**   You can use social networking sites, blogs, message boards, and online discussion groups to network with many people without ever leaving your home or office.

There are some disadvantages of using technology to market your business. Be aware of the following:

- **Ineffective emails**   If someone does not already know about your business, email might not be the best way to reach him or her. Many people delete mail from senders they do not know and use spam filters to keep such mail from reaching their inbox.
- **Loss of personal contact**   You lose personal contact with your customers if you rely only on technology to communicate with them. Many people hesitate to do business with someone they have not met.
- **Expense**   Developing and maintaining an effective website or social networking site can be very expensive and time-consuming.
- **Inefficient use of time**   Responding to numerous general inquiries that people email or post on your social networking site can be very time-consuming. If you take time to answer all of these inquiries, you can waste valuable time that you could be spending with "real" customers. It would be more efficient to have a FAQs (Frequently Asked Questions) page on your website that provides answers to commonly asked questions.

TRY IT OUT

You are starting a bakery specializing in cupcakes. You are trying to decide on the best technology to use to promote your business. Make a list of the goals for your promotional activities. Then determine the advantages and disadvantages of using different technology tools to help you meet the goals you listed. Describe the promotional plan you would use incorporating various types of technology.

SUMMARY

6.1 The Marketing Mix—Distribution

1. The four basic options for channels of distribution are: (1) manufacturer to consumer, (2) manufacturer to retailer to consumer, (3) manufacturer to wholesaler to retailer to consumer, and (4) manufacturer to agent to wholesaler to retailer to consumer.

2. Entrepreneurs should examine the different options for channels of distribution and choose the one that best meets the needs of their business.

3. Transportation, product storage and handling, and packaging needs are all factors that play an important role when choosing methods of physical distribution.

6.2 The Marketing Mix—Promotion

4. Advertising may be done on the Internet, on television, on radio, in the newspaper, through direct mailings, in magazines, and on billboards and signs. The best option for a business is the one that reaches the desired target market in the most cost-effective way.

5. Publicity is a nonpaid form of communication that calls attention to your business through media coverage. A business may generate publicity by submitting a press release, through public relations activities, and through self-promotion.

6.3 Selling and Promoting

6. A salesperson must identify the customer's needs, issues, and concerns so that they can be addressed throughout the sales process. To be successful, a salesperson must have a thorough knowledge of the features and benefits of the product or service.

7. Needs assessment involves determining the customer's needs and wants. Customers' buying decisions may be rational or emotional. Customers often use the problem-solving process to make buying decisions. The salesperson can assist customers through this process.

8. Offering an incentive to customers in order to increase sales is called sales promotion. Telemarketing is another effective way to let people know about your business. Visual marketing helps a company build a brand or an identity in the mind of consumers.

9. Evaluate promotional activities by looking at the volume of sales, direct responses to promotional activities, sales conversion rate, and return on investment.

WHAT DO YOU KNOW NOW?

Read *Ideas in Action* on page 153 again. Then answer the questions a second time. Have your responses changed? If so, how have they changed?

KEY TERMS REVIEW

Match each statement with the term that best defines it. Some terms may not be used.

1. The routes that products and services take from the time they are produced to the time they are consumed
2. The act of offering an incentive to customers in order to increase sales
3. Moves the product directly from the manufacturer to the consumer
4. Uses intermediaries that move products between the manufacturer and the consumer
5. Purchase decisions based on the desire to have a specific product or service
6. The act of establishing a favorable relationship with customers and the general public
7. Direct communication between a prospective buyer and a sales representative
8. Purchase decisions based on the logical reasoning of customers
9. A paid form of communication sent out by a business about a product or service
10. Involves the use of visual media to promote, sell, and distribute a product or service to a targeted audience
11. A written statement meant to inform the media of an event or product
12. A refund offered to people who purchase a product

a. advertising
b. channels of distribution
c. direct channel
d. distribution
e. emotional buying decisions
f. indirect channel
g. mass media
h. personal selling
i. physical distribution
j. press release
k. public relations
l. publicity
m. rational buying decisions
n. rebate
o. sales promotion
p. supply chain management
q. telemarketing
r. visual marketing

REVIEW YOUR KNOWLEDGE

13. Which of the following type of business is least likely to distribute its products or services directly to consumers?
    a. retail business
    b. service business
    c. manufacturing business
    d. none of the above directly distributes products to consumers
14. Which channel of distribution would be best for someone who makes and sells pottery at his or her home?
    a. manufacturer to consumer
    b. manufacturer to retailer to consumer
    c. manufacturer to wholesaler to retailer to consumer
    d. manufacturer to agent to wholesaler to retailer to consumer
15. **True or False** Agents and wholesalers serve as intermediaries that facilitate the flow of goods through direct channels of distribution.
16. Goods that arrive at their destination damaged probably have a problem with the _?_ in the physical distribution process.
17. Examples of promotion include
    a. advertising   c. sales promotion
    b. publicity   d. all of the above
18. An online ad that displays in a new window that opens in front of the current window is called a(n)
    a. interstitial ad   c. pop-up ad
    b. pop-under ad   d. banner ad

19. **True or False** Publicity is always good for a business.
20. If you have a local business that offers a service to consumers in your neighborhood, which of the following would be the best way for you to advertise?
    a. a commercial aired during the Super Bowl
    b. an advertisement on satellite radio
    c. an advertisement in the local newspaper
    d. a billboard on a major interstate highway
21. Which of the following is the least important in the sales process?
    a. customer's needs
    b. customer's issues
    c. customer's concerns
    d. customer's income
22. Which of the following would be the best way for you to promote your pressure washing business?
    a. free sample
    b. discount coupon
    c. contest
    d. gift with purchase
23. A salesperson who approaches all customers the same way is leaving out which important part of the sales process?
    a. needs assessment
    b. product knowledge
    c. rational buying decisions
    d. none of the above

APPLY WHAT YOU LEARNED

24. You are a home improvement contractor. What role will channels of distribution play in your business? (LO 6.1-1)
25. You are going to open a retail store that will offer gifts and accessories. Your target market is 13- to 15-year-old girls. Describe the promotional mix you will use for your business. (LO 6.2-1, LO 6.2-2, LO 6.3-3)

MAKE ACADEMIC CONNECTIONS

26. **MARKETING** Choose a product or service you would like to market. Who is your target market? Make a list of the features and benefits of the product or service that you would stress. Also list any product extensions you would offer. (LO 6.3-1)
27. **COMMUNICATION** You are opening a bowling alley and video arcade business. You are buying time on a local radio station to advertise. Write the commercial that will air on the radio. Then write a press release for local newspapers and radio and television stations. List some public relations activities that could promote your business. (LO 6.2-1, LO 6.2-2)
28. **RESEARCH** Many companies have reward programs for their customers. Research the reward program of a company with which you are familiar. Prepare a presentation about the program, including information on who is eligible, how customers participate, and the rewards available to participants. How does the reward program help build customer loyalty? Present your findings to the class. (LO 6.3-3)

29. **MATH** You have placed an ad on the Internet that is going to be charged using the CPA method at a rate of 50 cents per registered visitor. During one week, your website received 75,345 hits from visitors linking from the advertisement. There were 12,000 visitors who inquired about your product, and 7,432 of them registered their personal information with your website. How much will you have to pay the publisher of your ad? (LO 6.2-1)

What Would YOU DO?

You are the owner of Cookies For You. You have been selling your cookies in gift baskets designed for adults. Recently, you also decided to start offering cookie gift baskets for children. You are thinking about doing a promotional activity at a local day care center in which you will give free cookies to all of the children. However, with all of the recent news reports and stories about childhood obesity, you are not sure that you should be promoting cookies to children. You are concerned that your marketing strategy will be viewed negatively. What would you do? Is it your responsibility to monitor the eating habits of children, or is this something for which only their parents should be responsible? How can you promote your cookie gift baskets in a positive way?

BUILD YOUR BUSINESS PLAN PROJECT

This activity will help you complete the marketing plan for your business idea.

1. Determine the channels of distribution that you will use for your business. Include information on how you will get products from your suppliers as well as how you will distribute your products or services to your customers.
2. Develop selling strategies and company policies to ensure that the internal environment of your business promotes good customer relations.
3. Get advertising rates for a local radio station, television station, and newspaper. Also obtain rates for online advertising. Choose the medium that is best for your business and write an advertisement for it.
4. To generate publicity, write a press release that you will send to the media.
5. Determine what types of promotional activities you will use and how you will evaluate the effectiveness of these activities.
6. After you have completed your marketing plan, review it to be sure that the questions listed on page 130 in Chapter 5 are answered. If necessary, revise your marketing plan as needed to ensure that all of these questions are addressed.

"My dad's girlfriend recently attended a business conference and met another attendee who would like to be her business partner. Although she likes her prospective partner, she has hired a reputable private investigator to do a complete background check. She wants to be sure there's nothing in this person's background that could impede the progress of their business."

Private investigators are often hired by individuals and corporations to verify and analyze information about legal, financial, and personal matters. They provide a variety of services including child support investigations, employee background checks, and corporate asset protection.

Private investigators use a variety of tools when researching a case. They may search the Internet, make phone calls, interview people, and conduct surveillance when doing background investigations.

Employment Outlook
- An average rate of employment growth is expected.
- The need to protect property and confidential information will drive an ongoing need for private investigators.
- Internet scams and cybercrimes will lead to an additional demand for investigative services.

Job Titles
- Private Detective
- Surveillance Operative
- Assets Protection Investigator
- Financial Investigator
- Certified Legal Investigator

Needed Education/Skills
- Many private investigators are retired military or law enforcement professionals.
- Most states require licensing.
- An associate's degree or bachelor's degree in criminal justice may be required.
- Patience, resourcefulness, and inquisitiveness are necessary traits.

What's it like to work in Private Investigation? Otto, a self-employed private investigator, has spent the early part of his day performing hidden surveillance. His client, an industrial manufacturing firm, suspected fraudulent filing of a workers' compensation claim by an employee. The employee claimed that a recurring on-the-job back injury prohibited her from working. Otto has just finished his final surveillance of the employee. Today, she was playing tennis at a local park. Otto now has photos and video coverage of the employee in multiple scenarios performing physical activities that a back injury would prevent. With this information, Otto's client will be able to prove fraudulent filing of workers' compensation claims.

Otto is looking forward to dinner this evening, as the client is buying! The client, who is the owner of a local restaurant chain, hired Otto to investigate potential employee theft. Otto has been collecting data through hidden video cameras. Tonight, as he dines at the restaurant, he will focus his observation on one of the servers who is suspected of undercharging friends and family for their meals.

What about you? Would you enjoy lawfully tracking down information that could help individuals and companies do a better job of protecting their rights? What aspects of a career in private investigation do you find most exciting?

The DECA Marketing Communications Team Decision Making Event tests your knowledge of marketing communication that is intended to inform, remind, and/or persuade a target market. This is a case study event designed for two team members.

You are a marketing consultant for Fitness60, a new gym in a small city. At Fitness60, members take a 60-minute class under the guidance of a fitness instructor. During the class, members will spend time doing cardiovascular and weight resistance exercises, all while wearing an activity tracker. The instructor guides members through the workout. At the end of the session, the results from the activity tracker can be viewed by the member.

To celebrate the grand opening of Fitness60, the owner has decided to give a one-week free trial membership to anyone who pre-registers. Because the gym is unlike any other in the area, the owner believes people will need a free trial to help educate them about the gym's concept and to build excitement. The owner thinks that this sales promotion will help to spark a health trend in the community. The owner has asked you to develop a promotional plan, including public relations activities, for this free trial membership week.

Performance Indicators
- Explain the nature of a promotional plan
- Coordinate activities in the promotional mix
- Identify communications channels that are used in sales promotion
- Identify types of public relations activities
- Discuss internal and external audiences for public relations activities
- Describe factors used by marketers to position products/services
- Reinforce service orientation through communication

Go to the DECA website for more detailed information.

GIVE IT A TRY
Partner with a classmate. Set a timer for 30 minutes. Using the case study about Fitness60 and the performance indicators above, decide what you and your partner will do to assist the owner. During your 30-minute prep time, you may take notes, but you cannot use any reference materials. You can refer to your notes during your presentation. You will have ten minutes to present your plan to the owner (your teacher).

www.deca.org

MachineHeadz/iStockphoto.com

Select a Type of Ownership

7.1 DECIDE TO PURCHASE, JOIN, OR START A BUSINESS

7.2 CHOOSE A LEGAL FORM OF BUSINESS

7.3 LEGAL ISSUES AND BUSINESS OWNERSHIP

Generate a Buzz with Target Marketing

Tina Wells, CEO of Buzz Marketing Group

Tina Wells started her first business—The Buzz—when she was just 16 years old. Ten years later, she became CEO of Buzz Marketing Group®, which provides clients with data and marketing strategies focused on millennials, moms, and multicultural consumers.

Named one of *Entrepreneur* magazine's "Young Millionaires," Tina built her career working in the areas she loves—fashion and pop culture. At 16, she wrote reviews of companies and products that targeted teens for *The New Girl Times*, a newspaper for young girls. For her work, she received free products from more than 40 companies. After three months, she called on ten of her friends to help her, and they started The Buzz.

Tina noticed that companies were not connecting with the teen market, so she began submitting her reviews directly to the companies. She was amazed by the positive responses she received. A marketing director at one company told her that she had just paid someone $25,000 for the same type of information but that Tina's report was better.

Tina then realized she could get paid for doing what she loved, and Buzz Marketing Group (BuzzMG) was born. BuzzMG got its first paying client while Tina was a freshman at Hood College working toward a B.A. in Communication Arts.

Today, BuzzMG is headquartered in Tina's hometown of Voorhees, New Jersey. In addition to the staff, BuzzMG has a network of 9,000 momSpotters and 30,000 teenage and young adult buzzSpotters who research and report on what their peers are thinking and doing. The momSpotters and buzzSpotters help Tina and her staff stay on top of trends in her target markets.

Tina's advice for new entrepreneurs is to reinvest profits back into the business to keep it growing. This contributes to the success of the business. Tina's success certainly has made her an entrepreneurial role model.

WHAT DO YOU **KNOW?**

1. What unmet need did Tina find that led her to start a business?

2. How does BuzzMG keep on top of what is happening in its target markets?

3. Tina started out as a small business. Why has she been successful in growing her business? What obstacles do you think she faced?

7.1 DECIDE TO PURCHASE, JOIN, OR START A BUSINESS

The Essential Question What are the different ways that a person can become a business owner?

LEARNING OBJECTIVES

LO 7.1-1 List advantages and disadvantages of buying an existing business.

LO 7.1-2 Discuss franchise ownership.

LO 7.1-3 List advantages and disadvantages of joining a family business.

LO 7.1-4 List advantages and disadvantages of starting a new business.

KEY TERMS

- franchise
- initial franchise fee
- startup costs
- royalty fees
- advertising fees
- Franchise Disclosure Document

FOCUS ON SMALL BUSINESS

How can we get this dough rising?

Madge and Eva wanted to open a bakery. Madge found an ad for a bakery that was for sale. "If we purchase it, we would have the equipment and supplies we need," she told Eva. "If that's the Holcombe family bakery, we'd better stay away," Eva warned Madge. "I was there last week. No one was waiting on the customers, and everyone was getting upset. If we bought that bakery, we would have to do something to change people's opinions about the service."

"We could always start our own bakery," Eva suggested. "That may be hard to do," Madge replied. "We would have to find a location, buy everything we need, and build a customer base." "That's true," Eva said. "What if we buy a franchise?" Madge thought about it. "That's a possibility, but we'd have to follow the rules and regulations set by the franchise company." "Gosh, it sure isn't easy to get the dough rising, is it?" Eva replied.

WORK AS A TEAM What do you think would be some of the advantages and disadvantages to Madge and Eva of starting their own business, buying an existing business, or buying a franchise?

Svitlana-ua/Shutterstock.com

There are many ways to begin a business venture.

LO 7.1-1 Buy an Existing Business

When most people consider going into business for themselves, they think about starting a new business. However, purchasing an existing business could be a good option. Owners sell their businesses for a variety of reasons. Reasons can include insufficient sales or profits, new competition, fear of changing economic conditions, retirement, a dispute among partners, death or illness of a partner, and the owner's desire to do something different.

There are many ways to find businesses that are for sale. You may find advertisements in the local newspaper. You can also look online at classified advertisement websites such as Craigslist. You might decide to use a business broker who sells businesses for a living. Other people in your industry might know of businesses for sale. You might also learn about available businesses through leasing agents, lawyers and bankers, management consultants, the Small Business Administration (SBA), your local chamber of commerce, and bankruptcy announcements.

DEVELOP YOUR READING SKILLS

Before reading the chapter, make a list of questions you have about the different types of business ownership and the legal issues facing business owners. Try to find answers to your questions as you read the chapter.

Advantages of Buying an Existing Business

There are many advantages to buying an existing business.

1. **The existing business already has the necessary equipment, suppliers, and procedures in place**. It may also have built up *goodwill*, or customer loyalty. You may want to change some of the policies and procedures established by the former owner, but fine-tuning existing systems is likely to be much easier than creating systems from scratch.
2. **The seller of a business may train a new owner**. The previous owner or experienced employees may be willing to help the new owner learn about the company.
3. **There are prior records of revenues, expenses, and profits**. This means that financial planning will be easier and more reliable than it would be for a completely new business.
4. **Financial arrangements can be easier**. The seller of the business may accept an initial partial payment and allow the rest to be paid off in monthly installments. If bank financing is needed, getting it may be easier because banks are more likely to lend to an established business.

Disadvantages of Buying an Existing Business

Buying an existing business sounds like an easy way to become an entrepreneur, but it can be risky. There are disadvantages.

1. **Many businesses are for sale because they are not making a profit**. Owners often try to sell businesses that are not financially profitable.
2. **Serious problems may be inherited**. Businesses can have poor reputations with customers, have trouble with suppliers, be poorly located, or have other problems that may be difficult to overcome.
3. **Capital is required**. Many new entrepreneurs just do not have the money to purchase a mature business. Starting small may be their only option.
4. **There may be staff problems**. The new owner may have to deal with problem employees. Some employees may not like the change and decide to quit when the new owner takes over the business.

Steps in Buying a Business

Buying a business is a complicated process that requires serious thought. If you are considering buying a business, you will want to follow these steps:

1. **Write specific objectives about the kind of business you want to buy, and identify businesses for sale that meet your objectives.** This will help you find the right business for what you want to do.
2. **Meet with business sellers or brokers to investigate specific opportunities.** Ask about the history of the business, the reason for its sale, its financial performance, and the price the owner is asking for it.

What can you learn by visiting a business during its business hours?

3. **Visit during business hours to observe the business in action.** Inspect the facility closely to make sure that it meets your needs. Observe how the business operates when it is open to customers.
4. **Ask the owner to provide you with a complete financial accounting of operations for at least the past three years.** Analyzing these reports will help you see how much profit you can make and how much you will probably be paying out in expenses.
5. **Ask for important information in written form.** Get a list of all assets to be transferred to the new owner, a statement about any past or pending legal action against the business, a copy of the business lease or mortgage, and a list of all the suppliers. Have an accountant and a lawyer help you review all of the materials. Be suspicious if the owner refuses to provide any information that you request.
6. **Determine how you would finance the business.** Contact lending institutions and ask the seller if he or she would be willing to finance part or all of the purchase.
7. **Get expert help to determine a price to offer for the business.** An accountant or a *valuator*—an expert on determining the value of a business—can help. Present the offer in writing to the seller. If an agreement is reached, have a lawyer draw up a sales contract.

 CHECKPOINT

What are the advantages and disadvantages of buying an existing business?

LO 7.1-2 Franchise Ownership

Purchasing a franchise is another route by which you can become an entrepreneur. A **franchise** is a legal agreement that gives an individual the right to market a company's products or services in a particular area. A *franchisee* is the person who purchases a franchise agreement. A *franchisor* is the person or company that offers a franchise for purchase.

There are currently more than 770,000 franchises operating in the United States, and the number is growing. Franchising opportunities are available in virtually every field, from pet stores to restaurants to fitness centers. *The Franchise Handbook* lists more than 1,700 franchise opportunities by category. It also provides information about the costs and capital requirements. The handbook is published quarterly and is available in print and online. You can also obtain information from the International Franchise Association, the Small Business Administration, the U.S. Department of Commerce, the Federal Trade Commission, and various newspapers, magazines, and websites.

Operating Costs of a Franchise

If you decide to purchase a franchise, you will have to pay an initial franchise fee, startup costs, royalty fees, and advertising fees. The **initial franchise fee** is the amount the local franchise owner pays in return for the right to run the franchise. The fee can run anywhere from a few thousand to a few hundred thousand dollars. It is usually nonrefundable. **Startup costs** are the costs associated with beginning a business. They include the costs of renting a facility, equipping the outlet, and purchasing inventory. **Royalty fees** are weekly or monthly payments made by the local owner to the franchise company. These payments usually are a percentage of your franchise's income. **Advertising fees** are paid to the franchise company to support television, magazine, or other advertising of the franchise as a whole.

Jim Swanson purchased a Subway restaurant franchise. For the right to use the Subway name and logo, Jim paid a franchise fee of $15,000. In addition, Jim spent $70,000 renting restaurant space, purchasing equipment and supplies, and obtaining legal and accounting services. During its first year, Jim's franchise earned $36,000 in profits. He paid 12.5 percent, or $4,500, to Subway in royalty fees (8 percent) and advertising fees (4.5 percent). During Jim's second year in business, his restaurant earned $51,000, and he paid $6,375 in royalty and advertising fees.

Investigate the Franchise Opportunity

The Federal Trade Commission (FTC) regulates franchises and has established certain guidelines to assist those interested in buying a franchise. If you decide to purchase a franchise, you will have to complete an application to give to the franchisor. Once the franchisor has approved your application, you should receive two documents—the Franchise Disclosure Document and the franchise agreement.

The **Franchise Disclosure Document (FDD)** is a regulatory document describing a franchise opportunity that prospective franchisees must receive before they sign a contract. State and federal laws require that the franchisor provide these documents at least 14 days before the franchisee signs a contract. To help ensure that the franchisee is able to make a knowledgeable purchase, the FDD includes the following information:

- A brief history of the franchise, documenting who founded the company, when it began doing business, when and if it was incorporated, and when it first started franchising
- A brief summary of the officers, directors, and other executives
- The franchise fees and royalties
- An approximation of the initial costs of starting the franchise in addition to the franchise fees, including equipment, inventory, operating capital, and insurance
- The name, address, and phone number of at least 100 current franchisees; the number of franchises it anticipates selling in the next year; and the number of franchises that were sold, terminated, or transferred over the past three years
- A brief description of any major civil, criminal, or bankruptcy actions that the officers and executives have been involved in or that the franchise company is a party to
- The terms of the franchise agreement, such as initial terms of five to ten years with or without the option to renew for additional periods
- The reasons a franchisor may terminate before the contract expires, such as poor condition of the location, failure on the part of the franchisee to pay royalties in a timely manner, and excessive customer complaints
- The franchisor's responsibilities to the franchisee, such as providing a training manual, picking a suitable location, training the franchisee and/or an employee, helping plan or attending the grand opening, offering some sort of continuing assistance with advertising and managing the store, and licensing the use of certain trademarked symbols and names
- The franchisee's principal obligations under the franchise agreement and other related agreements

Before you sign a contract, you should review the franchise manual and meet the franchisor's personnel who are going to assist you. Be sure to verify everything with an attorney, a business adviser, and your accountant.

Evaluate a Franchise

Some of the things you should do when evaluating a franchise include the following:

1. **Study the disclosure document and proposed contract carefully**. Make sure all of the information listed above is included in the disclosure document. All costs and royalty fees should be provided.

2. **Interview current owners listed in the disclosure document carefully**. Ask them if the information in the disclosure document matches their experiences with the company. Be aware of *shills*, people listed in the document that are paid to give favorable reports.

3. **Investigate the franchisor's history and profitability**. Determine how long the franchisor has been in business and review its financial performance.

4. **Investigate claims about your potential earnings**. The company should provide you with the written basis for any claims made about potential earnings. Determine the projected demand for the franchised product or service in the area where you will locate. Does the demand match the potential earnings?

5. **Obtain from sellers in writing the number and percentage of owners who have done as well as they claim you will**. Sellers are required by law to provide this information.

Why is it important to research a franchise before you buy it?

6. **Listen carefully to sales presentations**. Be cautious of any sales presentation that pressures you to sign up immediately. A seller with a good offer does not use high-pressure sales tactics. Don't fall for a promise of easy money. Remember that success usually requires hard work.

7. **Shop around**. Compare franchises with other business opportunities. Different companies offer different benefits. Choose franchises that interest you, and request disclosure documents. Find out what services the franchisor offers. For example, will the franchisor help with marketing, merchandising, and site selection?

8. **Get the seller's promises in writing**. All promises made should be included in the written contract that you sign. Remember, the contract is a legally binding document.

9. **Determine what will happen if you want to cancel the franchise agreement**. Buying a franchise is a major investment, so you should determine the financial risks of canceling the franchise agreement.

10. **Remember that it is okay to ask for advice from professionals**. Lawyers, accountants, or business advisers can review the disclosure document and contract and give you their professional opinions about them. The money you spend for this service could save you from making a bad decision about investing in the franchise.

Advantages of Owning a Franchise

When thinking about owning a franchise, there are many advantages to consider.

1. **An entrepreneur is provided with an established product or service**. This attracts customers who are familiar with the franchise, allowing entrepreneurs to compete with other well-known companies.

2. **Franchisors offer management, technical, and other assistance**. This may include on-site training or classes, aid with starting the new business and handling daily operations, and tips on crisis management. Some franchisors even offer help on everything from site selection and building design to equipment purchase and recipes. Most also maintain toll-free telephone numbers that franchisees can call for advice.

3. **Equipment and supplies can be less expensive to purchase**. Large franchises may also be able to purchase in huge quantities. Some of the savings they enjoy as bulk purchasers are passed on to the franchisee.

4. **A guarantee of consistency attracts customers**. A franchise contract mandates a certain level of quality. Consumers know that they can walk into a franchise anywhere in the country and receive the same product or service. For example, a cheeseburger sold at a Wendy's in Long Beach, California, will be very similar to a cheeseburger sold at a Wendy's in Toledo, Ohio.

Disadvantages of Owning a Franchise

Although franchising sounds like a great idea, there are some disadvantages that you need to consider.

1. **Franchise fees can be costly and cut down on profits**. The initial capital needed to purchase a franchise business often is high. Also, some of the profits you earn as a franchise owner are returned to the franchisor as royalty fees.

2. **Owners of franchises have less freedom to make decisions than other entrepreneurs**. Many business decisions that entrepreneurs generally make themselves have already been made for franchisees. For example, franchisees must offer only certain products or services, charge prices set by the franchisor, and use the standard uniforms and packaging materials issued by the franchisor. Many entrepreneurs object to this control because it inhibits the freedom they sought as independent business owners.

3. **Franchisees are dependent on the performance of other franchisees in the chain**. A franchisee can benefit from the success of other franchisees. But if other franchisees run sloppy operations, customer opinions of the chain will decline. As a result, customers may stop going to a franchise, even if a specific store maintains high standards.

4. **The franchisor can terminate the franchise agreement**. If the franchisee fails to pay royalty payments or meet other conditions, the investment in the franchise can be lost. Similarly, when the franchise expires, the franchisor can choose not to renew the agreement.

 CHECKPOINT

What are some of the advantages and disadvantages of investing in a franchise?

LO 7.1-3 Enter a Family Business

The U.S. economy is dominated by family businesses. According to some estimates, as many as 90 percent of all businesses are owned by families. Many large companies, such as Walmart and Ford Motor Company, continue to be owned largely by people who are related to the company founder.

Advantages of a Family Business

Family businesses offer some unique advantages.

1. **Leadership is highly stable**. There is usually longevity in leadership in a family business, which provides stability. Leaders usually stay in the position for many years, until a life event such as retirement, an illness, or death.
2. **There is a high level of commitment and loyalty from employees**. Entrepreneurs who work for their family business enjoy the pride and sense of mission that comes with being part of a family enterprise. They are happy that their business will remain in the family for at least one more generation. Therefore, they are more committed to making the business succeed.
3. **A family business may offer more flexibility than other types of businesses**. In a family business, there may be more leeway to work a flexible or part-time schedule, or to choose your own hours.

Why do you think such a large percentage of businesses are family owned?

Disadvantages of a Family Business

Like any other type of business, family businesses have several drawbacks.

1. **Leaders and/or employees may be inadequate**. In a family business, business owners may automatically promote family members or give them a job even if they are not qualified for the position. This can result in poor business decisions. It also makes it difficult to retain good employees who are not members of the family.
2. **There is less freedom to make decisions**. Entrepreneurs who join their family business must be prepared to make compromises. Unlike individuals who start or buy their own companies, people who work for their families cannot make all of the decisions themselves. They may also be unable to set policies and procedures as they like.
3. **Family politics often enter into decision making**. The distinction between business life and private life is blurred in family businesses. As a result, family problems may end up affecting the business.

4. **There is often no exit strategy**. Business owners often do not plan how to keep the business operating after they leave the business or if no other family members want to take over the business. Then the family must decide whether to continue the business or sell it to a nonfamily member.

CHECKPOINT

What are some of the advantages and disadvantages of entering a family business?

LO 7.1-4   Starting Your Own Business

For one reason or another, joining a family business or operating a franchise may not be possible for you, or you might not be able to find a business to purchase. This means that to be an entrepreneur you will have to establish a business of your own.

Advantages of Starting Your Own Business

Starting your own business from scratch offers a number of benefits that purchasing an existing business, buying a franchise, or entering a family business doesn't.

1. **Working for yourself offers more freedom and independence**. Entrepreneurs who start their own business get to make decisions about everything from where to locate the business to how many employees to hire to what prices to charge.
2. **The business owner gets to keep all of the profits**. Unlike earning a wage as an employee, business owners can set their own salary based on profits.
3. **Starting a business offers a greater sense of personal satisfaction and achievement**. Entrepreneurs usually start businesses based on something they enjoy. Many are attracted to the challenge of creating something new and profiting from it.

Disadvantages of Starting Your Own Business

There are many risks to consider when you start your own business.

1. **There is a high level of risk and uncertainty**. The success of the business depends on the owner and his or her business talents. There is no certainty that customers will purchase the product or service being offered. If the business is not profitable, the owner can lose money.
2. **Financing for starting a new business can be difficult to obtain**. Many entrepreneurs who start their own business must obtain loans and/or use their own savings for capital.
3. **Starting a new business takes time and commitment**. Entrepreneurs who start their own business initially must work long hours to get the business up and running.

4. **Startup business owners have a high level of responsibility**. Initially, they are responsible for doing most of the work themselves. They also must make all business decisions, some of which may not have positive results.

CHECKPOINT

Why is it more difficult to start a new business than to take over an existing business or purchase a franchise?

7.1 ASSESSMENT

THINK ABOUT IT

1. When you purchase an existing business, why is it important to know the owner's reason for selling?

2. What extra expenses could you expect to pay when operating a franchise as compared to operating a nonfranchised company? Could you save money in expenses by operating a franchise? If so, how?

3. Your family owns a successful business that distributes flowers from around the world to local florists. Both of your parents work full time in the business. They have offered you a position in the company after you graduate from college. Will you accept their offer? Explain.

4. Do you think the advantages of starting a business from scratch outweigh the disadvantages? Why or why not?

MAKE ACADEMIC CONNECTIONS

5. **RESEARCH** Using local newspapers, periodicals, and the Internet, find advertisements for franchises. Make a list of the type of information that is included in the advertisements.

6. **COMMUNICATION** Locate a locally owned family business. Interview one of the family owners or employees to learn about the history of the business, the number of family members employed, and the pros and cons of working in a family business. Write a one-page report on what you learn.

Teamwork

Form teams. Brainstorm a list of reasons that business owners may decide to sell their businesses. Put a check mark next to the reasons that could negatively affect the buyer's chance for success.

The Essential Question Refer to The Essential Question on p. 186. A person can become a business owner by purchasing an existing business, purchasing a franchise, entering a family business, or starting their own new business venture.

CHOOSE A LEGAL FORM OF BUSINESS

The Essential Question Why is it important for entrepreneurs to understand each legal form of business?

LEARNING OBJECTIVES

LO 7.2-1 List advantages and disadvantages of a sole proprietorship.

LO 7.2-2 List advantages and disadvantages of a partnership.

LO 7.2-3 List advantages and disadvantages of a corporation.

KEY TERMS

- sole proprietorship
- partnership
- corporation
- share of stock
- board of directors
- dividends

FOCUS ON SMALL BUSINESS

Establish ownership.

Cheryl and Grayson are going to open a camp for dirt bike riders. It will be a place where people can come and ride their dirt bikes and camp overnight. Their long-range plan includes building cabins on the property that can be rented to the bikers.

Grayson asked Cheryl, "Do you think we should operate our business as a partnership or a corporation, since we can't be a sole proprietorship?" Cheryl thought about it a while and said, "You know, Grayson, there is a chance that someone could get hurt, and we would be responsible if the accident was on our property. Let's choose the form of ownership that would help protect us and others too!" "Good idea, Cheryl," Grayson replied. "Let's start investigating and see what we can find!"

WORK AS A TEAM Why do you think the possibility of someone getting hurt would be a big concern for Cheryl and Grayson? What other considerations do you think business owners should have when choosing a legal form for their business?

There are several forms of business ownership to consider.

©Marcel Jancovic/Shutterstock.com

LO 7.2-1 Sole Proprietorship

Once you decide to start your own business, you must decide what type of ownership the business will have. A sole proprietorship is a business that is owned exclusively by one person. Sole proprietorships enable one person to be in control of all business aspects. Sole proprietorships may be very small businesses with just a few employees, or they may be large businesses with hundreds of employees.

Advantages and Disadvantages of a Sole Proprietorship

The government exercises very little control over sole proprietorships, so such businesses can be established and run very simply. Accurate tax records and certain employment laws must be met. For example, certain types of businesses, such as restaurants, need a license to operate. But these are usually the only forms of government regulation. For this reason, the sole proprietorship is the most common form of ownership in the United States. As a sole proprietor, you get to make all of the business decisions and keep all of the profits.

There are disadvantages of sole proprietorships. It can be difficult to borrow or raise money for a sole proprietorship. You often are the only person investing money in the business. You also bear the burden of all of the risks. If a sole proprietorship fails and debts remain, the entrepreneur's personal assets may be taken to pay what is owed.

CHECKPOINT

Why are sole proprietorships a popular form of business ownership?

LO 7.2-2   Partnership

A business owned by two or more people is a **partnership**. Many entrepreneurs prefer to go into business with one or more partners so that they can share decision-making and management responsibilities as well as the risks involved with entrepreneurship.

Advantages and Disadvantages of a Partnership

Running a business as a partnership means that you will not have to come up with all of the capital alone. It also means that any losses the business incurs will be shared by all of the partners. Partners may offer different areas of expertise and knowledge, which can strengthen the business. Also, partnerships face very little government regulation.

Some entrepreneurs do not like partnerships for various reasons. They may not want to share responsibilities and profits with other people. They may also fear being held legally liable for the errors of their partners. Partnerships can lead to disagreements and end bitterly.

Partnership Agreement

When two or more entrepreneurs go into business together, they generally sign a *partnership agreement*, which sets down in writing the rights and responsibilities of all owners. A sample partnership agreement is shown on the next page. It identifies the following:

1. Name of the business or partnership
2. Names of the partners
3. Type and value of the investment each partner contributes

GENERAL PARTNERSHIP AGREEMENT FORMING
"SUNNY SIDE UP"

By agreement made this 21st day of September, 20--, we, Ana Ortiz, Keesha Gentry, and Thomas Chase, the undersigned, all of Palm Harbor, Florida, hereby join in general partnership to conduct a food service business and mutually agree to the following terms:

1.   That the partnership shall be called "Sunny Side Up" and have its principal place of business at 2013 Sand Drive, Palm Harbor, Florida, at which address books containing the full and accurate records of partnership transactions shall be kept and be accessible to any partner at any reasonable time.

2.   That the partnership shall continue in operation for an indefinite time until terminated by the death of a partner or by 90 days' notice, provided by one or more of the partners indicating his, her, or their desire to withdraw. Upon such notice, an accounting shall be conducted and a division of the partnership assets made unless a partner wishes to acquire the whole business by paying a price determined by an arbitrator whose selection shall be agreed to by all three partners. Said price shall include goodwill, and the paying of same shall entitle the payor to continue the partnership business under the same name.

3.   That each partner shall contribute to the partnership: $22,000 for initial working capital and the supplies and equipment.

4.   That in return for the capital contribution in item 3, each partner shall receive an undivided one-third interest in the partnership and its properties.

5.   That a fund of $75,000 be set up and retained from the profits of the partnership business as a reserve fund, it being agreed that this fund shall be constituted on not less than 15 percent of the monthly profits until said amount has been accumulated.

6.   That the profits of the business shall be divided equally between the partners, that the losses shall be attributed according to the subsequent agreement, and that a determination of said profits and losses shall be made and profit shares paid to each partner on a monthly basis.

7.   That the partnership account shall be kept in the First Florida Bank and that all withdrawals from same shall be by check bearing the signature of at least one of the partners.

8.   That each partner shall devote his or her full efforts to the partnership business and shall not engage in another business without the other partners' permission.

9.   That no partner shall cause to issue any commercial paper or shall enter into any agreements representing the partnership outside the normal conduct of the food service business without notice to the remaining partners and the consent of at least one other partner, and further that all managerial and person-nel decisions not covered by another section of this agreement shall be made with the assent of at least two of the partners.

   IN AGREEMENT HERETO, WE ARE

Ana Ortiz   Keesha Gentry   Thomas Chase

_Ana Ortiz_____   _Keesha Gentry_____   _Thomas Chase_____

4. Managerial responsibilities to be handled by each partner
5. Accounting methods to be used
6. Rights of each partner to review accounting documents
7. Division of profits and losses among the partners
8. Salaries to be withdrawn by the partners
9. Duration of the partnership
10. Conditions under which the partnership can be dissolved
11. Distribution of assets upon dissolution of the partnership
12. Procedure for dealing with the death of a partner

 CHECKPOINT

Name some advantages and disadvantages of a partnership.

What Went *Wrong?*

Partnership Woes

Stan and Peter met while working at a video production company. Stan was in charge of editorial and production. Peter ran the sales force. Stan decided to begin his own company and invited Peter to join him. SP Communications seemed like a perfect partnership. Peter would handle sales and administration, while Stan managed clients and directed production.

Things seemed to be going well until Peter decided he wanted to be a part of the creative process. He spent most of his time producing videos rather than looking for new business. As it turned out, Peter wasn't very good at the creative tasks he attempted. He made mistakes that reduced expected profits. In addition, he wasn't making new sales contacts, which was supposed to be his main job.

By the time Stan realized what was happening to the business, it was too late. What Stan thought were profits were the result of Peter not paying their bills. Peter left the business, and Stan was left with more than $150,000 in unpaid bills and other debts.

THINK CRITICALLY

1. How might Stan and Peter have avoided the problems that led to the end of their partnership?

2. Why is this a good example of the difficulty in maintaining partnerships between friends?

3. What types of things should be spelled out completely between partners at the beginning of the partnership?

Bonnin Studio/Shutterstock.com

Choose your partners wisely.

LO 7.2-3 Corporation

A **corporation** is a business that has the legal rights of a person but is independent of its owners. A **share of stock** is a unit of ownership in a corporation. There may be many owners, who are called *shareholders* or *stockholders*. The corporation, not the owners, pays taxes, enters into contracts, and is held liable for negligence.

An *open corporation* is one that offers its shares of stock for public sale. When going public through an initial public offering (IPO), the company must advertise the sale and file a registration statement with the Securities and Exchange Commission (SEC) with extensive details about the corporation and the proposed issue of stock. A *prospectus* is a condensed version of the registration statement that is shared with prospective buyers of newly offered stocks. A *close corporation* is one that does not offer its shares of stock for public sale. The business has only a few shareholders who may help run the business, similar to a partnership. Family-owned businesses are often close corporations.

Jim Munroe set up his company, Munroe Office Supply, as a corporation. He created 100 shares of stock worth $1,000 each. Jim then issued 15 shares to each of three outside investors, meaning they paid $45,000 total to be shareholders in his company. Jim kept the remaining 55 shares himself. This means that Jim owns 55 percent of his company, while outside investors own a total of 45 percent of the company. The individual or group that owns the most shares maintains control of the company.

Every corporation has a **board of directors**, which is a group of people who meet several times a year to make important decisions affecting the company. The board of directors is responsible for electing the corporation's officers, determining their salaries, and setting the corporation's rules for conducting business. The board of directors also decides how much the corporation should pay in dividends. **Dividends** are distributions of corporate profits to the shareholders. The company's officers, not the board of directors, are responsible for the day-to-day management of the corporation.

What role does the board of directors play in a corporation?

Advantages of a Corporation

Liability is the main reason entrepreneurs set up corporations. Liability is the amount owed to others. The shareholders' liability is limited to the amount of money each shareholder invested in the company when he or she purchased stock. The personal assets of shareholders may not be taken to pay the debts of the corporation.

If Munroe Office Supply goes bankrupt, leaving $150,000 in debt, each shareholder will lose only the amount he or she invested in the corporation. So the three outside people who invested $45,000 will lose their investment.

Jim will also lose his investment of $55,000. If Jim had set up his business as a sole proprietorship, he would have been liable for the $150,000 solely. If the business had been set up as a partnership among Jim and his friends, all four partners would have been liable for the $150,000.

Another advantage of corporations is that money can be raised by selling stock. Also, lending institutions are more willing to lend money to corporations than to sole proprietorships or partnerships. Finally, because shareholders do not directly affect the management of a corporation, the main shareholder of the company can change through the buying and selling of stock without disrupting the day-to-day business operations.

Disadvantages of a Corporation

Setting up a corporation is more complicated than setting up a sole proprietorship or a partnership. To incorporate, you will need the assistance of a lawyer, who will help you file *articles of incorporation* with the state official responsible for *chartering*, or registering, corporations. Because of this, establishing a corporation can be costly. Articles of incorporation must fully detail the purpose of the business. If the articles are not well written, the corporation's activities can be limited.

Corporations are subject to much more government regulation than are sole proprietorships or partnerships. Another drawback of incorporation is that income is taxed twice. A corporation pays taxes on its income, and shareholders pay taxes on the dividends they receive from the corporation. This means that the corporation's profits are taxed as corporate income and again as individual income. This is known as *double taxation*.

S Corporation

A small corporation can elect to be treated as an S corporation. An *S corporation* is a corporation organized under Subchapter S of the Internal Revenue Code. Unlike regular corporations, an S corporation is not taxed as a business; only the individual shareholders are taxed on the profits they earn. However, S corporations must follow the same formalities and recordkeeping procedures as regular corporations. They are also managed by a board of directors and officers like regular corporations.

Many companies establish themselves as S corporations because they lose money in their early years. The owners can use any losses suffered from the S corporation to offset other sources of personal income and receive a tax break.

Chanda Patel runs Forever Yours, a wedding consultant business. Like many new businesses, Forever Yours lost money in its first year when its expenses exceeded its revenues by $12,000. However, since Chanda set up her company as an S corporation, she was able to reduce her taxable income from other sources by $12,000.

 BE YOUR OWN BOSS

You have decided that you are going to start a new business giving horseback riding lessons. You need to decide which legal form you will use for your business. Choose a sole proprietorship, partnership, or corporation. Write a paragraph explaining why you chose the legal form you did and the advantages and disadvantages of your choice.

Limited Liability Company

A *limited liability company* (LLC) is a legal form of business that provides the benefits of partnership taxation and limited liability features of a corporation for all of the owners of the business. Owners of LLCs are known as members—not shareholders. Unlike shareholders, members can participate in the management of the business. LLCs are not taxed as a separate business entity. Instead, all profits and losses are "passed through" the business to each member of the LLC. LLC members report profits and losses on their personal federal tax returns, just like the owners of a partnership would. Disadvantages are that some state laws restrict the type of business that can be set up as an LLC and limit the life of an LLC.

 CHECKPOINT

What is the main benefit of setting up your business as a corporation?

7.2 ASSESSMENT

THINK ABOUT IT

1. Which do you think is more risky: a sole proprietorship or a partnership? Why?

2. What would be the advantages and disadvantages of forming a partnership with a friend?

3. Why do you think the government regulates corporations more closely than it does sole proprietorships or partnerships?

MAKE ACADEMIC CONNECTIONS

4. **MANAGEMENT** You and a friend plan to form a partnership and open a business. Prepare a partnership agreement for your business.

5. **MATH** Caren McHugh formed a corporation. To raise money, she created 500 shares of stock, each worth $75. Caren held 260 of the shares for herself and sold the rest in equal amounts to six investors. How many shares does each investor own? If the business fails and leaves $65,000 in debt, for how much would each investor be liable?

Teamwork

Working with teammates, create a chart listing all the forms of business ownership and the advantages and disadvantages of each one.

The Essential Question Refer to The Essential Question on p. 196. Entrepreneurs must weigh the pros and cons of each form of business ownership in order to select the type that will best meet their needs.

LEGAL ISSUES AND BUSINESS OWNERSHIP

The Essential Question Why should entrepreneurs understand the regulations, laws, and legal issues that may affect their business?

LEARNING OBJECTIVES

LO 7.3-1 Recognize how laws promote competition.

LO 7.3-2 Describe how entrepreneurs protect intellectual property.

LO 7.3-3 Identify regulations that protect the public and explain their impact on businesses.

LO 7.3-4 Describe some of the minor legal issues affecting entrepreneurs.

KEY TERMS

- patent
- copyright
- trademark
- contract

Why are there regulations?

James and Katie are starting an apparel company specializing in sportswear. They are trying to decide what they want their company logo to look like. "Let's put a 'swoosh' in our logo like the one Nike uses," James suggested. "James, we can't use that logo. It's a Nike trademark," Katie responded. "See the ™ symbol next to it? That means it's protected by a trademark and no one else can use it."

"Well, I guess we'd better keep thinking about what we want our trademark to be," answered James. "That's a good idea," Katie said. "And while we're at it, we'd better look into all of the rules and regulations that we need to follow. We don't want to start off on the wrong foot by unintentionally doing something illegal."

FOCUS ON SMALL BUSINESS

Petar Djordjevic/Shutterstock.com

Business owners must follow certain laws and regulations.

WORK AS A TEAM Did you realize that businesses have to follow rules and regulations? Do you think it's fair for government to regulate business?

LO 7.3-1 Regulations That Promote Competition

As an entrepreneur, you will learn that there are laws affecting almost every aspect of a business. Even the competition that businesses face is regulated by the government. To make sure that competition is fair, federal, state, and local governments have enacted various laws to help protect businesses.

Antitrust Legislation

Beginning in 1890, laws were created that made monopolies in certain industries illegal. A monopoly is also called a trust, so these laws were called antitrust laws. Antitrust laws also ban other types of business activities that do not promote competition. It is important to become familiar with these laws to determine how they affect your business.

SHERMAN ACT   This law makes it illegal for competitors to get together and set prices on the products or services they sell. This means that you and your competitors cannot jointly decide to keep prices at a certain level. Discussing prices with competitors is illegal. For example, if the owner of one business decides to raise his prices, he cannot ask the owner of a competing business to raise her prices by the same amount.

CLAYTON ACT   This law states that it is illegal for a business to require a customer to buy exclusively from it or to purchase one good in order to be able to purchase another good. A distributor of computers, for example, cannot force customers to buy software when they purchase a computer.

The Clayton Act also prevents anticompetitive mergers. A *merger* occurs when a company buys a competing firm. While most mergers allow the companies to create better quality goods at less expensive prices, some mergers limit competition and make price fixing easier.

ROBINSON–PATMAN ACT   This law protects small businesses from unfair pricing practices. It makes it illegal to discriminate by charging different prices to customers. A manufacturer, for example, may not sell its products at different prices to similar customers in similar situations when the effect of such sales will reduce competition. Differences in price may only be justified based on differences in quantities purchased (volume discounts), special distribution or legal requirements in different locations, or other economically sound reasons. If your business sells to other businesses, you must offer the same terms to all of those businesses. The law does not apply to retail stores where certain groups may be targeted by special promotions, such as giving discounts to senior citizens.

How does antitrust legislation affect pricing?

Lightpoet/Shutterstock.com

WHEELER–LEA ACT   This law bans unfair or deceptive actions or practices by businesses that may cause an unfair competitive advantage. False advertising is an example. This act also requires businesses to warn consumers about possible negative features of their products. Drug companies, for example, must let people know of any side effects they may experience from using a medication.

Government Agencies That Protect Competition

The Antitrust Division of the Justice Department and the Federal Trade Commission are two government agencies that work to make sure competition among businesses remains fair. Other agencies, such as the Federal Aviation Administration and the Food and Drug Administration, oversee business practices in particular industries.

JUSTICE DEPARTMENT   The Justice Department's Antitrust Division takes legal action against any business it believes has tried to monopolize an industry. It also prosecutes businesses that violate antitrust laws, which can lead to large fines and jail sentences.

FEDERAL TRADE COMMISSION   The Federal Trade Commission (FTC) deals with issues that touch the economic life of every American. The FTC administers most of the laws dealing with fair competition and pursues vigorous and effective law enforcement. Some of the activities the FTC monitors include false or misleading advertising, price setting by competitors, price discrimination, and misrepresentation of the quality, composition, or place of origin of a product. It is the only federal agency with both consumer protection and competition jurisdiction in broad sectors of the economy. In addition, the FTC does the following:

- Advances consumers' interests by sharing its expertise with federal and state legislatures and U.S. and international government agencies
- Develops policy and research tools through hearings, workshops, and conferences
- Creates practical and plain-language educational programs for consumers and businesses in a global marketplace with constantly changing technologies

CHECKPOINT

How do laws promote competition?

LO 7.3-2   Intellectual Property

Intellectual property is the original, creative work of an artist or inventor and may include such things as songs, novels, artistic designs, and inventions. Such works may be registered for special government protections—including patents, trademarks, trade names, and copyrights—that provide business owners with the exclusive use of the intellectual property in the United States and many foreign countries. Registration gives businesses or individuals the exclusive right to profit from what they have created. No one else can use their creations to make money. If you violate another person's patent, copyright, or trademark, you could be sued.

Patents

A **patent** is the grant of a property right to an inventor to exclude others from making, using, or selling his or her invention. The intent of a patent is to give the developer of a new product time to recover the development costs without having to worry about competition. Patents are issued by the U.S. Patent and Trademark Office and last for 20 years. During this period, no individual or business can copy or use the patented invention without the patent holder's permission. A *provisional patent application* allows an inventor one year to investigate the feasibility, marketability, and potential license interest of an invention before deciding to file a formal patent application. This allows the inventor to use the term *patent pending*, giving him or her a head start on other inventors who may file for the same invention.

Copyrights

A **copyright** is a form of intellectual property law that protects original works of authorship, including literary, dramatic, musical, and artistic works. Copyright law does not protect facts, ideas, systems, or methods of operation. A copyright lasts for the life of the author plus 70 years. After that time, individual works enter the public domain and can be reproduced by anyone without permission. For as long as the copyright is in effect, the copyright owner has the sole right to display, share, or perform the material, or license the use of the material for a royalty payment.

FAMOUS ENTREPRENEUR

JAMES W. BAKER In 1902, James W. Baker, a 28-year-old business teacher at Knoxville Business College, decided to write his own textbook based on his innovative approach to teaching bookkeeping. In just one year, *20th Century Bookkeeping and Office Practice* became an overwhelming success, which prompted Baker to form South-Western Educational Publishing. Soon South-Western became the leading publisher of business education textbooks for high school and college students. The company's success was attributed to Baker's customer service philosophy. He focused on helping teachers by offering them a strong curriculum, innovative instructional ideas, and real-world examples of business

James Baker

What led to James W. Baker's success as an entrepreneur?

concepts—strategies still used by South-Western (which is now part of Cengage Learning).

Baker's book, which was reintroduced in 1972 as *Century 21 Accounting Multicolumn Journal*, is the leading accounting high school textbook still today. The influence of this young entrepreneur has lasted for over 100 years, enriching the lives of business educators and students by exemplifying sound business practices, quality service, and a commitment to education.

THINK CRITICALLY

How did James W. Baker's entrepreneurial ideas help build a company that could last for over 100 years?

Trademarks

A trademark is a name, symbol, or special mark used to identify a business or brand of product. Products that are trademarked are identified by the ™ or ® symbol. Examples include Band-Aid® and Kleenex®. You cannot invent a new bandage and use the term Band-Aid in the product name. Nor can you use the "swoosh" mark that is trademarked by Nike in any product or business promotion you conduct.

 **CHECKPOINT**

How can entrepreneurs protect intellectual property rights?

LO 7.3-3   Laws That Protect Consumers

The government also has regulations that protect consumers. They include licenses, zoning regulations, and consumer protection laws.

Licenses

State and local governments require some businesses to have licenses. Beauty salons, restaurants, and health and fitness centers are just some of the companies that must carry licenses. If you own a business that requires a license, you and your employees may need to complete training requirements. You may also need to have regular inspections by state and local authorities. Failure to meet certain standards could mean the loss of your license and the closing of your business.

Zoning Laws

Local governments often establish zoning regulations that control what types of buildings can be built in specific areas. In many communities, certain areas are zoned for residential use only. This means that business buildings may not be built in those areas. Other areas may be zoned as commercial for retail businesses, as industrial, as agricultural, as multipurpose, and so on. Before choosing a location for your business, make sure that the area selected allows your type of business to operate there. Zoning laws help keep neighborhoods safe for their residents.

Consumer Protection Laws

Since the 1930s, Congress has passed numerous laws to protect consumers from harmful products and unfair business practices. These laws are enforced by a variety of government agencies. Following are just a few of the major laws that have been passed.

THE FEDERAL FOOD, DRUG, AND COSMETIC ACT OF 1938   This law bans the sale of impure, improperly labeled, falsely guaranteed, and unhealthful foods, drugs, and cosmetics. The Food and Drug Administration (FDA) enforces this law. The FDA has the power to force producers to stop manufacturing products that are unsafe.

How does the Consumer Product Safety Act impact businesses?

THE TRUTH-IN-LENDING ACT OF 1968   This law requires lenders to inform consumers about all costs of credit before an agreement is signed. Lenders must disclose the finance charge, which is the total dollar amount of all costs of credit, including interest, service charges, and other fees. Lenders must also disclose the annual percentage rate (APR). The APR is the finance charge calculated as a percentage of the amount borrowed. These numbers help consumers evaluate alternatives and determine the best option.

THE CONSUMER PRODUCT SAFETY ACT OF 1972   This law sets safety standards for products other than food and drugs. The act established the Consumer Product Safety Commission (CPSC). When the CPSC determines that a product is unsafe, it can force businesses to recall the product and stop selling it.

THE FAIR CREDIT BILLING ACT OF 1974   This law helps consumers correct credit card billing errors. Consumers who feel they have been charged incorrectly must write to the credit card issuer within 60 days of receipt of their bill and explain why they think the charge is wrong. The creditor must reply within 30 days and either correct the error or show why the amount is correct within 90 days. While the disputed charge is being investigated, it cannot accrue interest.

This law also gives the consumer a method for resolving problems relating to product quality. The first step in dealing with a product of inferior quality purchased with a credit card is to try to resolve the problem with the merchant. If it cannot be resolved, the consumer can withhold payment to the credit card company until the matter is settled.

 CHECKPOINT

What laws protect the public?

LO 7.3-4   Legal Issues Affecting Business

It is helpful to learn some basics about legal issues affecting businesses so that you can handle minor legal issues yourself. In other instances, you may want to obtain the services of a lawyer.

Contracts

A **contract** is a legally binding agreement between two or more persons or parties. As an entrepreneur, you will enter into contracts as you start and operate your business. For a contract to be considered legally binding, certain elements must be included.

- *Offer and acceptance* occurs when one party offers to do something and the other party accepts or agrees. If the second party makes a counteroffer, however, there is no agreement.

- *Consideration* is what is exchanged for the promise. For example, a payment is consideration and causes the contract to be binding.
- *Capacity* means the parties are legally able to enter into a binding agreement. Minors, intoxicated persons, and those with a mental deficiency cannot enter into a binding contract.
- *Legality* means that a contract cannot have anything in it that is illegal or that would result in illegal activities.
- *Genuine assent* means that the agreement is not based on deceit on the part of either party, certain mistakes of fact, or the use of unfair pressure exerted to obtain the offer or acceptance.

Some contracts must be in writing to be fully enforceable in court. In many cases, however, an oral contract is enforceable.

Torts Relating to Business Enterprises

A *tort* is a wrong against people or organizations for which the law grants a remedy. If someone commits a tort, the person injured as a result can sue and obtain compensation for damages. Torts may occur when manufacturers make defective products that injure users. Certain elements are common to most torts and must be proved in a court of law to establish liability.

- *Duty*—A legal obligation to do or not to do something
- *Breach*—A violation of the duty
- *Injury*—A harm that is recognized by the law
- *Causation*—Proof that the breach caused the injury

Agency Relationships

An *agency* is a relationship that allows one party to act in a way that legally binds another party. The *principal* is the person who authorizes another person, the *agent*, to enter into legal relationships on the principal's behalf. A common form of agency is when a salesperson for a business makes a contract with a customer on behalf of the business's owner.

Licenses

Depending on the business, a number of local, state, and federal permits and licenses will be required. For example, if the business prepares or sells food, it will likely need a health department permit from the local government. Every business also must have a legal name that is registered through the state. A legal name is needed to get a nine-digit Employer Identification Number (EIN) from the Internal Revenue Service (IRS). This number is used for purposes of identification and reporting employment taxes.

Hire a Lawyer

At some point, you may need to hire a lawyer to assist you with legal issues affecting your business, such as those listed in the table that follows. Your chamber of commerce may have a list of lawyers who specialize in small businesses.

HOW LAWYERS CAN HELP YOU		
Assist you in choosing a legal structure for your business	Create documents such as lease and purchase agreements and contracts	Develop partnership agreements
Inform you of regulations and licenses	Give advice on insurance coverage	Advise you on taxes
Prepare and file patent applications	Help you plan for your future (a will, retirement plans)	Defend you in a lawsuit or file one on your behalf

 CHECKPOINT

Name legal issues of which entrepreneurs should be aware.

 7.3 ASSESSMENT

THINK ABOUT IT

1. Think of three examples of how a business might misrepresent a product it sells. Explain each example.

2. Besides Band-Aid, Kleenex, and Nike, name three other products that are trademarked.

3. What is the purpose of zoning laws?

4. Explain the nature of agency relationships.

MAKE ACADEMIC CONNECTIONS

5. **RESEARCH** Conduct online research to find information on the process for applying for a patent. Also, find out how much a patent costs, how many patents have been issued to date, and what the criteria are for obtaining a patent. Prepare a short report on your findings.

6. **COMMUNICATION** Research a company that has violated one or more of the laws or regulations discussed in this lesson. Prepare a report describing the legal issues facing the business and the impact of the violation on both the business and the individual or group who experienced the violation.

Teamwork

Working in teams, create several business scenarios that involve violation of anti-trust laws. Role-play scenarios for the rest of the class and let them guess which antitrust law is being violated.

The Essential Question Refer to The Essential Question on p. 203. Entrepreneurs must understand the elements of antitrust legislation, laws, and legal issues because they affect almost every aspect of a business, specifically when dealing with consumers.

Sharpen Your 21st Century Entrepreneurial Skills

Using the Telephone for Business

Businesses rely on telephones for conducting business. Many changes have occurred in phone technology over the years. You will have to decide which of these technologies is best for your business.

1. Landline phones are still used by many businesses because of their reliability and voice quality. Some businesses might be in a location that does not have good cell reception or broadband access. Others just like the security of a landline.

2. Cell phones are a necessity for many small businesses and their employees. A cell phone can be used for basic functions, such as making and receiving calls and texting, but it does not have an operating system like a smartphone. Cell phones allow business owners to stay in touch with customers, suppliers, and colleagues from wherever they are. One issue that a business owner must address is whether to provide employees with a business cell phone.

3. Smartphones are also widely used by small businesses. They combine the capabilities of a standard cell phone and add many features of a computer, including mobile apps, GPS, email, and Internet access. They are much smaller and easier to carry around than a laptop. A business owner can use a smartphone to place and receive orders, make payments to creditors, and even deposit checks into bank accounts, all online.

4. Phone systems are available in a variety of configurations. Many small business phone systems today run on Internet Protocol (IP) networks, which connect employees, devices, and information resources. When choosing a small business phone system, you should understand what your users need. Some of the features to consider are videoconferencing, the ability to use the computer as a phone, an automated attendant, paging and intercom functions, integration with a customer relationship management (CRM) system, and unified messaging that delivers notifications by email, texts, or phone.

TRY IT OUT

You are opening a candy store in a local mall. You plan to have two employees working in the store and two buyers who work with vendors that supply the candy. Make a list of the ways that you and your employees will use the telephone in your business. Decide which type of telephone system you will choose. Then write guidelines that you will share with your employees regarding telephone usage.

SUMMARY

7.1 Decide to Purchase, Join, or Start a Business

1. An existing business has an established customer base and relationships with suppliers. The seller may train you, and prior records can make financial planning easier.

2. When evaluating a franchise opportunity, study the disclosure document, interview current owners, investigate the franchisor's history, investigate potential earnings claims, compare opportunities, get promises in writing, learn the risks of canceling the franchise, and seek advice from professionals.

3. Family businesses have stable leadership and high levels of employee commitment and loyalty. However, some family members may be unqualified, and family politics can negatively affect the business.

4. Entrepreneurs who start new businesses have more freedom and independence. However, there is increased risk because there is no established demand for the product or service and financing to start the business can be difficult to obtain.

7.2 Choose a Legal Form of Business

5. A sole proprietorship is the simplest and least expensive form of business ownership, but the owner may have trouble raising money for the business. Personal assets are at risk if the business fails.

6. A partnership is easy to start and faces little government regulation. However, a partner can be held legally liable for the actions of the other partner(s).

7. A corporation is more difficult to start, but it is easier to raise capital by issuing shares of stock. Owners' personal assets are not at risk.

7.3 Legal Issues and Business Ownership

8. Antitrust laws were developed to promote fair competition in business. The Antitrust Division of the U.S. Justice Department and the Federal Trade Commission (FTC) are government agencies that work to ensure fair competition.

9. Entrepreneurs can protect intellectual property by registering for patents, copyrights, and trademarks.

10. Laws that protect consumers include licensing, zoning regulations, and consumer protection laws.

11. Legal issues affecting a business include contracts, torts, and agencies.

WHAT DO YOU **KNOW NOW?**

Read *Ideas in Action* **on page 185 again. Then answer the questions a second time. Have your responses changed? If so, how have they changed?**

KEY TERMS REVIEW

Match each statement with the term that best defines it. Some terms may not be used.

1. A group of people who make decisions affecting a company
2. Paid to the franchise company to support television, magazine, or other advertising of the franchise as a whole
3. The grant of a property right to an inventor to exclude others from making, using, or selling his or her invention
4. A business that has the legal rights of a person but is independent of its owners
5. Distributions of corporate profits to shareholders
6. A legal agreement that gives an individual the right to market a company's products or services in a particular area
7. A regulatory document describing a franchise opportunity that prospective franchisees must receive
8. A unit of ownership in a corporation
9. Weekly or monthly payments made by the local owner to the franchise company
10. A form of intellectual property law that protects original works of authorship, including literary, dramatic, musical, and artistic works
11. A business that is owned exclusively by one person
12. A business owned by two or more people
13. A name, symbol, or special mark used to identify a business or brand of product
14. The costs associated with beginning a business
15. A legally binding agreement between two or more persons

a. advertising fees
b. board of directors
c. contract
d. copyright
e. corporation
f. dividends
g. franchise
h. Franchise Disclosure Document
i. initial franchise fee
j. partnership
k. patent
l. royalty fees
m. share of stock
n. sole proprietorship
o. startup costs
p. trademark

REVIEW YOUR KNOWLEDGE

16. Which of the following is *not* an advantage of buying an existing business?
    a. existing customer base
    b. seller can provide training
    c. seller may work out financing agreement
    d. capital is required
17. **True or False**   A franchise is an inexpensive way to get into business quickly.
18. The legal form of business that is the simplest to establish is the
    a. sole proprietorship
    b. partnership
    c. S corporation
    d. limited liability company
19. **True or False**   The board of directors of a corporation is responsible for the day-to-day management of the corporation.
20. You and several other business owners agree to raise the price of the paint you sell by $1.50 per gallon. You are in violation of the
    a. Sherman Act
    b. Clayton Act
    c. Robinson–Patman Act
    d. Wheeler–Lea Act
21. **True or False**   A patent grants property rights to an inventor for 70 years.

22. You want to advertise a special price on a product that you do not have in stock just to get customer traffic into your store. If you do so, you will be in violation of the
    a. Sherman Act
    b. Clayton Act
    c. Robinson–Patman Act
    d. Wheeler–Lea Act
23. For a contract to be legally binding, it must have which of the following elements when it is created?
    a. offer and acceptance, cooperation, capacity, legality
    b. offer and acceptance, consideration, capacity, legality
    c. genuine assent, consideration, cooperation, and legality
    d. amendment, consideration, capacity, and legality

APPLY WHAT YOU LEARNED

24. You are meeting with the owner of an ice-cream shop you would like to purchase. What specific questions are you going to ask her? What documents do you want to see? How will you evaluate whether or not to purchase this existing business? (LO 7.1-1)
25. You decide to start a business selling a new video game that you have developed. You plan to sell the game over the Internet. What intellectual property right issues should you consider? (LO 7.3-2)
26. You want to purchase a cleaning service franchise. The initial franchise fee is $19,500 and startup costs are $15,200. Advertising fees are $1,500. The royalty fee is 8 percent. If your estimated sales for the first year of operation are $56,500, how much is your profit after paying all costs and the royalty fee? (LO 7.1-2)

MAKE ACADEMIC CONNECTIONS

27. **MATH** Marta Vasquez is one of three partners in a car dealership. The division of profits and losses as specified in the partnership agreement is 60 percent for Marta, 25 percent for the second partner, and 15 percent for the third partner. The dealership recently lost a lawsuit and must pay damages of $1,200,000. What is Marta's liability? What is the liability of each of the other two partners? (LO 7.2-2)
28. **RESEARCH** Use the Internet, newspaper, magazines, and other materials to research business opportunities. Find two businesses for sale that interest you. Write a brief summary that describes each business. Which business do you think would be the better investment? Why? (LO 7.1-1)
29. **BUSINESS LAW** Conduct online research and find out the Federal Trade Commission (FTC) requirements and your state's requirements for disclosure documents prior to the purchase of a franchise. Write a paragraph outlining the requirements. (LO 7.1-2)
30. **GEOGRAPHY** China is a major source of intellectual property theft. Many counterfeit products are produced in China. Research this problem and learn how U.S. businesses can better protect themselves. Prepare a short presentation on your findings. (LO 7.3-2)

What Would YOU DO?

You receive a new iPod and $50 iTunes gift card for your birthday. You sign onto iTunes and download many of your favorite songs, quickly spending $50. One of your friends tells you about some websites where you can download all the music you want for free. You decide to talk to your parents about these sites. They explain that iTunes is a legal site and that the music artists receive royalties when you download from its site. The websites your friend told you about do not pay the artists the royalties due to them. When you tell your friend this, he still sees no harm in getting the music for free because he believes the artists have already made enough money. Will you continue to pay and use only iTunes or will you use the free websites? Why? Recording artists are entrepreneurs. If you were an entrepreneur, how would you feel if you did not get the money that was owed to you?

BUILD YOUR BUSINESS PLAN PROJECT

This activity will help you continue with the development of a business plan for your business idea.

1. Contact your state and local governments and obtain information about licensing and zoning regulations. How will these regulations affect your business?

2. To expand your business, you have decided to purchase similar businesses in your area. List the businesses in your area that compete with you. Write the reasons you would or would not consider buying each business.

3. Investigate a franchise opportunity available in your business field. Gather information about it, such as franchise fees, royalties, projected earnings, and operating costs.

4. You have a friend who is interested in being your business partner. Write the partnership agreement for the two of you.

5. Make a list of all the advantages and disadvantages of organizing your business as a corporation. Determine how much stock to sell and the value of each share.

6. How will you become an entrepreneur? Will you buy an existing business, purchase a franchise, enter a family business, or start your business from scratch? Determine which form of business organization you will use—sole proprietorship, partnership, corporation, S corporation, or limited liability company. Write the Ownership and Legal Structure section of your business plan as described in Chapter 3.

PLANNING A CAREER IN FRANCHISING

"This weekend when I visited a new restaurant to order a sub sandwich, my former babysitter was behind the counter. She had bought the restaurant from a franchisor. The franchisor taught her how to run the restaurant. It provided the training and support materials she needed. She said that, although the hours were long, the work was gratifying and profitable."

When purchasing a franchise, many people often use the services of a franchise consultant. Based on their client's strongest abilities, interests, price range, and business objectives, franchise consultants make recommendations to their client after evaluating the performance track records and products and services of various franchisors.

Some franchise consultants work on a fee-only basis whereby they receive a fee up front for their services. Others earn a commission from the franchisor.

Employment Outlook
- A faster-than-average rate of employment growth is expected.
- Career changes, as a result of an evolving business environment and downsizing, will increase the need for business counselors.

Job Titles
- Franchise Business Coach
- New Business Sales Leader
- Franchise Business Consultant
- Franchise Performance Coach

Needed Education/Skills
- A bachelor's degree in business is recommended.
- Prior management experience in training or sales is helpful.
- Strong interpersonal and analytical skills are needed.
- A desire to help others and an ability to gain trust is important.

What's it like to work in Franchising? Jasmine, a franchise consultant, is on the phone with a prospective new client. The client is looking to purchase a franchise but needs some guidance. By collecting data through informational interviews, structured assessments, and coaching sessions, Jasmine can help the client match her business objectives to an appropriate franchise.

Jasmine's next two phone calls are to two different windshield repair franchisors. Jasmine has a client whose testing results revealed that a windshield repair franchise is a good match for his interests and business objectives. Jasmine is setting up a meeting between the franchisors and her client. After her client talks with both franchisors, Jasmine will coach him through the decision-making process.

On the way home from work, Jasmine stops by a tutoring franchise that she helped one of her clients establish. She has a brief chat with the franchise owner to see if there are any business issues she can help resolve. By staying in touch with clients, Jasmine can help ensure the ongoing success of their franchise.

What about you? Would you like to help clients match their interests, goals, and resources with an appropriate franchising opportunity? What would you like or dislike about this career?

International Business Plan

Understanding different economic systems is an important skill for an entrepreneur. Entrepreneurs must make business decisions based on economic conditions. This event will help you apply entrepreneurship knowledge and skills while trying to start and operate a business on an international scale.

The DECA International Business Plan event centers around the creation of a new business venture in an international setting. Participants in this event may create any type of product or service or add a new product or service to an existing business. You must prepare a written proposal (limited to 30 pages) for your new business venture and give an oral presentation to a panel of judges. The presentation is limited to ten minutes, and the judges will have five minutes after the presentation to ask questions.

Performance Indicators
- Provide a clear and organized description of the business or product
- Demonstrate thorough analysis of the international business situation
- Explain the planned operations and financing of the proposed business or product
- Display a professional appearance, poise, and confidence
- Use effective presentation techniques and visual aids

Go to the DECA website for more detailed information.

GIVE IT A TRY
To help you develop your business plan for your international business, follow the steps below:
1. Organize into groups of two or three students. Select a new business or a new product or service for an existing business.
2. Write a one-page executive summary, or description, of your product or service.
3. Select the country in which you will establish your new business. Research the economy of that country. Be sure to research the country's economic system, governmental structure, labor and trade laws, geographic and demographic information, customs, and competition.
4. Decide what type of ownership your new business will have and give your rationale for this type of ownership.
5. Using presentation software, create a presentation to give to your classmates. Include all of the information that you researched.

www.deca.org

mangostock/Shutterstock.com

Locate and Set Up Your Business

8.1 CHOOSE A LOCATION

8.2 OBTAIN SPACE AND DESIGN THE PHYSICAL LAYOUT

8.3 PURCHASE EQUIPMENT, SUPPLIES, AND INVENTORY

Creativity Knows No Boundaries

Photo by Khoa Phan

Khoa Phan, video animator

While some entrepreneurs locate their businesses in large office buildings or warehouses, others need only a small space (maybe only a kitchen) to unleash their creativity. Video creator and entrepreneur Khoa Phan creates short videos for Vine, a Twitter-owned video-sharing app for social networking. Phan links together short, separate videos in a continuous loop for six- or seven-second video spots that can be viewed on Vine or Twitter, or embedded into a web page. His videos have become popular marketing tools. Phan has signed lucrative video-production deals with clients such as Snapple, MTV, Livestrong, and Peanuts Worldwide.

Phan was 23 when he began putting his videos on Vine, the day after Twitter bought the app. He's been going strong ever since. Mashable, a leading source for news, information, and resources for the "connected generation," lists Phan as one of the top ten people to follow on Vine.

His style—which is a mix of fun and salesmanship in fluid-construction-paper-stop-motion videos—has made him recognizable and marketable. His first post was a five-shot video of a Keurig machine brewing a cup of coffee. However, it was his second video that really got him noticed. In this video, turquoise construction-paper bubbles float across a dark wooden table. As each bubble is punctured by a finger, the words, "Have a good day" appear. This sentiment, along with the construction paper, has become his trademark.

"It just happened to become my style on Vine. I didn't really intend on using construction paper; it just kind of happened," Phan said. "I had some construction paper at home and figured, 'Well, use what you have.' I can also very easily manipulate construction paper and reuse it for future vines."

Phan's work has been covered by CNN and Bloomberg TV. He was a short-list finalist at the Tribeca Film Festival and was named Mashable's "Most Creative Stop-Motion Animator." Today Phan continues to work as a brand content creator and animator.

WHAT DO YOU KNOW?

1. Why is Khoa Phan's business well suited to operate out of his home?

2. Why do you think Phan's videos are so popular among clients?

3. What lessons can you learn from Phan's business model?

8.1 CHOOSE A LOCATION

The Essential Question How do entrepreneurs decide where to locate their business?

LEARNING OBJECTIVES

LO 8.1-1 Identify options for locating a retail business.

LO 8.1-2 Discuss factors to consider when choosing a location for a nonretail business.

LO 8.1-3 Identify the advantages and disadvantages of having a business online.

LO 8.1-4 Describe steps to take in selecting a site.

KEY TERMS

- industrial park
- enterprise zones
- e-commerce
- trade area

FOCUS ON SMALL BUSINESS

Good locations come at a price.

Gail worked very hard to get just the right product mix for her company, Fitness for You, which offers creative branding strategies and products to the fitness industry. Business was good, but profits were still not at the level she wanted. She examined her costs and realized that a large portion of her monthly expenses was for rental of her office space. She was located in an upscale office complex in Palm Beach, Florida. When she started looking at her customer base, she realized that most of her customer interaction was by phone or email and at trade shows and business meetings held away from her office. Many of her customers were located in other states.

WORK AS A TEAM How important do you think Gail's location is to the success of her business? What would you advise her to do about her location?

Carefully consider your location needs.

Rommel Canlas/Shutterstock.com

LO 8.1-1 Locating a Retail Business

Your location plan will help ensure that your product is available in the right location to reach your target customer. If you want to open a retail business, choosing the location for it will be one of the most important decisions that you will make as an entrepreneur. The wrong location could spell disaster, but the right location will help your business succeed from the start. The right location for your business depends on the kind of business you plan to operate and the type of customer you want to reach.

Another factor to consider is whether you will sell your products or services through inside sales or outside sales. If you are selling a product through inside sales, customers will come to your place of business to purchase the product. If you are using outside sales to sell your product, you will travel to the customer's residence or place of business. The way you offer your product or service will affect the location of your business.

Downtown Areas

In some communities, the downtown area represents an easily accessible, central location. Workers from downtown offices and professional businesses may shop at your business on their breaks or on their way to and from work. Rents vary widely from city to city, so you will want to do some research if you are thinking of using a downtown location.

Issues faced in many downtown areas include a higher crime rate, traffic jams, lack of free or convenient parking, and a lack of customers in the evening. Thus, some downtown areas have lost business to neighborhood, community, and regional shopping centers. But many cities are revitalizing their downtown shopping districts and are offering incentives to attract businesses back into the area.

Neighborhood Shopping Centers

Neighborhood shopping centers are small shopping centers that serve a certain neighborhood. They are often called strip malls. They generally consist of 3 to 15 stores and have a retail area of 30,000 to 150,000 square feet. They are typically anchored by a supermarket, which is supported by other stores offering convenience goods (food, pharmaceuticals, and miscellaneous items) and personal services. Examples of supporting stores include drugstores, dollar stores, and dry cleaners.

Neighborhood centers represent good locations for stores selling goods or services that people need to purchase frequently. Rent is usually low in these centers, making them ideal for small businesses. Customers of neighborhood shopping centers are mainly residents of the surrounding area who shop at these centers because of their convenience. However, it could be a disadvantage for your business if the only customers you have come from the immediate area.

Community Shopping Centers

Community shopping centers are larger than neighborhood centers and offer a wider range of goods. They usually have a retail area of 100,000 to 350,000 square feet. These shopping centers are designed to serve residents from many neighborhoods. Apparel, furniture, toy, sporting goods, and electronic stores are often located in community shopping centers. Community centers usually have one or two major anchor stores. Anchor stores can include the following:

- Small department stores (Kohl's, JCPenney)
- Discount department stores (Walmart, Kmart, Target)
- Large supermarkets (Kroger, Safeway, Publix)
- Super drugstores (Walgreens, Rite Aid, CVS)
- Home improvement stores (Home Depot, Lowe's)

DEVELOP YOUR READING SKILLS

As you read, make a chart showing the advantages and disadvantages of each type of location for retail, service, home-based, industrial, and online businesses.

Although rent in community shopping centers is generally higher than in neighborhood shopping centers, it is usually still affordable. Stores in community shopping centers can earn higher profits. Anchor stores advertise heavily and attract customers throughout the community. Other businesses in the shopping center typically benefit from the advertising. Customers shop at the anchor stores and then may browse and buy at the smaller stores also located in the shopping center.

Regional Shopping Centers

Regional shopping centers are designed to attract customers from an entire region. These large shopping areas usually have 40 to 100 stores and a retail area of 400,000 to 800,000 square feet. They are anchored by two or more large department stores, such as Macy's and Nordstrom. Regional centers offer a variety of products and services, although the majority of the stores sell apparel. Many regional shopping centers are malls. These malls tend to have higher-end stores that need to pull customers from a larger area in order to be profitable.

If your business requires a large amount of walk-in traffic to be successful, you may want to locate in a regional shopping center. Rents at these centers are high, however, making it more difficult to earn profits. Also, the distance to the shop may be too far for some consumers. For convenience, they may decide to patronize businesses closer to their homes.

Super-Regional Shopping Centers

Super-regional shopping centers are the largest classification of shopping centers. They have a retail area of over 800,000 square feet and house more than 100 stores that offer an extensive variety of merchandise and services. They are typically anchored by three or more large department stores. They serve a larger population base than the other types of shopping centers. Two of the largest super-regional

What are the advantages and disadvantages of locating a business in a shopping mall?

centers are the West Edmonton Mall in Edmonton, Canada (with over 800 stores), and the Mall of America in Bloomington, Minnesota (with over 500 stores).

Most tenants in these centers are large chain stores that can afford the very high rents charged. If convenience is a factor for your target market, customers may not be willing to travel a great distance to come to your store. Such centers usually are not recommended for new businesses because of the competition that exists among many similar businesses.

Stand-Alone Stores

Stand-alone stores can be located just outside of shopping centers or far away from other businesses. Large jewelers, auto parts stores, and flower and garden centers are often operated as stand-alone stores.

Businesses locate in stand-alone locations because rent is often less expensive than it is elsewhere. Also, a competing business is less likely to be right next door. However, because stand-alone stores often depend on drive-by traffic, they must have plenty of parking, good signs, and effective lighting if they are to be successful. Advertising is often necessary to earn a profit because people must have a specific reason to come to your business.

Warehouses

Some retail stores, such as appliance dealers or furniture sellers, operate in warehouses. Warehouses are generally one of the cheapest rental facilities because they are of basic construction with few frills inside or out. Locating your business in a low-rent warehouse may allow you to charge lower prices than your competitors. This can work to a retailer's advantage because customers are usually more concerned about getting the best price than about the appearance of the business. However, by locating your business away from other retailers, potential customers may not notice or be aware of you. For this reason, businesses that operate out of warehouses generally must advertise heavily.

 CHECKPOINT

What are the main options for locating a retail business?

LO 8.1-2 Locating a Nonretail Business

Location can be very important for nonretail businesses, which include service, wholesale, and manufacturing businesses. Owners of these types of businesses face different considerations when choosing a location.

Service Businesses

For some service businesses, such as restaurants and hair salons, location considerations are the same as for many retail businesses because they are offering an inside service. Owners of these types of businesses

When might the location of a service business not be a major factor?

have to be very careful when choosing a location. Convenience can be an important factor for the business's customers.

Location is much less important for other types of service businesses. Customers never actually visit businesses that offer outside services, such as plumbing or carpet-cleaning companies. Locating these kinds of businesses in expensive areas does not make sense. Being close to customers may be important, however, because customers are more likely to call a company located nearby. For example, a computer-repair service might choose to locate downtown to be closer to its customers—the businesses in the downtown area—so it can respond quickly to emergency calls.

Industrial Businesses

Industrial businesses, such as manufacturing and wholesale companies, ship their products directly to their customers, so customers rarely see their facilities. Industrial businesses do not need to operate in upscale locations that attract lots of consumer traffic. Availability of good employees and low cost are the key factors in determining where an industrial business locates.

Nonretail businesses sometimes locate in industrial parks. An **industrial park** is a section of land that is zoned for industrial businesses only. They are usually located where space is less expensive, away from housing developments and downtown areas. Communities sometimes subsidize rents in industrial parks in order to attract industrial businesses.

Industrial businesses may locate in enterprise zones. **Enterprise zones** are areas that suffer from lack of employment opportunities. Entrepreneurs who set up businesses in these areas may be eligible for favorable tax treatment based on the number of jobs their businesses create. Some businesses may find these tax benefits attractive. Others, however, may find that these benefits do not make up for the lack of an appropriate customer base or the increased risk of crime in those areas.

Home-Based Businesses

In recent years, there has been an increase in the number of home-based businesses. Some of the reasons that entrepreneurs decide to set up their business in their home include the following:

- **Cost savings** Separate rent, utility costs, and maintenance fees for the business are eliminated, so there is more capital available for promotional activities and the purchase of inventory.
- **More freedom** Home-based business owners do not have to sign a lease agreement for the business, so they are not subject to the restrictions and obligations of a lease.

- **Convenience** The owner can work more flexible hours and does not have to commute to and from another location.
- **Tax benefits** Operating a home office offers some tax savings. You can deduct a portion of your home's expenses, such as mortgage, property taxes, and repairs and maintenance, against your business income.

Locating a business at home is a great way to save money when starting a business. If the business outgrows its space, the owner can begin to look for an appropriate location outside the home.

Although operating a business from home offers a number of advantages, there are some disadvantages to operating a home-based business.

Why do you think the number of home-based businesses is growing?

- **Limited space** Lack of space can limit the expansion of the business.
- **Lack of separation between business and home life** A problem with a home-based business is that you are always at work. Thus, it may be hard to keep your business and family life separate.
- **Isolation** Many home business owners feel isolated from the business community and miss opportunities to network with colleagues.

 CHECKPOINT

What are some of the factors to consider when selecting a location for a nonretail business?

LO 8.1-3 Starting a Virtual or Online Business

The widespread use of technology and access to the Internet has changed the way that business is conducted. For entrepreneurs, the virtual or online world has created many new business opportunities. **E-commerce**, or electronic commerce, consists of buying and selling products or services over the Internet. Virtual or online businesses offer an alternative means of conducting business transactions that traditionally have been carried out by telephone, by mail, or face to face in a traditional retail setting.

Advantages of Virtual or Online Businesses

There are numerous benefits of running virtual or online businesses in comparison to running traditional brick-and-mortar operations.

How has e-commerce transformed the way companies conduct business?

- **Quick and easy setup**   Starting a business online allows a business to have an immediate presence.
- **Cost savings**   The cost of maintaining an online business is much less than the cost of buying or leasing a building. In addition, marketing, customer service, order processing, inventory, and personnel costs are much lower. For example, it is much more cost-effective to use email than direct mail to reach out to hundreds of customers. Because customers enter their own orders online, employee costs are kept to a minimum.
- **Large customer base**   A traditional business is limited by its location because it can reach only as far as its geographic boundaries. However, an online business can reach out to customers globally.
- **No time restrictions**   E-commerce can take place 24 hours a day, 7 days a week, including holidays.
- **Ease of data collection**   Collecting and managing information about customer behavior is quick and easy for an online business. A customer's movements and selections on the website can be tracked and used to improve customer relations.

Disadvantages of Virtual or Online Businesses
While there are many advantages of running online businesses, it also has some disadvantages.

- **Special expertise**   It takes knowledge of computers, programming, and the Internet to manage and maintain the website of an online business. You may have to hire a person or another company to handle these tasks.
- **Internet downtime**   You could stand to lose a lot of time and money if, for some reason, your website goes down. This could cause potential customers to take their business elsewhere.

- **Security breaches**   Security can be an issue with online businesses. Hackers may steal consumers' personal information.

Virtual or Online Business Precautions

To help ensure success, there are some precautions to take when setting up your online business.

- Do not use free web space. It is more professional to buy your own domain (web address) to get a single and specific name for your website.
- Use a creative website design that appeals to customers. It should reflect the image you want to project for your business. Don't use all text and no pictures.
- Be aware of the loading speed of your website. If it takes too long to load web pages, customers may get frustrated and exit the website.
- Don't leave outdated information on your website. Keep it current.

 CHECKPOINT

What are some benefits of having a virtual or online business?

LO 8.1-4   Selecting Your Site

Given all of the possible types of locations for different types of businesses, how do you decide where to locate? One way of identifying the options for your business location is to buy a map and mark your trade area. The trade area is the geographic area from which you expect to attract a majority of your customers. Indicate on the map all of the locations that might be appropriate for your business. Then using a different color marker or symbol, indicate the locations of all your direct competitors. Typically, you don't want to locate too close to them. Also mark the locations of businesses that do not directly compete with your business but may attract the same kind of customer. For example, if you want to open a poster store that will attract mostly teenagers, mark the locations of other stores that appeal to this target market, such as trendy clothing stores and music stores. It may be beneficial to be located near complementary businesses.

Location Type and Availability

The next step is to identify which type of location is right for your business. Do you want to locate in a community shopping center? A stand-alone store? Downtown? Determining which type of location you want will help narrow your search.

How can you find the right location for your business?

After deciding on the type of location, you must determine what spaces of this type are available in your trade area. You can find locations by driving around your trade area. Signs advertising an available building will often be hung in the front window or placed on the front lawn of the property. Websites, search engines, and the classified section in your local newspaper, may also be helpful in determining options that are open to you. You may also want to enlist the help of a realtor. Mark each possible location you find on your trade area map.

Evaluate the Location

After identifying the trade area for your business and the type of location you'd prefer, you should be able to compile a list of possible locations. Inspect and evaluate each location to see how it meets your needs. Factors to consider include the following:

- Hidden costs, including renovations, and taxes (state and local income and property taxes)
- Convenience for customers

What Went *Wrong?*

Right Space, Wrong Place

Jim Teal was the owner and operator of Jimmy T's Rib House, a barbecue rib restaurant. One day a commercial realtor advised Jim that a restaurant four times the size of his current space was on the market. The realtor said he could get Jim a good deal on the lease if he liked it.

Gelpi JM/Shutterstock.com

Jim knew that the city where the building was located had no other barbecue rib restaurant. He researched and verified the population numbers and demographics for the area. It was in a good neighborhood and on a main road, just off the freeway. He even did a traffic-flow study, and the numbers were terrific. Jim decided to lease the building.

Grand opening week went well. Then business began to drop off. Although there was plenty of traffic, Jimmy T's was on the wrong side of the street. Customers coming west from the freeway exit could not cross the center island, and there was a "No U-Turn" sign at the corner. When Jim tried to improve his visibility by adding signs to attract more freeway traffic, he found that city ordinances prevented it. After six months, Jim took his loss and closed the new restaurant.

Consider the pros and cons of a location.

THINK CRITICALLY

1. What questions about location should Jim have asked the realtor before assuming the lease?

2. Who else should Jim have questioned about the location?

- Proximity to suppliers and vendors
- Local labor market (number of potential employees in the area)
- Safety (crime rate) of the location
- Image projected by the location
- Room for growth in case of expansion
- Zoning laws

 CHECKPOINT

What are some of the factors you should consider when selecting a site for your business?

 ASSESSMENT

THINK ABOUT IT

1. Why do you think rents are lower in neighborhood shopping centers than in community and regional shopping centers?

2. Do you think advances in technology have influenced some new business owners' decision to operate from their homes? Why or why not?

3. When marking the trade area for your business, why should you indicate the locations of your competitors?

MAKE ACADEMIC CONNECTIONS

4. **PROBLEM SOLVING** Using a map of your area, mark the potential trade area for a new furniture superstore. Then use the six-step problem-solving model from Chapter 1 to determine at least two appropriate locations.

5. **COMMUNICATION** As a downtown business owner, you actively work to recruit other businesses to the area. Write a letter to the editor of your local newspaper about the advantages of locating a business downtown.

Teamwork

Work in teams to select an online business that your group will operate. Design a website for your business by describing the content and features you would include. Use word processing software, a graphics program, or web design software to create the proposed layout of the homepage.

The Essential Question Refer to The Essential Question on p. 220. Entrepreneurs should choose the best location according to the type of product they sell and the type of customer they want to reach. They must also consider factors such as competition, costs, proximity to suppliers and vendors, and zoning regulations.

8.2 OBTAIN SPACE AND DESIGN THE PHYSICAL LAYOUT

The Essential Question What should entrepreneurs consider before obtaining property and designing its layout?

LEARNING OBJECTIVES

LO 8.2-1 Compare purchase and lease options.

LO 8.2-2 Describe layout considerations for different types of businesses.

KEY TERMS

- tenant
- landlord
- gross lease
- net lease
- percentage lease
- visual merchandising

FOCUS ON SMALL BUSINESS

Store layout results in walking inventory.

Trying to create a fun, relaxing atmosphere in his clothing and accessories store, Justin decided to move the cash register into the far back corner of his store. That gave him more space for displays and merchandise up front. He was really excited about all he could do with the space.

Due to slow traffic in the store at times, there was often only one employee on duty. The next thing Justin knew, his inventory was "walking right out the door," and it wasn't with paying customers. Justin had created a perfect layout for shoplifters. He knew he had to make some changes.

The layout should meet the needs of the business and its customers.

WORK AS A TEAM What did Justin do wrong in changing the layout of his store? If Justin wants to keep the same layout, what suggestions can you make that would cut down on shoplifting?

LO 8.2-1 Lease or Buy Space

Unless you operate your business out of your home, you will have to lease or buy business property. There are advantages to buying space. Owning property offers a bigger tax advantage than leasing because you get a tax deduction on the interest you pay on your loan for the building. A loan payment on the building may be no more than a lease payment.

However, most entrepreneurs lack the money to purchase property for their businesses. Even entrepreneurs who can afford to purchase property generally prefer not to be locked into a particular location. Some leases require the owner of the building, not the owner of the business, to pay certain expenses, such as upkeep and maintenance of the building's exterior. For these reasons, most businesses lease space.

Commercial Leases

When leasing property, a contract is required. In a lease contract, there is a tenant and a landlord. The **tenant** is the person who pays rent to occupy space owned by someone else. The **landlord** is the person who owns and rents out buildings or space.

There are three kinds of commercial leases. Each kind requires different levels of responsibility from the tenant and the landlord.

1. In a **gross lease**, the tenant pays rent each month for the space occupied, and the landlord covers all property expenses for that space, such as property taxes, insurance on the building, and building maintenance.
2. A **net lease** occurs when the landlord pays building insurance, and the tenant pays rent, property taxes, and any other expenses.
3. With a **percentage lease**, the tenant pays a base rent each month, and the landlord also receives a percentage of the tenant's revenue each month. The percentage lease is most common for prime retail locations. This type of lease can be beneficial for both the landlord and tenant. The landlord shares in the business's profits, and the tenant has the advantage of a lower base rent, which can make rent more affordable during slow sales periods.

Commercial lease agreements are usually long and complex. You should never sign one without consulting an attorney. Your attorney will review your lease to make sure that it covers all conditions and costs, including the basic rent, maintenance fees, utility costs, insurance costs, and other items.

Compare Costs of Doing Business

Once you have selected some possible locations for your business, you need to compare the costs and benefits of leasing property at each location. To do so, you need to calculate how much rent you will be paying per customer.

Juan Martinez plans to open a music store. He finds two locations that meet his needs—one in a neighborhood shopping center and the other in the downtown area. To decide which location he should select, Juan determines the amount of rent he would pay and the number of projected customers for each location. Juan divides the amount of rent by the number of projected customers to determine the *rent per customer*.

	Downtown	Shopping Center
Rent per month	$ 925	$ 1,100
Projected customer traffic per month	÷8,500	÷12,000
Rent per customer	$ 0.11	$ 0.09

From his calculations, Juan determines that, although the total rent at the shopping center will be higher, he will be paying a lower rent per customer. Juan decides to lease space at the shopping center.

CHECKPOINT

Name three kinds of commercial leases.

LO 8.2-2   Design the Layout

After you have leased or purchased a facility, you will need to design your layout, or floor plan. Your layout must include enough space for employees, customers, merchandise, and equipment. It must also have space for restrooms, stockrooms, storage, and offices.

Create the Floor Plan

To create an accurate floor plan, start by taking measurements. Measure the height and width of the walls and any doorways and window frames. You'll also want to measure the furniture and other large pieces that will go in your business. It is not necessary to measure smaller items such as office chairs.

After you finish measuring, you're ready to draw your floor plan to scale. You can use floor planning software to design your layout, or you can prepare a scale drawing using graph paper. To create a scale drawing, let 1 inch represent 1 foot of actual space. For example, a 4-foot-by-3-foot closet would be represented by a 4-inch-by-3-inch rectangle. Indicate the planned use of each area. Also indicate the location of furniture, display cabinets, shelves, fixtures, and equipment. Your drawing will help you identify potential problems in your layout. It will also help you communicate with the people who may be helping you organize your space.

Sample Floor Plan

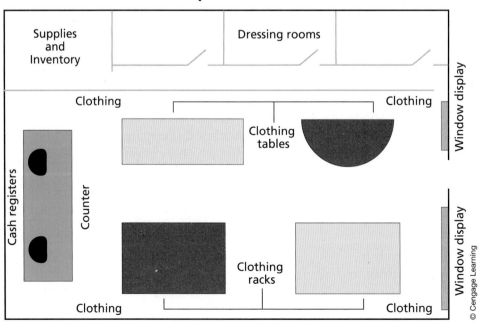

Decide on a layout, an outside sign, and window displays that match your image. For example, you will select a very different design for your store if you want to project an elegant image versus an outdoorsy image.

Layout of a Retail Business

For a retail business, visual merchandising is very important. **Visual merchandising** is the process of combining products, environments, and spaces into an appealing display to encourage the sale of products or services. The goal of your layout should be twofold: (1) to attract customers to your store and keep them coming back and (2) to meet the needs of your business.

Here are some ways you can send a positive message about your store.

1. Choose lighting that is appropriate for the kind of merchandise that you sell. Good lighting is important for any business where customers inspect merchandise closely.
2. Think carefully about window displays. Use them as a way to display new merchandise or seasonal items.
3. Make the entrance inviting. An entrance that is welcoming will draw customers into the store.
4. Leave at least 4 feet of aisle space. This makes it easy to move around in your store.

FAMOUS ENTREPRENEUR

RACHAEL RAY Sometimes success comes from being in the right place at the right time. And it always helps to be prepared! Just ask Rachael Ray, who says her life has been "a very happy, wonderful accident that I didn't and couldn't have planned."

The truth behind that statement is that Ray had extensive training in the food service industry before she became a TV star. She grew up in a family of restaurant owners. Starting at the candy counter of Macy's, she was promoted to manager of the Fresh Foods Department. She then helped to open and was store manager and buyer for Agata & Valentina, the prestigious New York gourmet marketplace.

She was discovered by the local CBS station while working for Cowan & Lobel, which was a

How did Rachael Ray build upon her early success?

Paul Drinkwater/NBC/NBCU Photo Bank/ NBCUniversal/Getty Images

large gourmet market in Albany, New York. As a way to increase grocery sales during the holidays, she began a series of cooking classes in which she showed people how to make meals in less than 30 minutes. The classes were so popular that the station signed her on to do a weekly "30 Minute Meals" segment for the evening news. The cooking segments eventually led to a contract with the Food Network and have spawned a best-selling series of cookbooks. In September 2006, Ray launched the daily one-hour, nationally syndicated show Rachael Ray.

THINK CRITICALLY
Even though Rachael Ray says her success was accidental, what steps did she take in her life that prepared her for her current position?

5. Use common sense when organizing the merchandise in your store. Customers should always easily find what they want. Inventory and supplies should also be well organized so that you can find things faster and serve your customers better.
6. Create attractive in-store displays. Customers are drawn to displayed merchandise.
7. Use wall space wisely. Wall space may be too high for customers to reach, but it can be used to display merchandise.
8. Place the cash register in a central location. Customers should not have to search for a cashier.

Layout of a Service Business

There are two types of service businesses:

1. Businesses where people come to the business location to receive a service (restaurants, hair salons, automobile repair services)
2. Businesses that travel to the customer's location and perform the service on-site (exterminators, plumbers, cleaning services)

The layout of the first type of service business should be considered just as carefully as that of a retail business. However, on-site service businesses are rarely visited by their customers, so an attractive layout is not important. Instead, organization should be a major consideration of on-site service businesses so that supplies are easy to find.

Layout of a Wholesale Business

Customers of wholesale businesses are concerned with price and quality, not physical appearance. Thus, a wholesale business needs only to have an efficient and well-organized layout. Wholesalers are constantly receiving and shipping large volumes of products. Wholesale businesses can do the following to facilitate shipping and receiving:

What factors influence the layout of a wholesale business?

YinYang/iStockphoto.com

1. Locate in a one-story warehouse.
2. Keep merchandise close to the shipping dock to minimize the distance it has to be moved.
3. Store the most popular items in the most accessible locations.
4. Be sure there are areas that can accommodate merchandise of all sizes.
5. Keep walkways free of merchandise so that employees can exit the building quickly in an emergency.
6. Store items safely. For instance, do not stack too many boxes on top of one another because they may fall if they become unsteady.

Layout of a Manufacturing Business

For manufacturing businesses, the layout should facilitate the production process. Attractiveness does not count. Important considerations include the following:

1. Work teams should be situated close together.
2. Supervisors should be able to easily observe the people they supervise. Their office should be located near the employees.
3. Exits should be clearly marked and easily accessible so that employees can quickly leave in the event of an emergency.
4. Any hazardous materials should be stored safely.
5. Equipment and machinery should be positioned in a way that reduces the chance of an accident.

CHECKPOINT

What should you consider when choosing a layout for a business?

8.2 ASSESSMENT

THINK ABOUT IT

1. What are the differences between a gross lease, net lease, and percentage lease? Which type of lease would you prefer? Explain why.

2. Why do you think it is important to draw a floor plan of your business before you begin setting up shop?

MAKE ACADEMIC CONNECTIONS

3. **RESEARCH** You are thinking about opening a bicycle sales and repair shop. Research layouts of other bicycle shops and determine what type of equipment and supplies would be included in the layout of your shop.

4. **MATH** Determine the rent per customer for each of the following:

Location	Rent per Month	Projected Customer Traffic per Month	Rent per Customer
Downtown	$1,200	9,500	?
Community shopping center	$2,800	18,000	?
Stand-alone store	$1,050	7,400	?

Teamwork

Working in teams, design the layout for a salon that has three stations used to cut men and women's hair, one room for massage therapy, two chairs for pedicures, and one manicure station.

The Essential Question Refer to The Essential Question on p. 230. Entrepreneurs should obtain property that has appropriate space and design its layout according to the type of business.

8.3 PURCHASE EQUIPMENT, SUPPLIES, AND INVENTORY

The Essential Question What should entrepreneurs consider when selecting vendors and purchasing inventory?

LEARNING OBJECTIVES

LO 8.3-1 Explain how to find and choose vendors for your business.
LO 8.3-2 List factors that determine the needed level of inventory.

KEY TERMS

- inventory
- vendors
- quote
- reorder point

Time for a new supplier.

Karen has operated Bear Creek Embroidery and Alterations as a home-based business for several years. She started small and was able to purchase her supplies from a local discount store. But now that her business is growing, she is buying larger quantities of supplies and materials. She often finds that the local discount store does not carry everything she needs and does not have large quantities of materials in stock.

Karen must find a new vendor for her supplies, but she's not sure where to start and how to ensure she gets the best price available.

WORK AS A TEAM How would you advise Karen to start looking for a new supplier? What information should Karen gather before contacting a supplier?

A growing business needs a reliable supplier.

Siede Preis/Photodisc/Getty Images

LO 8.3-1 Obtain Equipment and Supplies

Every business needs to analyze its operational needs and select equipment, supplies, and goods and services based on these needs. Machinery, computers, cash registers, and furniture are types of equipment. Supplies include items such as paper, pens, and pencils. **Inventory** consists of the products that a business sells to its customers as well as the materials needed to make those products. Without these things, a business cannot operate properly. If there is no inventory, what will you sell? If there is no paper, how will you send a letter? Suppliers or vendors can provide your business with everything you need to function.

To determine the equipment and supplies you need to start your business, make a list of what you think you will need. Your list should include standard items needed by all businesses as shown in the table below. It should also include items specific to your particular business. For example, if you opened a lawn care and landscaping business, you would need lawn fertilizer and mulch as part of your supplies and lawn mowers and leaf blowers as part of your equipment.

STANDARD EQUIPMENT AND SUPPLY NEEDS FOR MOST BUSINESSES	
Type	Items
Furniture	Desks, chairs, bookcases, filing cabinets, tables, computer stands
Fixtures	Lamps, overhead lights
Office Equipment	Computers, routers, modems, fax machines, telephones, printers, copiers, scanners
Office Supplies	Stationery, pens and pencils, scissors, tape, staplers, paper clips, binder clips, folders, calendars
Maintenance Supplies	Toilet paper, paper towels, hand soap, cleaning supplies
Kitchen Supplies	Coffee maker, small refrigerator, soft drinks, coffee, tea

© Cengage Learning

Once you have listed all of the items that you need, indicate how much of each item you require. Be sure to list the minimum quantity you need right now, not the amount you might need if your business succeeds. Being overly optimistic could leave you with many bills that will be difficult to pay if your sales fall short of your projections.

Identify Suppliers

To fill the standard and special needs of your business, you will need to research vendors. **Vendors** are companies that sell products and services to businesses. Vendors are also called *suppliers*. Valuable sources of vendor information include the following:

- Telephone directory advertising section
- Trade magazines (specialized magazines devoted to a particular industry), which carry vendor advertising
- Trade associations
- The Internet
- Other companies in your industry
- SBA and SCORE

Shira Silberg wants to open an assisted-living center for senior citizens. To find suppliers of furniture, linens, and other items, Shira looks through copies of trade magazines for advertisements from companies that target the nursing home industry. She also contacts nursing home trade associations and locates vendor websites for additional information. Finally, she contacts other assisted-living centers to find out which vendors they use.

What role do vendors like OfficeMax play in the operation of a business?

Evaluate Proposals

Most of the items you will need to start your business will be available from a variety of vendors. How will you decide among them? Before you make a purchase, contact several vendors and ask them to quote you a price for the merchandise that you are interested in purchasing. A quote is an estimate for how much you will pay for the merchandise or service. Also ask vendors about the quality of their merchandise, their financing terms, quantity discounts, and shipping and handling charges. Once you have all of the information you need, compare the various proposals. Choose the supplier that provides the best combination of products at a cost that fits your budget.

Shira contacts vendors and asks for price quotes. She then compares prices, service, quality of merchandise, discount options, and shipping and handling fees. Shira knows that the lowest price is not always the best option if paying a little more means receiving better quality and service. She decides on a higher-priced linen business because it offers additional services that meet the needs of her business.

 **CHECKPOINT**

What should you consider when selecting vendors for your business?

LO 8.3-2 Purchase Inventory

Retailing, wholesaling, and manufacturing businesses must purchase inventory before they can open for business. For retail and wholesale businesses, inventory is merchandise (a finished product) purchased with the intent of reselling it to customers. For manufacturing businesses, inventory consists of the business's finished product as well as the parts that go into producing the finished product.

Purchase Inventory for a Startup Business

Determining the amount of inventory to keep in stock is difficult for all business owners. It is particularly difficult for owners of new businesses, who do not yet know what their level of sales will be.

Chris Keating wants to open an art supplies store. Not knowing how high or low his sales will be at first, Chris doesn't want to purchase too much inventory and tie up his cash if he can't sell it quickly. Chris is also worried about finding space to store the inventory. Because of these concerns, Chris purchases just enough stock to fill his shelves.

BE YOUR OWN BOSS

You own a toy store. Some of the stuffed animals that you carry have become very popular with children, and you cannot keep them in stock. In the past, your reorder point was three and you never ran out of the animals, but now you are losing sales because of empty shelves. You know you could sell more stuffed animals if you had them. Outline a plan that will meet your business's inventory needs as well as your customers' needs.

Purchase Inventory for an Ongoing Business

Once your business is up and running, you will have a better idea of how much inventory you need to operate. To avoid running out of stock, you should track it and establish reorder points for each product. The **reorder point** is a predetermined level of inventory that signals when new stock should be ordered. How low you set the reorder point depends on how long it takes your supplier to get merchandise to you, how many units of the item you sell each month, and how important it is for you not to be out of stock.

Chris sells an average of 150 erasers a month at his art supplies store. Because he never wants to be out of stock, he sets his reorder point at 30. Every time his inventory of erasers falls at or below 30, he places an order to renew his stock of this item.

 CHECKPOINT

How do you determine how much inventory to keep in stock?

Why should a business keep track of its inventory?

THINK ABOUT IT

1. Why should you make a list of all the equipment and supplies you need to start your business?

2. Why is it important to obtain price quotes from several different vendors before selecting one? What questions should you ask them?

3. Explain the relationship between inventory and customer service.

MAKE ACADEMIC CONNECTIONS

4. **COMMUNICATION** You are a wholesale distributor of party supplies. A new store, Party Express, has asked you to submit a proposal for supplying its paper goods inventory. To prepare for a meeting with the Party Express management, make a list of questions you will ask them to get enough information for your proposal.

5. **MATH** You are going to open a personal fitness training business. You will work with clients in their homes. You have determined you need to purchase the following items: 10 sets of hand weights, 10 exercise bands, 4 exercise mats, 6 jump ropes, 4 heart rate monitors, 2 pairs of gym shoes, and 2 duffel bags. Using catalogs, the Internet, and other sources, find suppliers who can provide the items you need. Determine the unit cost and total cost for each item.

6. **RESEARCH** Use the Internet, trade magazines, newspapers, and other sources to make a list of goods and services that a web designer would need to start a business. Discuss your list in a small group and add additional items as needed.

Teamwork

Lee Torres is opening a retail pet store that carries high-quality pet foods and supplies. She does not plan to sell puppies or kittens but will have a large assortment of birds, tropical fish, and small animals (hamsters, guinea pigs, etc.) and the foods and accessories needed for them. The store will carry an assortment of books about selecting, training, breeding, and caring for pets. Lee will also offer grooming services for pets.

Working with teammates, make a list of all of the equipment and supplies Lee will need for her business. Use the Internet to compile a list of several vendors that sell pet products and supplies. Create a list of questions that Lee should ask the vendors. Finally, consider Lee's inventory needs. Decide which products Lee should order in large or small quantities and explain why. Compile a report to present to Lee.

The Essential Question Refer to The Essential Question on p. 236. Entrepreneurs should consider the operational needs of the business, the demands of their customers, and their budget when selecting vendors and purchasing inventory.

Sharpen Your 21st Century Entrepreneurial Skills

Email Etiquette

In today's world, businesses use email on a regular basis when dealing with vendors and customers. Using email to communicate can be more convenient, more economical, and faster than a phone call or letter. However, when conducting business via email, you should demonstrate professionalism by using proper email etiquette. The following guidelines are important to remember when sending emails:

1. **Use a professional email address.** The address you use should convey your name and/or the name of your company. Avoid funny email addresses that you may have for personal use.

2. **Use a clear, direct subject line.** The subject line should appropriately describe the message. Also, because people receive numerous emails, try to use a subject line that will catch their attention.

3. **Cover only one topic per email.** If you have several topics to discuss, send them in separate emails.

4. **Be courteous and professional in your message.** Use humor sparingly. What one person finds funny, another may find offensive. Remember, once the email is sent, you cannot get it back.

5. **Remember that business email is not private.** Email is monitored in many companies. Also, any email you send can easily be forwarded to someone else. Do not send anything that you would not want to be made public.

6. **Reply to emails in a timely manner.** Scan emails to see if the recipient needs you to reply by a certain time or date. Reply accordingly to avoid missing deadlines. As a general rule, try to reply to all other emails within 24 hours.

7. **Proofread every message.** Be sure that messages are clearly organized and grammatically correct. Write in complete sentences and always check spelling and punctuation.

8. **Provide an email signature.** An email signature is a block of text at the bottom of the message that includes your name and contact information such as a phone number, email address, or link to the company's website or social media page.

9. **Limit the number and size of attachments.** Large files can take too much time to open and can fill up the recipient's inbox.

TRY IT OUT

You want to send an email to a potential vendor asking for a quote for office supplies that you need for your new business. Compose the email that you would send. Be sure to follow the guidelines given above.

SUMMARY

8.1 Choose a Location

1. Options for locating retail businesses include downtown areas, neighborhood shopping centers, community shopping centers, regional shopping centers, super-regional shopping centers, stand-alone stores, and warehouses.

2. When choosing a location for service businesses that customers visit, the same factors must be considered as for retail businesses. For service businesses where the service is performed on-site, the business location is not as important.

3. For industrial businesses, availability of good employees and low cost are the key factors in choosing a location.

4. Advantages of operating a business out of the home include cost savings, more freedom, convenience, and tax benefits.

5. Benefits of starting a virtual or an online business include a quick and easy setup, cost savings, a large customer base, no time restrictions, and the ease of data collection.

6. Mapping your trade area with possible locations, the locations of competitors, and the locations of businesses that draw the same target customers can help you narrow your location options.

8.2 Obtain Space and Design the Physical Layout

7. To evaluate leases, compare the costs and expected benefits of various locations and the types of leases—gross, net, or percentage—offered. Calculating the rent per customer can help you determine which location is most cost-effective.

8. The layout of a business depends on the type of business. For retail businesses, the layout should be designed to attract and keep customers and to meet the needs of your business. For wholesale businesses, the aim of a layout is to store inventory in the most efficient manner. For manufacturing businesses, the layout should facilitate the production process.

8.3 Purchase Equipment, Supplies, and Inventory

9. Once you determine your equipment and supply needs, you will need to identify and evaluate a number of vendors by obtaining quotes.

10. To determine the amount of inventory to keep in stock and the reorder point, consider the amount of expected sales, the time it takes your supplier to get merchandise to you, and how important it is for you not to be out of stock for the item.

WHAT DO YOU KNOW NOW?

Read *Ideas in Action* on page 219 again. Then answer the questions a second time. Have your responses changed? If so, how have they changed?

KEY TERMS REVIEW

Match each statement with the term that best defines it. Some terms may not be used.

1. A section of land that is zoned for industrial businesses only
2. Companies that sell products and services to businesses
3. The geographic area from which a business expects to attract a majority of its customers
4. An estimate of how much you will pay for merchandise or services
5. The person who owns and rents out buildings or space
6. A type of lease in which the tenant pays rent each month for the space occupied, and the landlord covers all property expenses for that space
7. A type of lease in which the landlord pays building insurance and the tenant pays rent, property taxes, and any other expenses
8. Areas that suffer from lack of employment opportunities
9. Buying and selling products or services over the Internet
10. A predetermined level of inventory that signals when new stock should be ordered

REVIEW YOUR KNOWLEDGE

11. Which of the following is *not* a location option for a retail business?
    a. downtown area
    b. industrial park
    c. community shopping center
    d. warehouse
12. Which of the following service businesses would consider the same location factors as a retail business?
    a. exterminating company
    b. lawn service
    c. hair salon
    d. on-site computer repair service
13. Which of the following is *not* a good reason to locate a business in the home?
    a. saves money
    b. more freedom
    c. limited space
    d. convenience
14. **True or False**   Availability of parking would be an important consideration for the location of a coffee shop.
15. **True or False**   Most entrepreneurs start out by purchasing the site where their business will be located.
16. In which type of lease does a landlord receive a portion of the tenant's revenue each month in addition to a base rent?
    a. gross lease
    b. net lease
    c. percentage lease
    d. tenant–landlord lease
17. Which of the following is the *least* important consideration when organizing the layout of a retail business?
    a. lighting
    b. window displays
    c. aisle space
    d. organization of supplies

18. Which of the following is the *least* important consideration for the layout of a wholesale business?
    a. organization   c. safety
    b. efficiency   d. appearance
19. **True or False** When purchasing supplies, equipment, and inventory, it is always best to purchase from the lowest-cost vendor.
20. Which of the following is *not* considered inventory?
    a. dolls for a toy store
    b. component parts of a product
    c. vacuum cleaners owned by a maid service
    d. all of the above are considered inventory
21. Which of the following is the *least* important factor in determining the reorder point for a sale item in your store?
    a. the size of the item
    b. the time it takes to receive merchandise from your supplier
    c. how many units you sell each month
    d. how important it is to you to not run out of stock

APPLY WHAT YOU LEARNED

22. You are planning to open a bakery. Identify the trade area. What types of locations are available in your community? List the advantages and disadvantages of each. Are there competing bakeries in any of these locations? Are there other businesses that do not compete directly but attract the same kind of customer? What are these businesses? Why do you think these businesses chose this particular location? (LO 8.1-4)
23. You want to start an online business that offers photo gifts such as photo keychains, mugs, and calendars. Customers can upload their photos to your website. Then you will assemble the products and mail them to the customers. Describe the advantages of operating your business online. What should you consider when designing your website? (LO 8.1-3)

MAKE ACADEMIC CONNECTIONS

24. **MARKETING** Design the layout of a bookstore. Create a scale drawing of the space and show the placement of all the fixtures, shelves, furniture, and equipment. Describe how you will use visual merchandising to help promote a positive image for your store. (LO 8.2-2)
25. **MATH** You are choosing between a neighborhood shopping center and a stand-alone store for your shoe store. The monthly rent for the shopping center is $3,200, and the projected monthly customer traffic is 6,500. The monthly rent for the stand-alone location is $2,500, and the projected monthly traffic is 5,100. Which location will you choose and why? What other factors might you consider? (LO 8.2-1)

26. **RESEARCH** Interview the owners or managers of three to five local retail businesses. What do they see as advantages and disadvantages of their locations? (LO 8.1-1)

What Would YOU DO?

You are looking for a vendor to supply your new business with a computer, printer, and copy machine. You have contacted several vendors for quotes. One of the vendors offers you a "special" deal if you accept his quote before the end of the day. In addition to a competitive price for the equipment, he is offering you tickets to an NFL game in a private stadium suite. He wants you to agree to the deal without signing a contract and has asked that you pay him in cash. What would you do?

BUILD YOUR BUSINESS PLAN PROJECT

This activity will help you choose a location and vendors for your business idea.

1. Choose the location area that is best for your business. Why is it the best choice? Make a list of your reasons.
2. Using a local map, mark the trade area for your business. Mark the possible locations for your business and the locations of your competitors. Are there any businesses in the trade area that do not directly compete but attract a similar type of customer? If so, mark those on the map. For each area, write an evaluation that outlines why this would or would not be a good location for your business.
3. Determine if it will be more cost-effective for you to buy or lease space, to run your business from home, or to operate your business online. Consider rent-per-customer projections. Write a short paper justifying your decision.
4. Design the physical layout of your business. Use floor planning software or create a scale drawing of the space and show the placement of all the furniture, fixtures, and equipment. Indicate the planned use of each area. How does this layout meet your goals? Calculate the square footage requirements for the entire layout.
5. Analyze the equipment and supplies you will need to start and operate your business. Using the telephone book, trade magazines, the Internet, and other sources, locate five vendors. Contact the vendors (or use their website) to obtain information about their products, pricing, financial terms, quantity discounts, and shipping and handling charges. Using the prices from each vendor, calculate the total cost of all equipment and supplies you will need. How do the vendors compare? Which one will you select? Why?

Architecture & Construction

"My uncle is excited about the solar panels he recently had installed on the roof of his home. His city provided a $1,000 rebate for solar panel installation. As required by the rebate, the panels annually displace 1,500 kilowatt hours of grid-based power. My uncle's utility bills have decreased. He also feels good about doing his part to improve the environment."

Solar power is a renewable energy source that is rapidly increasing in popularity. By way of solar panels, sunlight is transformed into electricity. Recent technological advances have reduced the cost of solar panels, making it a viable source of electricity for both businesses and homeowners. States and cities often provide incentives, such as tax rebates, to those who choose to use solar power.

Solar panels are typically placed on roofs, where the greatest amount of sunlight is captured. Solar photovoltaic (PV) installers put solar panels in place. PV installers may work alone or as part of a team.

Employment Outlook
- A faster-than-average rate of employment growth is expected.
- The rapid increase in popularity of solar panels is expected to create new jobs.

Job Titles
- Solar Panel Installer
- PV Installer
- Solar Energy Project Manager
- Photovoltaic Lighting Designer

Needed Education/Skills
- A high school diploma is required, although most PV installers take courses at community colleges and technical schools.
- Although not mandatory, PV installers may obtain certification.
- Prior experience in construction is beneficial.
- Mechanical skills, physical stamina and strength, and being detail-oriented are essential.

What's it like to work in Solar Energy? Paige, an independent PV installer, has obtained installation contracts from a variety of companies. The companies that have contracted for Paige's services provide their clients with on-site consulting, ranging from determining the optimal location of solar panels, to the filing of paperwork for government-based rebate and tax credit programs, to providing a six-month follow-up visit to ensure proper functioning of panels.

Since Paige has many years of experience, she can install panels at residential, commercial, or industrial sites. For larger jobs, she is often part of a team of roofers, electricians, and other PV installers.

Next week, Paige is attending a conference that will focus on state and federal solar energy incentive programs. Becoming more knowledgeable about these issues is part of Paige's continuing education plan to prepare her to start her own solar energy consulting business.

What about you? Would you like to help clean up the environment by actively converting energy consumers to renewable, "green" energy sources? What do you find appealing about this career?

Understanding digital media is an important skill for a young entrepreneur. With advancements in social media and communication technology, it is important to understand how to market and advertise your business through the use of digital media.

The Digital Media Production Event is an individual event. You will create a one- to two-minute piece of digital media based on the given topic. The topic is selected by the BPA National Center and is available at the beginning of the school year. Please check BPA's *Workplace Skills Assessment Program Guidelines* for this school year's topic.

Performance Indicators

- Evaluate responsibilities needed to perform required tasks
- Demonstrate effective oral communication skills
- Demonstrate an understanding of developing promotions for a target audience
- Demonstrate utilization of various software applications
- Demonstrate knowledge of digital media
- Demonstrate knowledge of graphic design, including color, audio, and video

Go to the BPA website for more detailed information.

GIVE IT A TRY

1. Select one of the topics below.
   a. You have been asked by your local chamber of commerce to create a promotional video to inspire young entrepreneurs to start a business in your town.
   b. Your school's athletic program is seeking sponsors for the upcoming season. Create a promotional video that will demonstrate both the athletic and academic aspects of your school.
2. Using any form of software application available to you, create a digital media production that is one to two minutes in length. You may use audio, video, and animation—much like what you would see on a television commercial. Be sure that you comply with all federal and state copyright laws.
3. When you are finished with your digital product, present it to your class. During your presentation, describe how you made the video and explain how it will appeal to your target audience.

www.bpa.org

9

Plan and Track Your Finances

(9.1) FINANCING YOUR BUSINESS

(9.2) PRO FORMA FINANCIAL STATEMENTS

(9.3) RECORDKEEPING FOR BUSINESSES

IDEAS IN **ACTION**

Determination Leads to Success

Photo by Laren Helms

Robert Nay, CEO of Nay Games

The developer of the Bubble Ball app, Robert Nay, became an overnight success as a 14-year-old eighth grader. Bubble Ball is a multi-level physics game that challenges players to use objects and gravity to guide a ball to its destination. Within two weeks of launching, Bubble Ball had a million downloads and became the most popular free app on iTunes. "I was surprised by how well it was doing," Nay said.

Nay's love for computer programming prompted a friend to suggest he try making an iPhone app. Nay used the public library to research and work on Bubble Ball. After considering various app-creation programs, Nay settled on Corona SDK from Ansca Mobile, which enables users to create an app with the simple Lua coding language. Using Corona, Nay was able to build Bubble Ball within a couple of months. Nay said Corona was easy to use and let him publish for both Apple and Android devices. Still, Nay had to author 4,000 lines of code to create Bubble Ball, and it wasn't all fun and games.

"There were times when I ran into problems that seemed insurmountable," he said. "But then there were times when things just worked…. I proved to myself that I was able to create an app." Even with all the hard work, Nay says he enjoyed creating Bubble Ball, and that his story shows that you never know what success might come from trying something new.

Nay's startup costs were relatively low, since he did the research and development work himself. He did have to pay licensing fees to publish his games for use with Apple and Android as well as a licensing fee to use the Corona program to make Bubble Ball.

Offering Bubble Ball as a free app turned out to be a good marketing move. Its popularity has given Nay the brand recognition he needs to create new games that he can sell. He has set the stage for doing just that by starting his own company, Nay Games LLC, located in Spanish Fork, Utah. Others are taking notice as well. Nay has been interviewed by *ABC News*, *CNN*, and *Inc. Magazine*, and was put on the *Forbes* "30 Under 30" list of the brightest entrepreneurs under the age of 30.

WHAT DO YOU **KNOW?**

1. What makes Robert Nay's success so unusual?
2. How did Nay manage to create a mobile app without any prior app experience?
3. If Nay's company grows, what financial expenses do you think he will incur?

9.1 FINANCING YOUR BUSINESS

The Essential Question When starting a business, how can entrepreneurs assess their financial needs and get funding?

LEARNING OBJECTIVES

LO 9.1-1 Estimate your startup costs and personal net worth.

LO 9.1-2 Identify sources of equity capital for your business.

LO 9.1-3 Identify sources of debt capital for your business.

KEY TERMS

- net worth (owner's equity)
- assets
- liabilities
- debt-to-equity ratio
- equity capital
- debt capital
- collateral

FOCUS ON SMALL BUSINESS

Line up your financing.

Monty wanted to start his own meeting planning business. He compiled a list of all the things he would need to buy for his business. Monty realized that he was going to need some financial assistance because he did not have enough money saved to buy everything he needed. So he called his friend Sarah for some advice.

"Sarah, I need some help financing my new business. Who do you think I should ask?" Sarah had taken some business courses in school and remembered that there were many different avenues for funding a business. "Why don't you start with your friends and family and see if any of them are interested in investing in your business?" Sarah suggested. "If not, I've got lots more ideas!"

WORK AS A TEAM Do you think your friends and family members would be willing to loan money or invest in your business? If not, whom else could you approach for funding?

Determine if you need financial assistance.

LO 9.1-1 Assess Your Financial Needs

As you start a business, you will have many decisions to make regarding its financing. Your financial needs will vary depending on the size and type of business you start. If you are starting a very small business, you may be able to provide all of the startup money you will need. If your business will be large or require special equipment, you may need to look to others to help raise the startup money.

Before you can approach a lender or investor about financing your business, you will have to prepare some financial documents. First, you must estimate your startup costs and create a personal financial statement. Then you will prepare pro forma financial statements of the cash flow statement, income statement, and balance sheet. *Pro forma financial statements* are financial statements based on projections. (Pro forma financial statements are discussed in the next lesson.) These items allow potential lenders and investors to determine if your business is viable. They also help lenders decide whether the financing that you are requesting is reasonable.

Startup Costs

Itemizing your startup costs is an important part of determining how much money you need to start your business. You want to be sure you have accounted for all of the items you will need. Some common startup expenses include equipment and supplies, such as computers, printers, telephones, and paper; furniture and fixtures, such as desks and chairs; vehicles, such as delivery trucks; and legal, such as accounting and licensing fees.

Some entrepreneurs attempt to reduce start-up costs and shorten the product's development cycle. Companies using this approach are referred to as *lean startups*. This approach may involve releasing a "minimally viable product," which is a version of the product that has just enough features to satisfy early customers and to provide feedback for future development.

Felicia Walters plans to start a lighting fixture store. To help her determine how much money she will need to borrow, she calculates her startup costs, as shown in the table.

Personal Financial Statement

To determine if you have the resources you need to finance your business, begin by assessing your net worth. **Net worth** is the difference between **assets**, items of value that you own, and **liabilities**, amounts you owe to others. Net worth is also referred to as **owner's equity**. To calculate your net worth, you should prepare a *personal financial statement*. On the left side, list all of your assets with their value. Include cash, investments, and any property. Total the worth of these items. On the right side, list all of your liabilities and total the amount that you owe. Then subtract your total liabilities from your total assets to determine your net worth.

Felicia Walters prepares a personal financial statement to help her determine whether she is able to finance her new business. She finds that her net worth is $27,800, as shown on the next page. After comparing her startup costs to her net worth, Felicia determines that she will need to seek additional financial resources for her business.

STARTUP COSTS
Walters Electric

Item	Estimated Cost
Equipment and supplies	
Computers (3 @ $1,500)	$ 4,500
Scanner	175
Cash registers (2 @ $1,800)	3,600
Printer	400
Supplies	300
Subtotal	$ 8,975
Furniture and Fixtures	
Desks (4 @ $400)	$ 1,600
Chairs (8 @ $75)	600
Subtotal	$ 2,200
Vehicles	
Delivery truck	$10,000
Automobile	8,000
Subtotal	$18,000
Remodeling	
Drywall replacement	$ 1,000
Electrical work	2,500
Paint	1,000
Carpet	3,000
Subtotal	$ 7,500
Legal and accounting fees	$ 3,000
Total	$39,675

© Cengage Learning

PERSONAL FINANCIAL STATEMENT
Felicia Walters

Assets		Liabilities	
Cash	$ 5,000	Car loan	$ 6,900
Checking account	13,500	College loan	4,000
Certificate of Deposit	6,000	Credit cards	1,300
Stock	10,000		
Computer equipment	3,000		
Coin collection	2,500		
Total assets	$40,000	Total liabilities	$12,200

Total assets − Total liabilities = **Net worth**

$40,000 − $12,200 = $27,800

 CHECKPOINT

Why is the net worth of an entrepreneur important to potential investors in the business?

LO 9.1-2 Equity Capital

There are two types of financing available for your business—equity and debt financing. When obtaining financing, you must consider your company's **debt-to-equity ratio**, or the relation between the dollars you have borrowed (debt) and the dollars you have invested in your business (equity). This ratio measures how much money a company can safely borrow over time. The formula for debt-to-equity ratio is:

Total Liabilities ÷ Total Equity

A high ratio indicates that a business is mostly financed through debt, while a low ratio indicates that a business is primarily financed through equity. The debt-to-equity ratio can vary among industries, so comparisons of ratios among companies within the same industry should be made.

Lenders and investors look at the debt-to-equity ratio to assess risk. Lenders usually prefer low debt-to-equity ratios. A high debt-to-equity ratio indicates that a company may not be able to generate enough cash to meet its debt obligations. Thus, a bank runs the risk of not being repaid for its loan.

Equity capital is money invested in a business in return for a share in the profits of the business. Equity capital includes money invested by the owner. Entrepreneurs may seek additional equity capital when they do not qualify for other types of financing and are not able to fully finance their business out of their own savings. Other sources of equity capital include friends, relatives, venture capitalists, and crowdfunding. Equity capital can be raised by issuing stock.

An *initial public offering* (*IPO*) is the first time that the stock of a private company is offered to the public. IPOs often are issued by smaller, younger companies seeking capital to expand. However, they also can be done by large privately owned companies looking to become publicly traded.

Personal Contributions

Many entrepreneurs use their personal savings to finance the start of their business. Investing personal finances can help you get a loan from a bank. By investing your own money, you demonstrate to the bank that you have faith that your business will succeed. When you personally invest a small amount of capital to start and build a company, it is called *bootstrapping.*

Friends and Relatives

Friends and relatives can be a good source of equity capital. They know whether you are trustworthy and a good risk. Because of this, they may be willing to invest more money in your business than other sources in return for a share of the business profits.

FAMOUS ENTREPRENEUR

MARK CUBAN An icon of entrepreneurship and financial success, Mark Cuban became a self-made billionaire by age 40. As with many entrepreneurs, Cuban started at an early age. In high school, he earned money any way he could, but he had a focus on stamp and coin sales. Cuban started offering dance lessons to make college tuition payments. That endeavor soon led him to hosting large disco parties for a cover charge. After college, Cuban formed his own consulting business, MicroSolutions. Cuban was soon a leader in the computer and computer networking industry. In 1990, Cuban sold MicroSolutions to CompuServe for $6 million. Understanding that a new world awaited with the development of the Internet, Cuban and a business partner, Todd Wagner, started AudioNet in 1995, becoming the first website to stream audio content on the Internet. After changing the name to Broadcast.com, the firm went public in 1998 and soon saw its stock reach $200 a share. A year later, Wagner and Cuban sold Broadcast.com to Yahoo!, making Cuban $2 billion richer. In 2000, Cuban purchased NBA's Dallas Mavericks for $285 million.

Since his purchase of the Mavericks, Cuban launched the high-definition TV network "HDNet" (now AXS TV) in 2001, and he co-founded 2929 Entertainment, a film and television producer and distributor, in 2003. He has also ventured into television, producing his own reality show in 2004 and appearing as a "shark" investor on the hit TV series *Shark Tank*.

Why do entrepreneurs often have more than one business venture?

Disney ABC Television Group/Getty Images

THINK CRITICALLY

How did Mark Cuban's past business ventures help him launch new ventures?

Venture Capitalists

Some privately owned companies get financing through venture capitalists. A *venture capitalist* is an individual or a company that makes a living by investing in startup companies. Venture capitalists carefully research opportunities that they believe will make above-average profits. They are usually interested in companies that have the potential of earning hundreds of millions of dollars within a few years. The prospect of a company "going public" by offering shares of stock for sale to the general public also attracts venture capitalists. Because of the desired criteria, many small businesses have trouble attracting the interest of venture capitalists. The first major round of business financing by venture capitalists is the "A" Round Financing.

Crowdfunding

Equity-based crowdfunding is becoming an increasingly popular financing method for many entrepreneurs and small businesses. *Crowdfunding* is the use of the Internet to fund a business venture or project by raising money from a large number of people. The idea behind crowdfunding is to convince enough people to contribute to reach a target amount.

The funding campaign is typically conducted through a crowdfunding website, or "platform." Those seeking the contributions create an online profile. Their profile typically contains a short video and/or written description of the business venture, the target amount they'd like to raise, and the deadline for reaching the target. Individuals who are interested in supporting the business venture contribute money in exchange for a share of the company's profits.

CHECKPOINT

What is the significance of a business's debt-to-equity ratio?

LO 9.1-3   Debt Capital

Debt capital is money loaned to a business with the understanding that the money will be repaid within a certain time period, usually with interest. You can borrow money from friends, relatives, and banks.

Friends and Relatives

Serg Zastavkin/Shutterstock.com

What are the pros and cons of borrowing money from family and friends?

If friends and relatives are not interested in investing in your business with equity capital, they may be willing to loan you money. Before borrowing from a friend or relative, you should consider how the loan may affect your relationship. If you take a loan from friends or relatives, you should prepare a formal agreement that spells out the terms of the loan. Be sure both you and the individuals loaning the money understand exactly how much interest and principal you will pay each month. Also, specify what your obligations are to pay back the loan if your business is not successful. Sometimes someone who invests in small startups or entrepreneurs is called an *angel investor*.

Commercial Bank Loans

Most businesses take out loans from banks. Entrepreneurs usually have an established relationship with a bank and begin looking for funds there. There are different types of loans that banks offer their customers.

SECURED LOANS   Loans that are backed by collateral are called secured loans. **Collateral** is property that the borrower forfeits if he or she defaults on the loan. Banks demand collateral so that they have some recourse if the borrower fails to repay the loan. For example, suppose you take out a $25,000 business loan and use your home as collateral. If you fail to repay the loan, the bank has the right to take ownership of your home and sell it to collect the money that you owe. Banks accept different forms of collateral, including real estate, savings accounts, life insurance policies, stocks, and bonds.

Types of secured loans include the following:

1. **Line of credit**   An agreement by a bank to lend up to a certain amount of money whenever the borrower needs it is called a *line of credit*. Banks will charge a fee for this program whether or not money is actually borrowed. In addition, they will charge interest on the borrowed funds. Most businesses establish lines of credit so that funds are readily available to help them make purchases when necessary.
2. **Long-term loan**   A loan payable over a period longer than a year is a *long-term loan*. Long-term loans are generally made to help a business make improvements that will boost profits.
3. **Short-term loan**   A loan payable within one year is a *short-term loan*.
4. **Accounts receivable financing**   Many businesses allow their customers to charge merchandise and services and pay for them later. The balances owed by customers are called the business's *accounts receivable*. A bank usually will loan a business up to 85 percent of the total value of its accounts receivable if it feels its customers are good credit risks. The interest rate for accounts receivable financing is often higher than for other types of loans.
5. **Inventory financing**   When banks use a business's inventory as collateral for a loan, it is called *inventory financing*. Banks usually require that the value of the inventory be at least double the amount of the loan and that the business has already paid its vendors in full for the inventory. Banks are often not eager to make this kind of loan. If the business defaults, the bank ends up with inventory it may have trouble reselling.

UNSECURED LOANS   Loans that are not guaranteed with collateral are unsecured loans. These loans are made only to the bank's most creditworthy customers. Unsecured loans are usually made for very specific purposes. They are usually short-term loans that have to be repaid within a year. Unsecured lines of credit are also available for those who have good credit.

REASONS A BANK MAY NOT LEND MONEY   Banks use various guidelines to determine whether borrowers are a good risk. Some of the main reasons that banks turn down loan applicants include the following:

1. **The business is a startup.** Banks are often reluctant to lend money to startup businesses because new businesses have no record of repaying loans and could be at risk for default.
2. **Lack of a solid business plan.** Banks evaluate businesses based on their business plans. A company with a poorly written or poorly conceived business plan will not be able to obtain financing from a bank.
3. **Lack of adequate experience.** Banks want to be sure that the people setting up or running a business know what they are doing. You will have to show that you are familiar with the industry and have the management experience to run your own business.
4. **Lack of confidence in the borrower.** Even if your business plan looks solid and you have adequate experience, you may fail to qualify for financing if you make a bad impression on your banker. Make sure you dress and behave professionally, show up on time for appointments, and provide all information that your banker requests.
5. **Inadequate investment.** Banks are suspicious of entrepreneurs who do not invest their own money in the business.

Other Sources of Loans

Many government agencies can assist you with debt capital loans.

1. **Small Business Administration (SBA)**   The SBA offers a number of loan programs to assist entrepreneurs and small businesses. It does not make direct loans. Rather, it sets the guidelines for loans, which are made by its lending partners, such as banks and credit unions. The SBA guarantees that a percentage of these loans will be repaid. To receive an SBA-guaranteed loan, a business must meet certain eligibility requirements.
2. **Small Business Investment Companies (SBICs)**   SBICs are privately owned and operated investment firms that are licensed by the SBA to make loans to and invest capital with entrepreneurs.
3. **Department of Housing and Urban Development (HUD)**   HUD provides grants to cities to help improve impoverished areas. Cities use these grants to make loans to private developers, who in turn must use the loans to finance projects in needy areas.
4. **Economic Development Administration (EDA)**   The EDA is a division of the U.S. Department of Commerce that partners with distressed communities throughout the United States to foster job creation, collaboration, and innovation by lending money to businesses that operate in and benefit economically distressed parts of the country. Borrowing from the EDA is similar to borrowing from the SBA, but the application is more complicated, and the restrictions are tighter.

DID YOU KNOW?

In 2014, the SBA approved 52,044 loans in the amount of $19.19 billion to small businesses. Loans made to women increased by 14 percent over the previous year.

5. **State and Local Governments** Most states have economic development agencies and finance authorities that make or guarantee loans to small businesses. City, county, or municipal governments sometimes also make loans to local businesses.

Settlement Documents

Once financing is settled, a startup typically creates a *capitalization table*. This is a spreadsheet that shows the company's capitalization, or ownership stakes. Another document is the *term sheet*, which sets the conditions under which an investment will be made. This is done to ensure that the parties involved concur on major aspects of the agreement to lessen the likelihood of disputes.

 CHECKPOINT

Why might a bank turn down a business loan applicant?

 9.1 ASSESSMENT

THINK ABOUT IT

1. What are some of the challenges you might encounter if you get equity financing from friends and/or family members?

2. Why is a secured loan easier to get than an unsecured loan?

3. Why would a bank be more willing to grant an SBA-guaranteed loan to a new business?

MAKE ACADEMIC CONNECTIONS

4. **MATH** Tisha Appleton obtained an SBA-guaranteed loan from her bank for $45,000 for her new business. The SBA guaranteed 75 percent of the loan. How much does the bank risk losing if Tisha's business fails?

5. **COMMUNICATION** In one paragraph, summarize why a personal financial statement would be important for a bank to review when granting loan requests.

Teamwork

You want to start a home remodeling business. You need money to purchase tools and equipment and a new truck. Work in small groups to identify sources of financing. Role-play a scenario in which you meet with a potential investor. Explain your business idea and your need for funds, and make a request for funding.

The Essential Question Refer to The Essential Question on p. 250. Entrepreneurs can assess their financial needs by making a list of startup costs and creating a personal financial statement. They can use their own savings to finance the business or obtain money from friends, relatives, venture capitalists, crowdfunding sites, banks, and various government agencies.

9.2 PRO FORMA FINANCIAL STATEMENTS

The Essential Question Why is it essential for a new business to prepare pro forma financial statements?

LEARNING OBJECTIVES

LO 9.2-1 Prepare a pro forma cash flow statement.

LO 9.2-2 Prepare a pro forma income statement.

LO 9.2-3 Prepare pro forma balance sheet.

KEY TERMS

- cash flow statement
- income statement
- balance sheet
- accounts receivable
- accounts payable

FOCUS ON SMALL BUSINESS

Show me the money!

"So, Monty, how much money do you think your business will make?" asked Sarah. "And I'm supposed to know that how?" Monty replied. "Well, take a look at your pro forma financial statements," Sarah answered. "Well, Sarah, once again you are showing me how much I don't know!"

"There are financial statements you should prepare to help you estimate the finances of your business," Sarah responded. "The pro forma income statement estimates how much money will come in, how much you will spend, and the amount of any projected profit or loss. Some people even call it a profit/loss statement. There's also a pro forma cash flow statement and balance sheet. Come on, Monty, we've got work to do."

WORK AS A TEAM What types of information do you think that a business owner can get from pro forma financial statements? Why do you think pro forma financial statements should be included as part of a business plan?

Financial statements show how well your business is doing.

Andresr/Shutterstock.com

LO 9.2-1 Cash Flow Statement

Financial statements are important when you are trying to raise capital for your business. The financial statements you prepare for your business plan are pro forma financial statements and are based on projections. The cash flow statement, income statement, and balance sheet all tell you something different about the condition of your business.

For many, the cash flow statement is the most important financial statement. A **cash flow statement** is an accounting report that describes the way cash flows into and out of your business over a period of time. Because it deals with actual cash coming in and going out of a business, it shows how much money you have available to pay your bills and whether you have enough money to continue operating.

Forecast Receipts and Disbursements

To create a pro forma cash flow statement, you will need to estimate your monthly cash receipts and monthly cash disbursements. Cash receipts include cash sales, collected accounts receivable, tax refunds, and funds from bank loans and investors. When you forecast the amount of your cash receipts, you need to analyze the demand for each of your products and services. You also need to know the price you will charge for each item.

Felicia Walters estimates her total cash sales for her lighting fixture store by multiplying the quantity of each type of product she expects to sell by the price she has set for each item. In addition, Felicia estimates her other monthly cash receipts as shown below.

FORECASTED RECEIPTS
Walters Electric
January 20—

Cash sales

	Quantity Sold	Price	Total
CFL bulbs	20	$ 15	$ 300
Indoor light fixtures	10	155	1,550
Outdoor lights	6	175	1,050
Subtotal			$2,900
Accounts receivable			$ 300
Bank loan			$1,000
Total			$4,200

© Cengage Learning

Cash disbursements may include payments for cost of goods (what you pay manufacturers or wholesalers to get products and services to sell), accounts payable (credit accounts with suppliers), rent, salaries, taxes, office supplies, utilities, insurance, advertising, loans, and other expenses. Felicia's estimated monthly cash disbursements are shown in the table to the right.

Prepare the Cash Flow Statement

After making projections of cash receipts and disbursements, you can prepare your cash flow statement. You should create monthly pro forma cash flow statements for the first year of operation and annual statements for the second and third years to give your lender an estimate of your cash flow over time.

FORECASTED DISBURSEMENTS
Walters Electric
January 20—

Disbursement	Amount
Cost of goods	$2,400
Rent	900
Utilities	100
Salaries	2,000
Advertising	700
Supplies	100
Insurance	75
Payroll taxes	175
Other	50
Total	$6,500

© Cengage Learning

PRO FORMA CASH FLOW STATEMENT
Walters Electric
January–June 20—

	Jan	Feb	Mar	Apr	May	June
Cash receipts	$4,200	$5,410	$5,750	$6,320	$7,375	$8,130
Cash disbursements						
Cost of goods	$2,400	$2,520	$2,520	$2,640	$3,300	$3,480
Rent	900	900	900	900	900	900
Utilities	100	100	100	100	100	100
Salaries	2,000	2,000	2,000	2,000	2,000	2,000
Advertising	700	700	700	700	700	700
Supplies	100	115	130	150	150	150
Insurance	75	75	75	75	75	75
Payroll taxes	175	175	175	175	175	175
Other	50	50	50	50	50	50
Total disbursements	$6,500	$6,635	$6,650	$6,790	$7,450	$7,630
Cash Flow	−$2,300	−$1,225	−$ 900	−$ 470	−$ 75	$ 500

© Cengage Learning

Net cash flow is the difference between cash receipts and cash disbursements.

Cash receipts − Cash disbursements = Net cash flow

If cash receipts total more than cash disbursements, your business has a positive cash flow. You can put this money in the bank, pay down debt, or use it to expand your business. If cash disbursements total more than cash receipts, your business has a negative cash flow. You may have to borrow money or ask your creditors to give you more time to pay. Preparing pro forma statements helps you to anticipate when negative cash flows will occur, so you can plan for how to handle or avoid them. Felicia Walters' pro forma cash flow statement for the first six months is shown above.

Many entrepreneurs create two cash flow statements: one based on a worst-case scenario and the other based on a best-case scenario. For a worst-case scenario, you should project lower cash receipts and higher cash disbursements than you think you will have. For a best-case scenario, you should project the highest cash receipts and lowest cash disbursements that your business is likely to have.

Economic Effects on Cash Flow

Changes in the economy can have a dramatic effect on the cash flow of a business. During good economic times, many businesses see large amounts of cash flowing into their companies and experience positive cash flows. However, economic slowdowns cause many businesses to experience negative cash flows. When making projections, business owners should look at economic forecasts. Remembering that changing economic conditions can affect cash flows, it is best to err on the side of caution and make conservative estimates.

LO 9.2-2   Income Statement

An income statement shows the business's revenues and expenses incurred over a period of time and the resulting profit or loss. For this reason, it is sometimes called the *profit/loss statement*. An income statement helps you:

1. Examine how sales, expenses, and income are changing over time.
2. Forecast how well your business can expect to perform in the future.
3. Analyze your costs to determine where you may need to cut back.
4. Identify categories of expenditures you may want to increase or decrease, such as advertising.

While the cash flow statement deals with actual cash coming in and going out, the income statement shows revenues that you have not yet received and expenses that you have not yet paid. For example, suppose Walters Electric sells $5,000 worth of lighting in June. The company's monthly income statement would show income of $5,000. Felicia may not actually have received $5,000, because some customers may have paid on credit and will not make payments until July or August.

Customers are not the only people who defer payments. Felicia may purchase $1,500 worth of merchandise to sell but wait 30 days to pay the invoice. Because no cash has been paid for this purchase, it will not appear on the cash flow statement. In contrast, the income statement will show that Felicia incurred an expense of $1,500.

Prepare a Pro Forma Income Statement

Preparing a pro forma income statement for a number of years will help lenders see the long-term growth of your business. The pro forma income statement consists of the following parts:

- **Revenue**   The money that a company receives from its normal business operations is revenue. A business that manufactures a product receives revenue when it sells the product. A service business receives revenue when it performs a service for a customer. Interest earned from bank accounts and investments is also considered revenue.
- **Cost of goods sold**   The cost of the inventory that a business sells during a particular period is called cost of goods sold. Only businesses that have inventory will have this item on their income statements.
- **Gross profit**   The difference between revenue and cost of goods sold is the gross profit.

Why should a business estimate the amount of revenue it expects to earn?

PRO FORMA INCOME STATEMENT
Walters Electric, 20—

Item	Year 2	Year 3
Revenue	$115,000	$125,000
Cost of goods sold	55,400	60,000
Gross profit	$ 59,600	$ 65,000
Operating expenses:		
Salaries	$ 26,705	$ 27,315
Rent	10,800	10,800
Utilities	1,230	1,260
Advertising	1,200	1,200
Insurance	900	900
Supplies	600	615
Other	615	615
Total operating expenses	$ 42,050	$ 42,705
Net income before taxes	$ 17,550	$ 22,295
Taxes	7,020	8,918
Net income/loss after taxes	$ 10,530	$ 13,377

© Cengage Learning

- **Operating expenses** The costs necessary to operate a business are the operating expenses. They include salaries, rent, utilities, advertising, insurance, supplies, and other expenses. All businesses pay operating expenses.
- **Net income before taxes** Net income before taxes is the amount remaining after cost of goods sold and operating expenses are subtracted from revenue. It shows how much you earned before taxes.
- **Taxes** Taxes are usually listed separately from other expenses.
- **Net income/loss after taxes** After taxes are subtracted, the result is the net income or loss for the period.

Felicia Walters' pro forma income statement for years 2 and 3 is shown above.

 CHECKPOINT

What does an income statement show?

LO 9.2-3 Balance Sheet

A **balance sheet** is a financial statement that lists what a business owns, what it owes, and how much it is worth at a particular point in time. It does so by identifying the assets, liabilities, and owner's equity of the business. It is based on the accounting equation:

$$Assets = Liabilities + Owner's\ Equity$$

Assets are items of value owned by a business. They include items such as cash, equipment, and inventory. Liabilities are amounts that a business owes to others. They include loans and outstanding invoices. Owner's equity is the amount remaining after the value of all liabilities is subtracted from the value of all assets. A business that has more assets than liabilities has positive net worth. A business that has more liabilities than assets has negative net worth.

Prepare a Pro Forma Balance Sheet

You must estimate the amount of assets, liabilities, uncollectible accounts, and asset depreciation when preparing a pro forma balance sheet for your business. Felicia Walters' pro forma balance sheet is on the next page.

PRO FORMA BALANCE SHEET
Walters Electric
December 31, 20—

Assets		Liabilities	
Current assets		*Current liabilities*	
Cash	$ 1,000	Accounts payable	$12,000
Accounts receivable	8,000		
Less allowance for			
uncollectible accounts	–500	*Long-term liabilities*	
Inventory	14,000	Loans payable	$17,900
Total current assets	$22,500	**Total liabilities**	$29,900
Fixed assets			
Equipment	$ 8,975		
Less depreciation	–1,795		
Furniture	2,200		
Less depreciation	–220	**Owner's Equity**	
Vehicles	18,000		
Less depreciation	–3,600	Felicia Walters	$16,160
Total fixed assets	$23,560	**Total liabilities and**	
Total assets	$46,060	**owner's equity**	$46,060

TYPES OF ASSETS   Businesses usually separate assets into current assets and fixed assets. *Current assets*, often referred to as *liquid assets* because they can be converted to cash easily, include cash, inventory, and items that are used up in normal business operations, such as supplies. Another special type of current asset is accounts receivable. **Accounts receivable** are the amounts owed to a business by its credit customers. Accounts receivable are usually collected from customers within a few months and then converted into cash. *Fixed assets*, also referred to as *illiquid assets* because they cannot be converted into cash easily, are those that will be used for many years. They include buildings, furniture, and computers.

TYPES OF LIABILITIES   Businesses usually separate liabilities into long-term liabilities and current liabilities. *Long-term liabilities* are debts that are payable over a year or longer. A mortgage is a type of long-term liability. *Current liabilities* are debts that are due to be paid in full in less than a year. A special kind of current liability is accounts payable. **Accounts payable** are amounts owed to vendors for merchandise purchased on credit. Businesses can usually choose to pay later for merchandise they receive now. Because a business generally pays invoices from vendors within 30 to 90 days, accounts payable are a current liability.

REDUCTIONS IN ASSETS   Some customers will fail to pay for the merchandise they purchased on credit. The amount that a company estimates it will not receive from customers is known as the *allowance for uncollectible accounts*. This amount should be subtracted from the assets.

Business equipment will lose value over time just as a car loses value as it gets older. The lowering of an asset's value to reflect its current worth is called *depreciation*. Estimates for uncollectible accounts and depreciation should be included to ensure that the balance sheet provides an accurate picture of the business's net worth.

 CHECKPOINT

What is the accounting equation and how does it affect the balance sheet?

 9.2 ASSESSMENT

THINK ABOUT IT

1. What are the various types of revenue for a business?

2. What is the difference between a liquid asset and an illiquid asset and between a current liability and a long-term liability? Provide an example of each.

3. Green Golf Course has a positive cash flow only six months out of the year. What should the owner do with the extra cash during these months?

MAKE ACADEMIC CONNECTIONS

4. **PROBLEM SOLVING** You are trying to save money to buy a new tablet computer within the next six months. Create a pro forma cash flow statement to project your cash receipts and cash disbursements over the next six months. Do you project a positive cash flow? If not, how can you improve your cash flow?

5. **MATH** In May, Yoder's Bookstore had revenue of $5,000, cost of goods sold of $3,000, operating expenses of $800, and taxes of $400. Calculate Yoder's gross profit and final net income or loss.

6. **MATH** At the end of its first year of operations, Berganstein Sportswear had current assets of $13,000, fixed assets of $25,000, current liabilities of $7,000, and long-term liabilities of $14,000. What is the amount of owner's equity?

Teamwork

Working in a small group, research the current state and future forecasts of the U.S. economy. Prepare a brief presentation using visual aids to share what you have learned. Based on your findings, predict how the current state and future forecasts of the economy could affect the cash flow of a new business now and in coming years.

The Essential Question Refer to The Essential Question on p. 258. Each pro forma financial statement tells the owner something different about the projected finances of the business.

RECORDKEEPING FOR BUSINESSES

The Essential Question Why must entrepreneurs establish, maintain, and analyze appropriate accounting and business records?

LEARNING OBJECTIVES

LO 9.3-1 Differentiate between alternative methods of accounting.

LO 9.3-2 Describe the use of journals and ledgers in a recordkeeping system.

LO 9.3-3 Explain the importance of keeping accurate and up-to-date bank, payroll, and tax records.

KEY TERMS

- transaction
- journals
- account
- check register
- payroll

Keep it all straight.

After securing financing for his business, Monty was ready to get started. He purchased equipment and supplies and set up meetings with potential clients. Two months into his business, he was very surprised to find a notice from his bank informing him that he had written checks from a bank account that had no funds.

"How did this happen?" he asked Sarah. "Did you reconcile your bank statement last month? Have you been recording your business transactions and keeping your business records?" Sarah responded. Judging by Monty's puzzled look, Sarah knew the answer.

"Monty, financial recordkeeping is very important for a business owner. We need to get you some help from an accountant. In the meantime, I'll give you a few lessons in basic recordkeeping."

WORK AS A TEAM

Why do you think financial recordkeeping is essential to the success of a business? What types of records do business owners need to keep?

FOCUS ON SMALL BUSINESS

Good recordkeeping keeps everything in balance.

Africa Studio/Shutterstock.com

LO 9.3-1 Cash or Accrual Accounting Methods

The cash method and the accrual method are the two principal methods of reporting a business's revenue and expenses. The major difference between the two methods is the timing of when transactions, including sales and purchases, are recorded.

Cash Method

Under the *cash method*, revenue is not recorded until money (cash or a check) is actually received, and expenses are not recorded until they are actually paid. For example, if your home remodeling business installed windows in October but you did not receive the payment from the customer until December, you would not record the revenue until December. The cash flow statement is prepared using the cash method.

Accrual Method

Under the *accrual method*, transactions are recorded when the order is placed, the item is delivered, or the service is provided, regardless of when the money is actually received or paid. In other words, revenue is recorded when the sale occurs, and expenses are recorded when you receive the goods or services. You don't have to wait until you receive the money or pay money to record the transaction. If the accrual method is used in the home remodeling example above, you would record the revenue in October when you completed the work, not in December.

Choosing an Accounting Method

Typically, only very small businesses use the cash method. The accrual method is used by most companies because it offers a better picture of long-term profitability. The cash method does not report expenses that have been incurred but not yet paid and revenue that has been earned but not yet received. This distorts a company's profitability. Most small businesses (with sales of less than $5 million a year) are free to adopt either accounting method. However, a business must use the accrual method if:

- it has sales of more than $5 million a year, or
- it stocks an inventory of items that will be sold to the public and has sales over $1 million a year.

CHECKPOINT

What is the main difference between the cash and accrual methods of accounting?

LO 9.3-2 Recording Transactions

A transaction is any business activity that changes assets, liabilities, or net worth. Accurate recordkeeping of your business transactions will help you keep track of how much money you have earned, how much money you have spent, how much money you owe, and how much customers owe you. It will also help you create financial statements to determine your business's net worth and how much profit you have made.

Journals

Journals are accounting records of the transactions you make. There are five different journals that businesses use to record their transactions.

1. **Sales journal** This journal is used to record only sales of merchandise on account. Merchandise sold on account means that customers receive goods or services now that they will pay for later.
2. **Cash payments journal** This journal is used to record only cash payment transactions. Any cash, check, or electronic payment that a business makes is recorded in this journal.
3. **Cash receipts journal** This journal is used to record only cash receipt transactions. Cash sales and cash payments received from customers on their credit accounts are recorded in this journal.
4. **Purchases journal** This journal is used to record only purchases of merchandise on account. If you receive supplies today but pay for them later, you should record this transaction in the purchases journal.
5. **General journal** This journal is used to record any kind of transaction. Some businesses use a general journal to record all transactions, whereas some businesses use the general journal to record transactions that do not fit in the other four journals described above.

Ledgers

Businesses also use a general ledger that is made up of accounts. An **account** is an accounting record that provides financial detail for a particular business item, such as for cash, sales, rent, and utilities. The general ledger will have an account for every type of asset, liability, revenue, expense, and so forth. Transactions entered into the journals are posted, or transferred, to the general ledger accounts affected by the transactions, as shown in the ledger to the right. Posting is generally done every one to two days to keep the ledger current. The balances in the accounts will help you prepare the financial statements you will need to run your business effectively.

© Cengage Learning

SUBSIDIARY LEDGERS Some businesses choose to keep a more detailed record of certain general ledger accounts in a separate, supporting subsidiary ledger. A subsidiary ledger is commonly used for accounts payable to show in detail the transactions with each vendor from whom merchandise is purchased on account. Each vendor will have its own account showing transaction history and the current balance owed. A subsidiary ledger is also commonly used for accounts receivable with separate accounts showing each customer's transaction history and current balance due.

Why is it important to keep track of business transactions?

Kim Smith is the owner of Photo Memories. She wants to use subsidiary ledgers for accounts payable and accounts receivable to keep detailed records of transactions with her suppliers and customers. The detailed information in these subsidiary ledgers will be summarized and transferred to the accounts payable and accounts receivable accounts in the general ledger. The subsidiary ledgers make it easy for Kim to see at a glance her transactions with suppliers and customers.

AGING TABLES An *aging table* is a recordkeeping tool for tracking accounts receivable. It shows a business how long it is taking customers to pay their bills. Because accounts receivable can affect a company's cash flow positively or negatively, the collection period should be closely monitored to identify problem customers.

Kim can see by her aging table that one customer is more than 61 days past due on a bill. She decides not to ship this customer any more merchandise until he pays the outstanding bill.

Customer	Amount	0–30 days	31–60 days	Over 61 days
E. Kwon	$175.23	$175.23		
P. Mossett	$106.20		$106.20	
M. Stern	$82.34			$82.34
Totals	$363.77	$175.23	$106.20	$82.34
Percent of total	100%	48%	29%	23%

© Cengage Learning

✔ CHECKPOINT

What is the difference between a journal and a ledger?

LO 9.3-3 Business Records

Good recordkeeping can help you make smart business decisions. Incomplete or inaccurate records can cause you to mismanage your business or can cause serious legal problems. You will need to keep accurate banking, payroll, and tax records. These records may be kept manually or electronically.

Banking Records

You will need to open a separate checking account for your business. You will use your business account for all deposits and withdrawals related to your business.

When you open your checking account, you will receive a set of checks and a check register. A **check register** is a booklet in which you record the dates and amounts of the checks as well as the names of people or businesses to whom you have written the checks. You can also maintain a check register electronically using computer software.

What Went *Wrong?*

Don't Put All Your Eggs in One Basket

Billy Wong started Japanese Car Parts Distributors (JCP). The business grew, and in ten years it had 12 employees, thousands of parts in inventory, and hundreds of customers across the country.

Billy kept handwritten records for the business. Before long, his 18-year-old, computer-whiz son, Tommy, wouldn't let him ignore the advantages of computerizing his recordkeeping. So Billy gave Tommy the task of setting up a computer system and transferring the accounts, inventory, and financial information from his paper records to the new electronic format. Within a year, Billy stopped keeping handwritten records in favor of the computerized system. The business ran more smoothly than ever.

Tragedy struck the business one night when Tommy found robbers in the business office. Tommy was badly injured by the thieves and, sadly, he died. If this wasn't enough for Billy to handle, the thieves also stole the office computer.

Billy had left all the electronic recordkeeping to his son, and he had no idea whether Tommy had made backup copies of all the files that had been stored on the stolen computer. Billy found that it would take months of work and a large sum of money to set up a new computerized recordkeeping system.

imtmphoto/iStockphoto.com

Backing up computer files can prevent problems.

THINK CRITICALLY

1. Was Billy wrong to trust his young son with so much responsibility?
2. Would JCP's problems have been solved if the stolen computer had been found?

BALANCE YOUR ACCOUNT Every time you write a check, transfer money electronically, or make a deposit or withdrawal, you should balance your check register. Balancing your check register is important because it will prevent you from accidentally writing checks when you do not have enough money in your account to cover them. Writing bad checks is illegal. If your checks do not clear, your suppliers may stop shipping merchandise to you. Businesses and banks will charge you fees on accounts that have insufficient funds. If you use a computer program to keep your checkbook register, it will automatically balance your account after each transaction is recorded.

RECONCILE YOUR ACCOUNT Every month you will receive a bank statement that shows all of your deposits, checks paid, electronic money transfers, and bank fees. The bank statement balance will not be the same as your check register balance because of checks you have written that have not cleared the bank, deposits you have made after the bank statement was prepared, or bank fees you have not recorded in your check register. Thus, when you receive your bank statement, you should *reconcile* it with your check register to ensure your bank balance is accurate. There is often a bank reconciliation form on the back of the bank statement or on the bank's website that you can use to reconcile your account, or you can use a computer program.

Payroll Records

If you have employees working for you, you will have to maintain payroll records. A **payroll** is a list of people who receive salary or wage payments from a business. The payroll records will show how much your employees have earned during each pay period. They will also show deductions that may have been made from those earnings for taxes and benefits. There are many computer programs that can help you maintain these records. There are also many payroll service companies with which you can contract to handle payroll processing for you.

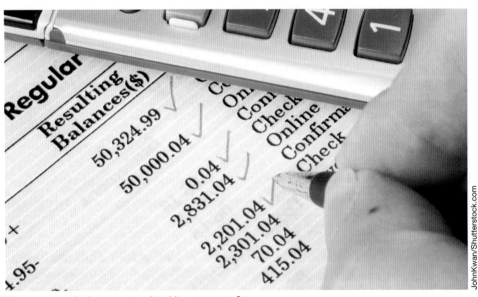

How can you balance your checking account?

You will need to complete a payroll register for every pay period. The register will include the following information for each employee:

- Employee name
- Number of hours worked
- Regular and overtime earnings
- Federal, state, and local taxes deducted
- Social Security and Medicare contributions deducted
- Deductions for benefits, such as health insurance, life insurance, and retirement savings plans.

After you create the payroll register, you will prepare payroll checks. Most businesses use voucher checks for their payrolls. *Voucher checks* have a statement of earnings and deductions attached to them. The statement shows employees how their pay was calculated.

Tax Records

You will have to make several different kinds of tax payments as a business owner. These include income taxes and payroll taxes, and may also include sales taxes.

INCOME TAX   Businesses that earn profits must pay income tax. These taxes are paid quarterly, or every three months. Income tax must be prepaid at the beginning of a quarter, so you will need to estimate your income taxes. If you fail to make these payments or you underestimate how much tax is due, you may have to pay a penalty. You could also be subject to criminal penalties for tax fraud.

PAYROLL TAXES AND DEDUCTIONS   By law, you are required to deduct taxes from your employees' paychecks and submit these taxes to the government. As an employer, you are also required to pay unemployment insurance taxes and a portion of Social Security and Medicare taxes based on the earnings of your employees. Your employees may ask you to take voluntary deductions from their earnings to cover health, dental, or vision insurance. If you deduct this money from employees' earnings, you are required to send it to the companies that are providing the insurance coverage.

SALES TAX   In most states, retail businesses are required to charge sales tax on goods or services. If you own a business that collects sales tax, every month you will have to deposit the tax you collect into a special bank account that belongs to the government. Sales taxes are based on a percentage of sales. The actual percentage charged varies from state to state and can vary within a state if the local county or city also assesses a sales tax.

 BE YOUR OWN BOSS

You own a home remodeling business in your community. You have one full-time employee working for you. Research the types of federal, state, and local taxes you will need to withhold from your employee's paycheck. Create a table listing the types of taxes to withhold. For each one, describe how you would determine the amount of taxes to withhold.

9.3 ASSESSMENT

THINK ABOUT IT

1. Why might a business prefer to use the accrual method instead of the cash method to record revenue and expenses?

2. Eliza Conner owns a small clothing boutique. Eliza uses her personal checking account for both business and personal needs. How would you convince Eliza that she should open a separate bank account for her business?

3. Why is it important to keep accurate payroll records?

MAKE ACADEMIC CONNECTIONS

4. **MATH** Scott Belville, owner of Flowers on Main, completed an aging table for his accounts receivable, similar to the one found on page 268. The column totals are shown below. Complete the "Percent of total" row for Scott. (Round answers to the nearest whole percent.)

Customer	Amount	0–30 Days	31–60 Days	Over 60 Days
Totals	$6,500	$2,300	$3,100	$1,100
Percent of total	__?__	__?__	__?__	__?__

5. **COMMUNICATION** Assume that you are Kim Smith, the owner of Photo Memories. Look at the aging table on page 268. You have decided that no more orders will be filled for Mark Stern until his account balance is paid in full. Write a letter to Mr. Stern to inform him of your decision. Provide payment options to help Mr. Stern pay off his account balance.

Teamwork

Working with team members, discuss the pros and cons of maintaining electronic records versus manual records for your business. What are some ways to resolve the cons of maintaining electronic records? Which method do you think is best? Why?

The Essential Question Refer to The Essential Question on p. 265. Accounting and business records help owners keep track of how much money they have earned and spent as well as how much they owe and are owed. Good record-keeping prevents mismanagement and allows owners to make smarter business decisions.

Sharpen Your 21st Century Entrepreneurial Skills

Online and Mobile Banking

Financial institutions are making their services more and more convenient and available for their customers. First there were ATMs, then online banking using a personal computer, and now mobile banking using a smartphone or other mobile device. As an entrepreneur, you will benefit from the flexibility and speed of handling your financial transactions online.

With online and mobile banking, you can make deposits and withdrawals, transfer funds from one account to another, view cleared checks and pending transactions, apply for a loan, pay a bill, and view the history of transactions and bank statements. You can even locate a nearby ATM or bank office, if you care to step into a brick-and-mortar building. You will need to download your bank's mobile app to complete some of these transactions.

Some banks offer specialized banking apps. For example, your bank's app may be able to track your location and send you special deals for restaurants and stores that you're near. Other apps allow you to send money to someone by entering the recipient's mobile number or email address. One helpful banking app helps you track your spending by allowing you to view and categorize every dollar you spend from your bank accounts.

To begin banking online, you will need to enroll in your bank's online banking service. You'll need a user name and a password. To help keep your account safe from hackers and thieves, create a sound password. Avoid using your initials or birthday. Use a combination of letters and numbers, and do change your password often. Most banks will ask you a few security questions that you'll need to answer. For example, the question may ask for the name of your best friend or your mother's maiden name.

Once logged in, you can set up email and/or text alerts that will tell you when your account balance reaches a certain amount or a payment is due, for example. You will be able to modify your account options at any time. Once enrolled, you'll find online and mobile banking easy and efficient, something every entrepreneur needs and appreciates in a busy day.

TRY IT OUT

Explore how online and mobile banking transactions are completed. If you have a bank account, sign up for online banking and watch a demo. As an alternative, do an online search using the search terms *online banking demo*. After watching the demo, write in your own words how to make a deposit and a withdrawal with both online and mobile banking. Then do an online search for mobile banking apps and list five that you think would be useful for entrepreneurs.

SUMMARY

9.1 Financing Your Business

1. As an entrepreneur, you must prepare a list of startup costs to determine how much money you will need to start your business. You should also prepare a personal financial statement based on the formula: Total assets − Total liabilities = Net worth.

2. Equity capital is money invested in a business in return for a share in the profits of the business. Sources of equity capital include personal contributions, friends and relatives, venture capitalists, and crowdfunding.

3. Debt capital is money loaned to a business that must be repaid within a certain period of time, usually with interest. Sources of debt capital include friends and relatives, commercial banks, and various government agencies such as the SBA. Bank loans may be secured, requiring that you provide collateral, or unsecured.

9.2 Pro Forma Financial Statements

4. The cash flow statement describes the way that cash flows into and out of your business and uses the following basic formula: Cash receipts − Cash disbursements = Net cash flow.

5. The income statement shows the business's revenues and expenses incurred over a period of time and the resulting profit or loss. It can help you forecast how well your business may perform in the future.

6. The balance sheet is a financial statement that lists what a business owns, what it owes, and how much it is worth at a particular point in time and is based on the accounting equation: Assets = Liabilities + Owner's Equity.

9.3 Recordkeeping for Businesses

7. Businesses can use the cash or accrual method for reporting revenue and expenses. The difference between the two methods is the timing of when transactions are recorded.

8. Businesses initially record transactions in journals. The transactions are then posted to accounts in the general ledger. More detailed records of certain general ledger accounts, such as accounts receivable and accounts payable, are kept in a subsidiary ledger.

9. You will need to keep accurate and up-to-date bank, payroll, and tax records. You will need to keep your bank records balanced and prepare a bank reconciliation each month. If you have employees, you will need to prepare a payroll register for every pay period. You will also have to pay income, payroll, and sales taxes at regular intervals.

WHAT DO YOU KNOW NOW?

Read *Ideas in Action* on page 249 again. Then answer the questions a second time. Have your responses changed? If so, how have they changed?

KEY TERMS REVIEW

Match each statement with the term that best defines it. Some terms may not be used.

1. The difference between assets and liabilities
2. Money invested in a business in return for a share in the profits of the business
3. A list of people who receive salary or wage payments from a business
4. An accounting report that describes the way that cash flows into and out of a business
5. Any business activity that changes assets, liabilities, or net worth
6. Amounts owed to a business by its credit customers
7. Amounts you owe to others
8. Money loaned to a business with the understanding that the money will be repaid, usually with interest
9. The relation between the dollars you have borrowed and the dollars you have invested in your business
10. Items of value that you own
11. A financial statement that shows a business's revenues and expenses incurred over a period of time and the resulting profit or loss
12. A financial statement that lists what a business owns, what it owes, and how much it is worth at a particular point in time

a. account
b. accounts payable
c. accounts receivable
d. assets
e. balance sheet
f. cash flow statement
g. check register
h. collateral
i. debt capital
j. debt-to-equity ratio
k. equity capital
l. income statement
m. journals
n. liabilities
o. net worth (owner's equity)
p. payroll
q. transaction

REVIEW YOUR KNOWLEDGE

13. Which of the following would be a startup cost?
    a. computer for a business
    b. monthly utility bill
    c. monthly rent expense
    d. weekly payroll
14. You have decided to try to finance your business with equity financing. Whom should you approach to invest in your business?
    a. local bank
    b. Small Business Administration (SBA)
    c. friends and family
    d. Department of Housing and Urban Development (HUD)
15. Which of the following would most likely be accepted as collateral for a secured loan of $25,000?
    a. $32,000 automobile that is paid for
    b. $12,000 of home equity
    c. $2,500 computer system
    d. apartment that you rent
16. Which of the following is *not* a reason that a bank may reject a loan application?
    a. business is a startup
    b. owner invested $30,000
    c. lack of a business plan
    d. lack of experience
17. **True or False**   Accounts receivable payments that are collected by businesses are converted to cash.

18. **True or False** If your cash receipts are less than your cash disbursements, your business has a negative cash flow.
19. Which of the following would *not* be included on a cash flow statement?
    a. sale to a customer on account
    b. payment received from a customer on account
    c. payment made to a vendor for new equipment
    d. funds of $4,000 received from a bank loan
20. Loans that are guaranteed with property are called ____?____.
21. In which of the following journals would you record a sale of merchandise if the customer pays you cash at the time of the sale?
    a. sales journal
    b. cash payments journal
    c. cash receipts journal
    d. purchases journal
22. **True or False** Taxes that you withhold from employees' paychecks are deposited into your bank account until the employee files an income tax return.
23. A potential investor or bank would want to see all of the following financial documents *except*
    a. cash flow statement
    b. startup costs
    c. personal financial statement
    d. journal

APPLY WHAT YOU LEARNED

24. You plan to open a retail sportswear store. You will hire several employees to help run the store. What types of journals do you need to keep for such a business? Why? What kinds of bank, payroll, and tax records will you have to maintain? How could you use a computer to help you keep and manage your records? (LO 9.3-2, LO 9.3-3)
25. You plan on opening Rashida's Beauty Salon. You have listed your projected monthly revenues, expenses, and taxes below. Prepare a pro forma income statement based on this information. (LO 9.2-2)

Revenue	$15,000	Insurance	$ 750
Cost of goods sold	2,550	Rent	1,000
Supplies	1,100	Utilities	650
Salaries	4,800	Taxes	1,050

MAKE ACADEMIC CONNECTIONS

26. **MATH** You own a store that sells video games. You owe $25,000 to video game vendors; you have a ten-year bank loan of $50,000; your bank account balance is $13,000; you own inventory worth $57,000; you have $2,000 in accounts receivable; and fixed assets are $22,000. What are your total assets, liabilities, and owner's equity? What is your debt-to-equity ratio? (LO 9.1-2, LO 9.2-3)
27. **COMMUNICATION** Conduct a phone interview with the manager of a local bank to find out what kinds of loans the bank offers to small businesses. Specifically, ask about secured loans, unsecured loans, and SBA-guaranteed loans. Write a one-page report on your findings. (LO 9.1-3)

What Would YOU DO?

You are preparing for a meeting with a loan officer to get financing for your new business. As you compile your resume, you think it might appear as if you do not have the adequate experience and skills to run your business successfully. You consider enhancing your resume by adding some additional job experiences that you haven't had in order to make it look better for potential investors and lenders. Do you think it will matter? Do you think anyone will ever actually check your job experiences or references? What might be the result if they do check? What would you do?

BUILD YOUR BUSINESS PLAN PROJECT

This activity will help you continue with the development of a business plan as you prepare your financial plan.

1. Estimate your startup costs for your business and prepare a personal financial statement to determine your net worth.

2. Determine how much money you need to begin your business. Decide if you will obtain equity and/or debt financing. Will you use your savings; raise money through crowdfunding; or borrow from friends and relatives, venture capitalists, a commercial bank, the SBA or other government agency, or a combination of these resources? Write why you think one or more of these financing methods will work for your business.

3. Determine your projected cash receipts and cash disbursements for the first year of your business. Prepare a pro forma cash flow statement. After doing so, prepare pro forma cash flow statements based on worst-case and best-case scenarios.

4. Decide if you will use the cash or accrual method of keeping records of revenue and expenses and explain why. Determine your projected revenue and operating expenses for the first year of your business. Estimate the amount of income taxes you will have to pay. Prepare a pro forma income statement.

5. Make a list of your assets and liabilities. Prepare a pro forma balance sheet.

6. Determine what types of journals you will keep for your business. For each type, give an example of a transaction that will be recorded in that journal. What accounts will your business have?

7. Contact two local banks and obtain information about commercial checking accounts. What are the interest rates? What types of special services or products are offered to small business owners?

8. Create a payroll register for your business. Contact your state and/or local government to find out what taxes must be deducted from employees' pay. Find out how the taxes are calculated. Are there any other deductions that will be made? If your state (or city) collects sales tax, find out what the rate is.

PLANNING A CAREER IN ACCOUNTING

"My brother, an accountant, got tired of the demanding hours required while working at a large accounting firm. Tax season was especially demanding on his family. His wife is an attorney with her own strenuous workload. They decided he should stay home with the kids and start a part-time business as an accountant for small businesses."

Accountants help individuals and corporations manage their finances. They examine financial statements to ensure that they are accurate and comply with laws and regulations and prepare tax returns.

In addition to examining and preparing financial documents, accountants meet with clients to review their findings. In some cases, they may have to prepare written reports.

Many accountants become a certified public accountant (CPA). This enhances job prospects.

Employment Outlook
- An average rate of employment growth is expected.
- Changes in accounting-related legislation will fuel demand for accountants to help corporations meet regulatory requirements.
- CPAs have the best prospects of employment.

Job Titles
- Accounting Manager
- Controller
- Financial Auditor
- Certified Public Accountant (CPA)
- Cost Accountant
- Certified Management Accountant (CMA)

Needed Education/Skills
- A bachelor's degree with a major in accounting or a related field is required.
- Certifications in various accounting specialties exist, such as certified public accountant (CPA) and certified management accountant (CMA). Continuing education is required in most states for those who are certified.
- Strong analytical, math, and communication skills are needed.

What's it like to work in Accounting? Boyd works as an independent accountant. He recently passed the national exam to become a CPA.

It is currently tax season. Today, Boyd is examining the financial records of a local home décor boutique to prepare its tax returns. He will analyze, compare, and interpret information related to the boutique's finances in order to minimize the business's tax liability while complying with laws and regulations. He will also assess the business's financial operations and suggest ways to reduce costs, enhance revenues, and improve profits. Boyd will prepare a written report with his findings and recommendations and present them at a meeting he is having with the owner of the business later this week.

After work, Boyd will attend a class at the local university. The class is a continuing education requirement for CPAs.

What about you? Would you like to help businesses improve their financial performance by helping them manage the financial portions of their business? Would you prefer to work for yourself or for a firm? Why?

Business Financial Plan

All entrepreneurs must have a solid financial plan for their business. Without one, it will be difficult to secure investors or bank loans to help cover startup expenses or expansions.

The FBLA Business Financial Plan is an event for either an individual member or teams of two or three members. For this event, members will use a case study to create a report that will establish and develop a complete financial plan for a business venture.

You are planning to open a one-stop-shop kitchen and cooking store where customers will be able to purchase a variety of items, including kitchen cabinets, cookware, cutlery, food storage containers, and virtually anything relating to kitchen and food preparation. Competition includes hardware stores, furniture stores, discount retailers, department stores, and other smaller kitchen-related stores.

Your niche concept is that everything available in these stores can be purchased in one location where customers can bundle deals on multiple products to save money. You plan to open your facility in a 15,000 square foot, stand-alone store and warehouse. You will need to purchase inventory for the store and stock the warehouse, as well as hire contractors, installers, and truck drivers to assist with the delivery and setup of the building and inventory.

Performance Competencies
- Explain the need for a business loan
- Evaluate the type of loan needed
- Explain the process for obtaining a business loan
- Arrange a report in a logical order in proper business format
- Demonstrate good written communication skills

Go to the FBLA website for more detailed information.

GIVE IT A TRY
Partner up with a classmate. Create a one- to three-page report that addresses the following topics for a financial business plan:

- Company description (overview of the business including type of business, form of ownership, location, goals, etc.)
- Target market
- Competitive analysis
- Financials including projected startup costs and future financial results

When you are finished, present your findings to your classmates for discussion.

www.fbla-pbl.org

Operations Management

10.1 OPERATING PROCEDURES

10.2 INVENTORY CONTROL

10.3 FINANCIAL MANAGEMENT

A Lack of Diversity in the Workplace

atipica.co

Laura Gómez founded Atipica. The name means "atypical" in Esperanto.

Entrepreneur Laura Gómez's personal and professional life was shaped by her childhood. Gómez was an undocumented immigrant from Mexico who arrived in the United States when she was ten years old. Today, she is a U.S. citizen with a bachelor's degree from the University of California at Berkeley and a master's degree from the University of California, San Diego. She has become one of the leading voices in the world of technology.

Gómez's multicultural background helped her succeed in her career. She has worked for well-known high-tech companies, including Hewlett-Packard, YouTube, and Twitter. At Twitter, she was one of the founding members of the international team that localized Twitter in 28 different languages. Gómez managed a team of 16 members that completed the project in less than 8 months. At Jawbone, a developer of human-centered wearable technology and audio devices, Gómez led the internationalization and localization efforts. While employed at these companies, Gómez recognized the lack of diversity. She believes that tech companies need to change their hiring patterns in order to have a more diverse, richer pool of ideas from employees.

Gómez has also started a variety of tech companies, including Digital Playbook, which specializes in brand design and digital sports marketing; Atipica, software-as-service startup that works toward greater diversity in the tech industry; and Vyv, a content-sharing site for the purpose of validating the accuracy of breaking news. One-third of Vyv's staff is female and two-thirds are Latin American or Middle Eastern.

Her commitment to diversity landed Gómez on the board of the Institute for Advanced Technology and Public Policy, where she sits alongside former U.S. Secretary of State George P. Shultz. She has been recognized by the U.S. State Department, *The Business Journals*, *USA Today*, *GQ Mexico*, and *Silicon Valley Latino* for her contributions to the tech industry. With all of her accomplishments, Gómez takes the most pride in helping others. She said, "For me it's really giving back to encourage people of diverse backgrounds, who might otherwise be intimidated, to enter the tech industry."

WHAT DO YOU KNOW?

1. How has Laura Gómez's multicultural background helped shape her professional life?

2. Why does Gómez believe workplace diversity is beneficial?

3. What would Gómez say is her most important accomplishment?

10.1 OPERATING PROCEDURES

The Essential Question How does a small business benefit from effective operating procedures both internally and externally?

LEARNING OBJECTIVES

LO 10.1-1 Define the five functions of management.
LO 10.1-2 Describe five types of policies that should be included in an operations manual.

KEY TERMS

- manager
- management
- organizational structure
- authoritative management
- democratic management
- operations manual

FOCUS ON SMALL
BUSINESS

Make the shift from entrepreneur to manager.

Avery had been running her alterations business alone. The business grew to the point that she was able to hire three employees. Because she now had others to help operate the business, Avery was looking forward to having more free time for herself. She decided to take a vacation.

Two days into her vacation, her cell phone was ringing nonstop. The three employees were fighting among themselves about who was supposed to do what. No one wanted to answer the phone at the shop, and customers were becoming frustrated trying to find out when their clothing alterations would be completed. Avery realized she needed to return home and get her business under control!

WORK AS A TEAM Discuss with your teammates the shift that must be made from entrepreneur to manager when the business hires employees. What skills do you think good managers should have?

Managers are responsible for business operations.

Piotr Marcinski/Shutterstock.com

LO 10.1-1 Management Functions

Once you open your business and have people working for you, you become a manager. A **manager** is the person responsible for planning, organizing, staffing, implementing, and controlling the operations of a business. These are functions that all managers must perform, no matter the size or type of business that they manage. **Management** is the process of achieving goals by establishing operating procedures that make effective use of people and other resources. All functions of management work together and are continuous.

Planning

Planning involves analyzing information, setting goals, and making decisions about what needs to be done to move the business forward. The planning activities must be performed in a timely manner. In business you often hear the saying, "time is money." If you waste time in the planning process, you can lose money for your business. There are three types of planning that should take place in any organization.

DEVELOP YOUR READING SKILLS

Before you begin reading, skim the chapter and note the headings and boldface words. Think about what you will be learning as you read the chapter.

- **Strategic planning**   Setting broad, long-range objectives to achieve the long-term goals of your business is called strategic planning. You should think three to five years ahead when doing strategic planning. Envision where you want your business to be at that time and what it will take to get you there.
- **Intermediate-range planning**   Preparing detailed plans and strategies for achieving goals within a one-year period is intermediate-range planning. You should include target dates for the completion of the tasks that will lead to the accomplishment of your goals.
- **Short-term planning**   Planning for the day-to-day operations of the business to achieve the goals and objectives set in intermediate-range planning is called short-term planning. Rules, policies, procedures, and budgets are important components of short-term planning.

Planning is an ongoing process. Entrepreneurs frequently refer back to their business plan for guidance. Likewise, the planning that you do once your business is up and running will help you maintain focus and keep your business on track. Once plans are in place, it does not mean they must be followed exactly. Plans can be revised as needs change.

Organizing

Organizing is identifying and arranging the work and resources needed to achieve the goals that have been set for your business. Included in the organizing function are the following:

- **Assignment of tasks**   As you start your business, you will have to determine how many employees you will need and what their duties will be.
- **Grouping of tasks into departments**   As your business grows, you will need to organize departments. You will have to decide which tasks are closely related and group them accordingly. Some of the department titles that businesses use include Accounting, Marketing, and Human Resources.
- **Organizational structure**   As your company grows, you will need an **organizational structure**, which is a plan that shows how the various jobs in a company relate to one another. It is often represented in a chart and indicates the working relationships within the business.
- **Allocation of resources across the organization**   Because resources are limited, there must be a plan for distributing and

using the available resources efficiently across the company. This is done by creating budgets based on requests from the departments within the company.

Staffing

Staffing includes all of the activities involved in obtaining, training, and compensating the employees of a business. Because a company is only as good as the people who work for it, the staffing function is critical to the success of a business.

Implementing

Implementing involves directing and leading people to accomplish the goals of the organization. Implementing is accomplished by communicating assignments and instructions to your employees. To effectively implement the work of the organization, managers must develop a management style that will motivate employees to perform at a high level. *Management style* is the way a manager behaves toward and works with employees. Managers use different styles based on the characteristics of the employees being managed, the type of work assignment, and the importance of the work being performed. An experienced and effective manager can change the style as needed.

AUTHORITATIVE MANAGEMENT   A management style in which the manager is directive and controlling is called **authoritative management**. This style is also called *directing* or *autocratic management*. The manager makes the major decisions and closely monitors the work of the employees to be sure the work is done correctly. This management style is often used in a crisis situation when there is not enough time to let the group participate in the decision-making process. It is also appropriate when working with a new group of employees who do not have previous experience in the type of work being performed.

DEMOCRATIC MANAGEMENT   A management style in which employees are involved in decision making and the manager provides less direction is called **democratic management**. This style is also called *participatory management*. A manager of a group of experienced employees who work well together does not have to be directive and controlling. Employees like to be involved in the planning and decision making that affects their work.

MIXED MANAGEMENT   Combining authoritative and democratic management styles is called mixed management. Different employees prefer different management styles. Some employees feel that if they are not involved in the decision-making process, then the manager does not trust them. Others prefer to be told what to do and want someone else to do the day-to-day decision making. An effective manager should be prepared to use mixed management to meet the needs of the business and its employees.

Controlling

Controlling is the process of setting standards for the operation of a business and ensuring that those standards are met. Some of the ways that you can determine if standards are being met are as follows:

- Compare actual revenues and expenses with what was projected
- Observe business operations and determine if they are running effectively
- Inspect products and services to ensure they are meeting performance and quality standards

If standards are not being met, it will be necessary for managers to make changes. Changes may include hiring new employees, upgrading to higher-quality production materials, or increasing the budget for a specific area. You may also decide to change operating procedures such as work processes and work flow. As part of the control function, you will routinely review your plans and make adjustments.

 CHECKPOINT

What are the functions of management?

LO 10.1-2 Operations Manual

As your business grows, you will find that an operations manual is an essential tool for operating your business efficiently. An **operations manual** contains all of the rules, policies, and procedures that a business should follow to function effectively. You can also have a separate *company* or *employee handbook* that details the rules, policies, and procedures that apply to employees. Just as you spent time developing your business plan, it is important to spend time detailing the operations of your business. By having this information in writing, it can be referenced easily and applied consistently to business operations.

Your operations manual should include the rules, policies, and procedures that guide your business practices. *Rules* outline the appropriate behavior and actions of those that work for you. All employees should be treated the same way when it comes to rules. *Policies* serve as guidelines for daily operations. They are established to make the business run efficiently and may apply to both employees and customers. *Procedures* are a series of steps and actions that employees must follow to complete an activity. They are instructions on how to perform a task correctly. Procedures are more specific than rules. As a business owner, it is important to remember that sometimes you have to make exceptions to rules, policies, and procedures because not all situations are the same.

What information should be included in an operations manual?

Operating Policies

You should set daily operating hours that are convenient for your customers. For many years, banks were open Monday through Friday from 9 A.M. to 5 P.M. when most people were working. In order to meet the needs of their working customers, many banks have extended hours to 6 P.M. or 7 P.M. and are open on Saturdays as well.

Customer Service Policies

Customer satisfaction is one of the main goals of any business. Products do not always meet the expectations of customers, and a service might not be performed to the customer's satisfaction the first time. Thus, it is important to have a policy for customers who need to return a product or have a follow-up service. A policy for replacements, refunds, or repairs will help maintain goodwill. Other customer service policies can include payment options regarding cash, checks, and credit cards.

Why is it important for a business to establish customer service policies?

Delivery Policies

Some businesses provide delivery services along with the sale of their products. Delivery is often provided for the convenience of the customer. For example, businesses that sell large appliances often provide delivery service, since most people are unable to transport the appliances themselves. Many restaurants offer delivery service for food. You will need to determine whether you will offer delivery services for the products you sell, whether you will charge a delivery fee, and whether you will guarantee delivery within a certain time frame.

Hiring Policies

A business must have a hiring policy. The policy may specify that all job applicants must complete an employment application and submit a resume and letters of reference. Testing may be required for some positions. Applicants may also have to submit to a background check or even a credit report check. The hiring policy may also specify who makes final hiring decisions.

Safety Policies

It is important that you have policies in place that provide for a safe environment for your customers and employees. Instruction in safety procedures should be part of employee training. Employees should know how to operate equipment safely and be required to wear the necessary protective gear. Employees should also be briefed on emergency plans for fires, tornadoes, and other disasters. Signs should be placed in strategic locations reminding employees of safety procedures in the workplace. You should also provide warnings to customers so that they do not enter employee-only areas. Caution cones can be placed where unsafe conditions exist.

 CHECKPOINT

What are the various policies that should be included in a business's operations manual?

 ASSESSMENT

THINK ABOUT IT

1. Why do you think it might be difficult for some entrepreneurs to become managers?

2. Why do you think it is important for a business to develop an operations manual?

MAKE ACADEMIC CONNECTIONS

3. **PROBLEM SOLVING**   You have been named manager of the children's department of a retail clothing store. Sales are down in the department. There are five employees in your department. Two have been working in the department for three years. The other three are new to the store and have no retail experience. Describe the management style you will use to lead the department.

4. **VISUAL ARTS**   When organizing a small business, a manager needs to consider the business's goals and divide tasks related to those goals among departments. Assume a sporting goods business wants to increase its sales. Develop a goal related to sales for each of the following departments: marketing, human resources, and accounting. Then based on each goal, create a flow chart that identifies tasks (steps) to be completed within each department.

Teamwork

Working in a small group, describe the traits of a perfect manager. Explain why each trait is important.

The Essential Question   Refer to The Essential Question on p. 282. Effective operating procedures benefit a small business internally by allowing the company to run more efficiently and making it easier for employees to do their jobs. This in turn benefits a business externally because employees are able to provide quality service to customers.

10.2 INVENTORY CONTROL

The Essential Question What is inventory, and why is it important for a small business to track and manage its inventory?

LEARNING OBJECTIVES

LO 10.2-1 Prepare a purchasing plan for inventory.

LO 10.2-2 Describe the periodic and perpetual inventory methods.

LO 10.2-3 Determine how much inventory to keep in stock.

KEY TERMS

- periodic inventory method
- perpetual inventory method
- stock card
- point-of-sale software system
- stock turnover rate

FOCUS ON SMALL BUSINESS

How much to buy?

Matthew was starting his own frame store, Matt's Frames. He had previously worked part time in a framing store and had learned a great deal about the business.

Matthew considered how much inventory he would need initially. He knew from experience that the first few months of the year would be slow but that business would pick up as Mother's Day and graduations approached. Business would also pick up in the summer during the height of the wedding season. Another sales peak would occur during the holiday season.

Because he was opening his store in February, Matthew decided he would start out with a small inventory of basic framing supplies and focus on specialty frames that people might want for Valentine's Day. Then he would increase his inventory of frames and frame supplies for the spring and summer seasons.

Business owners must carefully plan to meet inventory needs.

WORK AS A TEAM Do you think that Matthew is doing the right thing by starting out with only basic framing supplies? Why do you think he intends to increase his supplies as spring and summer approach?

LO 10.2-1 Meet Inventory Needs

Inventory is the stock of goods that a business has for sale. Successful inventory control involves balancing the costs of inventory with the benefits of having inventory in stock. Maintaining inventory is costly to a business, and it must be well managed if you are going to make a profit. Direct costs of inventory include storage, insurance, and taxes, in addition to the purchase price of the inventory. Some of the concerns about inventory that managers must address include the following:

- Maintaining a wide assortment of stock but keeping adequate quantities of fast-moving items
- Increasing inventory turnover but maintaining a high level of service
- Keeping stock levels as low as possible without sacrificing service or performance as a result of stockouts
- Obtaining lower prices by making bulk purchases but not ending up with slow-moving inventory
- Having adequate inventory on hand but not ending up with out-of-date items

How can a store meet both its inventory needs and its customers' needs?

Pavel L Photo and Video/Shutterstock.com

Purchasing Plan

The most important aspect of inventory control is having items in stock when they are needed. This involves planning ahead to determine inventory needs, placing purchase orders for the items in advance, and scheduling deliveries to arrive at the point in time when you need the items. Inventory control also involves determining when you need the most inventory in stock, establishing *reorder points* (the minimum amounts of inventory you want to have before you place a new order), and determining when you should discontinue stocking an item.

The amount of inventory you need to purchase can be calculated from the sales forecast. You must look at how many units you need to add to the inventory you already have in stock to reach your sales objective. The formula for calculating inventory needs is as follows:

Beginning inventory + Purchases − Sales = Ending inventory

Alan has a beginning inventory worth $40,000 in his automobile parts store and expects to sell $80,000 over a period of six months. He wants to have $25,000 of inventory at the end of the six-month period. Alan uses the formula to calculate his purchases.

Beginning inventory	+	Purchases	−	Sales	=	Ending inventory
$40,000	+	?	−	$80,000	=	$25,000
	+	?	−	$40,000	=	$25,000
	+	?			=	$25,000 + $40,000
	+	?			=	$65,000

Alan must purchase $65,000 in inventory during the six-month period. However, he does not want to purchase the entire inventory and have it delivered at the same time because he does not have the cash to pay for it all at once, nor does he have the storage space. Alan decides to make his major purchases in the spring when people are beginning to get their cars ready for vacations and summer travel. He knows from past experience that he will sell more from March through June and that January and February are slower months.

Based on this information, Alan prepares a detailed purchase plan to show how much inventory he will purchase each month during the six-month period.

PURCHASE PLAN FOR AUTOMOBILE PARTS

	January	February	March	April	May	June	Total
Beginning inventory	$40,000	$33,500	$29,500	$25,300	$25,600	$25,050	
+ Purchases	4,500	4,500	10,800	16,800	14,200	14,200	$65,000
− Sales	(11,000)	(8,500)	(15,000)	(16,500)	(14,750)	(14,250)	$80,000
= Ending inventory	$33,500	$29,500	$25,300	$25,600	$25,050	$25,000	

© Cengage Learning

 CHECKPOINT

What are some inventory control concerns managers have?

LO 10.2-2   Track Your Inventory

Most businesses must keep the products they sell in stock as a convenience to their customers. To avoid running out of items your customers want, you will need to keep track of your inventory levels. You will also need to determine how much you can afford to keep in stock at any given time.

Tracking your inventory can be done in two different ways. You can use the periodic inventory method or the perpetual inventory method.

Periodic Inventory Method

The **periodic inventory method** involves taking a physical count of your merchandise at regular intervals, such as weekly or monthly. This method will tell you how many units of each item remain in stock. You can then compare your inventory counts to your established re-order points to determine which items need to be restocked. This method is commonly used by small businesses with limited inventory.

When taking a physical count, you will need to record the date on which you are taking the inventory, the stock number of each item, a description of each item, and the actual number of units in stock. At least two people should be involved in taking a physical count. One person should count the items on the shelves while the other records the information.

Perpetual Inventory Method

The **perpetual inventory method** keeps track of inventory levels on a daily basis. This method can make your business more efficient. It can also ensure that you never run out of stock.

The perpetual inventory method uses stock cards or a computer to track inventory. A **stock card** is a paper inventory record for a single item. Businesses that sell hundreds of items usually track inventory electronically. Retail businesses can use Radio Frequency Identification (RFID) tag readers or bar code scanners to scan inventory items at the point of sale. Cash registers with a **point-of-sale (POS) software system** update inventory records as each sale happens. With a POS system, you will always have an up-to-date inventory balance. You will also get detailed information on sales that will assist you in the decision-making process for inventory control. You can analyze the sales data, determine how well each item you have in stock is selling, and adjust your purchasing accordingly.

Regardless of whether you use stock cards or maintain electronic inventory records, you should record the following information:

- A description of the item
- A stock number for identification purposes
- Any receipt of inventory, the number of units received, and the date of the transaction
- Any sale of inventory, the number of units sold, and the date of the transaction
- The amount of inventory you currently have
- The minimum amount you want to keep in inventory (reorder point)
- The maximum amount you want in inventory at any time

Even with the perpetual inventory method, you will need to take a physical count of your inventory at least once or twice a year. Your actual inventory may differ from that listed in your perpetual inventory system. The difference can be caused by many things, such as failure to record sales, theft, or damage to merchandise.

Lei Woo owns a toy store. Lei uses her computer to track inventory levels on a daily basis. She creates a low stock report, which shows the items she needs to reorder. It also shows how many units of each item Lei needs to order so that she can restock to the maximum level.

LOW STOCK REPORT				
ITEM	STOCK NUMBER	MAXIMUM	REORDER POINT	NEED TO ORDER
Building blocks	Q323	15	7	8
Doll houses	K393	4	2	2
Playing cards	S222	25	12	13
Stickers	S494	50	20	30

© Cengage Learning

CHECKPOINT

How does the periodic inventory method differ from the perpetual inventory method?

LO 10.2-3 Manage Your Inventory

The level of inventory you keep in stock depends on three factors:

- The costs of carrying inventory
- The costs of lost sales due to being out of stock
- Your stock turnover rate

BE YOUR OWN BOSS

You own a small hardware store located on the Gulf Coast. Weather forecasters are predicting higher-than-average hurricane activity in your region for the upcoming season. You know that if a hurricane comes to your area, there will be a high demand for plywood, generators, batteries, and other hurricane preparedness supplies. You have limited storage space and limited funds to invest in inventory, but you realize the chance to increase sales and profits. Outline a plan for managing your inventory needs. Explain your decisions.

Costs of Carrying Inventory

Holding inventory can be very costly. These costs are known as *carrying costs*. A business with inventory will always have carrying costs. Carrying costs can become too high if you have too much inventory. Costs can increase for many reasons.

- **Obsolescence**   Inventory can be held too long and become old and outdated. People do not want to buy a computer made two years ago or products that have reached their expiration dates. You may be stuck with merchandise you cannot sell.
- **Deterioration**   Inventory can deteriorate, forcing you to throw it away or sell it at a discount. For example, if you own a garden store, some plants will need to be sold within a few weeks because they will begin to die.
- **Interest fees**   Vendors charge interest on money due to them. If you cannot pay your vendors until you sell your inventory, you will incur an extra expense.
- **Insurance**   You will need to carry insurance against theft, fire, and other disasters. Insurance premiums increase as the value of the inventory insured increases.
- **Storage**   Inventory takes up space—space that you may be leasing on a square-foot basis. If you run out of room, you will need to lease additional space.

Costs of Being Out of Stock

Being out of stock can cost you money. If you are out of the items that your customers want, you will lose sales. If customers repeatedly fail to find what they are seeking at your business, you could also lose customer loyalty. Establishing reorder points is a way to avoid stockouts.

Stock Turnover Rate

The **stock turnover rate** is the rate at which the inventory of a product is sold and replaced with new inventory. It shows how many times a year you sell all of your merchandise. To calculate the stock turnover rate, divide sales by inventory. For example, if a frame shop maintains an inventory of 20 for a particular frame and sells 100 of those frames in a year, the stock turnover rate for that frame is 5, computed as follows:

$$\text{Sales} \div \text{Inventory} = \text{Stock turnover rate}$$
$$100 \div 20 = 5$$

Stock turnover rates vary from industry to industry. For example, restaurants and grocery stores will have a high stock turnover rate, whereas car dealerships and furniture stores will have a low stock turnover rate. You can find the turnover rates for various industries by conducting online research, contacting the trade association for your industry, or talking to other entrepreneurs in your field.

Turnover rates can help you determine how much inventory to keep in stock. To find out how many months of inventory you should keep in stock, divide 12 (the number of months in a year) by the stock turnover rate.

FAMOUS ENTREPRENEUR

DAYMOND JOHN As founder, president, and CEO of FUBU ("For Us By Us"), Daymond John has helped revolutionize the fashion industry. John's entrepreneurial talents were exhibited early on. By age 10, he started repairing and selling bicycles that people had left out with their trash. In high school, John participated in a co-op program that allowed him to work a full-time job and attend school on an alternating weekly basis, which he credits with instilling an entrepreneurial spirit.

Later in life, John's love of hip-hop music and fashion led him to a new entrepreneurial venture. When shopping for a hat that he saw in a hip-hop music video, John was surprised by the $20 price tag. He asked his mother to teach him how to sew so that he could make the distinctive hats. He began selling them on the streets of Queens for $10, earning as much as $800 in a single day. Realizing the potential, John recruited some neighborhood friends to work with him. They created a distinctive logo, and FUBU was born. Working from the basement of John's mother's house, they began

What lessons can be learned from Daymond John's success?

Cindy Ord/Getty Images Entertainment/Getty Images

sewing the FUBU logo on hats, sweatshirts, and t-shirts. John and his partners' hard work paid off in 1994 when they attended an industry trade show in Las Vegas. Despite not being able to afford a booth, they left the trade show with over $300,000 in orders for FUBU products. Soon after, FUBU's popularity exploded. The company signed contracts with Macy's and JCPenney and a distribution deal with electronics manufacturer Samsung. By 1998, FUBU had over $350 million in revenues. Currently, FUBU has amassed over $6 billion in product sales, and John has a net worth of over $250 million.

Over the last decade, John has branched out into other endeavors. He wrote his first book in 2007, joined the hit TV show *Shark Tank* as a "shark" investor in 2009, and has become one of the world's most highly sought-after business and motivational speakers.

THINK CRITICALLY
What inventory challenges do you think John experienced with the initial success of FUBU?

Brad Wilson owns a retail store. The stock turnover rate in his industry is 6. This means that he needs to keep two months worth of inventory in stock at all times.

Months in year	÷	Stock turnover rate	=	Months of inventory to stock
12	÷	6	=	2

 CHECKPOINT

What three factors determine the amount of inventory a business keeps in stock?

 ASSESSMENT

THINK ABOUT IT

1. Why do you think a purchasing plan is essential to good inventory management?

2. What do you think are the benefits of using the periodic inventory method? The perpetual method?

3. Do you think you could still manage your inventory well if you did not know the turnover rate for a product? Why or why not?

MAKE ACADEMIC CONNECTIONS

4. **TECHNOLOGY** You own a grocery store in your town. Your business uses the perpetual inventory method. Use spreadsheet software to create an inventory tracking report for at least five inventory items a grocery store would carry.

5. **MATH** Refer to the low stock report on page 291. Suppose that building blocks cost $3.45 per unit, doll houses cost $23.60 per unit, playing cards cost $1.32 per unit, and stickers cost $0.30 per unit. How much would Lei Woo have to pay to replenish her inventory to the maximum level?

Teamwork

Working with teammates, make a list of ten items that you would sell in a hobby store that caters to teenagers. This is a new business with no inventory on hand. Decide how many of each item you think you could sell in a six-month period (July–December). Based on this information, make a purchasing plan for the hobby store showing how much inventory you would purchase each month.

The Essential Question Refer to The Essential Question on p. 288. Inventory is the stock of goods that a business has for sale. It is important for a small business to track and manage its inventory because having too much or not enough inventory reduces profitability.

FINANCIAL MANAGEMENT

10.3

The Essential Question Why does a business need to manage its cash flow and analyze financial statements?

LEARNING OBJECTIVES

LO 10.3-1 Describe strategies for managing cash flow.

LO 10.3-2 Evaluate a business's performance through financial statement analysis.

KEY TERMS
- cash budget
- gross sales
- net sales

Cash flows in and out.

Lars is an independent contractor in the construction business. He has a good handle on his finances and has built cash equity in his business. He has recently completed two big contracts and is eagerly awaiting his next. Lars realizes that demand for his services will be less in the winter months and could also decrease as a result of changes in the economy.

Realizing that there could be months when he does not have money coming in, Lars begins to think about the cash in his bank account. Although he has cash in the bank today, he knows he has to plan for tomorrow. He needs to manage his cash flow to ensure he can cover his expenses during slower months. Lars understands that when he gets a big construction contract, he needs to set aside some of the money for a time when he doesn't have any contracts lined up.

WORK AS A TEAM Why do you think cash flow is important to a business owner? List the kinds of businesses that you think might have cash flow issues similar to those in Lars' profession.

FOCUS ON SMALL BUSINESS

Vetkit/iStockphoto.com

Seasonal businesses must plan their cash flow.

LO 10.3-1 Manage Your Cash Flow

As the owner of your own business, you will need to make sure that you have enough cash to make purchases and pay expenses. To do so, you will have to create a cash budget. You will also have to learn how to manage your cash flow.

Create a Cash Budget

A **cash budget** should show the projections of your cash coming in and going out. To ensure accuracy, it should be based on actual past revenues and operating expenses. A cash budget looks very similar to a cash flow statement, but it has slight differences. Three columns are used to show the estimated cash flow, the actual cash flow, and the difference between the two. This information can help you budget your financial resources. For example, if your cash budget shows you will be short of cash in six months, you can begin arranging financing or generating capital now. If your cash budget shows you will have a surplus of cash two years from now, you might use that information in planning how to expand your business.

Many companies use spreadsheets to prepare their cash budgets. The spreadsheet will automatically perform calculations on the amounts that you provide. This allows you to see the outcomes of changes in your cash flow instantly.

Mark Matson owns a snow removal business that he runs from his home. He uses a spreadsheet to create a budget for the first three months of the coming year, which is shown below.

MARK'S SNOW REMOVAL SERVICE CASH BUDGET, Jan–Mar, 20—

	A	B	C	D
		Estimated	Actual	Difference
1	Cash receipts			
2	Cash sales	$2,000	$4,000	$2,000
3	Accounts receivable payments	$11,150	$13,150	$2,000
4	Tax refund	$850	$850	$0
5	Total cash receipts	$14,000	$18,000	$4,000
6	Cash disbursements			
7	Salaries	$4,500	$5,500	−$1,000
8	Gasoline	$2,500	$3,125	−$625
9	Vehicle maintenance	$350	$400	−$50
10	Utilities	$50	$50	$0
11	Advertising	$150	$300	−$150
12	Insurance	$500	$500	$0
13	Other	$250	$250	$0
14	Total cash disbursements	$8,300	$10,125	−$1,825
15	Net cash increase/decrease	$5,700	$7,875	$2,175

Improve Your Cash Flow

Two businesses with the same level of sales and expenses may have very different cash flows. One business may have a positive cash flow, while the other may have a negative cash flow and be unable to cover its expenses. The difference may reflect a different pattern of cash receipts and disbursements.

If your cash receipts will not cover required cash disbursements, you will need to take action to improve your cash flow. You can increase cash receipts, decrease cash disbursements, or perform both actions.

INCREASE CASH RECEIPTS One way to improve your cash receipts is to decrease your accounts receivable by getting customers who owe you money to pay more quickly. To encourage faster payment, you can do the following:

- Offer discounts on bills paid right away.
- Establish tighter credit policies (decrease the amount of time your customers have to pay their bills from 60 days to 30 days).
- Establish a follow-up system for collecting unpaid accounts receivable. For example, consider hiring a collection agency to track down customers who are considerably late with their payments.
- Hold shipments to customers with large unpaid bills or insist that such orders be paid in advance.

Businesses can have cash flow problems if they start off with too little capital. If your cash flow is inadequate, you may want to increase cash receipts by obtaining more capital. This means securing a loan, investing more of your own money in the business, or finding investors who will provide you with capital in return for a share of your future profits.

What Went *Wrong?*

Too Big, To Fast

Webvan was founded in 1996 by Louis Borders, who also co-founded the Borders bookstore chain. Webvan was an online grocery ordering and delivery service. Initially, this service was offered in ten U.S. markets. The company's long-range plans included expansion into 26 cities. The company started with investments of more than $396 million from venture capitalists. It then raised $375 million in its initial public offering of stock in 1999. At one point, Webvan was worth $1.2 billion, but problems soon surfaced. Customers did not sign up as founders hoped they would. But the biggest problem Webvan faced was rapidly disappearing cash reserves.

Too many cash disbursements can lead to business failure.

It placed a $1 billion order to build high-tech warehouses, bought a fleet of delivery trucks, purchased state-of-the-art computer systems, and acquired another grocery delivery startup called HomeGrocer. In addition, the management team of Webvan did not have anyone with experience in the supermarket industry. Webvan simply tried to grow its business too fast. By 2001, Webvan had $830 million in losses and was forced to file for bankruptcy.

THINK CRITICALLY

1. What are some of the problems that Webvan faced during its short-lived operation?
2. Webvan started with a large amount of cash reserves. What caused Webvan to end up with cash flow problems?
3. What changes in operations do you think Webvan could have made that might have helped it be successful?

What effect can inventory have on cash disbursements?

DECREASE CASH DISBURSEMENTS

Another way of improving the cash flow of your business is to reduce your disbursements. This can be done by gaining better control over your inventory and payroll, reducing expenses, or slowing the rate at which you pay your bills.

Inventory is a large business expense over which you have some control. Reducing this expense will improve your cash flow. As stated earlier, carrying inventory is costly. If your business has cash flow problems, make sure that you are not holding too much inventory. Decreasing the amount of inventory you carry will reduce your accounts payable because you will not be purchasing as much.

Payroll is another large category of expense for businesses. Reducing your payroll can improve your cash flow. Payroll expenses can be decreased by reducing the size of your workforce or reducing the number of hours that employees work. It is important to determine your workforce needs before you start making reductions in this area.

Many expenses, such as rent and insurance, are fixed, so you cannot reduce them. However, you can reduce variable expenses, such as advertising, to help improve your cash flow.

Most of your suppliers will offer credit terms. This means that they may agree to accept payment at a later date if you pay interest charges. Depending on your cash flow needs, you may want to take advantage of the longest possible credit terms or use a credit card for purchases.

Mark Matson usually pays cash for gasoline and oil for his snowplow trucks. However, at the beginning of the winter season in December, his expenses are particularly high and cash receipts low, so he charges his expenses to his credit card. By delaying payment until the following month, Mark improves his cash flow in December. When the credit card bill comes in January, he will have received payment from his customers for the work he did in December and will not have a problem paying the bill.

 CHECKPOINT

What are some ways you can improve your cash flow?

LO 10.3-2 Prepare and Analyze Financial Statements

To run your own business, you have to be able to understand and analyze financial statements to determine how well your business is performing. Your records and statements can help you analyze your profits, debts, and equity. They also can assist you in making management decisions.

Prepare Financial Statements

When you are starting a business, you will prepare pro forma financial statements based on projections. Once your business is up and running, you will prepare financial statements that show actual financial performance. These financial statements will contain more detailed financial information than the pro forma statements because the business's finances will change as the business grows.

CASH FLOW STATEMENT   The cash flow statement shows the cash inflows (receipts) and cash outflows (disbursements) for a business during a specific period of time. This statement shows the actual cash that a business receives and how that cash is used. Unlike the income statement, which reports revenues not yet received and expenses not yet paid, the cash flow statement reports actual amounts, making it the most valuable financial statement for many business owners.

INCOME STATEMENT   The income statement reports revenues, expenses, and the net income or loss over a specific period of time, such as a month, a quarter, or a year. Many businesses will prepare an income statement monthly in order to closely monitor revenues and expenses.

BALANCE SHEET   The three most important elements of a company's financial strength are its assets, liabilities, and owner's equity. The value of assets, liabilities, and owner's equity on a specific date is reported on the balance sheet. The balance sheet is usually prepared monthly and at year-end.

Analyze Sales

You must know how to use the information in your financial statements to determine the level of sales you need to achieve to earn a profit. Your sales records show sales trends and patterns. You can use these records to forecast future sales and make good business decisions.

ANALYZE SALES BY PRODUCT   Analyzing your sales by product can help you make decisions about the kind of inventory to stock. It can help you increase sales and profits.

Emily Lee owns a garden and patio store. Her store has four departments: outdoor furniture, outdoor grills, plants, and garden tools. Emily's sales figures show that almost 57 percent of her annual sales come from the outdoor furniture department, calculated as follows:

DEPARTMENTAL SALES • LEE GARDEN AND PATIO

Department	Sales	Percent of total*
Outdoor furniture	$110,000	56.7
Outdoor grills	37,000	19.0
Plants	24,000	12.4
Garden tools	23,000	11.9
Total	$194,000	100.0

*Rounded

Sales of outdoor furniture ÷ Total sales = Percent of sales
$110,000 ÷ $194,000 = 56.7%

The plants department accounts for only a little over 12 percent of sales. Based on these data, Emily decides to reduce the size of the plants department and increase her inventory of outdoor furniture.

Analyze Net Profit on Sales

Your income statement shows whether or not your business is earning a profit. It also tells you how profitable your business is. This information can be very useful in helping you set and meet profit goals. The rate of profit that a business earns is often shown as the ratio of its net profit to its sales. This ratio is calculated by dividing net income after taxes by net sales.

Net income after taxes ÷ Net sales = Net profit on sales

In order to calculate net profit on sales, a business must first perform calculations to determine net sales and net income after taxes. All of these calculations are found on the income statement.

INCOME STATEMENT
Hendrick's Auto Supplies, 20—

Revenue from sales	
Gross sales	$235,000
Returns	3,200
Net sales	$231,800
Cost of goods sold	150,000
Gross profit	$ 81,800
Operating expenses	
Salaries	$ 26,200
Rent	8,400
Utilities	1,500
Advertising	1,100
Insurance	1,000
Supplies	700
Other	1,000
Total operating expenses	$ 39,900
Net income from operations	$ 41,900
Interest expense	2,400
Net income before taxes	$ 39,500
Taxes	12,245
Net income/loss after taxes	$ 27,255

CALCULATE NET SALES Jack Hendrick owns a retail store that sells automotive supplies. He wants to find out his net profit on sales. First, he must determine his gross sales and net sales. **Gross sales** is the dollar amount of all sales. **Net sales** is the dollar amount of all sales with any returns subtracted. Jack sold $235,000 worth of merchandise and had $3,200 worth of merchandise returned. Therefore, his net sales amount is $231,800.

Gross sales − Returns = Net sales
$235,000 − $3,200 = $231,800

CALCULATE NET INCOME AFTER TAXES Three calculations must be performed to determine your net income after taxes. You must calculate the (1) gross profit, (2) net income from operations, and (3) net income before taxes.

Gross profit is profit before operating expenses are deducted. Last year, Jack spent $150,000 for merchandise that he sold. This amount represents his cost of goods sold. Jack subtracts his cost of goods sold from his net sales to find his gross profit.

Net sales − Cost of goods sold = Gross profit
$231,800 − $150,000 = $81,800

Jack's operating expenses include rent, salaries, and similar business expenses. Last year, his operating costs were $39,900. Gross profit minus operating expenses equals net income from operations.

Gross profit − Operating expenses = Net income from operations
$81,800 − $39,900 = $41,900

To calculate net income before taxes, Jack has to subtract one more expense that has not yet been taken into account: interest on loans he has obtained. Last year, Jack paid $2,400 in interest. He subtracts this from his net income from operations to get his net income before taxes.

If a company has no additional expenses, such as interest expense, the net income from operations equals the net income before taxes.

Net income from operations	−	Interest expense	=	Net income before taxes
$41,900	−	$2,400	=	$39,500

To compute his after-tax income, Jack subtracts the amount he paid in income tax last year, $12,245, from his net income before taxes. This gives him his net income after taxes for his automotive supply business.

Net income before taxes	−	Income tax paid	=	Net income after taxes
$39,500	−	$12,245	=	$27,255

CALCULATE AND ANALYZE NET PROFIT ON SALES After net sales and net income after taxes have been calculated, the net-profit-on-sales ratio can be calculated. This calculation helps determine how profitable your business is. Jack determines that his profits represent 11.8 percent of his net sales.

Net income after taxes	÷	Net sales	=	Net profit on sales
$27,255	÷	$231,800	=	11.8%

Jack can use this figure to assess his profits in two ways. First, he can compare his profit ratio this year with his profit ratio in previous years. If his profit ratio has declined, his business has become less profitable. If his profit ratio has increased, his business has become more profitable. Jack can also compare his profit ratio with average profit ratios in his industry. If his profit ratio is lower than the industry average, he may want to figure out how he can improve his profitability.

Set and Meet Profit Goals

To run your business effectively, you need to set profit goals that reflect the amount of profit you hope to earn from your business in a particular year.

Jack Hendrick would like to increase his profit ratio to 15 percent. He decides to try to increase his sales and reduce his expenses. He begins a frequent-buyer program and offers discounts on bulk purchases. Jack will try to reduce his cost of goods sold by purchasing his inventory in larger quantities to get a discount from suppliers.

Perform Breakeven Analysis

Breakeven analysis is a useful tool for determining how increases in sales (revenues) will affect your profits, as shown in the graph. The breakeven point is the volume of sales that must be made to cover all of the expenses (costs) of a business. Below the breakeven point, your

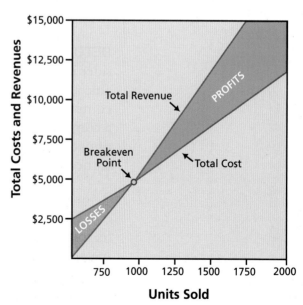

expenses will exceed your revenues and you will lose money. Once you reach the breakeven point, your sales will equal all of your expenses. This means that at this level of sales, you will neither make nor lose money. Once you exceed the breakeven point, you will begin to earn profits.

Analyze Debt and Equity

When analyzing a company's financial health, it is important to look at its mix of debt and equity. The balance sheet, as shown on the next page, contains most of the data needed for this analysis. There are four key areas an entrepreneur should review using data from the balance sheet.

1. *Ability to pay debt as it comes due.* Does the company have enough money to meet its short-term commitments?
2. *Return on assets.* Is the company providing a good rate of return on assets?
3. *Amount of debt the company is using.* Using debt increases the risks that a company faces, but it could also increase the expected return on the owners' equity investment.
4. *Rate of return on the owners' equity investment.* All decisions ultimately affect the rate of return earned by the owners on their equity investment in the business.

ABILITY TO PAY DEBT   A business that has enough money to pay off any debt owed is described as being liquid. The liquidity of a business depends on the availability of cash to meet debt obligations. The current ratio is used to measure a company's liquidity. The ratio compares a company's current assets to its current liabilities.

Current assets ÷ Current liabilities = Current ratio

Hendrick's Auto Supplies has current assets of $125,410 and current liabilities of $59,610. Its current ratio equals 2.10. This means that it has $2.10 in current assets for each $1 in current liabilities. A standard current ratio is close to 2, meaning that the company has twice as many assets as liabilities.

RETURN ON ASSETS   An important factor for a company to consider is its return on assets (ROA). The ROA indicates how profitable a company is relative to the total amount of assets invested in the company. It is usually expressed as a percentage. Assets are invested in a company for the purpose of producing net income. A comparison of net income to total assets reveals the rate of return that is being earned on the entire company's assets.

Net income ÷ Total assets = Return on assets

Hendrick's Auto Supplies has net income totaling $27,255, and its total assets equal $206,770. Its ROA is 0.1318, or 13.18%, which means that the company earned over $0.13 for each $1 of assets. The higher the ROA, the better. A higher number indicates a company more effectively used its assets to generate profits.

BALANCE SHEET
Hendrick's Auto Supplies
December 31, 20—

Assets		Liabilities	
Current assets		*Current liabilities*	
Cash	$ 24,720	Accounts payable	$ 37,390
Accounts receivable	47,400	Notes payable	22,220
Less allowance for		Total current liabilities	$ 59,610
uncollectible accounts	–1,500		
Inventory	54,790	*Long-term liabilities*	
Total current assets	$125,410	Loans payable	$ 42,000
		Total liabilities	$101,610
Fixed assets			
Equipment	$ 37,975		
Less depreciation	–3,975		
Furniture	32,280		
Less depreciation	–3,320		
Vehicles	24,000	**Owner's Equity**	
Less depreciation	–5,600	Jack Hendrick	$105,160
Total fixed assets	$ 81,360	**Total liabilities and**	
Total assets	$206,770	**owner's equity**	$206,770

DEBT RATIO   The amount of debt (total liabilities), relative to total assets, used to finance a business should be examined. The more debt a business has, the more risk it is taking. Because debt is a fixed cost, it has to be repaid no matter how much profit the company earns. The debt ratio is calculated using the following formula:

Total debt ÷ Total assets = Debt ratio

Hendrick's total debt (liabilities) is $101,610, and its total assets are $206,770. Its debt ratio is 0.4914. This means that it has approximately $0.49 in debt for each $1 of assets. For good financial health, the ratio should be 1 or less, which indicates the company's debt does not exceed its assets.

RETURN ON EQUITY   The owner's (or shareholders') profitability can be measured by the return on equity (ROE). The ROE is the rate of return the owners are receiving on their equity investment. It reveals how much profit a company earned in comparison to the total amount of owner's equity reported on the balance sheet. It is usually expressed as a percentage. A business that has a high ROE is likely to be more capable of generating cash internally. The formula for ROE is as follows:

Net income ÷ Owner's equity = Return on equity

Hendrick's net income totals $27,255, and its owner's equity totals $105,160. Its ROE is 0.2592, or 25.92%. A company's ROE should be as good as the average ROE for other companies in the same industry. If the industry average is 30%, then the owner of Hendrick's Auto Supplies is not receiving a return on his investment equivalent to that of owners of comparable businesses.

CHECKPOINT

What does a company's ROA measure? Should this number be high or low?

 **10.3 ASSESSMENT**

THINK ABOUT IT

1. How will constructing a cash budget using an electronic spreadsheet make this financial report more helpful?

2. What would be the benefit of preparing an income statement monthly instead of once a year?

3. Which goals do you think are more important to meet: sales goals or profit goals? Explain your answer.

MAKE ACADEMIC CONNECTIONS

4. **PROBLEM SOLVING** If your business is experiencing a negative cash flow, how might you use the six-step problem-solving model (from Chapter 1) to help find a solution?

5. **MATH** Using the following data, calculate the current ratio, ROA, debt ratio, and ROE for Hallman Printers.

Current assets	$170,000	Current liabilities	$100,000
Total assets	450,000	Total liabilities	150,000
Net income	50,000	Owner's equity	300,000

6. **MATH** Refer to Mark's snow removal cash budget on page 296. Assume that gas prices rise over the next three months and Mark's actual gas expenses increase by 3 percent. If all other items are constant, what would be his new net cash increase/decrease?

Teamwork

Working in a small group, use the Internet to locate a copy of an annual report for a business. Review all of the financial statements that are included in the annual report. Calculate the net profit on sales, current ratio, debt ratio, ROA, and ROE. Based on your calculations, write an analysis of the financial condition of the business.

The Essential Question Refer to The Essential Question on p. 295. A business must manage its cash flow to ensure it has enough money to make purchases and pay expenses. By analyzing financial statements, a business can determine how well it is doing by measuring profitability, debt, and equity.

Sharpen Your 21st Century Entrepreneurial Skills

Internal Accounting Controls

As an entrepreneur, you will have to establish internal accounting controls to promote and protect sound management practices. Internal controls help prevent and detect fraud. Following internal accounting control procedures will significantly increase the likelihood that

- Financial information is reliable so that it can be used for decision making
- Assets and records of the business are not stolen, misused, or accidentally destroyed
- The company's policies are followed
- Government regulations are met

Some of the most effective types of internal accounting controls include the following:

1. **Segregation of duties** Different individuals should be assigned responsibility for different elements of related activities, especially those involved with recordkeeping. There should be a system of checks and balances. For example, the person who writes the checks should not be the person who signs the checks.

2. **Proper authorization** Transactions and activities must follow established procedures. For example, a company's return policy may serve as an official authorization to refund money to a customer.

3. **Adequate documentation and records** There must be documentation and records for all transactions to ensure that financial information is reported correctly. Checks should be numbered and all checks should be accounted for. There should also be documentation to back up each check that is written.

4. **Physical control** Having physical controls helps protect the company's assets and records. These may include electronic or mechanical controls (a safe, employee ID cards, security system) or computer-related controls (file backup and recovery procedures).

5. **Independent checks** Audits should be performed by personnel who did not do the work being audited. For example, a supervisor may verify the accuracy of a retail clerk's cash drawer at the end of the day.

TRY IT OUT

Conduct online research to find an article about a business that recently experienced financial problems as a result of its accounting procedures. Does it appear that internal controls were in place? Summarize the problems that occurred and the end results or actions taken by the business or others.

SUMMARY

10.1 Operating Procedures

1. Managers are responsible for planning, organizing, staffing, implementing, and controlling the operations of a business.
2. A detailed operations manual is essential for a business's success. It should include rules, policies, and procedures. Policies may include operating policies, customer service policies, delivery policies, hiring policies, and safety policies.

10.2 Inventory Control

3. A purchasing plan will assist with inventory control by ensuring you have items in stock when they are needed. It helps you calculate ending inventory needs based on beginning inventory, purchases, and sales.
4. You can track inventory using the periodic or perpetual inventory methods. The periodic inventory method involves taking a physical count of merchandise at regular intervals, such as weekly or monthly. The perpetual inventory method tracks inventory levels on a daily basis.
5. The level of inventory you keep in stock depends on three factors: the costs of carrying inventory, the costs of losing sales due to being out of stock, and your stock turnover rate.

10.3 Financial Management

6. To manage cash flow, begin by creating a cash budget, which shows the projections of your cash coming in and going out. You can improve your cash flow by increasing cash receipts, decreasing cash disbursements, or performing both actions.
7. When starting a business, you prepare pro forma statements based on projections. Once your business is operating, you will prepare financial statements based on actual performance. The three financial statements most commonly prepared by businesses are the cash flow statement, income statement, and balance sheet.
8. You can examine your business's finances by analyzing your sales by product; analyzing your net profit on sales; performing a breakeven analysis; and analyzing debt and equity by computing your current ratio, ROA, debt ratio, and ROE.

Read *Ideas in Action* on page 281 again. Then answer the questions a second time. Have your responses changed? If so, how have they changed?

KEY TERMS REVIEW

Match each statement with the term that best defines it. Some terms may not be used.

1. The process of achieving goals by establishing operating procedures that make effective use of people and other resources
2. The rate at which inventory of a product is sold and replaced with new inventory
3. The dollar amount of all sales with any returns subtracted
4. A plan that shows how the various jobs in a company relate to one another
5. Keeps track of inventory levels on a daily basis
6. Involves taking a physical count of your merchandise at regular intervals, such as weekly or monthly
7. A management style in which employees are involved in decision making and the manager provides less direction
8. Shows the projections of your cash coming in and going out
9. Contains all of the rules, policies, and procedures that a business should follow in order to function effectively
10. A system that updates inventory records as each sale happens
11. The person responsible for planning, organizing, staffing, implementing, and controlling the operations of a business
12. A management style in which the manager is directive and controlling

a. authoritative management
b. cash budget
c. democratic management
d. gross sales
e. management
f. manager
g. net sales
h. operations manual
i. organizational structure
j. periodic inventory method
k. perpetual inventory method
l. point-of-sale software system
m. stock card
n. stock turnover rate

REVIEW YOUR KNOWLEDGE

13. Preparing detailed plans that will provide strategies for achieving goals and objectives in a one-year period is
    a. strategic planning
    b. intermediate-range planning
    c. short-term planning
    d. none of the above
14. Which of the following functions of management would apply when grouping tasks into departments?
    a. planning   c. implementing
    b. organizing   d. controlling
15. Jorge is supervising new employees with no experience in food service at a concession stand in an amusement park. Which management style should he use?
    a. authoritative management   c. mixed management
    b. democratic management   d. participatory management
16. **True or False**   The organizational structure outlines all of the rules, policies, and procedures that a business must follow.
17. A store that has very limited inventory commonly uses the ___?___ inventory method.
18. **True or False**   A point-of-sale (POS) software system makes it easier to analyze your inventory records at the end of the day.

19. The level of inventory you keep in stock depends on all of the following except
   a. the costs of carrying inventory
   b. the costs of lost sales due to being out of stock
   c. your stock turnover rate
   d. your net-profit-on-sales ratio
20. If you want to improve your cash flow by increasing cash receipts, which of the following strategies could you try?
   a. offer discounts on bills paid right away
   b. establish tighter credit policies
   c. hold shipments to customers with large unpaid bills
   d. all of the above

APPLY WHAT YOU LEARNED

21. You received a $500 payment from a customer in the form of a check, which you deposited in your bank account. Several days later, you received a notice from your bank that the customer's checking account did not have the funds to cover it. You needed that money to help you cover your monthly rent. What will you do? (LO 10.3-1)
22. You want to analyze your sales by product for your hardware store. Your total sales are $140,750. The sales of each department in your store are given below. What percent of sales does each department generate for your store? (LO 10.3-2)

Seasonal merchandise	$25,525
Lumber	40,211
Tools	38,524
Lighting	15,235
Kitchen cabinets	21,255

MAKE ACADEMIC CONNECTIONS

23. **MATH** You own a bookstore. The stock turnover rate in the bookstore business is 4. How many months' worth of inventory must you keep on hand? (LO 10.2-3)
24. **MATH** You own a pet-supply store. Last year, you sold $42,000 in dog food and $53,000 in cat food. Returns totaled $5,000. The cost of goods sold was $13,000 on the dog food and $14,000 on the cat food. Operating expenses were $13,000 for salaries, $4,500 for rent, $1,200 for insurance, $1,000 for utilities, $900 for advertising, and $600 for other. Taxes were $10,500. What is your net income after taxes? What is your net-profit-on-sales ratio? (LO 10.3-2)
25. **COMMUNICATION** An operations manual is an important tool to keep your business running smoothly. It should contain policies related to operations, customer service, delivery, hiring, and safety. For your pet-supply store in Problem 24, write three policies for each of the areas listed above. (LO 10.1-2)

26. **COMMUNICATION**   You and a partner own a kitchen equipment store. You would like to implement a point-of-sale (POS) software system. Write a letter to persuade your partner to make this change. Identify advantages of using a POS software system. (LO 10.2-2)

What Would YOU DO?

You asked two of your employees to work extra hours over the weekend to perform a physical count of inventory. You are certain that there were three plasma television sets in stock prior to having the employees take inventory. However, when the inventory was completed, the list showed only two plasma television sets in stock. You checked the stockroom, and you found only two. You have always trusted your employees. What would you do? Will you confront the employees? If so, how will you approach them? Working with a partner, role-play the conversations you will have with the employees.

BUILD YOUR BUSINESS PLAN PROJECT

This activity will help you plan the operations management of your business.

1. Describe the management style you will use for managing your business. Will you always use the same style? How will you determine when to use a different style?
2. Locate and contact two professionals in your area who specialize in strategic planning. What are their credentials? What are their fees? Do you think it would be helpful to utilize the services of a strategic planner? Why or why not?
3. Develop an operating procedures manual for your business. Include the rules, policies, and procedures that your business will follow to run effectively.
4. If your business has an inventory, list all of the items you will have in inventory and your cost for each. Create a purchasing plan for your inventory.
5. Set up inventory records for your business using either a paper system or an electronic system. Be sure to list all of the items discussed in Lesson 10.2. How did you determine your reorder point? What inventory carrying costs are relevant to your business? How can you reduce your carrying costs?
6. Analyze your sales by creating a table that lists each of your products and the total sales (or estimated sales) for each. What is the percentage of total sales for each product? Based on this information, will you make any changes to your inventory?
7. Develop internal accounting controls for your business. Explain why you chose the controls you did.

"My stepsister, who is a high school senior this year, has become our household computer expert. She recently attended a summer technology camp sponsored by a national computer retailer that provides a variety of computer support services. The camp was established as a way to help fulfill future labor needs. After completing camp, she's become the 'go to' person in our house for any high-tech gadget issues."

Computer service specialists help resolve a variety of complex technological issues that affect computer efficiency and reliability. This ranges from repairing computer parts, such as a hard drive or monitor, to removing spyware and viruses. They must be familiar with various operating systems and software packages. Some computer service specialists work from repair shops, while others travel to customers' locations.

Employment Outlook
- A faster-than-average rate of employment growth is anticipated.
- The use of the newest forms of technology, which are often complex, will help fuel demand.
- Growing demand will be somewhat offset by the trend to outsource tech support jobs to foreign countries with lower wage rates.

Job Titles
- Software Support Specialist
- Help Desk Analyst
- Application Specialist
- Technical Support Associate
- MIS Support Technician

Needed Education/Skills
- Education requirements vary. A bachelor's degree is required for some computer service specialist positions, while an associate's degree is adequate for some jobs.
- To keep up with changes in technology, many computer support specialists continue their education throughout their careers.
- Strong customer-service, problem-solving, and troubleshooting skills are needed.

What's it like to work in Computer Repair? Milo is a computer service specialist. He has his own business and provides on-site repair services.

Today, Milo is updating the rates on his company website. These rates include the trip charge to arrive at a client's home or place of business, the one-hour minimum labor charge, and the additional fees for a partial hour beyond the one-hour minimum.

After receiving a call from a frantic client, Milo dashes off to the client's home. The client, who has a home-based consulting business, has a hard drive that is failing. The client accidentally dropped his flash drive into a cup of coffee, and he has no backup for his files. Consequently, he needs help retrieving critical files from his hard drive.

After saving the files to a new flash drive, Milo suggests to his client that he consider investing in an automated data backup service. For a monthly fee, designated data can be automatically saved to a personalized website that would be password accessible for security purposes.

What about you? Would you like to help a variety of individuals and businesses solve their computer technology problems? What would you find appealing (or not appealing) about this job?

The Personal Financial Literacy Event measures your personal finance knowledge. Entrepreneurs must understand and know how to keep their business funds separate from their personal funds. Managing your personal funds in a stress-free manner will allow you to concentrate more of your time and energy on your business. This event includes a role-play scenario in which students will demonstrate how to manage their financial resources effectively.

You are about to graduate from high school and have decided that you will live in an off-campus apartment during college. You signed a 12-month lease in just your name, and the rent is $1,100 per month. Trash pickup and recycling is included, but you will have to pay for all other utilities. You have already signed up for basic cable, Internet service, and a $19/month renter's insurance policy.

The rent at the apartment is too expensive for just you, so you decide to get a roommate. Today, you are meeting a potential roommate to discuss the rent and other financial expectations of the living arrangement. You need to decide which household expenses will be shared and which will be each individual's responsibility. You will also discuss how you plan to pay those expenses. It is important that you leave the meeting with an understanding of who will be financially responsible for all aspects of living on your own for the first time.

Performance Indicators

- Recognize the responsibilities associated with personal financial decisions
- Apply communication strategies when discussing financial issues
- Analyze the requirements of contractual obligations
- Describe how to use different payment methods
- Justify reasons to use property and liability insurance
- Use a personal financial plan

Go to the DECA website for more detailed information.

GIVE IT A TRY

Working with a partner, read the scenario above. Set a timer for ten minutes. Create a skit that will showcase a meeting between potential roommates. Be sure to address the performance indicators above. Present your skit to the class.

www.deca.org

Vm/iStockphoto.com

Human Resource Management

(11.1) **IDENTIFY YOUR STAFFING NEEDS**

(11.2) **STAFF YOUR BUSINESS**

(11.3) **DIRECT AND CONTROL HUMAN RESOURCES**

Working for a Worthy Cause

Marcio Jose Sanchez/AP Images

Shubham Banerjee, founder of Braigo Labs Inc.

Shubham Banerjee, a 12-year-old seventh grader from Santa Clara, California, combined his love of LEGO Mindstorms robotics with a desire to make a difference in the world. He created an affordable printer for the visually impaired.

People who are visually impaired read with their fingertips, using a system called braille that has raised dots representing letters, numbers, and punctuation. When Shubham learned that braille printers cost more than $2,000, he took action. Shubham used a LEGO Mindstorms EV3 kit and high-level programming skills to create a functioning braille-type printer for about $350. He calls his printer Braigo, a combination of braille and LEGO.

"Technology should help us to make our life easier and not become a burden due to high cost," he said. To ensure the printer is affordable to those in need, Shubham publishes free instructions online and keeps the coding open-source so that others can improve on his original idea.

Braigo has a small computer and three motors that move a pushpin up and down over a sheet of paper, poking indents that are a mirror image of braille lettering. Readers who are visually impaired can flip the paper over and read the bumps.

As a new startup, Shubham relied on a loan from his parents to begin his project. It didn't take long for word to get around, and soon Intel Capital invested in Shubham's company, Braigo Labs Inc. A whole team of mentors and coaches from different walks of life came on board, and more investors followed. Today Braigo Labs is staffed with engineers, professors, and company executives who provide a variety of technical and product experiences. They all came together to take the Braigo printer to the next level.

Shubham and his printer have won numerous awards, including being named one of the ten greatest inventions of the year by *Popular Science* in 2015. "It feels amazing," Shubham says about being able to make life easier for the visually impaired. "I'm really proud of myself."

WHAT DO YOU KNOW?

1. What makes Shubham a good entrepreneur?
2. Why do you think so many people wanted to invest in and work for Braigo Labs?
3. How does a company like Braigo Labs benefit by having employees with a variety of experiences?

11.1 IDENTIFY YOUR STAFFING NEEDS

The Essential Question What must entrepreneurs consider when staffing their business?

LEARNING OBJECTIVES

LO 11.1-1 Explain how to determine staffing needs for a business.

LO 11.1-2 Describe options for recruiting employees.

LO 11.1-3 Identify alternatives to hiring permanent employees.

KEY TERMS

- staffing
- job description
- job analysis
- chain of command
- recruit
- freelancers
- interns

FOCUS ON SMALL BUSINESS

Hire help.

Emanuel started his excavation contracting business six months ago. He soon had more business than he could handle. He decided he needed help and posted a "Help Wanted" sign in front of his business. People began calling and stopping by, continually interrupting his work. They wanted to know what type of work he had and how much it would pay. Emanuel didn't really know what to tell them. He had not thought through the details of the posted position.

Emanuel took down his sign to determine exactly what type of help he needed. In addition to his excavation work, Emanuel had a large amount of paperwork to do. He realized that if he had help with the administrative tasks, he would have more time to devote to other areas of his business. He could also use someone else with excavation experience to help him.

Think about your staffing needs before posting a "Help Wanted" sign.

WORK AS A TEAM What do you think Emanuel should have done before posting the "Help Wanted" sign? What types of positions could Emanuel add? Do you think using a sign in front of his business is the best way for Emanuel to attract qualified job applicants?

LO 11.1-1 Staffing

The management functions of staffing, implementing, and controlling can be directly applied to the people who work for your business. The people who work for your business are your *human resources*. You may not need to hire employees when you first start your business. But as your business grows, you will find the need for employees. Good employees and a well-run human resource management program are as important to your business as are capital, equipment, and inventory.

Staffing involves determining the number of employees you need and defining a process for hiring them. To find out your staffing needs, ask yourself the following four questions:

1. What kinds of employees do I need?
2. What skills am I missing?
3. What skills do I need daily?
4. What skills do I need occasionally?

To answer these questions, list all of the duties in your business. Then try to identify how much time is needed to perform each of these duties. Your list should help you identify whether you need part-time, full-time, or temporary workers. You can also determine whether you need managers or assistants and how many employees you need.

Job Descriptions

A *job* is a collection of tasks and duties that an employee is responsible for completing. A *task* is a specific work activity that is performed, such as answering the telephone or answering email. Many positions include a variety of tasks that are sometimes referred to as *functions*. A **job description** is a written statement listing the tasks and responsibilities of a position. Job descriptions also can indicate whom the position reports to, educational and professional experience required, and salary range.

Job descriptions are written after conducting a **job analysis**, which is the process of determining the tasks and sequence of tasks necessary to perform a job. A job analysis helps a business determine which employees are the best fit for specific jobs. You will need to understand exactly what every job entails so that you can determine what the important tasks of the job are, how they are carried out, the

---

SAMPLE JOB DESCRIPTION

Title: Account Executive
Tasks and Responsibilities: Plans, coordinates, and directs advertising campaigns for clients of advertising agency. Works with clients to determine advertising requirements and budgetary limitations. Coordinates activities of workers engaged in marketing research, writing copy, laying out artwork, purchasing media time and space, developing special displays and promotional items, and performing other media-production activities.
Qualifications: Bachelor's degree with courses in marketing, leadership, communication, business, and advertising; sales experience; interpersonal and written communication skills; neat professional appearance; characteristics of self-motivation, organization, persistence, and independence
Reports to: Marketing Manager
Salary Range: $30,000 to $50,000, depending on experience

necessary qualifications needed to complete the job successfully, and how much money to offer job applicants. Job descriptions also can be used to measure how well an employee performs a job when conducting performance evaluations.

Organizational Structure

Once your company has several employees, you will need an organizational structure. An *organizational structure* is a plan that shows how the various jobs in a company relate to one another and is often displayed in an *organizational chart*. The organizational chart can also help you analyze your staffing needs. Using the chart during planning can help you identify the number and types of employees you need. When planning, you can list positions and primary responsibilities of each. Then as employees are hired, you can fill in the names.

The organizational chart shows the **chain of command**, or who reports to whom in the company. In a small business, all employees may report directly to the company owner. In large companies, lower-level employees usually report to a supervisor. This kind of organizational structure ensures that the owner is not called upon to deal with relatively unimportant issues that could be handled more efficiently by a lower-level manager.

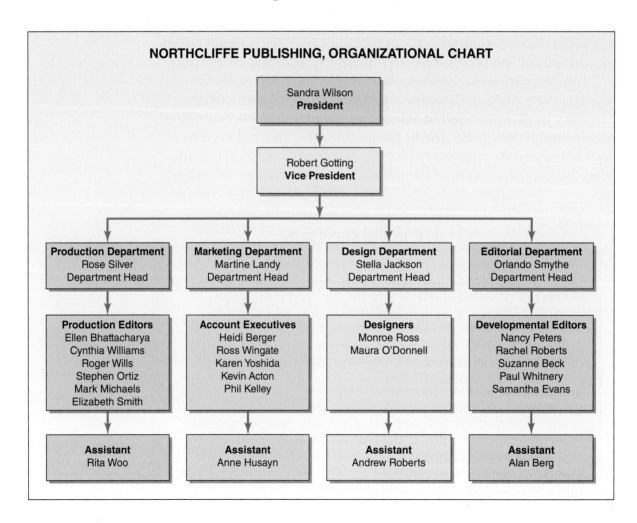

NORTHCLIFFE PUBLISHING, ORGANIZATIONAL CHART

Sandra Wilson — **President**

Robert Gotting — **Vice President**

Production Department Rose Silver Department Head	**Marketing Department** Martine Landy Department Head	**Design Department** Stella Jackson Department Head	**Editorial Department** Orlando Smythe Department Head
Production Editors Ellen Bhattacharya Cynthia Williams Roger Wills Stephen Ortiz Mark Michaels Elizabeth Smith	**Account Executives** Heidi Berger Ross Wingate Karen Yoshida Kevin Acton Phil Kelley	**Designers** Monroe Ross Maura O'Donnell	**Developmental Editors** Nancy Peters Rachel Roberts Suzanne Beck Paul Whitnery Samantha Evans
Assistant Rita Woo	**Assistant** Anne Husayn	**Assistant** Andrew Roberts	**Assistant** Alan Berg

LO 11.1-2   Recruiting

To **recruit** is to look for people to hire and attract them to the business. As the owner of a small business, it may be difficult for you to attract experienced employees to work for your business. They will have opportunities to work for larger, established businesses that can offer them higher pay and better benefits.

You can use a variety of resources for recruiting, including online sources, employment agencies, college placement centers, in-store advertising, classified advertisements, and referrals. Recruiting from a variety of resources helps attract a diverse pool of candidates.

Online Sources

Today people often use the Internet to look for a job, so online recruitment is used by many companies. Career and employment websites, also known as *job boards*, allow you to post a job and then search the resumes that are submitted in response to the posting. Some job boards have a database of resumes that you can review when you are looking for someone to fill a specific job. Popular employment websites include Indeed.com, Monster.com, and CareerBuilder.

Industry-specific career sites are becoming popular as well. For example, Dice.com lists job openings for information technology professionals. JobsOnTheMenu.com specializes in jobs in the food service and restaurant industries. Because they are career-specific, employers can focus only on those candidates in a specialized market.

You may also have a website for your business. If you do, you may have a "Human Resources" or "Careers" section where you can post job openings and allow applicants to apply directly on the website.

Social media sites, such as Facebook, Twitter, and LinkedIn, and mobile apps are becoming an increasingly popular way to recruit employees. Recent surveys revealed that 70 percent of job seekers use social networking sites to look for jobs, and 43 percent of job seekers use their smartphone or other mobile device to search for jobs.

Employment Agencies

Employment agencies find employees for businesses. These firms try to match people looking for jobs with businesses looking for employees. They charge businesses and/or the job seekers a fee when they are successful in making a match. Some businesses may use a *headhunter*, which is an employment specialist who seeks out highly qualified professionals to fill positions. Seeking applicants through an employment agency or a headhunter saves time for the employer in screening applicants, but the cost can be high.

Career Centers

Most colleges and universities operate career centers. These offices collect information on career and employment opportunities, which they make available to their students and recent graduates. Many have websites on which employers can post job openings for students and alumni. They also hold career fairs that give employers the opportunity to meet and talk with students who are looking for jobs. Generally, college and university career centers do not charge a fee for their services.

In-Store Advertising

Have you ever walked into a store and seen a sign that says "Help Wanted" or "Now Hiring"? This is another method of advertising that businesses use. When you post a sign, interested applicants will come into your business and fill out an application form. Before placing a sign in the window, be sure you will have time to deal with the many people who may stop or call to inquire about the position.

Classified Advertisements

Classified advertisements are a good way to attract a large number of applicants at a low cost. This type of advertising typically runs in the classifieds section of newspapers and other publications and on Internet classifieds sites such as Craigslist.

The advertisement that you use is called a *want ad*. The ad should briefly describe the position and the education and experience requirements. It should also identify any special job requirements, such as a willingness to travel or to work evenings. Close your ad with contact information for your business and instructions on how to apply for the position. For example, you may want them to email a resume and cover letter or complete an application at your place of business or on your website.

Do you think a classified ad is a good way to find job candidates? Why or why not?

Referrals

One of the best ways that entrepreneurs find qualified applicants is by acting on referrals from family, friends, acquaintances, or other employees. While employment sites and classified ads still collect the highest number of applicants, statistics show that referrals, by far, garner the highest number of qualified hires. Using referrals from trusted sources cuts down on screening time and, thus, recruitment costs.

 **CHECKPOINT**

What resources can you use for recruiting employees?

LO 11.1-3   Alternatives to Adding Staff

Adding employees to your payroll is costly. It takes time and money to recruit staff and to track, report, and pay their salaries, benefits, and tax withholdings. In many cases, you may need help but not have sufficient work to keep a permanent full-time employee busy. For these reasons, you may want to consider alternatives to permanent employees, such as hiring freelancers, interns, and temporary workers.

Freelancers

Freelancers are people who provide specialty services to a number of different businesses on an hourly basis or by the job. Freelancers are also called *independent contractors*. Examples of freelancers include bookkeepers, accountants, lawyers, graphic designers, window display artists, and advertising copywriters. Business owners use freelancers when they need to get a job done but do not have enough of the required type of work to warrant hiring a permanent employee. A freelancer is different from an employee, because the business does not have to pay any benefits to the freelancer. In addition, the business does not have control over the actions of the freelancer. The freelancer can decide what methods to use to accomplish a task as long as the completed job meets the business's specifications.

Interns

Interns are students who work for little or no pay in order to gain experience in a particular field. Internships are typically short-term in nature. It is the company's responsibility to provide on-the-job training and real-world experience. The company may need to meet certain requirements to qualify as an internship site and work with the school's intern coordinator to ensure program requirements are met.

Students often use an internship to determine if they have an interest in a particular career, to gain school credit for graduation purposes, or to create a network of contacts. Some interns find permanent, paid employment with these companies. This saves employers' time and money because interns will have the needed experience.

Temporary Workers

Businesses that need additional help often use temporary workers. Some temporary workers are seasonal employees. Other temporary workers are substitutes for employees who are sick or on a leave of absence. Temporary employment agencies provide trained workers for various kinds of businesses. A business that uses a temporary employee pays a fee to the agency. The agency in turn manages the worker's salary and benefits.

 CHECKPOINT

What are some alternatives to hiring permanent employees?

 11.1 ASSESSMENT

THINK ABOUT IT

1. Why is it important for a company to have an organizational structure that allows the owner to focus on long-term issues?

2. List some advantages of using an employment agency to fill job openings.

3. What would be some disadvantages of hiring freelancers and temporary workers?

MAKE ACADEMIC CONNECTIONS

4. **PROBLEM SOLVING** Create an organizational chart for a 30-person local package delivery service. First, determine all of the types of employees the business would have. Then create the chart based on your decisions.

5. **RESEARCH** Create a resource guide containing names of employment agencies, college career centers, and online career websites that you could use to help meet the staffing needs of your business. Include contact information such as URLs, addresses, and phone numbers.

Teamwork

Form teams and choose a business in your community. Discuss the various job positions that may be held at this business. Select one position and develop a recruiting plan to hire a new employee. Design a want ad that could be used for the recruiting method you select. If you select referrals as the best recruiting method, design a referral request form that could be sent to family, friends, acquaintances, and current employees.

The Essential Question Refer to The Essential Question on p. 314. Entrepreneurs should consider the kinds of employees needed, the skills that are needed for the business, and the best ways to recruit such employees.

STAFF YOUR BUSINESS

11.2

The Essential Question What can entrepreneurs do to make sure they hire and retain the best employees?

LEARNING OBJECTIVES

LO 11.2-1 List and describe the steps in the hiring process.
LO 11.2-2 Describe compensation packages for employees.
LO 11.2-3 Identify laws protecting employee rights.

KEY TERMS

- wages
- salary
- bonus
- profit sharing
- commission
- benefits

Who to hire?

FOCUS ON SMALL **BUSINESS**

Emanuel took a good look at his business needs and decided that he would hire an administrative assistant to help him. If he had someone in the office to answer the phone, schedule work, and handle the billing, it would allow him to spend more time at excavation job sites. He put an ad in the local newspaper and had several candidates contact him. Now he had to decide whom to interview.

Emanuel's sister, JoAnna, had run her own business for several years, so he went to her for advice. JoAnna recommended that he have candidates submit a resume and complete an application form. He could review the provided information to determine who is really qualified for the job. Then he could set up interviews with the best candidates.

"So, JoAnna," Emanuel asked, "do you have an application form lying around here anywhere?"

WORK AS A TEAM Do you think that JoAnna gave Emanuel good advice about selecting candidates to interview? Why or why not?

Consider the skills needed to improve your business.

LO 11.2-1 The Hiring Process

Hiring the best people available and retaining them is important for the success of your business. However, hiring employees is often difficult because it requires making very important decisions based on fairly limited information. Bad hiring choices can result in lost time and money—losses that many businesses cannot afford.

So how should you decide whom to hire? There are generally four steps involved in the hiring process: (1) screening candidates,

(2) reviewing and verifying information on job applications, (3) interviewing the best candidates, and (4) making a job offer.

Screen Candidates

The first step in the hiring process is to screen candidates to eliminate people who are not right for the job. This allows you to focus on the most qualified candidates. The job description identifies the specific qualifications needed to perform a particular job. You need to match the job candidate's experience and skills with the job description. You should also look for personal characteristics that would make a person a desirable employee. However, you cannot screen on *protected classes*, which are characteristics of a person that cannot be targeted for discrimination. Protected classes include such things as race, gender, religion, ethnicity, national origin, and marital status.

Review and Verify Information on Job Applications

You will need to have potential candidates complete a job application. There are standard application forms that you can use, or you can design one that will meet your specific needs. The application allows you to gather information that might not be included on a resume. If you decide to design your own application, you can use the job description as a guide to gather the information you need about the candidate's experience.

Why is it important to contact the references and/or past employers provided by a job applicant?

Once you have applications and resumes from candidates, you may need to narrow the pool down even further. Look more closely at each candidate's qualifications. Also, verify that the information provided is correct. Request that the candidates provide an official transcript from schools they attended. Check the candidate's credit score and criminal record. Contact any references and/or past employers that are listed. Ask what they can tell you about the person. Describe the job opening and ask if the candidate would perform well in such a position. Other questions can revolve around the candidate's personal qualities, such as interpersonal skills and punctuality.

Interview the Best Candidates

The job interview provides you with the opportunity to determine whether a prospective employee would improve your ability to meet customer needs. It is also your chance to make your small business appealing to a prospective employee. Making the most of the job interview is as important for you as it is for the job candidate. Today, telephone and Skype interviews are common in the hiring process. They can help you determine who you want to bring in for a face-to-face interview.

SELL YOUR BUSINESS   During the interview, make your small business appear inviting and appealing to prospective employees.

- **Share your values and plans for the business.** Help the applicants understand your vision for the business.
- **Talk about the significance of working in a new business.** Emphasize the importance of the contributions the applicant would make in the development and growth of a new business. Give a realistic preview of the position to avoid job dissatisfaction later.
- **Explain the atmosphere in which the candidate would work.** Make sure the applicant understands that a small business can foster an environment of flexibility and caring. Some people would rather work in a small business that is not as structured as a large corporation.
- **Describe your bonus system.** With a small startup business, you may not be able to pay a large salary, but you can offer an attractive bonus or benefits package. Explain that if the business does well, you will share some of the profits with those who help you succeed.

MAKE THE INTERVIEW EFFECTIVE   To ensure that you use your time during the interview effectively, follow these basic rules:

1. **Be prepared.** Make a list of open-ended questions you want to ask. Review the candidate's resume and job application again just before the interview begins.
2. **Be courteous.** Do not be late for the interview. Avoid taking phone calls during the interview. Try to put job candidates at ease by offering them something to drink. Make them feel welcome in your office.
3. **Avoid dominating the interview.** Remember that the interview is your opportunity to get to know the job candidate. To do so, be sure to allow the applicant plenty of time to speak.
4. **Take notes.** Throughout the interview, jot down your impressions of the candidate as well as any interesting information he or she reveals.

SAMPLE INTERVIEW QUESTIONS

1. What interests you about the job?
2. How can your skills and experience benefit the company?
3. What are your career plans? How does this job fit in with those plans?
4. What other positions have you held? What did you like and dislike about those positions?
5. What were your achievements at your previous jobs?
6. Why did you leave your last job?
7. How do you think your education has prepared you for this job?
8. What kind of work do you enjoy most? What makes a job enjoyable for you?
9. Describe a situation where you had to manage conflicting priorities.

---

5. **Look for warning signs**. Indications that a person may not be a good worker include frequent job changes, unexplained gaps in employment, and critical comments about previous employers.
6. **Don't make snap judgments**. Don't rule out a candidate until the interview is over.
7. **Remain pleasant and positive throughout the interview**. At the end of the interview, thank the candidate for coming and let him or her know when you plan to make a decision.
8. **Write a summary of your impressions of the candidate**. Write your summary immediately after the interview while your thoughts are still fresh. Put this document in the candidate's file.

Make a Job Offer

When you have decided to make a job offer, contact the person by phone. Let the person know you were impressed with his or her credentials. Be sure to emphasize how much you would like the applicant to join your company. Clearly state the starting salary, benefits, and terms of employment. If the first applicant declines your offer, extend the offer to your second choice and then to your third choice, if necessary.

Once a candidate accepts your offer, contact the remaining candidates. Thank them for interviewing with your business and politely let them know that you have given the job to another applicant.

 **CHECKPOINT**

What are the four steps in the hiring process?

LO 11.2-2 Compensation Package

As an entrepreneur with paid employees, you will need to create a compensation package. The package will include some type of pay and may also provide a variety of benefits. The benefits you offer can influence a candidate's decision on whether to take a position with a company.

Types of Pay

There are many ways you can choose to pay your employees. The terms *wages* and *salary* are often used interchangeably, but there is a difference. Wages are payments for labor or services that are made on an hourly, daily, or per-unit basis. The paycheck for a person earning a wage will vary depending on how many hours are worked or how many units are manufactured. A salary is an amount paid for a job position stated on an annual basis. Regardless of the number of hours the person filling the position works, the amount of money the salaried employee is paid does not vary. Wages and salaries can be paid weekly, biweekly, or monthly. In most markets, wages and salaries are competitively determined. This means that an employer who offers much less than the going wage or salary rate is not likely to find qualified workers. To offer competitive wages or salaries, you will have to find out how much similar businesses in your area are paying their employees. You should also find out what people are earning in jobs with similar qualifications.

Employees may also receive a **bonus**, which is a financial reward made in addition to a regular wage or salary. Bonuses usually hinge on reaching an established goal. **Profit sharing** is another compensation arrangement in which employees are paid a portion of the company's profits.

Some employees are on commission-based salary plans. A **commission** is a percentage of a sale paid to a salesperson. A commission-based salary varies from month to month depending on sales. Those receiving this type of salary may be paid using a commission-only plan or a combination plan.

COMMISSION-ONLY PLAN   Some employees, especially those in sales, receive all of their salaries in commission. Commission-only plans are good for employers because commissions are paid only when sales are made. Some employees may not want to accept a commission-only position, because they are not comfortable with the uncertainty of not knowing what their actual pay will be from pay period to pay period.

Lyn Kovacs works entirely on commission. Last year, Lyn sold $490,000 worth of electronic devices. She received 10 percent of her sales as commission. Her annual salary was $49,000, as calculated below.

Amount sold × Percent of commission = Amount of commission

$490,000   ×   0.10   = $49,000

COMBINATION PLAN   An employee may be on a combination plan. A combination plan includes a base salary plus commission.

Hector Marquez sells men's clothing at a local department store. He earns $8.00 an hour, plus 10 percent of whatever he sells. Last

Dmitry Kalinovsky/Shutterstock.com

Why are salespeople paid using a commission plan?

month, Hector worked 158 hours and sold $11,500 worth of clothing. His total monthly compensation was $2,414, calculated as follows:

Base pay	+	Commission	=	Total pay
(Hours × Hourly wage)	+	(10% × Sales)	=	Total pay
(158 × $8.00)	+	(0.10 × $11,500)	=	Total pay
$1,264.00	+	$1,150.00	=	$2,414.00

Benefits

Benefits are rewards, other than cash, given to employees. They may include paid time off, insurance, and a retirement plan.

PAID TIME OFF Almost all employers offer paid time off to their employees. Examples of paid time off include paid vacation, paid holidays, sick leave, and personal days. These kinds of leave represent costs to employers, because employees are paid while they are not working.

Businesses handle vacation in various ways. Many offer one or two weeks of paid vacation a year to new employees. Employees usually gain more vacation time the longer they work at a business. Some businesses let employees carry over unused vacation days from year to year, whereas others require employees to use up their vacation time each year.

Most employers offer paid holidays to their employees. Paid holidays typically include Christmas Day, Thanksgiving Day, Fourth of July, Labor Day, and Memorial Day. Many businesses grant other holidays as well.

Some companies offer sick leave to employees to give them time off due to illness or to care for a sick child or other family member. The number of days of sick leave provided varies from business to business. In addition to sick leave, companies may offer personal days, which are paid time away from work for personal reasons. Personal days help workers meet outside demands on their time.

INSURANCE Health insurance is often viewed as the most important part of a benefits package. *Health insurance* pays specified amounts of money to cover medical expenses or treatments. Health insurance plans offered by employers vary but typically cover the cost of medical office visits for illness and checkups, hospitalization, emergency room services, and prescription drugs. In addition to basic health insurance, businesses may also offer other kinds of insurance, such as dental insurance, vision insurance, life insurance, and accident and disability insurance.

The cost to businesses to provide insurance coverage can be quite high. The Affordable Care Act (ACA) requires businesses with 50 or more full-time equivalent employees to provide health insurance or pay a penalty. Most insurance plans require employees to pay a portion of the cost.

Kurhan/Shutterstock.com

Why do you think employers offer their employees paid vacation time?

RETIREMENT PLANS   Some businesses help employees save for retirement by offering 401(k) plans. Employees who participate in 401(k) plans have a percentage of their earned income withheld by the employer to be deposited into a professionally managed investment account. Some employers will match employees' 401(k) contributions as much as 50 cents per dollar invested. The funds will continue to grow tax-free until they are withdrawn by the retiree upon reaching retirement age.

Pension plans are another type of employer-sponsored retirement savings plan. A pension plan pays an employee a fixed sum after retirement that is predetermined by a formula based on the employee's earnings history and years of service. Pension plans are typically funded solely by the employer and, thus, are more costly to the company. Because of this, they are not as common as they once were.

 CHECKPOINT

What may be included in a compensation package for employees?

LO 11.2-3   Regulations That Protect Employees

There are many laws governing the workplace. Certain laws place restrictions on employers and provide guidance in employer–employee relations. They provide employees with legal remedies in response to employer violations, such as discrimination. Other laws protect employees' rights to safe working conditions and reasonable accommodations for disabilities, disease, and family issues. Some of these laws established special commissions and agencies to enforce them.

It is important to consider these regulations as you develop your staffing plan. Small businesses often run into human resource management issues because the person doing the hiring is not a trained personnel specialist who is familiar with these laws.

National Labor Relations Act (NLRA) of 1935

Congress passed the National Labor Relations Act (NLRA) to protect the rights of employees and employers in the process of negotiating employment contracts. It guarantees workers the right to join a *union*, which is an organization that represents employees and bargains on their behalf for better working conditions and terms of employment. The contract negotiation process between the employer and the union is known as *collective bargaining*. The National Labor Relations Board (NLRB) supervises and controls all aspects of labor relations including formation of a union and the implementation and carrying out of collective bargaining agreements.

Entrepreneurs prefer to operate independently and usually are not unionized. However, some small businesses do negotiate labor contracts and employ unionized personnel.

Fair Labor Standards Act (FLSA) of 1938

The Fair Labor Standards Act (FLSA) defines the employment relationship between an employee and employer. It distinguishes between an employee and an independent contractor, who has a business of his or her own. An employee is dependent on the business for which he or she works. When an employee relationship exists as defined by the FLSA, the employee must be paid at least minimum wage. The act established the national minimum wage. Congress reviews the minimum wage every few years and makes adjustments when warranted.

The FLSA also established the maximum number of hours employees can work. It requires that employees earn overtime pay for hours worked in excess of 40 hours a week. In addition, the act includes rules for workers under the age of 16.

Civil Rights Act of 1964

Title VII of the Civil Rights Act prohibits discrimination on the basis of race, color, religion, sex, or national origin in hiring, promotion, discharge, pay, fringe benefits, job training, classification, referral, and other aspects of employment. This law is enforced by the Equal

FAMOUS ENTREPRENEUR

J. K. ROWLING Ask successful people how to succeed, and they will always tell you to do what you love. For a fortunate few, that formula works. Such is the case with J. K. Rowling, creator of *Harry Potter* and one of the most successful writers in the world today.

Rowling always wanted to be a writer. Her favorite subject in school was English, and she liked studying languages too. Rowling went to Exeter University and studied French. Her parents thought languages would lead to a career as a bilingual secretary. However, she discovered that she liked nothing about being a secretary and spent time working on stories at the computer when she thought no one was looking. Such misbehavior eventually got her fired, so Rowling went abroad to teach English as a foreign language in Portugal. With her

What can you learn about entrepreneurship from J. K. Rowling's experiences?

Cindy Ord/Getty Images Entertainment/Getty Images

mornings free, she began work on her third novel after giving up on two others when she realized how bad they were.

When she left Portugal, her suitcase was filled with stories about Harry Potter. She settled in Edinburgh, Scotland, and decided to finish the novel and try to get it published before starting work as a French teacher. A publisher bought the book one year after it was finished. Since then, Rowling has published six more *Harry Potter* books. The books have sold more than 400 million copies, becoming the best-selling book series in history, and were adapted into a blockbuster film franchise.

THINK CRITICALLY

J. K. Rowling found great success as a writer, but her experience as an employee was not very successful. Why do you think this is often the case with entrepreneurs?

Employment Opportunity Commission (EEOC), a government agency established by Congress in 1972 to regulate labor laws. The Civil Rights Act also includes protection against sexual harassment. Businesses should incorporate the following strategies in the workplace to avoid sexual harassment and liability claims:

- Establish clear policies and procedures and communicate them to employees
- Require employees to report incidents of harassment immediately
- Investigate all complaints thoroughly
- Take action against violations and maintain confidentiality
- Contact an attorney if a lawsuit is likely to be filed

Age Discrimination in Employment Act of 1967

The purpose of this act is to promote employment of older persons (40 and over) based on their ability rather than their age. It prohibits arbitrary age discrimination in employment, including hiring, promotion, discharge, and compensation.

Occupational Safety and Health Act (OSH Act) of 1970

The Occupational Safety and Health Act (OSH Act) requires that employers maintain safe working conditions for their employees. To comply with the act's regulations, you must keep records that show the steps you have taken to protect the welfare of your workers and to keep your workplace safe. If employees have to work with dangerous equipment or substances, you must provide them with special training. If the Occupational Safety and Health Administration (OSHA) suspects that your business has unsafe practices, its inspectors will examine your facility and may require you to make changes.

Hurst Photo/Shutterstock.com

What is the purpose of the Occupational Safety and Health Act?

Americans with Disabilities Act (ADA) of 1990

The Americans with Disabilities Act (ADA) bans discrimination against employees based on disabilities. It requires businesses with 15 or more employees to accommodate the needs of employees with disabilities, even if the firms currently do not have disabled employees. The intent of the ADA is to protect job applicants and employees who are legally disabled but are qualified for a specific job. An employee is qualified if he or she can carry out the necessary functions of the job with some type of reasonable accommodation.

Family and Medical Leave Act (FMLA) of 1993

This act requires businesses with more than 50 employees to provide them up to 12 weeks of unpaid leave if a serious health condition

affects the employee, the employee's child, or the employee's parent or spouse. This act also makes it possible for male and female employees to take leave in the event of a birth or adoption of a child. To be eligible, an employee must have been employed by the business for at least one year.

CHECKPOINT

Why do we need laws to help protect the rights of employees?

THINK ABOUT IT

1. What makes the hiring process challenging?

2. Why is the compensation package important to potential employees?

3. Why is it important for you as a small business owner to have an understanding of the laws designed to protect employees?

MAKE ACADEMIC CONNECTIONS

4. **RESEARCH**   Find and compare three ads for the same type of job. Are the qualifications requested the same? If not, how are they different? Is any mention of compensation made? If so, how is it structured? Conduct online research to find the going wage for this position. What do you think is a fair wage for this job?

5. **MATH**   You have an open position for an entry-level salesperson in your company. You offer a salary of $25,000 per year. You discover that another company with a similar sales position offers a combination plan of $13,000 per year plus a commission of 15 percent of sales. Average annual sales are $90,000. Which job has the potential for higher earnings? Do you need to adjust your salary? Why or why not?

Teamwork

When interviewing job candidates, there are questions you cannot legally ask. Using the library or the Internet, research the guidelines for the types of questions you can and cannot ask. Working with teammates, think of a position in a company and make a list of interview questions adhering to the guidelines. Role-play an interview for the position.

The Essential Question   Refer to The Essential Question on p. 321. When staffing a business, entrepreneurs should follow a hiring process, offer attractive compensation packages, and be aware of the various federal laws that guide employer–employee relations.

DIRECT AND CONTROL HUMAN RESOURCES

11.3

The Essential Question What do the implementing and controlling functions of management involve?

LEARNING OBJECTIVES

LO 11.3-1 Explain how to implement your staffing plan.

LO 11.3-2 Discuss ways to motivate your employees.

LO 11.3-3 Describe the control function of management as it applies to human resources.

KEY TERMS

- delegate
- performance evaluation

You've hired someone, now what?

FOCUS ON SMALL **BUSINESS**

Emanuel carefully screened the applicants for the administrative assistant position, interviewed a couple of candidates, and offered the job to Vivian. Vivian reported to work bright and early on a Monday morning. Emanuel reviewed her job description with her, showed her how the phone system works, and then headed out to do some excavation work.

He hadn't been gone an hour when his cell phone started ringing. It was Vivian. She was in a panic because she had received several calls about excavation services. Customers wanted to know the costs and when they could be scheduled for service. Vivian didn't know what to tell them, and some customers became impatient and demanding. Emanuel quickly turned his truck around and headed back to his shop. On the way there, he tried to figure out what to do.

Well-trained employees help a business succeed.

WORK AS A TEAM What mistakes do you think Emanuel made after hiring Vivian? What does he need to do now?

LO 11.3-1   Implement Your Staffing Plan

Once you have people working for you, you become a manager. This means that you will no longer focus all of your efforts on doing your own job. You will be *implementing*, which involves directing and leading employees to accomplish the goals of the organization. As a manager, you will have to exhibit leadership and motivate your employees.

To manage your staff effectively, you need to understand the levels of management, apply appropriate leadership styles, enforce policies, and provide training. This will help you create a workforce that is dedicated to meeting customer needs and increasing sales.

Understand the Levels of Management

There are three basic levels of management. The amount of responsibility varies with each level of management. As the manager moves up, the amount of responsibility increases.

1. *Lower (supervisory) level.* Lower-level, or first-line, managers work directly with the employees on the job. They are responsible for implementing the plans of middle management. They assign tasks, guide and supervise employees, and ensure quality.
2. *Middle (executive) level.* Middle managers serve as a liaison between the lower-level and top-level managers. They are responsible for implementing the goals of top management. Examples of middle-level managers include general managers and department managers.
3. *Top (administrative) level.* Top management has the highest level of responsibility. They are responsible for establishing the vision for the company, developing goals and company policies, and controlling and overseeing the entire company. Examples of top-level managers include the company's president, vice president, and CEO.

The number of managers at each level will vary depending on the size of the company. In a new business venture, the entrepreneur may serve in all levels of management. A large corporation may have many individuals working as executive- and supervisory-level managers.

Apply Leadership Styles

When you are a manager, workers will look to you as a leader. Leaders direct employees in different ways. Some leaders focus on the task to be completed. To make sure the job gets done in the best way possible, they give direct orders and expect employees to follow them. Workers know exactly what is expected of them. Other leaders focus on keeping employees satisfied and the workplace harmonious. By building good relationships, these leaders believe that workers will function as a well-organized team. They empower workers to make their own decisions rather than just follow orders. Empowerment reduces delays in the flow of work and reduces the workload of the manager. You will need to adopt the leadership style that helps you run the business most effectively.

Enforce Employee Policies

As the owner of your own business, you will establish policies concerning vacations, holidays, hours, compensation, benefits, behavior, and other issues

BE YOUR OWN BOSS

You own a floral design studio. Last year, you promoted Philip, one of your designers, to manager of the studio. Philip had shown excellent design skills and was eager to take on new responsibilities. Recently, Philip has become increasingly protective of information regarding the day-to-day management of the floral shop. Several major problems with important customers have surfaced that Philip knew about but had not shared with you. Business from two of these customers has decreased during the last quarter. Also, several staff members have come to you privately with complaints about Philip's management practices. Tina, who has worked for you for over ten years, is threatening to quit. Use the six-step problem-solving method (see Chapter 1) to determine how you will handle the issues with Philip.

affecting your workers. You will need to make sure that all of your employees are familiar with these policies. You may need to gently remind employees of policies if they fail to follow them.

Many companies communicate policies to staff by creating an employee handbook. These handbooks can be just a few pages long or they can fill a small binder, depending on the size of the company and the number of policies.

Train Your Employees

You will need to develop a training program for your new employees. This program should begin as soon as they are hired. Training should not end when the employee learns how things are done. Continuous training ensures that employees are always knowledgeable and up to date on changes affecting the business. This benefits both the employee and the company.

There are many ways to provide training to employees. You may use different techniques for different job responsibilities. You will need to decide which is best for you, your business, and the employee. Some of the more common training methods include the following:

- **On-the-job training** Employees learn new responsibilities by actually performing them at their place of business.
- **Coaching** Employees receive feedback and instruction from their manager on a constant basis.
- **Mentoring** An employee teams up with a more experienced employee to learn a job. The mentor helps the employee by providing advice and instruction when needed.
- **Conferences and seminars** Employees attend professional development conferences and seminars to learn about new techniques and trends from an expert in the field.

After training, you need to make sure that employees are using what they learned during the training. Assessing the effectiveness of the training program is helpful when planning future training programs.

Depending on your business, you or your employees may need a state occupational license. Obtaining the license usually requires training and passing a test. Doctors, attorneys, real estate agents, insurance sales reps, hairdressers, and food handlers are among the occupations that need licenses.

Why are conferences and seminars valuable training methods?

CHECKPOINT

What should be included in the implementation of a staffing plan?

LO 11.3-2 Motivate Your Employees

To get the most out of your employees, you will have to motivate them. You can do so in several ways.

1. **Pay employees well.** When employees feel they are compensated well, they will be happier. They will perform to the best of their ability.
2. **Treat employees fairly.** Everyone wants to be treated well. Be sure to treat everyone the same.
3. **Recognize employees for the work they do.** Offer public recognition for a job well done. Praise employees frequently.
4. **Empower employees.** When employees are involved in decision making, they often work harder and take pride in the fact that their input makes a difference.

Delegate Responsibility

To manage effectively, you must delegate. To **delegate** is to let others share workloads and responsibilities. Many entrepreneurs have difficulty delegating responsibility. However, as a business owner, it is important to recognize when tasks can be assigned to others to lighten your work load.

What Went *Wrong?*

Whom Do You Trust?

Sandy Warren formed Motiva International, a sales motivation and consulting company. Sandy felt it was very important to involve her employees in all business operations. At weekly meetings, she shared and discussed confidential company details with the company's 18 employees. However, Sandy soon learned that there were some things that should not be shared.

The company was experiencing some cash flow problems, and Sandy discussed this with the employees. Employees became concerned that they would not get paid, which distracted them from their job duties. Because work wasn't getting done, customer relations suffered. At another meeting, Sandy told her employees about a deal she was about to close with a new client. One excited employee told someone outside the company about the new client. This leak of information enabled a competitor to develop a stronger proposal and steal away the new client. Losing that deal forced Sandy to lay off employees, go deeper into debt, and finally dissolve the company.

Carefully consider what information to share with employees.

Mediaphotos/iStockphoto.com

THINK CRITICALLY

1. How do you determine what company information should be reserved for management and withheld from employees?
2. Would you have fired the employee who leaked the information regarding the potential new client? Why or why not?

Employees who are given more responsibility are better motivated and contribute more to the company. Delegating responsibility to them allows you to make the most of their experience, talents, and skills.

As a business owner, delegating allows you to focus on more important tasks, such as expanding into new markets or offering new products. Assigning duties that can be performed by others will free up your time.

Finally, delegating is essential if a company is to grow. When your business is small, you may be able to manage it by yourself. But if the company is to expand, you must let managers take on more responsibility.

Listen to Employees

Some entrepreneurs fail to listen to their employees. In doing so, they miss out on an opportunity to take advantage of valuable ideas and resources that can help them increase profits.

The people who work for you are very familiar with your business and may be able to offer fresh ideas. Listening to new points of view may help you come up with new, creative solutions. If you value the opinions of your employees, they will feel they are a valuable asset to your company. Being appreciated will keep them motivated to do a good job for you.

CHECKPOINT

How can you motivate employees?

LO 11.3-3   Control Human Resources

The controlling function of management involves setting standards for the operation of a business and ensuring those standards are met. In the area of human resources, it is necessary to establish performance standards for employees and then evaluate employees periodically to

Yuri Arcurs/iStockphoto.com

Why should a manager encourage employees to share their opinions and ideas?

be sure they are meeting the performance standards. This process can help you identify outstanding employees who should be promoted and problem employees who should be dismissed.

Evaluate Employees

Most businesses perform an employee review once or twice a year in which they analyze each employee's performance. The job description should be used when evaluating how well an employee has fulfilled all of his or her job responsibilities. Other aspects that may be evaluated include dependability, punctuality, attitude toward job and coworkers, and success in achieving predetermined objectives.

A **performance evaluation** serves as a management control tool that helps determine whether the objectives for a particular job are being met. The evaluation process is also useful to the employee. It helps the employee recognize strengths and see where there is room for improvement. As part of the process, plans for mentoring, training, and practice should be put in place to help improve the employee's performance in areas where needed.

Performance reviews should be conducted face to face. During the performance review, the reviewer should focus on the positive aspects of the employee's performance. Productivity should be reviewed, and the employee and reviewer should work together to set new objectives for the upcoming period. The review should be recorded on an appraisal form, as shown on the next page. The form should include the employee's name and job title as well as the manager's name, the date range the review covers, job responsibilities and attributes, comments, goals for the next year, and a section outlining plans for employee development. A ranking method can be used to rate how well the employee has performed. A copy of the appraisal form should be kept in the employee's file for future reference or in case there is a dispute.

Why are performance evaluations important to both the employer and employee?

Promote Employees

Having a promotion policy is important. If your employees know there is a potential career path within the company, they are more likely to remain interested in working for your business and strive for a promotion.

When promoting an employee, be sure you make the decision fairly to avoid problems among employees. Base your decision on work-related factors, such as the employee's skills and performance. For example, reasons for promotion may include a high volume of sales or exceptional customer service.

PERFORMANCE APPRAISAL

DATE: January 21, 20--
NAME: Daniel Tisdale
JOB TITLE: Marketing Director

Reports To: Laureen Stiles
Review Period: 1/1 to 12/31

ATTRIBUTE	WELL ABOVE STANDARD	ABOVE STANDARD	STANDARD	BELOW STANDARD	FAR BELOW STANDARD
Quantity of work		✓			
Knowledge of work		✓			
Ability to organize			✓		
Ability to meet deadlines			✓		
Dependability	✓				
Judgment			✓		
Initiative	✓				
Communication				✓	
Management of others			✓		
Teamwork			✓		

COMMENTS

You have done an outstanding job of increasing sales. Your hard work, dependability, and initiative are very much appreciated.

AREAS FOR IMPROVEMENT:

1. Increase technical knowledge to improve the quality and quantity of work.

2. Improve written communication skills by enrolling in a business writing course.

3. Improve management skills, in particular by delegating more responsibility to your marketing assistants.

4. Increase ability to participate as part of team.

GOALS FOR COMING YEAR:

1. Increase store sales 12 percent.

2. Oversee completion of company website.

3. Generate online sales of $75,000.

Employee: Daniel Tisdale

Manager: Laureen Stiles

Daniel Tisdale

Laureen Stiles

Dismiss Employees

Some employees may not work out. In fact, they may end up hurting your business. How will you handle such situations? As soon as you notice an employee not performing well or causing problems, discuss the situation with him or her. Form a specific action plan with the employee that will help him or her meet expectations. If there is still no improvement, you will need to dismiss that employee. Once you decide to dismiss an employee, do so immediately. Record the reasons for the dismissal in the employee's file.

 CHECKPOINT

Why is it important to conduct employee performance evaluations at regular intervals?

 11.3 ASSESSMENT

THINK ABOUT IT

1. How does a leader's role differ based on his or her leadership style? How does the leadership style affect employees?

2. Why do many entrepreneurs find it difficult to delegate?

3. Why do you think it is important to keep a copy of an employee's performance appraisal form?

MAKE ACADEMIC CONNECTIONS

4. **PROBLEM SOLVING** You own a clothing store and currently employ two sales assistants. You have just hired a new sales assistant. Develop a training program for your new employee so she will learn all aspects of the business, including operating the cash register, assisting customers, and opening and closing the store.

5. **COMMUNICATION** With a partner, design a performance appraisal form based on a career and job title of your choice. Then role-play an employee and employer participating in a performance review. Assume the employee is a good worker who deserves a promotion. Complete the performance appraisal form.

Teamwork

You manage a department in a business that is in the midst of change. Your employees have heard many rumors about job changes, possible layoffs, and pay reductions. Morale in the department is at an all-time low. Working with teammates, develop a plan to motivate your employees to achieve high performance standards and keep a good attitude in the midst of all the changes. Share your motivational plan with the rest of the class.

The Essential Question Refer to The Essential Question on p. 331. Implementing involves directing and leading employees to accomplish the goals of the organization. Controlling involves setting standards, such as performance standards, for the operation of a business and ensuring those standards are met.

Sharpen Your 21st Century Entrepreneurial Skills

Leadership Skills

As an entrepreneur and a manager, you need to demonstrate good leadership skills. If you want your business to grow, you must be able to lead and influence others to help you carry out your business vision. A manager who can get individual employees and groups to work well together to accomplish objectives is considered to be an effective leader.

An effective leader has a variety of traits and characteristics, including the following:

1. **Communication** Listen, speak, and write effectively.
2. **Understanding** Respect the feelings and needs of fellow workers.
3. **Initiative** Have the ambition and motivation to see a project through to the end.
4. **Dependability** Be reliable and follow through on commitments.
5. **Judgment** Make decisions carefully, objectively, and fairly.
6. **Objectivity** Look at all sides of an issue before making a decision.
7. **Confidence** Make decisions and take responsibility for the results.
8. **Consistency** Do not be too emotional or unpredictable.
9. **Cooperation** Work well with others.
10. **Honesty** Behave ethically and be truthful.
11. **Courage** Be willing to take reasonable risks and make unpopular decisions.
12. **Intelligence** Have the knowledge, understanding, and skills needed to perform well.
13. **Flexibility** Be able to adapt to new and unpredictable situations that may arise.
14. **Creativity** Be able to think outside the box for new solutions.

Not all people are natural-born leaders. However, everyone has the potential to lead, and everyone can develop skills to become an effective leader.

TRY IT OUT

Leadership styles vary from person to person. Choose two individuals who have played leadership roles in history and research their leadership styles. Prepare a report that illustrates how they exhibited each of the characteristics described above.

SUMMARY

11.1 Identify Your Staffing Needs

1. To determine staffing needs, list all of the duties in your business, identify how much time is needed to perform each duty, determine the skills and qualifications that employees need, and write job descriptions that list the specific responsibilities of each position. You should also create an organizational structure and chart to show the relationships between the various jobs in the company.

2. To recruit new employees, you may use online sources, employment agencies, career centers, in-store advertising, classified advertisements, and referrals.

3. In addition to hiring permanent employees, you can also hire freelancers, interns, or temporary workers.

11.2 Staff Your Business

4. The four steps in the hiring process are: (1) screen candidates, (2) review and verify information on job applications, (3) interview the best candidates, and (4) make a job offer.

5. A compensation package should include a method of pay and may provide a variety of benefits. Types of pay include wages, salary, commission only, or a combination of salary plus commission. Bonuses and profit sharing are other compensation methods. Benefits may include paid time off for vacation and sickness; health, dental, vision, life, and disability insurance; and retirement plans.

6. Employers must follow all laws and regulations that are created to protect employees from unfair labor practices.

11.3 Direct and Control Human Resources

7. Implementing your staffing plan effectively requires that you understand the levels of management, apply appropriate leadership styles, enforce employee policies, and offer training.

8. There are several ways to motivate employees, including paying them well, treating them fairly, recognizing them for good work, empowering them, delegating responsibility, and listening to them.

9. You should create a procedure for evaluating employees. Outstanding employees should be promoted when opportunities become available, and problem employees should be dismissed.

WHAT DO YOU KNOW NOW?

Read *Ideas in Action* on page 313 again. Then answer the questions a second time. Have your responses changed? If so, how have they changed?

KEY TERMS REVIEW

Match each statement with the term that best defines it. Some terms may not be used.

1. The process of determining the tasks and sequence of tasks necessary to perform a job
2. A management control tool that helps determine whether the objectives for a particular job are being met
3. To look for people to hire and attract them to the business
4. A percentage of a sale paid to a salesperson
5. People who provide specialty services to a number of different businesses on an hourly basis or by the job
6. An amount paid for a job position stated on an annual basis
7. A financial reward for employment service in addition to a regular wage or salary
8. To let others share workloads and responsibilities
9. The process of determining the number of employees you need and defining a process for hiring them
10. Payments for labor or services that are made on an hourly, daily, or per-unit basis
11. A written statement listing the tasks and responsibilities of a position

a. benefits
b. bonus
c. chain of command
d. commission
e. delegate
f. freelancers
g. interns
h. job analysis
i. job description
j. performance evaluation
k. profit sharing
l. recruit
m. salary
n. staffing
o. wages

REVIEW YOUR KNOWLEDGE

12. **True or False**   Good employees and a well-run human resource management program are as important to your business as are capital, equipment, and inventory.
13. A collection of tasks and duties that an employee is responsible for completing is a
    a. job
    b. job description
    c. job analysis
    d. duties and task list
14. **True or False**   The job analysis helps people in a company understand who reports to whom.
15. If you live in a very small community with a limited pool of available workers, what would be the *best* way to recruit employees from other nearby communities?
    a. online advertisement
    b. in-store advertising
    c. classified ad in the local paper
    d. career center for a university 300 miles away
16. **True or False**   During the screening process, you determine which candidates are most qualified for the position you are trying to fill.
17. **True or False**   As long as a job candidate has the appropriate skills needed, it is not necessary to verify that the information provided on his or her resume and job application is correct.
18. Which of the following would *not* be included in a job offer?
    a. job analysis
    b. starting salary
    c. terms of employment
    d. benefits package

19. You interviewed a candidate for a sales position in your swimming pool sales and installation business. Sales are usually high in the spring and summer and then drop off in the fall and winter. The candidate has a family and needs a steady income but likes the idea of earning more pay if he makes a large number of sales. Which payment method do you think he would prefer?
    a. wage
    b. salary
    c. commission only
    d. combination plan

20. **True or False**   The Occupational Safety and Health Act requires that employers maintain safe working conditions.

21. Which of the following levels of management is responsible for assigning tasks to employees and ensuring quality?
    a. supervisory-level
    b. administrative-level
    c. executive-level
    d. middle-level

22. Which of the following is *not* a way to motivate employees?
    a. pay them well
    b. treat them fairly
    c. recognize them for good work
    d. make all decisions for them

APPLY WHAT YOU LEARNED

23. You will hire three people to help in your custom drapery business: an administrative assistant, a seamstress, and an interior designer/salesperson. What qualifications and skills do each of these employees need? Write a job description for each position. Establish a compensation package for each position, describing the type of pay and benefits. Then using Internet sources, plan a training session for one of your employees to help improve his or her job skills. (LO 11.1-1, LO 11.2-2, LO 11.3-1)

24. Describe how you will recruit each of the employees in your custom drapery business above. Create a want ad and prepare a list of interview questions for each position. (LO 11.1-2, LO 11.2-1)

MAKE ACADEMIC CONNECTIONS

25. **MATH**   Kate Smith sells vacuum cleaners and is compensated under a combination plan. She earns $9.75 per hour, plus 15 percent of whatever she sells. Last month, Kate worked 160 hours and sold 9 vacuum cleaners. Five of the vacuum cleaners were high-end models priced at $1,100 each. The other four vacuum cleaners were $450 each. What is Kate's compensation for last month? (LO 11.2-2)

26. **PROBLEM SOLVING**   One of your employees is upset that another employee received a promotion. She thinks she should have received the promotion because she has worked there longer and has always had good performance evaluations. What are some reasons that a newer employee would receive the promotion? How will you handle the situation? (LO 11.3-3)

What Would YOU DO?

You want to hire a new sales assistant for your company. You checked with the local college career center, and it sent several qualified applicants for an interview. You are really impressed with one of the candidates, and you want to hire him for the position. Before making the job offer, you decide to check the Internet to see if the candidate has a profile on a social media site in order to find out more about his background and interests. You quickly find his Facebook page and are shocked at some of the pictures and comments he has posted. What would you do? Would you hire him anyway, or would this change your impression of him?

BUILD YOUR BUSINESS PLAN PROJECT

This activity will help you determine the staffing needs for your business. This information will help you develop the Operations section of your business plan.

1. Assume your business will grow over the next year and you will need to add employees. Make a list of at least three job positions that need to be filled. Is each position a full-time job, part-time job, or temporary work? For each position, write a detailed job description. Create an organizational chart for your business based on these new positions.

2. Write a classified advertisement for each of the positions you will need to fill. What employee characteristics and qualifications are you seeking? Write the interview questions that you will ask the candidates for each position. Write a list of questions you will ask their references and/or previous employers.

3. For each position, create a complete compensation package that outlines wages or salary and any nonsalary benefits. Explain why you have structured the compensation package as such.

4. Add employee policies concerning vacation, holidays, hours, behavior, and any other employee issues to the operating procedures manual you previously created in Chapter 10.

5. In what ways will you train new and existing employees for your business? What aspects of your business require training, and what type of training is the best for each aspect? Write a short report about your decisions.

6. Determine the ways you plan to motivate your employees. Create at least one method of publicly acknowledging employees for good work. Record your ideas.

7. Create a sample performance appraisal form. Will this form be the same for each position? Why or why not?

PLANNING A CAREER IN PHOTOGRAPHY

Arts, A/V Technology & Communications

"My aunt got married last weekend. She hired a professional photographer for the occasion. During the reception, the photographer set up a laptop on a table that had photos of the ceremony streaming on screen. It was really fun to see pictures of the ceremony while we were still celebrating the wedding."

Photographers take pictures of people, events, and products. They produce and preserve images to record an event. Photographers often specialize by topic. Areas of specialization include news, commercial, fine arts, portrait, or special event photography.

Today, most photographers use digital cameras instead of traditional film cameras. Digital cameras capture images electronically. This allows photographers to transfer the images to a computer where they can use software to modify or enhance them through color correction and other specialized effects.

Employment Outlook

- A slower-than-average rate of employment growth is anticipated.
- Competition for positions is fierce as improvements in digital technology have reduced barriers of entry into this profession.
- Demand for portrait photographers will remain high, whereas declines in the news industry will reduce demand for news photographers.

Job Titles

- News Photographer
- Online Photographer
- Event Photographer
- Portrait Photographer

Needed Education/Skills

- Creativity and a solid understanding of photography are essential.
- Strong artistic ability and interpersonal and customer-service skills are required.
- Computer skills for digital photo manipulation are needed.
- Developing a portfolio of work for prospective clients to view is necessary.

What's it like to work in Photography? Keisha is a school teacher who works as a freelance photographer on the weekends and in the summer to earn extra money. She specializes in portraits and ceremonies such as weddings and reunions.

On Sunday afternoon, Keisha went to a local park to take a combination of candid and posed pictures for a family reunion. That evening, she loaded the photos on her website. Although Keisha earned a fee for taking photos at the reunion, she will generate additional revenue when family members purchase either individual photos or customized albums.

Monday morning, Keisha met with a newly engaged couple who are potential clients. After discussing the logistical details of the wedding, Keisha went to her website to show the couple a few albums from prior weddings. Providing digital copies of the photos online and arranging them in albums makes it easy for clients to review photos.

What about you? Would you like to help individuals record special events through the use of photography? What kind of photography interests you?

Interview Skills

Every entrepreneur must possess interviewing skills, whether as the interviewer or the interviewee. The Interview Skills event allows BPA members the opportunity to develop, practice, and demonstrate effective job interviewing skills.

The Interview Skills event requires that you prepare a job application, resume, and cover letter for a job for which you are currently qualified. All of the information contained in the resume, cover letter, and application must reflect your real-life skills and abilities. You should not make up previous jobs or credentials, but you may use a fictitious personal address and telephone number.

Performance Indicators

- Apply technical writing skills to produce a cover letter and resume
- Demonstrate knowledge of employability search
- Apply research to determine qualifications for a job
- Produce a cover letter and resume
- Complete a job application
- Describe knowledge of job advancement
- Demonstrate interpersonal skills

Go to the BPA website for more detailed information.

GIVE IT A TRY

Use the Organizational Chart found in the BPA *Style & Reference Manual* to select a job for which you are currently qualified. (Your teacher can access the manual through the BPA website.) Prepare a resume using the one shown in Chapter 3 on page 87 as a guide. Then prepare a cover letter for the job you selected. Your cover letter should tell your potential new employer why you are the perfect fit for the job. Identify key skills that make you qualified. The letter should be addressed to the company below. Proofread all of your work for correct spelling, grammar, and punctuation.

Ms. Julie Smith, Manager
Human Resource Department
Professional Business Associates
5454 Cleveland Avenue
Columbus, OH 43231-4021

After completing your resume and cover letter, work with a partner to develop a mock interview for the job.

www.bpa.org

bikeriderlondon/Shutterstock.com

Risk Management

12.1 BUSINESS RISKS

12.2 INSURE AGAINST RISKS

12.3 OTHER RISKS

Making Friends Is Her Business

Photo by Kate Robbins

Catherine Cook, Vice President, Brand Strategy at MeetMe

When Catherine Cook was 15, her family moved to New Jersey. She and her brother Dave, 16, were faced with meeting new people. "Dave and I were flipping through the school's yearbook to see if we recognized anyone, and we were shocked at how useless the information was," Catherine said.

Wanting a way to make new friends led Catherine and Dave to create a social network. She enlisted the help of her older brother, Geoff, who had recently graduated from Harvard, and the trio launched myYearbook, a social networking site. Using Elance, an online staffing system, Catherine and Dave found developers to work with in Mumbai, India. Then they got busy thinking up ways to engage users with teen-oriented games and quizzes.

Catherine continued her work on myYearbook through high school and during college at Georgetown University. Competition from other social networking sites, such as MySpace and Facebook, spurred myYearbook to position itself with a unique marketing message: "Facebook is about the friends you already have; myYearbook is about making new friends."

As revenue grew, myYearbook faced another risk—entering the international market. Most of myYearbook's users were in North America, so Catherine and her brothers looked for ways to expand globally. Six years after starting myYearbook, the three siblings became multimillionaires when they sold the company for $100 million of combined stock and cash to Florida-based Quepasa, a company that runs social networking sites targeting Latinos.

The name was changed to MeetMe, and the site now has more than 100 million registered users, most of whom are ages 18 to 35. MeetMe is a mobile first company, with more than 1 million people using MeetMe's mobile applications every day. Catherine, now in her early twenties, is vice president of brand strategy at MeetMe. She still communicates directly with users to learn what they want. "I have always been, and still am, one of the most active members on the site. Every new member gets a friend request from me, which is why I now have more than a million friends," she said.

WHAT DO YOU KNOW?

1. What need was Catherine trying to meet when she started myYearbook?
2. What business risks did Catherine face when starting and growing the company?
3. Why was it important for myYearbook to go global?

12.1 BUSINESS RISKS

The Essential Question What types of risk do businesses face, and how can they deal with those risks?

LEARNING OBJECTIVES

LO 12.1-1 Explain how business owners can identify and deal with risks.

LO 12.1-2 Discuss types of theft and security precautions to take to protect your business.

KEY TERMS

- risk
- risk management
- risk assessment
- shoplifting
- bounced check

FOCUS ON SMALL BUSINESS

What if disaster strikes?

"Kristin," Ty asked his partner, "what do you think would happen to our web hosting business if our computers or computer data were stolen or hacked into?"

"Wow, Ty, we've never really thought about that," Kristin replied. "We just come in every day and do our work. We do back up our work periodically, but we just use flash drives."

"I know," Ty responded, "I started thinking about it after I read about a business that had all of its computers stolen one night. And I realized we have no emergency plan in place."

"We sure don't, but I bet we will have something figured out by tomorrow!" Kristin said.

Businesses must address computer security risks.

WORK AS A TEAM What risks do you think Ty and Kristin would face if all of their computers were destroyed or computer data were compromised? What steps do you think they should take to be prepared in case this would happen?

LO 12.1-1 Dealing with Business Risks

As an independent businessperson, you will face many risks. **Risk** is the possibility of some kind of loss. When you own a business, you need to consider the kinds of events that could pose a risk to your business and develop plans for handling them.

Categorize Risks

Risks can be categorized as human risk, natural risk, and economic risk. *Human risks* are those caused by the actions of individuals, such as employees or customers. Examples include shoplifting, employee theft, robbery, credit card fraud, and bounced checks. *Natural risks* are caused by acts of nature. Examples are storms, fires, floods, and earthquakes. The occurrence of any of these could bring about tremendous loss to a business. *Economic risks* occur because of changes in business conditions. Examples include political instability, increased competition, and inflation.

Prepare to Face Risks

As an entrepreneur, you must be prepared to face all kinds of risks. You will need to decide the best strategy for dealing with risks. **Risk management** is taking action to prevent or reduce the possibility of loss to your business. You can avoid risk, assume risk, or transfer risk.

You may decide to avoid the risk. For example, if you think a product you are developing will not meet market needs, you may decide to avoid financial risks caused by low sales by halting production of the product.

You may decide to assume the risk if you determine the risk is low. If your market research indicates the product you are developing will be successful with your target market, you will most likely produce and sell the product even though there is still a chance of lower sales than expected.

Transferring the risk is another option. You will be able to protect yourself against the financial losses from some risks by purchasing insurance. Insurance transfers the risk of financial loss to the insurance company.

You never know when a disaster may strike, but you should have a plan of action in place when it does to help you recover and restart business operations quickly. To prepare for risks, you should do the following:

1. Determine what can go wrong.
2. Develop a plan.
3. Communicate your plan.

DETERMINE WHAT CAN GO WRONG As a business owner, the first thing you need to do is conduct a risk assessment. A **risk assessment** involves looking at all aspects of your business and determining the risks you face. During this assessment, you should do the following:

- Learn the risks your business faces.
- Decide how the risks would affect your business.
- Prioritize the risks by the impact they will have on your business.

DEVELOP A PLAN Once you have identified the risks that could affect your business, you should develop a written plan for dealing with them. When developing a risk management plan, you may have to comply with certain laws. For example, the Occupational Safety and Health Administration (OSHA) requires businesses to have an evacuation plan for emergencies.

There are many good sources available to help you establish an effective risk management plan. If you are developing an emergency action

DEVELOP YOUR READING SKILLS

As you read, use the SQ3R method.
- **S**urvey the chapter to get an idea of what you will be reading.
- Make a list of **Q**uestions about the chapter that come to mind as you survey.
- **R**ead the chapter.
- **R**ecall what you have read.
- **R**eview the material by discussing it with a classmate.

Why is it important to have a plan for handling risks?

plan, the National Safety Council, a nongovernmental organization that promotes safety, is a good source. It recommends that the following items be included in your emergency action plan:

- Chain-of-command information, including names and job titles of the people responsible for making decisions, monitoring response actions, and recovering back-to-normal operations
- The names of individuals responsible for assessing the degree of risk to life and property and who should be notified for different types of emergencies
- The preferred method for reporting fires and other emergencies
- Specific instructions for shutting down equipment and other business activities and procedures for employees who must shut down equipment before they evacuate the facility
- Facility evacuation procedures, including maps showing the best and alternate exit routes
- Specific training for those who are responsible for responding to emergencies

Be sure to have a recovery plan in place if you suffer a setback. A *recovery plan* will enable you to get back to business as quickly as possible. If you suffer a loss due to a fire, have a plan for temporarily relocating, getting replacement equipment, and retrieving lost data. If one of your suppliers is out of stock of a component needed in the production of your product, have another supplier lined up. A recovery plan will help you continue to meet your customers' needs.

Review your risk management plan periodically. As your business develops and grows, risks facing your business may change. Revise your risk management plan to accommodate your changing needs.

COMMUNICATE YOUR PLAN Let your managers and employees know about your plan for handling risks. To ensure your plan is carried out properly, assign activities and responsibilities to the appropriate people. For example, to protect against the risk of a faulty product, assign the production manager the task of checking the quality of the finished product. If you plan to run an advertisement for an upcoming sale, make sure someone is responsible for placing the ad in the appropriate media at the appropriate time to avoid the risk of lost sales. If you want to protect your computer system from the risks of viruses and computer hackers, you can work with a computer security expert. To address the risks related to emergencies, provide training to all employees to show them what to do in the event of any type of emergency. Work with your managers and employees to be sure all risks are addressed.

LO 12.1-2 Types of Theft

One of the biggest risks that businesses face is theft. Shoplifters and employees may steal your merchandise. Burglars may break into your business and steal your equipment. Customers may use stolen credit cards or write checks when they don't have money in their account. Once you have identified the theft risks you face, you can determine what security precautions you need to take.

Shoplifting

Shoplifting is the act of knowingly taking items from a business without paying. Customers shoplift millions of dollars in merchandise every year. The problem exists in virtually every type of retail business.

If you own a retail business, you will have to take steps to prevent or reduce shoplifting. Some of the things you can do include the following:

- Instruct your employees to watch for customers who appear suspicious.
- Hire security guards or off-duty police officers to patrol your store.
- Post signs indicating that you prosecute shoplifters.
- Ask incoming customers to leave their bags behind the counter.
- Install electronic devices, such as mounted video cameras, electronic merchandise tags, and point-of-exit sensors, to detect shoplifters.

Employee Theft

As an entrepreneur, you need to be aware of the possibility of employee theft. Although most employees are hardworking and honest, there are a few who will take things from your business, such as office supplies, equipment, merchandise, and even money. These employees can negatively impact your business financially.

You need to take steps to prevent the problem from occurring. You also need to know how to detect the problem and handle it once it is evident. Adopting the following procedures may help:

1. **Prevent dishonest employees from joining your company.** Screen job applicants very carefully. Consider using a company that specializes in verifying job applicants' educational backgrounds and searching their criminal records, driver's license reports, civil court records, and credit reports.
2. **Install surveillance systems.** Often the mere knowledge that they are being recorded by a video camera deters employees from stealing.

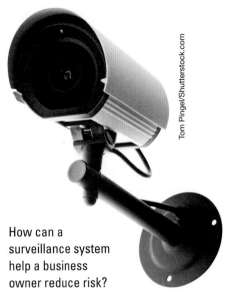

How can a surveillance system help a business owner reduce risk?

3. **Establish a tough company policy regarding employee theft**. Your company policy should detail the consequences of employee theft. Make sure that all employees are aware of the policy.

4. **Be on the lookout**. Watch for cash discrepancies, missing merchandise or supplies, vehicles parked close to loading areas, and other signs that something may be wrong. Keep an eye on employees who seem to work at odd hours, perform their jobs poorly, or complain unreasonably. Ask questions if an employee has an unexplained close relationship with a supplier or customer.

Robbery

Almost all businesses are vulnerable to robberies. It is simply a risk of being open for business, but there are preventative measures you can take. You can locate your business in what is considered a safe area of town to guard against being robbed. You can also install deadbolt locks and burglar alarms and keep the outside of your business well lit at night. To limit losses in the event of a robbery, many businesses keep a minimal amount of cash in the cash register. Once more than a certain amount is received, the cash is transferred to a safe. Some businesses also use surveillance cameras, which deter prospective robbers.

Credit Card Fraud

Business owners lose millions of dollars every year because of stolen credit cards. If a purchase is made on a stolen credit card, a business may not be able to collect the money. To prevent stolen credit cards from being used to purchase goods, you can install an electronic credit authorizer. This machine checks to see if a credit card is valid. If the card has been reported stolen or if the cardholder has exceeded the credit limit, authorization will not be granted.

Bounced Checks

A **bounced check** is a check that the bank returns to the payee (the person or business to whom the check is made payable) because the check writer's checking account has insufficient funds to cover the check amount. Bounced checks are also called *bad checks*.

⊙ **BE YOUR OWN BOSS**

You are the owner and manager of a diner located along a busy interstate highway. You do a good business with travelers passing through as well as locals who eat at your diner regularly. Recently, there have been several robberies during operating hours in nearby businesses. Your local customers are beginning to get a little nervous about coming to your diner. Outline a plan to minimize your risk of robbery. Include ways to make your customers feel safe.

Preventing losses from bad checks is difficult. To minimize losses, you can accept checks drawn on in-state banks only. You can also charge a fee if a customer writes a bad check. Asking for identification, such as a driver's license, can help you track down the check writer so that you can collect the money due. If bad checks are a serious problem in your area, you may decide not to accept checks at all.

CHECKPOINT

How can you protect your business from theft?

12.1 ASSESSMENT

THINK ABOUT IT

1. What are the categories of business risks? Provide three examples of each.

2. What are some steps that you can take to minimize employee theft?

3. You own a pizza shop. You suspect that one of your delivery people is charging customers more than what they actually owe and keeping the difference. How would you handle this situation?

MAKE ACADEMIC CONNECTIONS

4. **MATH**   At closing, the Old World Café's cash register receipts totaled $884. The cash in the register equaled $534, and the credit card slips equaled $237. How much of the proceeds are not accounted for? What might explain the difference?

5. **COMMUNICATION**   Think about your school as if it were a business. Make a list of the risks that students, faculty, staff, and others face at your school. Also, include risks to the property. Then develop a risk management plan for your school. Be sure to address each component of an effective risk management plan as described in the lesson. Share your plan with the class.

Teamwork

Last year, the holiday season profits at Ray's Sporting Goods were reduced significantly because of shoplifting. Form teams and brainstorm ways to approach the problem this year. Put together a proposal containing your recommendations for Ray. Share your recommendations with the rest of the class.

The Essential Question   Refer to The Essential Question on p. 348. There are three main types of risk businesses face—human, natural, and economic risks. It is critical for a business to create a risk management plan to address the actions of the business and the employees in the event these risks occur.

12.2 INSURE AGAINST RISKS

The Essential Question What is an insurable risk, and what types of insurance protect against these risks?

LEARNING OBJECTIVES

LO 12.2-1 Classify risks faced by business owners.

LO 12.2-2 Explain why some business risks are uninsurable.

LO 12.2-3 Determine the different types of insurance you need for your business.

LO 12.2-4 Explain how to approach an insurance purchase.

KEY TERMS

- pure risk
- speculative risk
- controllable risk
- uncontrollable risk
- insurable risk
- premium

FOCUS ON SMALL BUSINESS

A river runs through it.

Carlos thought he had found the perfect location for his new restaurant. He wanted to have a large outdoor patio with a great view, and this location had exactly what he wanted. The patio looked out over a river, and there were many beautiful shade trees. Carlos decided to talk to the owner of the previous restaurant that had occupied the site. He told Carlos that his restaurant had flourished until the river flooded and caused extensive water damage. The owner made the repairs but was never able to recover financially, so he went out of business. This concerned Carlos and made him wonder if this was really the ideal spot.

WORK AS A TEAM What do you think Carlos should do? If he decides to locate here, what can he do to protect his investment?

Without taking precautions, some businesses may be forced to close.

LO 12.2-1 Classification of Risk

As a business owner, you are at risk from more than just criminal activity. A fire could destroy your building. An accident could injure an employee. A broken water pipe could ruin your inventory. Business owners face many types of risk that can be classified based on the result of the risk, controllability of the risk, and insurability of the risk.

Result of the Risk

A **pure risk** presents the chance of loss but no opportunity for gain. If you have a vehicle that is used in your business, every time it goes out on the road there is the risk of an accident. If there is an accident, a loss will likely be suffered. However, if an accident is avoided, there is no opportunity for gain.

A speculative risk offers you the chance to gain as well as lose from the event or activity. Investing in the stock market is a good example of a speculative risk. When you invest money, you have the chance to make money if the stock price rises. However, if the stock price falls, you risk the chance of losing money.

Controllability of the Risk

A controllable risk is one that can be reduced or possibly even avoided by actions you take. Installing a security system in your business could lessen the risk of your business being robbed.

An uncontrollable risk is one on which actions have no effect. The weather cannot be controlled, but it can have a tremendous effect on some businesses. If a hurricane hits a resort town, a dramatic decrease in business and loss of profit will result. But if the weather is sunny and warm, tourism will flourish and business owners may make a profit.

Insurability of the Risk

A risk is an insurable risk if it is a pure risk faced by a large number of people and the amount of the loss can be predicted. Buildings that house businesses are susceptible to fire. Nearly all businesses face this risk, and past statistics can help insurance companies predict the amount of loss and percentage of businesses that will suffer fire losses annually. Insurance companies can sell fire insurance to help cover losses. A premium is a payment made to an insurance company to cover the cost of insurance. The premiums of all those insured are pooled and used to help those who incur losses.

If there is a risk that a loss will occur and the amount of the loss cannot be predicted, the risk is *uninsurable*. An insurance company would have no way of determining the premiums to charge or the amount of funds to pool to cover unpredictable losses. A business may move to a new location, and customers may not follow. The loss of income that could result cannot be predicted and, thus, is not insurable.

Dariush M/Shutterstock.com

Why is a fire an insurable risk?

LO 12.2-2 Uninsurable Risks

Sometimes things happen in the business world that are not covered by insurance, which can be very costly to a business. Insurance does not cover risks that cannot be reasonably predicted or for which the financial loss to the business cannot be calculated. These risks are tied to economic conditions, consumer demand, competitors' actions, technology changes, local factors, and business operations.

Economic Conditions

Managers must constantly study economic conditions. Changes in economic conditions can result from an increase or decrease in competition, shifts in population, inflation or recession, and government regulations. World events can also result in economic changes. The terrorist acts of September 11, 2001, caused a dramatic downturn in the U.S. economy, resulting in major cutbacks and layoffs by businesses. This decreased the amount of disposable income for many Americans, which resulted in losses for many entrepreneurs. When the economy takes a downward turn, a business must respond quickly by cutting production and expenses.

How might the actions of a competitor affect a business?

Consumer Demand

Businesses produce products and services that they think consumers want to buy. Business owners must research consumer needs and wants. If they can predict a change in demand, they may be able to profit by producing and selling a new product or service. However, if consumer demands change suddenly, the company may end up with products in its inventory that it cannot sell. This commonly occurs following the holiday season. The popularity of a "hot" toy that every child wants declines quickly as a new "hot" toy rises in popularity.

Competitors' Actions

Business is competitive. As a business owner, you must be aware of your competitors and their actions. A major advertising campaign or a drop in price by your competitors may result in a change in your volume of sales. You must be ready to respond to actions by your competitors to minimize the risk to your business. For example, fast-food restaurant chains are constantly revamping their value menus to match items their competitors are selling at lower prices.

Technology Changes

As a business owner, you need to stay up to date on technology trends. Evaluate new technology and see if it can help your business. Updates to technology can be a major expense but can alternatively provide efficiencies in business operations that help you serve customers better. If customers view your business as outdated, you may lose customer loyalty and sales to your competition.

Local Factors

If there is an increase in local taxes or a change in local business regulations, it can affect your business. If a local government makes improvements to the infrastructure, such as road or utility improvements, it can help your business in the long term. In the short term, it may result in a loss of business because ongoing construction could cause customers to detour around your business.

Business Operations

The management of a business contributes directly to its success or failure. A business that is poorly managed can have high employee turnover, poor customer service, higher expenses, and other problems. Poorly trained employees can also cause operational problems. Managers and employees must work together to ensure success.

CHECKPOINT

Why are some risks uninsurable?

LO 12.2-3   Types of Insurance

There are many options for insurance. You will have to examine the risks you identify and their potential impact on your business to determine if you need to insure against the risk.

Business Insurance

Insurance companies selling business insurance offer policies that combine protection from all major property and liability risks in one package. These coverages are also sold separately. Package policies are created for businesses that generally face the same kind and degree of risk. Many small and mid-sized businesses purchase a package known as a business owner's policy (BOP), which typically includes the following:

- **Property insurance**   This type of insurance provides coverage for damage to buildings and the contents inside the buildings, such as furniture, fixtures, equipment, and merchandise.
- **Business interruption insurance**   This type of insurance covers the loss of income resulting from a fire or other catastrophe that disrupts the operation of the business. It can also cover the extra expense of operating out of a temporary location.

- **Liability protection** This type of insurance covers your company's legal responsibility for the harm it may cause to others as a result of what you and your employees do or fail to do in your business operations. Harm may involve bodily injury or property damage due to defective products, faulty installations, and errors in services provided.

BOPs do not cover auto insurance, workers' compensation, or health and disability insurance. They also do not cover professional liability, which involves claims of negligent actions by business professionals such as doctors. You will need separate insurance policies to cover these items.

Life Insurance

Life insurance is paid in the event of the death of the insured. It is intended to provide financial support for families should the income earner die. A business owner may buy life insurance so that his or her heirs have enough money to continue the business.

Other Kinds of Insurance

Other types of insurance that you may want to purchase include flood, crime, and renters insurance. Flood protection is not standard with property insurance, so you may have to purchase it separately. Crime insurance protects against losses resulting from crime, such as robbery, computer fraud, or employee theft. Renters insurance covers the contents owned by the renter inside the leased space. The actual owner of the building would purchase insurance for the building. Depending on your business and its location, you may or may not decide to purchase these additional kinds of protection.

 **CHECKPOINT**

What types of insurance can you purchase for your business?

LO 12.2-4 Buy Insurance

Buying insurance is one of the best ways you can prepare for the unexpected, but it can be complicated. Is it possible to have too much or too little insurance? An insurance agent can be of help.

Choose an Insurance Agent

Insurance is sold by agents. An agent can be independent and represent many different insurance companies or work for a single insurance company. Before selecting an insurance provider, talk to an agent who represents more than one insurer or ask representatives of several different companies to talk with you about their policies.

The market for insurance is competitive, so many agents will be eager to sell you insurance. To get the best price, contact a few agents and compare prices and policies among insurers. In addition, check the financial strength of the company each agent represents. This will indicate the company's ability to meet its obligations to policyholders. You may already have an agent you trust with your car insurance or other types of insurance whom you can contact.

Determine the Coverage You Need

To determine the kinds and amounts of coverage you need, start by making a list of the property you own. Include equipment, inventory, vehicles, and other significant assets, and put a value next to each. Then think about the kinds of risk you would like to insure against. If, for example, your business is located near a river, you may want to purchase flood insurance. If you live in a low-crime area, you may decide against insurance that covers break-ins. Understand, however, the implications of not having insurance if something should happen.

The next step is determining how much coverage you need. Be sure you have enough insurance to cover any and all debts you may have incurred while starting your business. Insurance agents earn

What Went *Wrong?*

Up in Flames!

Leslie recently opened a candle store, "Wick's End," by taking out a $25,000 loan to help pay for equipment, supplies, and renovations to an existing store. She hired two part-time employees to help her run the store.

Leslie took out a BOP for $15,000 worth of coverage. She was making enough money to pay her monthly expenses and payroll but not enough to save at this point. With the holiday season just around the corner, she anticipated that she would have more incoming revenue. With the additional revenue, she could increase the level of coverage.

Leslie would often light candles in the store. One night, in a rush to close the store, Leslie left two candles burning near the front windows. A spark from the wick of one of the candles engulfed the curtains in flames. The fire spread, literally destroying the entire store. The part of the store not destroyed by fire had heavy water and smoke damage.

Leslie still owed almost $20,000 on her loan. All of her equipment and inventory, estimated at $10,000, were destroyed in the fire. Because she had only $15,000 of insurance coverage, she was forced to close Wick's End and take a job elsewhere to pay off her debt.

THINK CRITICALLY

1. Do you think Leslie was prepared to deal with business risks?
2. What mistake did Leslie make when purchasing insurance?

Don't cut costs by buying less insurance coverage than you need.

commissions on the amount of coverage they sell. To make sure you need all the coverage your agent suggests, talk to other business owners in your area or counselors from SCORE or the SBA.

CHECKPOINT

How can you determine how much insurance you need?

ASSESSMENT

THINK ABOUT IT

1. What factors must be considered when classifying risks?

2. Provide three examples of risks that are uninsurable.

3. Tim Stanton just opened a surf shop on the beach in Florida. He has purchased property insurance to cover possible losses against his building, fixtures, equipment, merchandise, and other assets. Against what additional risks should he consider insuring his business?

4. What factors should you consider when choosing an insurance agent?

MAKE ACADEMIC CONNECTIONS

5. **MATH**   You have taken out a loan for $50,000 to start your business. As a condition of the loan, your bank requires you to carry property insurance for at least the amount of the loan. Your property is valued at a total of $100,000. Your agent recommends you carry property insurance covering at least 80 percent of your property's value. If annual insurance premiums are $15 per $1,000 of coverage, how much will you pay for insurance to satisfy your bank loan requirement? How much will you pay if you follow your agent's recommendation?

6. **COMMUNICATION**   You have just opened an insurance agency that specializes in insuring businesses. Write a sales letter to prospective customers introducing yourself and your services.

Teamwork

Choose a partner. One partner should assume the role of an entrepreneur who just took out a loan to open a roller skating rink. The other should play the role of an insurance agent who must educate the new owner about the types of insurance available. Working together, use the Internet and other resources to research information about the types of insurance a skating rink should carry. Then role-play the conversation between the insurance agent and the business owner.

The Essential Question   Refer to The Essential Question on p. 354. An insurable risk is one faced by many people for which the amount of loss can be predicted. Property insurance provides protection against risks to a business's building and its contents. Liability insurance protects a business should injury or property damage occur to others as a result of business operations.

OTHER RISKS

The Essential Question What are some hidden risks that could negatively impact a business?

LEARNING OBJECTIVES

LO 12.3-1 Identify risks associated with credit.

LO 12.3-2 Explain how to manage risks at work.

LO 12.3-3 Describe strategies to reduce the risks of doing business internationally.

KEY TERMS

- trade credit
- consumer credit
- workers' compensation
- exchange rate

Risks are everywhere!

Dale realized that there were many risks he would face as the business owner of a new sporting goods store. He called his friend Monica for some advice. Monica had been in business for almost two years and had gained valuable business experience.

"Dale, it's good that you came to me," Monica replied. "I've got lots of information for you. I know you have learned about insurable and uninsurable risks, but there are some hidden risks you might not think about. I thought I could increase sales and provide customers a convenient service by offering them a store credit account, but you wouldn't believe how many people never paid their bills! Then my maintenance employee fell off a ladder while painting. He had to spend two weeks in the hospital. I could go on and on."

"Yes, Monica, I think you have given me plenty to think about. There are many more risks to consider than I was aware of!" Dale replied.

WORK AS A TEAM What do you think Dale can learn from Monica's experiences? What can Dale do to minimize the risks that Monica mentioned?

Beware of hidden risks.

LO 12.3-1 Risks of Credit

As a business begins operation, there will be costs that will be too expensive for the entrepreneur to pay all at once. Credit makes it possible for the entrepreneur to make these costly purchases. The business owner will also have to make decisions about extending credit to customers. When a business extends credit to customers, it is entering into a debtor–creditor relationship. For example, when

Why would a business offer its own credit card if it risks not being paid?

a person purchases an appliance and finances the cost, the business and purchaser now have a debtor–creditor relationship. Examples of debtor–creditor relationships include loans of all types, credit lines, and the use of credit cards.

Debtor–creditor relationships that involve extending credit can help increase a business's sales. However, a business will need to decide if extending credit will result in an overall increase in profits. Although credit is useful to a business when buying or selling, there are risks involved. It is important for you as an entrepreneur to understand these risks.

Types of Credit

Credit can be categorized according to whom the credit is offered. Like bank loans, the credit a business offers its customers can be secured or unsecured.

TRADE CREDIT When one business allows another business to buy now and pay later, it is offering **trade credit**. Many purchases a business owner will make from other businesses will be made with trade credit. The negotiated price of products purchased on trade credit will often be higher than the cash price. This is necessary because there is a lapse of time that occurs from when the sale is negotiated to when the products are actually delivered and the supplier is paid. Because of this delay in receiving payment, the supplier charges a higher price. As the business owner, you will need to be sure that you have the money to cover your debts when they are due in order to protect your credit record.

On March 29, Raul Garcia places an order with Bear Creek Embroidery for three-dozen golf shirts with his company logo embroidered on them. On April 1, Bear Creek Embroidery negotiates the purchase of three-dozen shirts from Alternative Apparel on credit. The shirts are delivered to Bear Creek on April 15. Two weeks later, Bear Creek ships the shirts with the logos to Raul. It takes one week for the shirts to arrive and one week for Raul to process and pay Bear Creek's invoice.

The trade credit that Alternative Apparel extends to Bear Creek allows 60 days for payment. This enables Bear Creek to receive the shirts, add the logo, ship the shirts, and receive payment from Raul in time to send payment to Alternative Apparel.

Why do many businesses offer installment loans to their customers?

CONSUMER CREDIT When a retail business allows its customers to buy merchandise now and pay for it later, it is offering **consumer credit**. Consumer credit is offered in two basic forms: loans and credit cards. A loan gives the individual a lump sum of money to spend and pay back over time with interest. If a loan is secured, it is backed by something of value (collateral) that can be taken and sold if the loan is not repaid. One type of secured loan offered by retail establishments is an *installment loan* that is paid back with interest in equal monthly amounts over a specified period of time. Many cars and home appliances are financed with installment loans, with the financed item serving as the collateral.

An unsecured loan is granted based on the credit history of the individual. This type of loan is not backed by collateral. Most credit cards are considered unsecured loans. When a business offers its own credit card to customers, it will not receive payment for a month or more after the sale is made. Therefore, the business will need to make other arrangements to ensure it has money to cover expenses associated with the sale of the merchandise. If the customer does not pay, then the business owner can attempt to collect the money or take back the goods that were purchased.

Collection difficulties are one reason a business chooses to accept credit cards that are issued by banks or credit card companies, such as Visa, Discover, or MasterCard. The credit card company will pay the business for the amount of the purchase. The business is charged a fee by the credit card company that is a percentage of total credit sales. The credit card company is then responsible for collecting the amount charged from the customer.

If Raul Garcia offers a credit card to his customers, then Raul is responsible for collecting payment from the customer. However, if the customer pays with a Discover card, Raul gets his money from Discover, and Discover bears the burden of collecting payment from the customer.

Credit Policies

Once a business decides to offer credit to customers (businesses or consumers), policies must be established to help reduce risks. Policies should specify to whom credit will be extended, what products may be purchased on credit, and what the terms of the credit will be. The terms include the amount of credit, the rate of interest charged, and the length of time before payment is required.

It will be very important for the entrepreneur to determine what type of customer will be approved for credit. Most businesses offering credit cards to consumers have them complete a credit application to determine whether they are *creditworthy*, or able to pay. Some things to consider in determining who is creditworthy include the following:

- Previous credit history
- Employment record
- Assets owned
- Money available for making payments (checking and savings accounts)
- Financial references

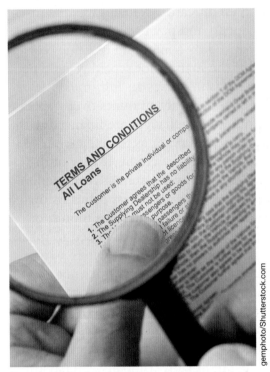

How can a business owner reduce the risks of offering credit?

Even though a business is careful about deciding which customers are creditworthy, there is still the risk that some customers will not pay their account balances, resulting in *uncollectible accounts*. If credit is extended to individuals who are not able to pay, the business loses all the money invested in the product. If the product is recovered, money will still be lost because used merchandise cannot be resold at the original selling price.

Businesses that offer credit may charge the customer interest on the balance due to cover the cost of the credit service. When accounts are paid on time, the interest is income for the business and increases the overall profit of the business. However, uncollectible accounts are an expense to the business and decrease profits. Collection procedures must be established and followed carefully. This will ensure that customers are billed on time. Procedures should state how to handle customers who do not pay on time or do not pay at all.

CHECKPOINT

What types of consumer credit might a business offer?

LO 12.3-2 Risks on the Job

Different occupations have different risks associated with them. Due to the nature of the work that is performed, some workplaces are considered to be dangerous. Some of the most dangerous occupations in America include fishers, loggers, aircraft pilots, construction workers, farmers and ranchers, roofers, and garbage collectors. Other occupations, although not classified as dangerous, do have health and safety risks associated with them. Individuals who work in hospitals can be exposed to viruses and bacteria that can cause disease or infection. Night clerks can be a target for a robbery. Even using a computer for long stretches of time can cause injury. *Repetitive stress injuries* result from performing the same activity repeatedly for long periods of time. They can be very painful and cause disabling injuries. With some exceptions, any harm suffered by employees at the workplace is considered to be a work-related injury.

Many businesses are making health and wellness a priority by offering healthful lunch options, fitness classes, and other preventive services like health fairs. The Affordable Care Act (ACA) offers incentives, such as tax breaks and tax credits, to some small businesses to help them provide health benefits to employees. Businesses are addressing safety concerns by offering training and certification courses to their employees.

Workers' Compensation

Workers' compensation is an insurance program that provides coverage to employees who suffer work-related injuries or illness. Workers' compensation laws vary from state to state but generally provide for the payment of medical bills, a percentage of lost wages, and vocational retraining if an employee is unable to resume his or her former job. Workers' compensation will also pay a death benefit to compensate survivors if an on-the-job injury results in the death of a worker.

Once employees accept workers' compensation benefits, they cannot sue their employer unless there is proof that the employer knew about the unsafe condition causing the accident and did not do anything to fix it.

Most employers are required by law to provide workers' compensation insurance. In some states, small businesses are exempt from workers' compensation requirements and employees working for them are not covered. Also, business owners, independent contractors, occasional or seasonal workers, domestic workers in private homes, agricultural workers, and unpaid volunteers are not covered by workers' compensation in some states.

Employers must notify employees of their right to compensation for work-related injuries and illnesses. Employees must also be notified that they cannot be fired for filing a claim and that workers' compensation premiums cannot be deducted from their pay. Most employers display a poster in the workplace containing this information.

COVERAGE PROVIDED Medical expenses for employees injured on the job should be covered by workers' compensation. If an employee is out of work for more than a few days, a percentage of lost wages

Why are employers responsible for carrying insurance on their employees?

may also be covered. Lost wage payments are usually about two-thirds of the employee's income, not to exceed state limits. If an employee is left permanently disabled from a work-related injury, the employee may be eligible for a lump-sum payment or long-term benefits. This depends on whether the employee can perform other work that pays as well as the former position. If a worker cannot earn as much as before the injury, the worker may be eligible for a long-term payment. If the worker is completely and permanently disabled, the worker may be eligible for Social Security benefits.

INJURIES NOT COVERED   Although laws vary from state to state, generally, the following injuries would not be covered by workers' compensation insurance:

- Injuries individuals afflict on themselves
- Injuries suffered under the influence of alcohol or illegal drugs
- Injuries suffered during a fight that the injured employee started
- Injuries suffered while disobeying orders or violating employer policy
- Injuries suffered while committing a crime
- Injuries suffered while not on the job

FILING A CLAIM   There are certain steps that must be followed in the event of an injury or illness at the workplace. Be sure that you are familiar with these steps so that you know what you and your employee should do in the event of an accident at your business.

1. **The injured employee must notify the employer**. The employer must be notified immediately after the accident. Check your state law to determine the time limit that employees have for reporting an accident or illness.

2. **The employee must follow doctor's orders.** If the employee does not follow the doctor's orders, it could be grounds for denying workers' compensation coverage. The doctor should put any special requirements for the employee in writing. Be sure the employee goes to the doctor that handles the workers' compensation cases for your business.

3. **The employee must file the claim.** The employer must provide the employee with the proper forms, but it is the employee's responsibility to file the claim.

CHECKPOINT

What is the purpose of workers' compensation insurance?

LO 12.3-3   Risks in International Business

When you start working with businesses and customers in other countries, there are risks that you may face. The stability of the economic system in other countries depends on the government's management of its economy. An unstable government can negatively impact businesses within its borders. It can also lead to difficulties for foreign companies doing business there. The cultural and social environments of these countries will also have a great influence on your international business activities. Doing business in a foreign country can present challenges for several reasons.

1. **You may not speak the language of the countries you are targeting.** If you cannot communicate with buyers or consumers, how can you sell your service or product? Misunderstandings are likely to occur.

2. **You may not be familiar with the laws, customs, and cultures of foreign countries.** In the United States, looking directly at people while speaking to them is a sign of respect. In some other countries, it is a sign of disrespect. If you fail to recognize these cultural differences, you risk offending those with whom you are trying to do business.

3. **You may have to change your products or services to meet the needs of global trade.** Consumers abroad have different needs and wants than do consumers in the United States. What sells in this country will not necessarily appeal to foreign customers. You will need to consider this when you develop and sell products or services in other countries.

4. **You will have to deal with different currency systems.** The amount of one country's currency that can be traded for one unit of currency in another country is the **exchange rate**. These rates change daily depending on the country's economic and political stability. The value of currency is affected by supply and demand. If a country's money is believed to have a solid value, people will

accept it as payment, and its value will increase. However, if a country is having financial difficulties, its currency will lose value compared to the currency of other countries.

5. **Your travel and shipping expenses may be high**. International flights can be very expensive. Sending or receiving packages overseas can also be costly.

Strategies for Dealing with International Markets

If you decide to conduct business globally, you should develop a plan that outlines your goals and identifies your risks. Analyze the foreign target market and perform research to learn more about the risks of doing business abroad.

Strategies recommended for dealing with the risks of international business include the following:

1. **Seek government assistance to answer your questions about international business**. Government agencies such as the SBA and the International Trade Administration can provide counseling, locate buyers overseas, and promote U.S. products and services.

FAMOUS ENTREPRENEUR

MARY J. BLIGE Called the "Queen of Hip-Hop Soul," Mary J. Blige is credited with pioneering the musical marriage of hip-hop and R&B. She is undeniably one of the greatest singers of her generation.

Mary's musical journey began at age 17 when she recorded a song at a recording booth in the Galleria Mall in White Plains, New York. The recording passed through several hands before it reached the president and CEO of Uptown Records, Andre Harrell. He met with Mary and signed her to the label in 1989. She was the youngest and first female artist of the company. Three years later, Mary released her debut album, which instantly became a huge success. Since then, Mary has sold more than 50 million albums and 25 million singles worldwide; worked with renowned artists such as Beyoncé, Rod Stewart,

Why do you think creativity is an important attribute for entrepreneurs?

and Andrea Bocelli; and received 9 Grammy Awards and a record 30 Grammy nominations.

In addition to her achievements as a singer, Mary has also made her mark as an entrepreneur. In 2004, Mary began her own record label, Matriarch Records. In 2009, she launched an eyewear line, Melodies by MJB. In 2010, she launched her first perfume, My Life, on the Home Shopping Network (HSN). The perfume broke HSN sales records by selling 65,000 bottles during its premiere. Mary is also the co-founder of the Foundation for the Advancement of Women Now (FFAWN), whose mission is to educate and empower women by providing scholarships, grants, and career development opportunities.

THINK CRITICALLY
What risks has Mary J. Blige taken to further her career?

2. **Conduct business in many different countries**. If you are doing business in only one country and something happens in that country, such as political upheaval, you run the risk of losing all sales and profits.

3. **Work with local business partners**. If you partner with a company that is located in the country you are targeting, your company will be better received by locals in that country.

4. **Comply with international labor standards**. Many Americans feel that the United States should require compliance with international labor standards as part of international trade agreements. Americans consider unfair labor practices in other countries morally wrong and believe that low labor standards create unfair competition for U.S. labor. Many also believe that the United States should not allow products to be imported when they have been produced under conditions that violate international labor standards. A strong majority of Americans have indicated they would pay higher prices for products to ensure that the products are not manufactured in substandard conditions.

5. **Employ local management**. If you hire managers from the country you are targeting, they will have a better understanding of the cultural and political scene of the country. They will be able to assist you in any product modifications or changes in business practices you need to make to work with the foreign market. Local management also can assist with labor issues, such as how much to pay employees, whether to work with a labor union, how to establish trust with employees, and how to deal with the ethical issues of the country.

6. **Learn about the other country's culture**. Research the country's cultural customs and beliefs. Develop cultural sensitivity.

When doing business in another country, why should you learn about its customs and culture?

 ASSESSMENT

THINK ABOUT IT

1. What are the risks and benefits involved when a business accepts (uses) and extends credit?

2. How can businesses promote health and safety among employees?

3. Why are some workplace injuries not covered by workers' compensation insurance?

4. What are some strategies you can use to reduce the risks involved with international business?

MAKE ACADEMIC CONNECTIONS

5. **COMMUNICATION** Working with a partner, role-play situations in which debtor–creditor relationships are created.

6. **MANAGEMENT** You are planning to open a retail store that will sell home appliances and furnishings. Decide what type of consumer credit you will offer, and develop a credit policy. Present your decisions to the class.

7. **RESEARCH** Choose three countries with different currency systems. Research online the exchange rate for each country's currency in relation to the U.S. dollar. Prepare a chart showing how they compare. Research the reasons why the value of the currency is such in relation to the U.S. dollar. Write a summary explaining what factors influence the exchange rates.

Teamwork

Many employers think workers abuse workers' compensation insurance. They may hire people to investigate workers who are on medical leave to determine if they are conducting themselves in any way that is not consistent with the injuries they have claimed. Based on the investigation, the employer may have a case for discontinuing the employee's workers' compensation claim. Working with teammates, discuss whether you think it is ethical for employers to spy on employees. What can be done to keep workers from abusing workers' compensation insurance?

The Essential Question Refer to The Essential Question on p. 361. There are many hidden risks that businesses must consider, including risks related to accepting trade credit and extending consumer credit, dealing with health and safety issues in the workplace, and conducting international business.

Sharpen Your 21st Century Entrepreneurial Skills

Respect Cultural Diversity

In today's global economy, you will come in contact with many people from cultures different than your own. You may work with people from different cultures. You may also buy from and sell to people from different cultures. As an entrepreneur, you need to appreciate different cultures. If you are open to other cultures, you can attract more customers. And by understanding the needs and wants of people from different cultures, you can market your business more effectively.

There are ways you can embrace cultural diversity. These include, but are not limited to, the following:

1. **Focus on similarities rather than differences.** Most people, regardless of their culture, want the same things in life.

2. **Avoid stereotyping people.** Don't assume that all people from an ethnic or cultural group hold the same values and opinions, behave the same way, or like the same things.

3. **Learn about different cultures.** Learning about a different culture will make you more comfortable around people from that culture. Learn how people in a different culture live and work.

4. **Make friends with someone from a different culture.** The friendship will help you begin to appreciate other cultures.

5. **Try to understand and identify with other people's feelings.** Try to see the world through the eyes of people from different cultures. Try to understand cultural views that are different from your own.

TRY IT OUT

You make and sell jewelry and watches for both men and women. You are ready to expand your business globally. Choose a country in which you would like to compete and research it. What aspects of the country's culture could affect your business? What is the value of that country's currency in relation to the U.S. currency? How will this affect your business? Will you need to make modifications to your products in order to sell them in that country?

Present the information you learned about the other country to your classmates. Explain how your products will compete in this country's marketplace.

SUMMARY

12.1 Business Risks

1. Risks can be categorized as human, natural, or economic. Occurrence of these types of risk can bring about loss to a business. To prepare for risks, you should (1) determine what can go wrong, (2) develop a plan, and (3) communicate your plan to employees and first responders.

2. Theft is one of the biggest risks faced by business owners. Types of theft include shoplifting, employee theft, robbery, credit card fraud, and bounced checks. Business owners can take precautions to prevent these risks.

12.2 Insure Against Risks

3. Classifications of risk faced by businesses are based on the result of the risk (pure or speculative), controllability of the risk (controllable or uncontrollable), and the insurability of the risk (insurable or uninsurable).

4. Insurance does not cover risks that cannot be reasonably predicted or risks in which the financial loss cannot be calculated. Such risks are tied to economic conditions, consumer demand, competitors' actions, technology changes, local factors, and business operations.

5. You will have to analyze the risks your business faces to determine the types of insurance to buy. A typical business owner's policy (BOP) covers property damage, business interruption, and liability. Life, flood, crime, and renters insurance are also available.

6. Before committing to an insurance purchase, compare prices and policies and seek advice from experienced business owners.

12.3 Other Risks

7. Although beneficial to you as a business owner and to your customers, credit has risks. You must analyze the potential risks to determine if it is wise for you to accept (use) and/or extend credit.

8. Workers' compensation insurance covers employees' medical expenses and lost wages incurred as a result of workplace injuries and illnesses.

9. To reduce international business risks, companies should seek government assistance, conduct business in more than one country, involve local business partners, comply with international labor standards, employ local management, and learn about the culture.

Read *Ideas in Action* on page 347 again. Then answer the questions a second time. Have your responses changed? If so, how have they changed?

KEY TERMS REVIEW

Match each statement with the term that best defines it. Some terms may not be used.

1. The possibility of some kind of loss
2. Taking action to prevent or reduce the possibility of loss to your business
3. Looking at all aspects of your business and determining the risks you face
4. The act of knowingly taking items from a business without paying
5. A payment to cover the cost of insurance
6. A risk that presents the chance of loss but no opportunity for gain
7. A risk on which actions have no effect
8. A pure risk faced by a large number of people and for which the amount of loss can be predicted
9. When one business allows another business to buy now and pay later
10. An insurance program that provides coverage to employees who suffer work-related injuries or illnesses

a. bounced check
b. consumer credit
c. controllable risk
d. exchange rate
e. insurable risk
f. premium
g. pure risk
h. risk
i. risk assessment
j. risk management
k. shoplifting
l. speculative risk
m. trade credit
n. uncontrollable risk
o. workers' compensation

REVIEW YOUR KNOWLEDGE

11. **True or False**   Businesses can avoid all possible risks by purchasing insurance.
12. Conducting a risk assessment involves all of the following actions *except*
    a. learn the risks your business faces
    b. decide how risks will affect your business
    c. prioritize the risks by the impact they will have on your business
    d. communicate your plan
13. **True or False**   Credit card fraud is an example of an economic risk.
14. If there is a risk that a loss will occur and the amount of the loss cannot be predicted, the risk is __?__ .
15. **True or False**   A credit card offered by a home furnishings center is an example of an installment loan.
16. Which of the following is *not* a risk associated with doing business in another country?
    a. language barriers
    b. different laws, customs, and cultures
    c. high travel and shipping costs
    d. all of the above are risks
17. A __?__ plan will enable you to get back to business as quickly as possible after a disaster.
18. Which of the following is *not* a strategy for dealing with a risk?
    a. avoid the risk   c. transfer the risk
    b. assign the risk   d. assume the risk
19. **True or False**   A speculative risk is classified as uninsurable.

20. Which of the following types of insurance would cover the cost to repair your office building if it were damaged by fire?
    a. property insurance
    b. disability insurance
    c. liability insurance
    d. life insurance
21. A change in the way websites are accessed that requires new, expensive computer equipment is an example of a risk related to
    a. economic conditions
    b. consumer demand
    c. competitors' actions
    d. technology changes
22. Which of the following types of insurance would cover losses your business incurred as a result of selling a faulty product that injured someone?
    a. property insurance
    b. disability insurance
    c. liability insurance
    d. life insurance
23. **True or False** The credit that a retail business extends to customers is called trade credit because they are trading money for goods.
24. **True or False** The negotiated price of products purchased with trade credit will often be higher than the cash price for those same products.
25. **True or False** Not all injuries that occur at work are covered by workers' compensation insurance.
26. Which of the following is *not* a strategy for dealing with a global risk?
    a. conduct business in only one country to minimize the risk
    b. seek government assistance
    c. work with local business partners
    d. employ local management
27. **True or False** If you are leasing a building for your business, you do not need to carry renters insurance because the owner of the building is required to carry insurance.

APPLY WHAT YOU LEARNED

28. You plan to open a horseback riding training center with a horse boarding facility. Make a chart and list the types of risk you will face. Categorize the risks as human, natural, or economic. Classify risks as controllable or uncontrollable and insurable or uninsurable. If the risk is insurable, list the type of insurance that you could purchase to protect against the risk. (LO 12.1-1, LO 12.2-1, LO 12.2-3)
29. Make a list of accidents and injuries that workers in a hospital could experience. Write "yes" next to the accidents and injuries that would be covered by workers' compensation insurance. Write "no" next to those that would not be covered. (LO 12.3-2)
30. You own a clothing boutique and have recently expanded into catalog sales. Many of your products will be sold abroad. As your business expands, you will need additional manufacturing sources. You are looking in other countries. Explain the labor issues that will be of concern to you. (LO 12.3-3)

MAKE ACADEMIC CONNECTIONS

31. **MATH** You are trying to decide whether to purchase security equipment for your business or hire a security guard. The cost of the security equipment is $15,000, and it has a useful life of 3 years. If you hire a security guard, it will cost you $50 per hour for 3 hours each day. Calculate and compare the annual cost of each and decide which will be the most cost-effective for your business. (LO 12.1-2)

32. **COMMUNICATION** More businesses are addressing health and safety concerns in the workplace. Conduct research to learn about new ways businesses are working to improve the health and safety of their employees. Prepare a two-page report. (LO 12.3-2)

What Would YOU DO?

Your business is growing and you have recently hired five new employees. Your business has been exempt from paying workers' compensation insurance premiums, but with the addition of new employees, you will no longer be exempt. You do not agree with the workers' compensation program because of the added expense to your business. You are thinking about not paying the premiums. Would this be fair to your employees? What would happen if one of your employees had a serious injury on the job and you did not have workers' compensation insurance?

BUILD YOUR BUSINESS PLAN PROJECT

This activity will help you continue with the development of a business plan by outlining your risk management strategy.

1. Identify risks faced by your business and establish a plan for dealing with them. Describe how the business will prevent shoplifting, employee theft, robberies, credit card fraud, and bad checks. Research how much it will cost to buy special security equipment or hire a guard. Present your proposal to the class. Prepare to defend your strategies.

2. Contact an insurance agent to obtain information on insuring your business. What types of insurance do you need? How much coverage should you buy?

3. Research workers' compensation laws for your state. Explain how you will meet your responsibilities under these laws.

4. What are some other cultures you will be exposed to in your business? Research one of these cultures and find out information about the lifestyle and business practices associated with this culture. What cultural issues will affect your business? How will you market your product or service to this and other cultures?

PLANNING A CAREER IN INSURANCE

"After returning from the grocery, our neighbor came home to a big mess. The laundry he had tossed into the machine prior to leaving the house had been off-balance. During the spin cycle, the water hose became loose and caused a huge water leak. Although he did his best to dry out the floors, he ultimately had to replace the hardwood flooring in the rooms bordering the laundry room. Fortunately his homeowners insurance covered the costs."

Insurance agents sell and service insurance policies. They spend much of their time explaining policies to help their clients obtain appropriate coverage for specific risks. Insurance agents also help policyholders settle claims.

Insurance agents may work for a single insurance company (captive agents), or they may work for an insurance brokerage (independent insurance agents). Captive agents sell only policies provided by the company that employs them. Independent insurance agents sell the policies of several companies.

Employment Outlook
- An average rate of employment growth is anticipated.
- Employment growth will likely be strongest for independent sales agents and for agents who sell health insurance.

Job Titles
- Insurance Broker
- Financial Services Agent
- Claims Adjuster
- Agency Specialist
- Property and Casualty Underwriter

Needed Education/Skills
- As insurance policies are complex, a bachelor's degree with a business or mathematics focus is often preferred.
- A state license is required to sell insurance and continuing education is often mandatory.
- Professional certification is available to demonstrate competency in specialized areas.
- Strong analytical and communication skills are essential.

What's it like to work in Insurance? Narelle, an independent insurance agent, is comparing auto insurance policies from a variety of policy providers for her new client—a young driver. As an independent agent, Narelle matches the needs of her clients to the policies that provide the best combination of rates and coverage. Narelle knows that by providing her young client with economical, effective coverage as well as courteous service, she can probably secure him as a new long-term client.

After lunch, Narelle finishes the handouts she is preparing for tomorrow's lunch seminar at a local SBA meeting. She is planning to discuss the appropriate types of coverage for each stage of business development. Narelle has learned that participation in professional meetings often results in valuable sales leads, which are essential to her ongoing success.

What about you? Would you like to help individuals and businesses identify and plan for their risks? What aspects of this job do you find appealing?

Global Marketing Team

Entrepreneurs set out not only to follow their dreams, but also to make money. Profit is the key to sustaining business. Entrepreneurs can maximize their profit by effectively marketing their businesses and appropriately pricing their goods. The BPA Global Marketing Team event focuses on developing a business marketing plan, including pricing strategies and promotional plans.

Your marketing team has been tasked with developing a new professional soccer team in a city of your choice. To introduce this new team, you have set up a soccer match with an already established international team in their home country.

Performance Indicators
- Demonstrate an understanding of management and international business concepts
- Create a marketing plan
- Identify the customer base, including consumer and business markets
- Demonstrate successful pricing strategies
- Work effectively as part of a team
- Demonstrate effective written and oral communication skills

Go to the BPA website for more detailed information.

GIVE IT A TRY
Work with one or two partners to create a two- to three-page marketing plan for the new soccer team that you will present to your class. The marketing plan should include the following areas:
- Description of the customers (target market) and their needs
- Description of the product (soccer team), including justification for locating in your city
- Description of pricing strategy
- Competition, including other sports and entertainment events in your city
- Marketing mix, including a description of the promotional international soccer match
- Economic, social, legal, and technological trends
- Human resource requirements
- Marketing timeline

www.bpa.org

Yuri_Arcurs/iStockphoto.com

Management for the Future

(13.1) **GROWTH STRATEGIES**

(13.2) **ETHICAL AND SOCIAL ISSUES**

(13.3) **GLOBAL TRENDS AND OPPORTUNITIES**

Finding Success by Helping Others

Photo by McKinley Wiley

Jose Vasquez, President and CEO of Quéz Media

Jose Vasquez has a passion—to open doors for entrepreneurs. This is what he does as president and CEO of Quéz Media, a full-service digital advertising and branding agency that helps clients create innovative marketing strategies. He is also the founder of, and contributor to, buildbrandblast.com, a resource blog for entrepreneurs that explores aspects of entrepreneurship from startup to success.

Jose takes pride in helping other companies prosper. "For me, it's always been about growing businesses and helping others. You can label me an entrepreneur, but the more people I can help along the way, the more it helps me grow myself," he said. Jose believes in the power of community and diversity. He has served on the Boards of Directors at the Northeast Ohio Hispanic Chamber of Commerce and Esperanza, Inc., among others. He is chairman for the Hispanic Business Center and also an alumnus of Leadership Ohio and Goldman Sachs 10KSB (10,000 Small Businesses).

In the five years since he started Quéz Media, Jose has built the business to include 22 employees and a satellite office in São Paulo, Brazil. The company has worked on marketing materials for Cox Communications, Nestle, and Energy Choice Ohio, among other companies.

Before Jose launched Quéz Media, he worked in various business fields, providing him with knowledge of operations, technology, sales, and marketing. The experience he gained gave him the insight to build his own company and to help other startups turn their dreams into results with more customers and higher sales.

To what does Jose attribute his ongoing success? "I always strive for continued education, so I never stop acquiring new skills and information. I get involved in as many entrepreneurship-based community events and classes as I can and regularly engage with other entrepreneurs in the area." That's good advice for young, aspiring entrepreneurs.

WHAT DO YOU KNOW?

1. Why might entrepreneurs want to read Jose's blog, buildbrandblast.com?

2. What do you think Jose meant when he said, "...the more people I can help along the way, the more it helps me grow myself"?

3. What do you think about Jose's advice for aspiring entrepreneurs?

13.1 GROWTH STRATEGIES

The Essential Question How can a business owner expand the business and maintain a presence in the market?

LEARNING OBJECTIVES

LO 13.1-1 Discuss factors to consider when expanding a business.

LO 13.1-2 List and describe product life cycle stages and steps involved in product development.

KEY TERMS

- market penetration
- market development
- product life cycle
- prototype

FOCUS ON SMALL BUSINESS

Know when to grow.

Mary Ardapple, owner of Apple's Bakery in Peoria, Illinois, has moved her business three times since she opened it in 1989. Her menu has expanded and now has three times its original offerings. She even makes her baked goods available to those outside the Peoria area through an online store. Mary is not content to conduct business as usual and is always looking for new opportunities. Recently, she added gluten-free items to her offerings. Throughout all the moves and expansions, Mary and her team have not forgotten the company's original motto, "Where smiles are made from scratch!"

WORK AS A TEAM
How do you think Mary knew when her business was ready to expand each time? Do you think it is important for Mary and her team to always remember their original motto?

Denise Kappa/Shutterstock.com

Business expansion should be carefully planned.

LO 13.1-1 Expanding Your Business

Sooner or later, you will consider expanding your business. Some businesses have difficulty growing; others expand too quickly. To expand successfully, you will need to determine both when and how to expand. You will also need to control your growth.

Before deciding to grow your business, be sure that all of your operations are functioning well. Unresolved operational issues will only get bigger and cause more problems when the business gets larger. You also need to be sure that you take care of your current customers when you begin growing your business. Remember, they helped you get where you are.

Determine When to Expand

Determining when to expand depends on two main factors: the condition of your business and the economic conditions in the market in which your business competes.

CONSIDER THE CONDITION OF YOUR BUSINESS How do you determine when it is time to expand your business? Some of the signs you should look for include the following:

- Your business is recognized by your community and industry.
- Your sales are rising.
- You have a customer base that regularly buys from you.
- You are hiring more employees and now have managers.
- You need more space.

ASSESS ECONOMIC CONDITIONS If the condition of your business shows that you should expand, you should next analyze the economic climate that controls the business. Ask the following questions:

- How is the national economy doing? Are people worried about spending money, or are they spending freely?
- What are the economic conditions in your industry or region?
- Have the demographics of your market changed?
- Is demand for your product or service expected to remain strong?
- Does your business face new competition?

Choose a Growth Strategy

You can expand your business in various ways. You can get more people to buy your products or services. You can expand into other geographic areas. You can find new products and services to sell. You can also combine with another company in a merger or acquisition.

PENETRATE THE MARKET Market penetration involves increasing the market share for a product or service within a given market in a given area. You can increase sales by increasing the number of people in your target market who buy from you. If total sales for your target market are $500,000 and your business attracts 5 percent of that market, your sales will be $25,000. If you raise your market share to 15 percent, your sales will be $75,000.

You can also increase your market share by increasing your advertising; offering customers special deals, such as frequent-buyer cards, incentives to purchase, and discounts; and offering superior customer service.

EXPAND GEOGRAPHICALLY Geographic expansion occurs when you decide to market your service or product in another town, city, county, state, or country. By expanding into a new geographic market, you expand your customer base. However, before deciding to expand, you need to research the new location and analyze your competition to be sure you can effectively compete in the new area.

DIVERSIFY WITH NEW PRODUCTS OR SERVICES Market development is a strategy for expanding the target market of a business.

DEVELOP YOUR READING SKILLS

While reading, write notes highlighting the main ideas. At the end of each section, review what you have written and fill in any gaps. Focus on the important points and support them with relevant details.

A business expands its target market by diversifying, which means selling new products or services in addition to what it already offers.

A company may choose to diversify its products or services by pursuing a horizontal growth strategy. A *horizontal growth strategy* involves adding new products and services that complement the company's current product line. For example, a musical instrument store can undertake a horizontal growth strategy by adding a sheet music department or offering music lessons. You can also grow horizontally by opening more locations. Other companies expand using a *vertical growth strategy*, whereby a company expands into new operations to decrease its dependence on other firms in the supply chain. For example, a retailer may purchase its own trucks and distribution facilities instead of hiring a freight company.

Businesses can fail if they diversify into the wrong areas. Use the following guidelines to make sure that your business diversifies successfully.

What Went *Wrong?*

Makeup Test

Sarah-Jane Stevens founded Charisma Cosmetics. Her company targeted professional cosmetics dealers serving makeup artists in the film, TV, and theater industries. Charisma Cosmetics had an excellent reputation as a high-quality manufacturer, a loyal customer base, and a major share of the market. However, competitors were slowly chipping away at Charisma's market. To remain competitive, Sarah-Jane rolled out a new brand, Picture-Perfect by Charisma. This brand was specifically designed to be sold in department stores.

The new strategy angered the professional cosmetics dealers who were the core customers of Charisma Cosmetics. Their competitive advantage had been to provide better products that were not available elsewhere. With Charisma's Picture-Perfect brand on the market, they no longer had the same competitive edge.

"We were determined to grow, and we strayed from our root value of 'don't be bigger, be better,'" Sarah-Jane said. Just eight months after getting into the department store market, Sarah-Jane got out. The company ended up losing hundreds of thousands of dollars in developing and marketing the Picture-Perfect brand.

Consider the risks when growing your business.

THINK CRITICALLY

1. What problems were created by the Picture-Perfect by Charisma brand?
2. How might Sarah-Jane have expanded without angering her dealers?

- Do not go into areas that you know nothing about.
- Choose a product or service that complements what you already sell.
- Don't neglect your original product or service line.
- Avoid allocating too much capital to new areas before you know if they will be profitable.

MERGERS AND ACQUISITIONS If your start-up is successful, you may grow the business through a merger or acquisition. You also may find that another company is interested in your business. If the two companies agree to combine as a single company it is a *merger*. If one of the companies is clearly established as the new owner, it is an *acquisition*. Under either scenario, your role in the new company may end or change.

Control Your Growth

Growing rapidly may sound like a great thing for a business, but uncontrolled growth can be just as bad as no growth at all. Businesses that grow too quickly often find that they don't have the resources to support their growth. They can lack money, employees, supplies, and more. As a result, they often overextend themselves. Sometimes they are even forced to go out of business.

To make sure that your business expands successfully, you will have to control its growth. This means you will need to come up with a plan for expansion that includes strategies for the following:

- attaining measurable objectives and goals (examples are reaching sales goals, increasing your customer base, and opening another store)
- hiring managers and supervisors
- financing expansion
- obtaining resources for expansion (capital, equipment, inventory, materials, and supplies)

 CHECKPOINT

What growth strategies can a business use to expand?

LO 13.1-2 Product Life Cycle and Development

A business must constantly monitor the sales of products and develop new products. Consumer interest in most products will decline over time. A business must keep developing new products in order to maintain a presence in the market.

Stages of a Product Life Cycle

The stages that a product goes through from the time it is introduced to when it is no longer sold is called its **product life cycle**. A product goes through four stages in its life cycle: introduction, growth, maturity, and decline. The stage of the life cycle can be determined by the type of competition that the product is facing.

97/iStockphoto.com

Why do products have a life cycle?

INTRODUCTION   The first stage of the product life cycle is the introduction of a new product into the market. At this stage, the product is quite different from existing products, so customers are not aware of it or how it can satisfy their needs. The price may be high during this stage as the company tries to recover development expenses. The competition, if any, for the product at this stage consists of older, established products.

GROWTH   If a product is successful in the introductory phase, it will enter the growth stage as sales begin to increase. The product will be distributed more widely as more consumers start to buy it. Competitors will see the opportunity for sales and introduce their own product. Each competitor's product needs to have different features and options in order to position it in the market as a better product. There will be a wider range of prices for the product during this stage due to competition.

MATURITY   During the maturity stage of the life cycle, sales peak and profits begin to decline. The product is in high demand and many companies offer it, so competition is very intense. Pricing becomes an important factor at this stage since customers view products on the market as being similar. Businesses will offer discounts or sale prices to encourage customers to buy their brand. Companies will make sure their product is easy for customers to find. During the maturity stage, a great deal of money will be spent on promotion because companies want to keep their brand in the minds of customers.

DECLINE   The decline stage occurs when consumers decide that a product is no longer meeting their needs or when they discover new and better products. Sales and profits will drop. During this stage, there is little opportunity for product improvement. If the product is not contributing a profit, no more money will be invested in it. Distribution is cut to only areas where the product is still profitable. Many times the price is cut during the decline stage. Promotion is decreased and targeted specifically to loyal customers in an effort to keep them as long as possible.

New Product Development

To stay competitive in the market, a business must develop new products or services to offer to customers. The business will need to find out early in the development process whether the product is likely to be successful before investing too much money in it. It is also important for the business to determine that the product meets an important market need, can be produced efficiently and at a reasonable cost, and will be competitive with other products in the market.

Product development involves the following steps: (1) idea development, (2) idea screening, (3) strategy development, (4) financial analysis, (5) product development and testing, and (6) product marketing.

IDEA DEVELOPMENT   The first, and often the most difficult, step in product development is finding ideas for new products. Employees or customers can generate ideas. Many times salespeople will hear wishes and complaints from customers about what they would like to see and not see in products. If the salesperson shares this information with the development department, it can lead to ideas for new products.

IDEA SCREENING   After ideas have been developed, they are screened to select the ones that have the greatest chance of being successful. Questions to be answered during the screening process include the following:

- Has a market been identified for the product?
- Is the competition in the market reasonable?
- Are resources available to produce the product?
- Is the product legal and safe?
- Can a quality product be produced at a reasonable cost?

STRATEGY DEVELOPMENT   Once an idea has been determined to be reasonable, the business will create and test a sample marketing strategy. The business performs research to identify the appropriate target market and to be sure that there are customers with adequate income who are looking to satisfy a need that the product meets. Questions asked during this stage include the following:

- What is the likely demand for the product?
- How would the introduction of the product affect existing products? Would the new product take away market share from existing products that the company offers?
- Would current customers benefit from the product?
- Would the product enhance the image of the company's overall product mix?

FINANCIAL ANALYSIS   If it is determined that a new product idea will meet a market need and can be developed, the company will perform a financial analysis. Costs of production and marketing, sales projections for the target market, and resulting profits are calculated. Spreadsheet programs are often used to perform these calculations. Questions to be answered at this stage include the following:

- What impact could the new product have on total sales, profits, market share, and return on investment?
- Would the new product affect current employees in any way? For example, would it require employees to learn new and different skills, the hiring of more people, or a reduction in the size of the workforce?
- Would any new facilities be needed?
- How might competitors respond?
- What is the risk of failure? Is the company willing to take the risk?

PRODUCT DEVELOPMENT AND TESTING   When a manufacturer sees a market opportunity and decides to develop a new product, it makes a **prototype**, which is a full-scale model of a new product. After testing the prototype in the laboratory and making final adjustments, the company designs the production process, obtains needed equipment and materials, and trains production personnel. The product is then test-marketed in selected areas. If it receives a positive response, the manufacturer places the product into full production. If not, the manufacturer drops it.

PRODUCT MARKETING   Introduction of the product into the target market is the last step in the product development cycle and the first step of the product's life cycle. Before this takes place, many other things must be done. The marketing mix elements must be planned,

Why is it necessary to perform a financial analysis when developing a new product?

and there must be an adequate supply of the product on hand to meet the target market's needs.

When the product is introduced into the market, the company will have to monitor its life cycle. Many new products fail even though the product development steps have been followed carefully. Products may not match the needs of customers, or customers may not see what differentiates the product from other products on the market. The product may be priced too high or too low, poorly distributed, or improperly promoted.

 CHECKPOINT

Why must a business be concerned with the life cycle of a product and with new product development?

 ASSESSMENT

THINK ABOUT IT

1. What factors should you consider before deciding to expand your business?

2. What is the difference between a horizontal and vertical growth strategy? Provide an example of a company that uses each type of strategy.

3. Why is it important to control the growth of your business?

4. List the stages of the product life cycle, and provide an example of a product in each stage.

MAKE ACADEMIC CONNECTIONS

5. **MATH** Tony Balducci owns a deli and sandwich shop. Total sales for his target market are $1.75 million per year. If he attracts 12 percent of the market, what will his sales be? What will sales be if he increases market share to 18 percent?

6. **PROBLEM SOLVING** You own a successful hair salon and want to expand the business. Outline a growth strategy for your business.

Teamwork

Form teams. List examples of business growth that you have seen. Classify the examples as market penetration, geographic expansion, or market development.

The Essential Question Refer to The Essential Question on p. 380. To expand successfully, a business owner will need to determine both when and how to expand. He or she will also need to control the business's growth. A business must keep developing new products in order to maintain a presence in the market.

13.2 ETHICAL AND SOCIAL ISSUES

The Essential Question Why is it important for an entrepreneur to be ethical and socially and environmentally responsible?

LEARNING OBJECTIVES

LO 13.2-1 Define ethics.

LO 13.2-2 Recognize the need for ethical practices in business.

LO 13.2-3 Discuss an entrepreneur's social responsibilities.

LO 13.2-4 List ways to meet a business's environmental responsibilities.

KEY TERMS

- ethics
- code of ethics
- business ethics

FOCUS ON SMALL BUSINESS

Make a difference.

While traveling to Argentina in 2006, Blake Mycoskie noticed that many of the children were running through the streets barefooted. Blake discovered that a lack of shoes was a huge problem in Argentina and other developing countries. Wanting to help, Blake decided to create TOMS, a business that operates using a unique business model it calls "One for One®"—for every pair of shoes sold, TOMS provides a new pair of shoes free of charge to the shoeless youth of Argentina and other developing nations. Since 2006, TOMS has provided over 35 million pair of shoes to children in need.

In recent years, Blake has expanded the business's product line to include eyewear. When TOMS sells a pair of eyewear, it provides prescription glasses, medical treatment, and/or sight-saving surgery for people in developing countries. Blake hopes that TOMS's success will inspire other companies to adopt the same business model.

Businesses have a social responsibility.

WORK AS A TEAM What do you think about TOMS's One for One business model? Are you willing to pay more for a product if you know that someone in need will benefit from your purchase?

LO 13.2-1 What Is Ethics?

Ethics is the study of moral choices and values. It involves choosing between right and wrong. Behaving ethically means behaving in an honest and fair manner. As the owner of a business, you will have to make ethical decisions about the way you want to run your business.

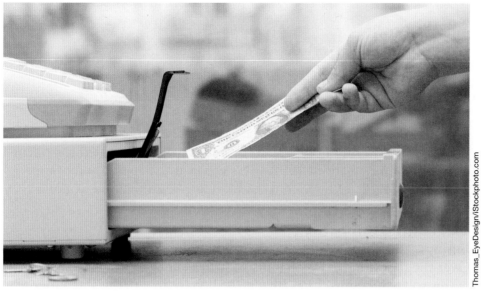

Why is ethics an important trait among employees?

Culture and Ethics

Different cultures define ethical behavior differently. In some countries, it is considered unethical to take bribes. In other countries, paying bribes may be an accepted business practice. In some countries, employers may treat employees badly. In other countries, employees have established rights that employers are expected to respect.

Codes of Ethics

Even within the same culture, individuals develop different standards, or codes, of ethics. A **code of ethics** is a set of standards or rules that outlines the ethical behavior demanded by an individual, a business, or a culture. Some individuals have a very high code of ethics and do what is right in every situation. Other individuals do not develop a code of ethics at all. They act without thinking whether their actions are right or wrong.

Individuals who have a high code of ethics also tend to have a strong *work ethic*, which can be demonstrated through certain traits.

- **Reliability** Workers with a strong work ethic do what they say they are going to do, showing that they are dependable.
- **Dedication** Employees who are dedicated work hard and are committed to their jobs. They recognize the importance of working to improve the overall success of the company.
- **Productivity** Highly productive employees perform well, often getting more work done quicker than others who lack a strong work ethic.
- **Cooperation** Because they recognize the value of teamwork, employees with a high work ethic make an effort to work well with others.
- **Character** Those who have a code of ethics demonstrate integrity, honesty, trustworthiness, and self-discipline. They treat others fairly and with respect.

LO 13.2-2 Ethics and Business

Ethical questions arise in every type of business. Large corporations, small companies, and home-based businesses all deal with ethical dilemmas at one time or another. **Business ethics** is the application of the principles of right and wrong to issues that come up in the workplace.

Set High Standards

Business and ethics used to be considered unrelated to each other. Over the past hundred years, this view has changed dramatically. Businesses today recognize that they must behave in an ethical manner. Doing so demonstrates professionalism.

MYTHS ABOUT BUSINESS AND ETHICS Some people believe that entrepreneurs need not concern themselves with ethical issues. They believe that their only goal should be increasing profits. They may treat someone or another business unfairly and use the excuse that "it is just business." They might think that acting ethically can hurt their profits. But, in fact, using ethics in business can make customers and suppliers more willing to do business with you.

CONSUMER AWARENESS Consumers and business owners are both sensitive to business ethics. Because consumers are so aware of ethical issues, businesses find ways to show customers that they practice ethics in their daily operations. For example, manufacturers of some shampoos and cosmetics print on their packaging that they do not test their products on animals. Consumers who have strong opinions about animal rights may be more willing to purchase such products.

Establish an Ethical Workplace

As the owner of your business, you are responsible for inspiring your employees to behave ethically. You will want to establish an ethical workplace for several reasons.

1. You want to do the right thing.
2. You want to serve as a role model to others.
3. You want to be proud of the way you conduct yourself, and you want others to be proud of you.
4. Ethical behavior is good for business because it gains the trust of customers.
5. Employees are more likely to act ethically if they see the business owner acting in an ethical manner.
6. Acting ethically reduces the possibility of being sued.

ENSURE CONFIDENTIALITY Confidentiality is defined by the International Organization for Standardization (ISO) as "ensuring that information is accessible only to those authorized to have access" and is an important part of information security. As an entrepreneur, you will be responsible for protecting confidential information obtained from employees, clients, and customers and ensuring that it does not fall into the wrong hands. Laws govern the type of information that you can collect from customers and keep, as well as the type of information you can request from your employees.

CREATE A WRITTEN CODE OF ETHICS One way that you can communicate your ethical beliefs to the people who work for you is by creating a written code of ethics. Such guidelines will help you and your employees make ethical decisions. A written code of ethics also communicates your company's standards of conduct to customers, suppliers, investors, and the general public.

You should create a code of ethics as soon as you begin your business, even if you are your business's only employee. You should also establish company policies and procedures that specify how you and your employees should behave in certain situations. For example, if an employee is offered a gift from a supplier, the employee can refer to the company's written code of ethics to determine whether the gift can be accepted. Oftentimes, large gifts are not permitted because they make an employee feel obligated to purchase from that supplier when it may not be the best choice to meet the business's needs. Established guidelines help company employees solve ethical dilemmas.

To create an ethical code for your business, think about ethical dilemmas that may arise and come up with solutions for dealing with them. Talk to other business owners to see what kinds of ethical problems they have encountered.

How does a business benefit from doing business ethically?

CHECKPOINT

Why should a business have a written code of ethics?

LO 13.2-3 Social Responsibilities

Entrepreneurs have personal responsibilities to the people they work and deal with, to the government, to the communities in which they are located, and even to the environment. What are these responsibilities, and how can you meet them?

Responsibilities to Customers

Your customers are your most important asset. You will need to treat them properly, or they will no longer use your services or buy your products. When dealing with customers, you should do the following:

1. **Treat all customers with respect**. No one likes to be treated badly.
2. **Be honest**. Never take unfair advantage of customers who do not know everything about the product or service they want to buy. Help your customers make good purchasing decisions.
3. **Avoid exaggerating the merits of your products or services**. Customers who are not happy with what they purchase will not do business with you again.
4. **Inform customers of possible dangers of the products you sell**. Remember that this is also a legal requirement.
5. **Handle all disputes fairly**. Try to see the customer's side of an issue when there is a disagreement.

Responsibilities to Suppliers

You depend on your suppliers for the goods you need to manufacture or sell your products. To maintain good relationships with them, you will need to do the following:

1. **Treat all suppliers with respect**. If you respect them, they will respect you.
2. **Avoid spreading rumors or incorrect information about suppliers**. Do not discuss nonfactual information with others. Rumors can damage a business's reputation.
3. **Give suppliers time to fill your order**. Try not to wait until the last minute to ask for merchandise.
4. **Handle all disputes fairly**. Try to see both sides of the issue and work out a solution that is fair to both of you.
5. **If you change suppliers, let your current supplier know the reason**. This is a courtesy to the supplier and a good business practice. The supplier will appreciate the feedback to use in developing future competitive strategies.

Responsibilities to Creditors and Investors

Creditors and investors have shown faith in your ability to succeed. To repay them for their confidence in you, you should run your business as effectively as possible. You should also let creditors and investors know when things are not going well. Never conceal risks you are facing.

Why does a business have a responsibility to the community in which it operates?

Responsibilities to Government

Federal, state, and local legislatures all create administrative agencies to carry out laws. The federal Social Security Administration, your state's department of motor vehicles, and your county's zoning commission are all administrative agencies. These administrative agencies are sometimes authorized to create rules and regulations, also called administrative laws. As an entrepreneur, you will need to comply with all federal, state, local, and administrative laws that affect your business.

Responsibilities to Your Community

Business owners have a special responsibility to contribute to their communities. They can do so in various ways, including donating money, products, and services. They can also get involved in community issues or activities.

CONTRIBUTE MONEY Business owners should donate money to charities, cultural institutions, and causes in which they believe. It is their responsibility to give something back to the community. Not all business owners can make large contributions, but any donation is welcomed.

DONATE PRODUCTS OR SERVICES Some businesses donate the products or services their business sells. For example, many used clothing stores donate unsold clothes to charities. Restaurants may donate leftover food to the local soup kitchen.

GET INVOLVED Entrepreneurs can contribute to their community in other ways as well. Some get involved in issues affecting their local governments, such as changes in zoning laws and the establishment of local parks. Others get involved by sponsoring local events or organizations, such as a school sports team.

DID YOU KNOW?

According to the Foundation Center, in a recent year the five largest corporate foundations ranked by total giving were as follows:
- Novartis Patient Assistance Foundation, Inc., $453 million
- Wells Fargo Foundation, $186.8 million
- The Walmart Foundation, $182.9 million
- The Bank of America Charitable Foundation, Inc., $175.3 million
- GE Foundation, $124.5 million

CHECKPOINT

What responsibilities do entrepreneurs have to customers, investors, and the community?

LO 13.2-4 Respect the Environment

Damage to the environment comes from many different sources. The burning of coal and oil for energy pollutes the air. Release of toxic chemicals pollutes the ground, air, and water. Disposal of billions of tons of garbage every year also creates environmental problems.

In 1970, the federal government created the Environmental Protection Agency (EPA) to enforce the laws governing the environment. Environmental law is designed to regulate the interaction of humans and the natural environment. Its purpose is to reduce the impacts of human activity, both on the natural environment and on human beings. Environmental law covers two major areas: (1) pollution control and correction of problem and (2) resource conservation and management.

Businesses have a major impact on the environment. To meet their environmental responsibilities, entrepreneurs should do the following:

1. **Protect the environment from pollutants.** Don't knowingly dump hazardous material on the ground or in lakes and rivers.

Would you be more likely to buy products that are less harmful to the environment? Why or why not?

2. **Conserve nonrenewable resources, such as coal and oil, by using them efficiently.** Nonrenewable resources are not easily replaced once they are gone. It takes hundreds of years to regenerate a nonrenewable resource. Use alternative resources when available.

3. **Reduce waste and dispose of waste responsibly.** Recycle materials such as paper, plastic, aluminum, glass, and steel. Package products using recyclable or biodegradable materials.

4. **Use environmentally safe and sustainable energy sources to meet business needs.** Electricity is a good example. It can be replaced quickly and is not a major source of pollution.

5. **Sell products that cause as little damage to the environment as possible.** For example, don't sell a car-wash solution that harms plant life.

CHECKPOINT

How can business owners protect the environment?

THINK ABOUT IT

1. All employees should practice ethical behavior. Think of some ethical dilemmas that a convenience store clerk might encounter. Then describe how the clerk could handle these situations.

2. Is it important for entrepreneurs to always act in an ethical manner? Why or why not? How are ethical behavior and professionalism related?

3. At what point do you think a business owner should tell creditors and investors of a new risk the business is facing? Why?

4. What is the purpose of the EPA? Do you think environmental laws are needed? Why or why not?

MAKE ACADEMIC CONNECTIONS

5. **RESEARCH** Confidentiality of information is important to your employees and customers. Conduct research on laws governing the type of information that you can keep on file about your customers and the type of information that you can request from employees and job applicants. Prepare a PowerPoint presentation based on your findings.

6. **MATH** Jade Yorida will donate 12 percent of her company's net income to the community if she makes her profit projections of a 5 percent increase over the previous year's net income of $235,000. Assuming Jade meets her projections, how much will she donate?

7. **RESEARCH** There have been many cases in recent years of businesses and individuals who have not practiced ethical behavior. Research a business or an individual who has been caught practicing unethical behavior and prepare a report on your findings.

8. **BUSINESS LAW** Conduct online research to learn about recent EPA legislation. Prepare a one-page report describing how this legislation has or will affect businesses. Explain what businesses will need to do to comply with the new law.

9. **COMMUNICATION** Work with a partner to create a role-play that demonstrates work ethics in the workplace. Be sure to exhibit the traits commonly found among those who have strong work ethics.

Teamwork

Working with teammates, brainstorm five ethical dilemmas that entrepreneurs might face. Then determine what decisions you would make if you were faced with these problems. Share your thoughts with the class.

The Essential Question Refer to The Essential Question on p. 388. Customers, investors, and suppliers are more willing to do business with companies that behave in an ethical manner and that meet social and environmental responsibilities.

13.3 GLOBAL TRENDS AND OPPORTUNITIES

The Essential Question What should an entrepreneur know and do before expanding globally?

LEARNING OBJECTIVES

LO 13.3-1 Discuss the reasons and methods for participating in the global economy.

LO 13.3-2 Determine whether international business is right for you.

LO 13.3-3 Identify trade regulations that affect international business.

KEY TERMS

- exports
- imports
- trade barriers
- quota
- tariff
- qualitative restriction

FOCUS ON SMALL BUSINESS

Explore international markets.

Monika has worked and grown her candy business for three years. She sells chocolate and mint candies that are very popular in her store and with her online customers. She recently visited friends in Vienna, Austria, and took them some of her candy as a gift. They loved her candy, as did their friends. Monika began to wonder if there would be a market for her candy in other countries. She went to her friend Lazlo for advice because he had experience selling antiques in the United States and other countries.

WORK AS A TEAM

What advice do you think Lazlo might give Monika? What things should Monika research before deciding to sell her candy outside of the United States?

Selling globally can be a way to grow your business.

LO 13.3-1 Exports and Imports

The global marketplace has dramatically changed the way that businesses operate. It has made business more competitive, and it has opened new opportunities for companies, including small entrepreneurial businesses. As the global marketplace continues to expand, entrepreneurs can take advantage of even more opportunities.

International trade is one way you can become part of the global marketplace. This means you would export or import the products or services you sell or use in your business.

Why might direct exporting be more difficult than indirect exporting?

Exporting

Products and services that are produced in one country and sent to another country to be sold are **exports**. The United States exports agricultural products, automobiles, machinery, computers, and more. These products are shipped to countries all over the world. The most commonly exported services include hospitality (hotels and food service), entertainment (movies, television production, and amusement parks), and financial services (banks, insurance, and real estate).

DIRECT EXPORTING   You can find buyers or distributors in foreign markets and ship your products to them. This is called *direct exporting.* For direct exporting, you may need to hire salespeople who live in or travel to the foreign countries.

INDIRECT EXPORTING   Because it can be difficult to make contacts with buyers in other countries, some businesses use *commissioned agents* who act as brokers to find foreign buyers for products and services. Exporting through commissioned agents is *indirect exporting.*

SELLING WORLDWIDE THROUGH THE WEB   Another way to get involved in exporting is through the Internet. The Internet has made doing business in other countries much easier. Businesses can translate and modify their websites to appeal to foreign customers. They can fill individual orders and ship them directly to the foreign customer's address.

Importing

Products and services that are brought from another country to be sold are **imports**. The United States imports many products, such as automobiles from Europe, Japan, and Korea and oil from the Middle East.

Entrepreneurs may decide to import products to sell or to use in the production of their product. Price and quality are usually factors in their decision to import. Consumers like low prices and demand high quality.

CHECKPOINT

Why do entrepreneurs participate in exporting and importing?

LO 13.3-2   Is International Business Right for You?

Not every business can succeed internationally. You need to consider the pros and cons of competing globally. Then you must determine whether there is a market for your business in other countries and write an international business plan.

Reasons for Competing Globally

As discussed in Chapter 12, there are many risks to consider when competing in the global marketplace, but there are also many benefits, including the following:

1. **Increased sales**   You can attract new buyers and broaden your customer base. You may also import unique products that local customers can buy.
2. **Reduced costs**   Manufacturers in other countries can produce goods less expensively because of low labor costs or availability of raw materials. This can mean a savings for you in the form of a lower price.

How can a company lower its costs by doing business in another country?

3. **Decreased dependence on current markets and suppliers**
   If the economy in the United States suddenly worsens, foreign markets and suppliers might help keep your profits high. Selling products and services abroad can also help you stabilize seasonal market fluctuations.

Analyze the Market

Analyzing whether there is an international market for your product will be very similar to how you analyzed your current target market and target customers. In addition to the kind of analysis you learned about in Chapter 4, you will need to consider other factors, including political, economic, social, and cultural issues. Additional taxes and regulations are also things to research and consider.

Various resources are available that can help you learn about doing business abroad.

- Trade fairs and seminars sponsored by the U.S. Department of Commerce
- Trade statistics from the U.S. Census Bureau and the Small Business Administration
- Federal or state government market studies on your industry's potential abroad

Write an International Business Plan

An international business plan is an extension of your business plan. It sets forth your goals for international expansion and defines the strategies for achieving those goals. Your plan should indicate the following:

- Why you want to expand your business into the global marketplace
- Which foreign markets you plan to enter and why
- What revenues your venture is expected to earn
- How you plan to finance your global expansion
- What costs (travel, shipping, marketing) you expect to have
- How you plan to market and sell your products or services abroad
- How you plan to deliver your products or services to foreign markets
- What legal requirements you must meet to sell your products or services abroad

 BE YOUR OWN BOSS

You manufacture toys for small children. You have found a manufacturer overseas that will make your toys for less than half of what you pay to have them manufactured in the United States. You are considering using the overseas manufacturer, but you want to be sure it uses quality materials, provides safe working conditions, and does not use child labor. Use the six-step problem-solving model discussed in Chapter 1 to determine if you will use the overseas manufacturer.

 CHECKPOINT

Name three reasons why businesses decide to expand globally.

LO 13.3-3 Government Regulation of International Trade

Some governments establish **trade barriers**, which are methods for keeping foreign businesses from competing with domestic producers. Quotas, tariffs, and qualitative restrictions are trade barriers. You should research trade barriers that may affect your global expansion.

Quotas

A **quota** is a limit on the amount of a product that can be imported into a country over a particular period of time. Japan places quotas on the number of foreign automobiles that can be imported to help protect Japanese car makers from foreign competitors.

Tariffs

A **tariff** is a tax on imports. Governments use tariffs to protect domestic manufacturers of products that compete with imports. For example, the United States places a tariff on imported sugar. Foreign companies that sell sugar in the United States must pay a tax. This makes their product more expensive and less competitive with sugar produced in the United States.

Qualitative Restrictions

A **qualitative restriction** is a standard of quality that an imported product must meet before it can be sold. A qualitative restriction can keep foreign businesses from competing with domestic producers. It is also used to protect consumers. For example, the United States requires that all meat sold in this country meet certain sanitary regulations and that imported toys meet U.S. safety requirements.

The North American Free Trade Agreement

The North American Free Trade Agreement (NAFTA) removed most barriers to trade and investment between the United States, Mexico, and Canada. U.S. businesses can sell their products and services in Canada and Mexico just as they would in the United States. It also means that the United States imposes no quotas or tariffs on imports from Canada and Mexico. NAFTA makes it much easier to export and import products and services within North America.

Government Assistance

Dozens of different government agencies are available to answer your questions about doing business overseas. They include the following:

- **Office of International Trade (OIT)** The OIT is the Small Business Administration's office for the support of small business international trade development. It works with other federal agencies and public- and private-sector groups to encourage small business exports and to assist small businesses seeking to export.

- **International Trade Administration (ITA)** The ITA is an agency of the U.S. Department of Commerce. It promotes trading and investing, strengthens industry competitiveness, and ensures fair trade. The ITA works to improve the global business environment and helps U.S. organizations compete at home and abroad.
- **Bureau of Industry and Security (BIS)** The BIS is another agency of the U.S. Department of Commerce. Its mission is to advance U.S. national security, foreign policy, and economic objectives by ensuring an effective export control and treaty compliance system and promoting continued U.S. strategic technology leadership.

FAMOUS ENTREPRENEUR

MICHELLE PHAN Many consider Michelle Phan to be a digital pioneer in the world of fashion and beauty. Through her video tutorials on YouTube, she has taught and inspired countless women to become their own best makeup artist. With a growing global community of over 7.5 million subscribers, Michelle's videos have been viewed more than 1 billion times, making her one of the most-watched talents in the digital world.

Michelle's success from her YouTube channel has allowed her to launch other lucrative entrepreneurial ventures in the world of beauty and makeup. In 2011, Michelle co-founded "ipsy," a monthly beauty products subscription service. For a monthly fee, subscribers receive a Glam Bag with beauty product samples. Ipsy quickly became the world's largest online beauty community, boasting over 1 million subscribers in the United States and Canada. The company spends little on marketing because most of ipsy's subscribers are viewers of Michelle's YouTube tutorials. In 2013, Michelle teamed with cosmetics giant L'Oréal to launch her own makeup line, "em Cosmetics." In 2014, Michelle published her first book, *Make Up:*

How did Michelle Phan's YouTube channel help her break new ground as an entrepreneur?

Your Life Guide to Beauty, Style, and Success—Online and Off.

Most recently, Michelle has branched out into other fields. In 2014, she partnered with Cutting Edge Group, a music financing and services provider, to launch a new record label. Shift Music Group uses the power of social media to spread awareness of new and existing artists. In 2015, she announced a partnership with production company Endemol Beyond to create a global online video network called ICON. The network produces original content from a variety of big-name creators in beauty, fashion, wellness, food, and travel and is distributed across a number of social media platforms.

THINK CRITICALLY

Michelle Phan's YouTube channel allows her to reach people globally with her makeup lessons. Since her business expanded to include beauty samples and her own line of cosmetics, what type of challenges do you think she might face if people from other countries want to order her products?

Steve Rogers Photography/Getty Images

In addition to these agencies, the federal government offers many programs that help U.S. businesses operate in foreign markets. The programs include export counseling, export financing, and technical assistance.

CHECKPOINT

Describe how governments can regulate international trade.

13.3 ASSESSMENT

THINK ABOUT IT

1. As an entrepreneur, what do you think are the pros and cons of competing globally?

2. Do you think it is in our country's best interest to have U.S. companies engage in international trade? Why or why not?

3. What do you think would happen to the U.S. economy if there were no quotas on imported goods?

MAKE ACADEMIC CONNECTIONS

4. **MATH** A government in an Asian country applies a 20 percent tariff to all electronic goods imported to the country. If it collects $24 million in tariffs for these goods, what was their total value?

5. **HISTORY** Research NAFTA and write a one-page report on what you learn. State your opinion on whether or not NAFTA is beneficial to the United States.

Teamwork

You own a clothing boutique and have recently expanded into online sales to sell your products abroad. Select a country in which you want to sell. Working with team members, determine what method of exporting you will use. Discuss some of the government regulations that will affect your business. Think about how you might obtain further information about these regulations. Share your team's ideas with the rest of the class.

The Essential Question Refer to The Essential Question on p. 396. An entrepreneur must know whether there is a market for the business in other countries. If there is, he or she must decide whether to export products. The entrepreneur should also write an international business plan, research existing trade barriers that may affect the business, and seek government assistance to answer questions.

Sharpen Your 21st Century Entrepreneurial Skills

Time Management

You have learned that an entrepreneur has many responsibilities. You are probably wondering how you can fit everything into one day! Good time-management skills are essential to the success of your business. The following techniques can help you be more effective.

- **Establish a plan**. A plan forces you to think ahead, which helps you manage your time more effectively. A plan should list all of the routine tasks of your business as well as those tasks related to growing your business.
- **Prioritize your tasks**. Prepare a "to do" list containing all of the tasks outlined in your plan. Prioritize the tasks from high to low priority. Assign due dates to each task. Review your list at the beginning and end of each day. Cross off tasks that have been completed, add new tasks that have come up, and reprioritize your list of tasks as necessary.
- **Use planning tools**. Planning tools include things such as organizers and calendars. There are various computer programs and apps available for planning purposes. Using these will help you stay organized and improve your productivity.
- **Delegate**. There may be tasks that can be handled more efficiently by others. Delegating allows you to focus on more important issues.
- **Eliminate distractions**. Getting things done requires focus. Distractions such as phone calls, emails, and Internet browsing can eat up valuable time when you are trying to complete tasks. Turn off your phone if necessary and let your calls go to voice mail. Set aside a specific time to view and answer your email.
- **Schedule down time**. Remember to allow for personal time. Take time out for physical and leisure activities. Also, take breaks occasionally during each workday. If you are working too much and overly stressed, you will not be an effective leader.

TRY IT OUT

Before you can schedule your time, you need to understand how you use your time. Use a spreadsheet or smartphone app to keep track of your daily activities for one week. At the end of the week, review how you spent your time. Identify time wasters and things that you can eliminate from your routine in order to make more productive use of your time. Write a short report describing what you have learned about the way you use your time. Explain whether you plan to make any changes in your daily routine.

SUMMARY

13.1 Growth Strategies

1. Determining when to expand your business depends on two main factors: the condition of your business and the economic conditions in the market in which your business competes.
2. Growth strategies include market penetration, geographic expansion, and market development.
3. Businesses that experience uncontrolled growth may find themselves overextended with inadequate resources to support the new level of business. You will want to create a plan for growth.
4. The stages of the product life cycle include introduction, growth, maturity, and decline. Steps in new product development include: (1) idea development, (2) idea screening, (3) strategy development, (4) financial analysis, (5) product development and testing, and (6) product marketing.

13.2 Ethical and Social Issues

5. Ethics is the study of moral choices and values.
6. Entrepreneurs should create a written code of ethics to establish appropriate behavior in the workplace.
7. An entrepreneur has social responsibilities involving customers, suppliers, creditors, investors, the government, and the community.
8. The purpose of environmental law is to reduce the impacts of human activity on the natural environment and human beings. It covers (1) pollution control and correction and (2) resource conservation and management.

13.3 Global Trends and Opportunities

9. Entrepreneurs participate in the global marketplace through direct and indirect exporting, importing, and selling through the Web.
10. To decide if international business is right for you, consider the pros and cons of competing globally, determine whether there is a market for your business in other countries, and write an international business plan.
11. Trade regulations that will affect your international business include quotas, tariffs, and qualitative restrictions established by the countries in which you will be doing business.

WHAT DO YOU KNOW NOW?

Read *Ideas in Action* on page 379 again. Then answer the questions a second time. Have your responses changed? If so, how have they changed?

KEY TERMS REVIEW

Match each statement with the term that best defines it. Some terms may not be used.

1. The application of the principles of right and wrong to issues that come up in the workplace
2. A strategy for expanding the target market of a business
3. A limit on the amount of a product that can be imported into a country over a particular period of time
4. Products and services that are brought from another country to be sold
5. Increasing the market share for a product or service within a given market in a given area
6. Products and services that are produced in one country and sent to another country to be sold
7. A set of standards or rules that outlines the ethical behavior demanded by an individual, a business, or a culture
8. Methods for keeping foreign businesses from competing with domestic producers
9. A tax on imports
10. A standard of quality an imported product must meet before it can be sold

a. business ethics
b. code of ethics
c. ethics
d. exports
e. imports
f. market development
g. market penetration
h. product life cycle
i. prototype
j. qualitative restriction
k. quota
l. tariff
m. trade barriers

REVIEW YOUR KNOWLEDGE

11. **True or False** The condition of your business and the economic conditions of the market in which you compete help determine when you should expand your business.
12. Which of the following is *not* a factor to consider when analyzing the economic climate that controls your business?
    a. the national economy
    b. new competition
    c. demographic changes
    d. prices you charge
13. Deciding to increase your advertising and improving your customer service are examples of growing your business through
    a. market penetration
    b. geographic expansion
    c. market development
    d. none of the above
14. **True or False** For a business to diversify successfully, it needs to develop products that are unrelated to the products it already sells.
15. **True or False** During the introduction stage of a product's life cycle, people are familiar with the product and what it can do for them.
16. A prototype of a product is created during which stage of new product development?
    a. idea screening
    b. strategy development
    c. product development and testing
    d. product marketing
17. **True or False** Culture has no effect on the ethics of an individual.

18. **True or False**   Ethical behavior is good for business because it gains the trust of customers.

19. As an entrepreneur, you have a personal responsibility to all of the following *except*
   a. the government
   b. your customers
   c. your investors
   d. your competitors

20. Which of the following is *not* an example of fulfilling environmental responsibilities?
   a. using solar energy to power your heating and cooling systems
   b. disposing of paper used by your business in the dumpster
   c. selling a laundry detergent with stain-removing enzymes that do not harm water ecosystems
   d. following federal guidelines for disposing of hazardous waste

21. **True or False**   Global competition has had no impact on the way businesses operate.

22. NAFTA removed most barriers to trade and investment between the United States and
   a. China and Japan
   b. Mexico and Cuba
   c. Mexico and Canada
   d. Canada and Korea

APPLY WHAT YOU LEARNED

23. You publish a cooking magazine that is circulated in your local metro area. How can you expand your business? What growth strategy will you employ? Write a plan for growth that includes setting and achieving measurable objectives, hiring managers, financing the expansion, and obtaining resources for expansion. (LO 13.1-1)

24. You have opened a delicatessen in your town. What are some of the responsibilities you have to your customers? In what ways can your business benefit the community? How do you think fulfilling these responsibilities will help your business? (LO 13.2-2)

MAKE ACADEMIC CONNECTIONS

25. **MATH**   You have a business selling concrete to contractors. One of your suppliers in China has quoted a price of $4.00 per 50-pound bag. Your U.S. supplier is charging $4.50 per 50-pound bag. Both suppliers have agreed to cover shipping costs, but the foreign company must pay a 12.5 percent tariff on each bag shipped and will pass that cost on to you. Which supplier will you buy from and why? (LO 13.3-3)

26. **RESEARCH**   Choose a business that has recently introduced a new product to the market. Research the company and find out what other products it had on the market before the introduction of the new product. Was the new product introduced to replace an existing product or to capture a new market? Report your findings. (LO 13.1-2)

What Would YOU DO?

You are an independent contractor hired by the state to inspect paving work done on a highway. The paving company had to complete the job on time or pay a fine to the state. To meet the deadline, the paving company did not follow all of the specifications in the contract. The president of the company has asked you to approve the job in exchange for a large sum of money. What would you do? What are the ethical issues you face? What do you think would be the best way to resolve the issue? Who will be affected by your decisions?

BUILD YOUR
BUSINESS PLAN PROJECT

This activity will help you think about growing your business, conducting business ethically, and expanding your business globally. You will also finalize the business plan that you have been working on throughout the book.

1. What will indicate that you are ready to expand your business? Give specific examples, such as your sales growing by 20 percent or your business outgrowing its current location.
2. What effect can the present economy have on your business? Write a growth plan that includes strategies for attaining measurable objectives, hiring managers, financing expansion, and obtaining resources for expansion.
3. Write a code of ethics for your business that includes company policies and procedures for dealing with particular situations. What are some situations that are specific to your type of business that may pose an ethical dilemma?
4. Write an environmental policy for your business. Consider how EPA rulings might affect your business. What are some of the actions your business will take to protect the environment? Are these actions required by law? If not, why will you incorporate them into your policy?
5. What global opportunities exist for your business? Choose two global markets into which you could expand. Compare and contrast the two markets and decide which would be the best market for you to enter. Describe the strategy you would use to enter the market. List the specific benefits and risks of global expansion for your business.
6. Put it all together! Now that you have researched the different aspects of starting your own business, you are ready to use the information you have gathered in the *Build Your Business Plan Project* to compile your business plan. Refer to the outline of a business plan in Chapter 3 on page 79 to help you organize it. Present your final plan to a group of potential investors from your school and/or community.

*Transportation,
Distribution
& Logistics*

"My mom's husband has a job that requires travel to a lot of big cities. He often arranges to have a limousine pick him up at the airport and take him to his destination. It saves him a great deal of time to have the limo driver waiting for him when he arrives. At his level in the organization, it makes sense financially to pay a bit more for his transportation to get him to his meetings as quickly as possible."

Chauffeurs are individuals who provide transportation to clients on a prearranged basis. They operate limousines, vans, or private cars. Chauffeurs may be employed by an individual, family, business, or government agency. Some chauffeurs may have multiple duties for an employer. Additional duties might include personal security, household help, or administrative assistance.

Employment Outlook
- A faster-than-average rate of employment growth is anticipated.
- Employment growth is expected due to an increasing amount of corporate travel.
- About a quarter of chauffeurs are self-employed.
- Large, thriving cities will offer the best opportunities.

Job Titles
- Limousine Driver
- Airport Limousine Driver
- Company Chauffeur
- Personal Chauffeur
- Luxury Car Driver

Needed Education/Skills
- A high school diploma is preferred.

- A good driving record is necessary.
- A chauffeur's license is required. Licensing requirements vary by state.
- Training that covers local traffic laws, driver safety, and local street layout may be required.
- Good customer service skills, as well as dependability and professionalism, are required.

What's it like to work in Transportation? Pedro has been leasing his limousine for two years. Paying a monthly fee to the limousine company entitles Pedro to full use of the vehicle, even when he isn't working. His monthly payment also covers routine vehicle maintenance and insurance fees. Pedro is saving money for a down payment on his own limousine.

Tonight, Pedro is scheduled to drive a bride and groom from their wedding ceremony to their reception. After the reception, he will drive them to their hotel.

For the first three days of next week, Pedro is scheduled to provide transportation for a repeat client. The client, an executive who visits Pedro's city each month, often books Pedro's time for a series of days. When Pedro isn't driving the client to a destination, he often runs errands for the client.

What about you? Would you enjoy driving an array of clients on a variety of trips throughout your city? What are the pros and cons of a career as a chauffeur?

Business Ethics

Entrepreneurs must make ethical decisions every day. These decisions can impact their profession, personal lives, and families. By being aware of ethical situations that can occur in the workplace, entrepreneurs can be better prepared to handle ethical dilemmas. The FBLA Business Ethics event gives you an opportunity to research a specific topic related to ethics.

For the Business Ethics event, a team of two to three members will make a presentation to a panel of judges. The current year's topic can be found on the FBLA website. You will have seven minutes to make your presentation to a panel of judges, and a three-minute question-and-answer session will follow.

Performance Competencies

- Demonstrate an understanding of ethics
- Make recommendations based on ethical decision making
- Demonstrate effective problem-solving skills
- Demonstrate effective oral communication skills
- Explain content logically and systematically

Go to the FBLA website for more detailed information.

GIVE IT A TRY

Your task is to work together in teams of two or three students to research and discuss the ethical dilemma faced by businesses doing business globally with manufacturers that use sweatshops and child labor. You should use primary and secondary sources to secure your information and you should be able to cite where you found the data. Once your research is complete, you should perform the following tasks:

1. Write a 500-word synopsis of your research. You should cite sources when needed. The references (sources) section is not included in the 500-word count.
2. Prepare a five- to seven-minute oral presentation on your research findings. Your classmates and teacher will serve as judges. You may use visual aids; but books, other bound materials, props, and equipment are not allowed.
3. At the end of your presentation, your classmates and teacher will ask you questions about your research.

www.fbla-pbl.org

GLOSSARY

A

Account an accounting record that provides financial detail for a particular business item, such as for cash, sales, rent, and utilities

Accounts payable amounts owed by a business to its vendors for merchandise purchased on credit

Accounts receivable the amounts owed to a business by its credit customers

Acquisition two companies combine with one of them clearly established as the new owner

Advertising a paid form of communication sent out by a business about a product or service; it keeps a product or service in the public's eye by creating a sense of awareness and helps the business convey a positive image

Advertising fees fees paid to a franchise company to support television, magazine, or other advertising of the franchise as a whole

Aptitude the ability to learn a particular kind of job

Assets items of value that you own

Authoritative management a management style in which the manager is directive and controlling

B

Balance sheet a financial statement that lists what a business owns, what it owes, and how much it is worth at a particular point in time

Benefits rewards, other than cash, given to employees, including paid time off, insurance, and a retirement plan

Board of directors a group of people who meet several times a year to make important decisions affecting the company

Bonus a financial reward made in addition to a regular wage or salary that usually hinges on reaching an established goal

Bootstrapping personally investing a small amount of capital to start and build a company

Bounced check a check that a bank returns to the payee (the person or business to whom the check is made payable) because the check writer's checking account has insufficient funds to cover the amount

Brainstorming a creative problem-solving technique that involves generating a large number of fresh ideas

Brand the name, symbol, or design used to identify a product

Business ethics the application of the principles of right and wrong to issues that come up in the workplace

Business model describes the way the company generates revenue and makes a profit

Business plan a written document that describes all the steps necessary for opening and operating a successful business

C

Canvas a graphic tool that maps the key elements about the company's products or services

Capitalism the private ownership of resources by individuals rather than by the government

Capitalization table a spreadsheet that shows the company's capitalization, or ownership stakes

Cash budget a financial report that shows the projections of cash coming in and going out of a business

Cash flow statement an accounting report that describes the way cash flows into and out of a business over a period of time

Chain of command the working relationships within a business—who reports to whom—often shown in an organizational chart

Channels of distribution routes that products and services take from the time they are produced to the time they are consumed

Check register a booklet in which an account holder records the dates and amounts of the checks as well as the names of people or businesses to whom he or she has written the checks

Code of ethics a set of standards or rules that outlines the ethical behavior demanded by an individual, a business, or a culture

Collateral property that a borrower forfeits to the bank providing the loan if he or she defaults on the loan

Commission a percentage of a sale paid to a salesperson

Competition-based pricing pricing that is determined by considering what competitors charge for the same product or service

Competitive analysis identifying and examining the characteristics of a competing firm

Consumer credit offered when a retail business allows its customers to buy merchandise now and pay for it later

Contract a legally binding agreement between two or more persons or parties

Controllable risk risk that can be reduced or possibly even avoided by taking action

Copyright a form of intellectual property law that protects original works of authorship, including literary, dramatic, musical, and artistic works

Corporation a business that has the legal rights of a person but is independent of its owners

Cost-based pricing pricing that is determined by using the wholesale cost of an item as the basis for the price charged

Cover letter a letter that introduces and explains an accompanying document or set of documents

Customer profile a description of the characteristics of the person or company that is likely to purchase a product or service

Customer relationship management (CRM) a company's efforts to understand customers as individuals instead of as part of a group

D

Debt capital money loaned to a business with the understanding that the money will be repaid within a certain time period, usually with interest

Debt-to-equity ratio the relation between the dollars borrowed (debt) and the dollars invested in a business (equity)

Delegate to let others share workloads and responsibilities

Demand the quantity of a good or service that consumers are willing to buy at a given price

Demand-based pricing pricing that is determined by how much customers are willing to pay for a product or service

Democratic management a management style in which employees are involved in decision making and the manager provides less direction

Demographics data that describe a group of people in terms of age, marital status, family size, ethnicity, gender, profession, education, and income

Direct channel a distribution channel that moves the product directly from the manufacturer to the consumer

Direct competition a business that makes most of its money selling the same or similar products or services to the same market as other businesses

Discount pricing pricing strategy that offers customers a reduced price to encourage them to buy

Distribution an important component of supply chain management that involves the locations and methods used to make products and services available to customers

Dividends distributions of corporate profits to the shareholders

E

E-commerce electronic commerce consisting of buying and selling products or services over the Internet

Economic decision making the process of choosing which needs and wants, among several, will be satisfied using the resources on hand

Economic resources means through which goods and services are produced

Economies of scale the cost advantages obtained by a business due to expansion

Emotional buying decisions based on the desire to have a specific product or service

Employees people who are hired to work for someone else

Enterprise zones areas that suffer from lack of employment opportunities

Entrepreneurs people who own, operate, and take the risk of a business venture

Entrepreneurship process of running a business of one's own

Equilibrium price and quantity point at which the supply and demand curves meet

Equity capital money invested in a business in return for a share in the profits of the business

Ethics the study of moral choices and values; involves choosing between right and wrong

Exchange rate the amount of one country's currency that can be traded for one unit of currency in another country

Executive summary a short restatement of the report portion of a business plan

Exit strategy a harvest strategy, or the way an entrepreneur intends to extract, or harvest, his or her money from a business after it is operating successfully

Exports products and services that are produced in one country and sent to another country to be sold

F

Features product characteristics that will satisfy customer needs

Fixed costs costs that must be paid regardless of how much of a good or service is produced

Focus group an in-depth interview with a group of target customers who provide valuable ideas on products or services

Franchise a legal agreement that gives an individual the right to market a company's products or services in a particular area

Franchise Disclosure Document (FDD) a regulatory document describing a franchise opportunity that prospective franchisees must receive before they sign a contract

Freelancers people who provide specialty services to a number of different businesses on an hourly basis or by the job

G

Geographic data data that help a business determine where its potential customers live and how far they will travel to visit the business

Gross lease a contract stating that the tenant pays rent each month for the space occupied and the landlord covers all property expenses for that space

Gross sales the dollar amount of all sales

I

Ideas thoughts or concepts that come from creative thinking

Imports products and services that are brought from one country into another country to be sold

Income statement a financial statement that shows the business's revenues and expenses incurred over a period of time and the resulting profit or loss

Indirect channel a distribution channel that uses intermediaries, such as agents and wholesalers, to move products between the manufacturer and the consumer

Indirect competition a business that makes only a small amount of money selling the same or similar products and services to the same market as other businesses

Industrial park a section of land that is zoned for industrial businesses only; usually located where space is less expensive, away from housing developments and downtown areas

Initial franchise fee the amount the local franchise owner pays in return for the right to run the franchise

Initial public offering (IPO) the first time the stock of a private company is offered to the public

Insurable risk a pure risk that is faced by a large number of people and for which the amount of the loss can be predicted

Intellectual property the original, creative work of an artist or inventor, including such things as songs, novels, artistic designs, and inventions

Interns students who work for little or no pay in order to gain experience in a particular field

Inventory the products and materials needed to make the products that a business sells to its customers

J

Job analysis the process of determining the tasks and sequence of tasks necessary to perform a job

Job description a written statement listing the tasks and responsibilities of a position; also covers to whom the position reports, educational and professional experience required, and salary range

Journals accounting records of the transactions you make; there are five different journals that businesses use to record their transactions: sales, cash payments, cash receipts, purchases, and general journals

L

Landlord the person who owns and rents out buildings or space

Liabilities amounts you owe to others

M

Management the process of achieving goals by establishing operating procedures that make effective use of people and other resources

Manager the person responsible for planning, organizing, staffing, implementing, and controlling the operations of a business

Marginal benefit measures the advantages of producing one additional unit of a good or service

Marginal cost measures the disadvantages of producing one additional unit of a good or service

Market development a strategy for expanding the target market of a business

Market penetration a strategy for increasing the market share for a product or service within a given market in a given area

Market research a system for collecting, recording, and analyzing information about customers, competitors, products, and services

Market segments groups of customers within a large market who share common characteristics

Market share business's percentage of the total sales generated by all companies in the same market

Marketing all of the processes—planning, pricing, promoting, distributing, and selling—utilized by a company to place its product in the hands of potential customers

Marketing concept uses the needs of customers as the primary focus during the planning, production, distribution, and promotion of a product or service

Marketing mix blending of the product, price, distribution, and promotion used to reach a target market

Marketing plan defines the market, identifies customers and competitors, outlines a strategy for attracting and keeping customers, and recognizes and anticipates change

Marketing strategy plan that identifies how marketing goals will be achieved

Mass media any means of communication that reaches very large numbers of people

Merger two companies agree to combine as a single company

Minimally viable product a version of a product that has just enough features to satisfy early customers and to provide feedback for future development

N

Needs things that a person must have in order to survive

Net lease a contract stating that the landlord pays building insurance and the tenant pays rent, property taxes, and any other expenses

Net sales the dollar amount of all sales with any returns subtracted

Net worth the difference between what is owned, called *assets*, and what is owed, called *liabilities*

O

Operations manual contains all of the rules, policies, and procedures that a business should follow in order to function effectively

Opportunities possibilities that arise from existing conditions

Opportunity cost value of the next-best alternative

Organizational structure a plan that shows how the various jobs in a company relate to one another; often represented in a chart indicating the working relationships within the business

Owner's equity *net worth*, or the difference between *assets* and *liabilities*

P

Partnership a business owned by two or more people

Patent the grant of a property right to an inventor to exclude others from making, using, or selling his or her invention

Payroll a list of people who receive salary or wage payments from a business

Percentage lease a contract stating that the tenant pays a base rent each month and the landlord receives a percentage of the tenant's revenue each month

Performance evaluation a management control tool that helps determine whether the objectives for a particular job are being met

Periodic inventory method involves taking a physical count of a business's merchandise at regular intervals, such as weekly or monthly

Perpetual inventory method keeps track of inventory levels on a daily basis

Personal selling direct communication between a prospective buyer and a sales representative in which the sales representative attempts to influence the prospective buyer in a purchase situation

Physical distribution includes transportation, storage, handling, and packaging of products within a channel of distribution

Pivoting a company reexamines its ideas for a product until it comes up with something successful; also can be used as a tool to discover additional growth

Point-of-sale (POS) software system cash registers used with a software system that updates inventory records as each sale happens

Positioning creating an image for a product in the customer's mind

Premium payment made to an insurance company to cover the cost of insurance

Press release a written statement meant to inform the media of an event or product

Primary data information collected for the very first time to fit a specific purpose

Pro forma financial statement a financial statement based on projected revenues and expenses

Problem-solving model a formal process used to help solve problems in a logical manner

Product life cycle the stages that a product goes through from the time it is introduced to when it is no longer sold; a product goes through four stages in its life cycle: introduction, growth, maturity, and decline

Product mix different products and services that a business sells

Profit difference between the revenues earned by a business and the costs of operating the business

Profit sharing a compensation arrangement in which employees are paid a portion of the company's profits

Prototype a full-scale model of a new product

Psychographics data that describe a group of people in terms of their tastes, opinions, personality traits, and lifestyle habits

Psychological pricing pricing strategy based on the belief that certain prices have an impact on how customers perceive a product

Public relations the act of establishing a favorable relationship with customers and the general public

Publicity a nonpaid form of communication that calls attention to a business through media coverage

Pure risk risk that presents the chance of loss but no opportunity for gain

Q

Qualitative restriction a standard of quality that an imported product must meet before it can be sold

Quota a limit on the amount of a product that can be imported into a country over a particular period of time

Quote an estimate for how much a business will pay for merchandise or service

R

Rational buying decisions based on the logical reasoning of customers

Rebate a refund offered to people who purchase a product

Recruit to look for people to hire and attract them to the business

Reorder point a predetermined level of inventory that signals when new stock should be ordered

Return on investment (ROI) amount earned as a result of the investment, usually expressed as a percentage

Risk the possibility of some kind of loss

Risk assessment involves looking at all aspects of a business and determining the risks it faces

Risk management involves taking action to prevent or reduce the possibility of loss to a business

Royalty fees weekly or monthly payments made by the local owner to the franchise company; these payments usually are a percentage of a franchise's income

S

Salary an amount paid for a job position stated on an annual basis

Sales promotion an incentive offered to customers in order to increase sales; examples include contests, free samples, rebates, coupons, special events, gift certificates, and frequent-buyer rewards

Scarcity occurs when people's needs and wants are unlimited and the resources to produce the goods and services to meet those needs and wants are limited

SCORE a nonprofit association made up of working and retired business professionals who volunteer their time to provide small businesses and entrepreneurs with free, real-world advice and know-how

Secondary data data found in already-published sources

Self-assessment evaluation of your strengths and weaknesses

Share of stock a unit of ownership in a corporation

Shoplifting the act of knowingly taking items from a business without paying

Short-term loan a loan payable within one year

Small Business Administration (SBA) an independent agency of the federal government that was created to provide support to entrepreneurs and small businesses

Small Business Development Centers (SBDCs) centers that provide technical assistance to small businesses and aspiring entrepreneurs

Social media marketing a form of Internet marketing that utilizes social networking sites as a marketing tool

Sole proprietorship a business that is owned exclusively by one person

Speculative risk risk that offers the chance to gain as well as lose from the event or activity

Staffing involves determining the number of employees that a company needs and defining a process for hiring them

Startup costs the costs associated with beginning a business, including the costs of renting a facility, equipping the outlet, and purchasing inventory

Statement of purpose a brief explanation of why the writer of a business plan is asking for a loan and an explanation of what he or she plans to do with the money

Stock card a paper inventory record for a single item

Stock turnover rate the rate at which the inventory of a product is sold and replaced with new inventory

Supply the quantity of a good or service a producer is willing to produce at different prices

Supply chain management the coordination of manufacturers, suppliers, and retailers working together to meet a customer need for a product or service

Survey a list of questions to ask customers to find out demographic and psychographic information; can be conducted by mail, over the phone, on the Internet, or in person

T

Target market the individuals or companies that are interested in a particular product or service and are willing and able to pay for it

Tariff a tax on imports that governments use to protect domestic manufacturers of products that compete with imports

Telemarketing using the phone to market a product or service

Tenant the person who pays rent to occupy space owned by someone else

Term sheet sets the conditions under which an investment will be made

Trade area the geographic area from which a business expects to attract a majority of its customers

Trade associations organizations made up of professionals in a specific industry

Trade barriers methods for keeping foreign businesses from competing with domestic producers

Trade credit offered when one business allows another business to buy now and pay later

Trade shows special meetings where companies of the same or related industry display their products

Trademark a name, symbol, or special mark used to identify a business or brand of product

Transaction any business activity that changes assets, liabilities, or net worth

U

Uncontrollable risk risk on which actions have no effect, such as the weather

Use-based data data that help a business determine how often potential customers use a particular service

V

Value proposition graphic illustration of a company's product or service and the wants and needs of potential customers

Variable costs costs that go up and down depending on the quantity of the good or service produced

Vendors companies that sell products and services to businesses

Visual marketing the use of visual media to promote, sell, and distribute a product or service to a targeted audience

Visual merchandising the process of combining products, environments, and spaces into an appealing display to encourage the sale of products or services

W

Wages payments for labor or services that are made on an hourly, daily, or per-unit basis

Wants things that a person thinks he or she must have in order to be satisfied

Workers' compensation an insurance program that provides coverage to employees who suffer work-related injuries or illnesses

INDEX

I